easy

Computer Basics, Windows Vista® Edition

Michael Miller

Contents

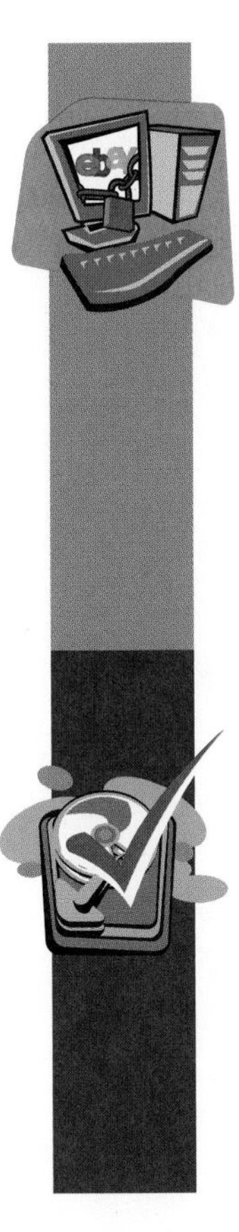

EASY COMPUTER BASICS, WINDOWS VISTA® EDITION

ISBN-13: 978-0-7897-3789-2
ISBN-10: 0-7897-3789-2
UK ISBN-13: 978-0-7897-3798-4
UK ISBN-10: 0-7897-3798-1

Library of Congress Cataloging-in-Publication Data

Miller, Michael, 1958-
Easy computer basics : Windows Vista edition / Michael Miller.
p. cm.
ISBN 0-7897-3789-2
1. Microsoft Windows (Computer file) 2. Microcomputers. I. Title.
QA76.5M5314135 2008
004.165—dc22

2008006984

Printed in the United States of America

First Printing: April 2008

TRADEMARKS

All terms mentioned in this book that are known to be trademarks or service marks have been appropriately capitalized. Que Publishing cannot attest to the accuracy of this information. Use of a term in this book should not be regarded as affecting the validity of any trademark or service mark.

WARNING AND DISCLAIMER

Every effort has been made to make this book as complete and as accurate as possible, but no warranty or fitness is implied. The information provided is on an "as is" basis. The author and the publisher shall have neither liability nor responsibility to any person or entity with respect to any loss or damages arising from the information contained in this book.

BULK SALES

Que Publishing offers excellent discounts on this book when ordered in quantity for bulk purchases or special sales. For more information, please contact

U.S. Corporate and Government Sales
1-800-382-3419
corpsales@pearsontechgroup.com

For sales outside of the U.S., please contact

International Sales
international@pearson.com

THIS BOOK IS SAFARI ENABLED

The Safari® Enabled icon on the cover of your favorite technology book means the book is available through Safari Bookshelf. When you buy this book, you get free access to the online edition for 45 days.

Safari Bookshelf is an electronic reference library that lets you easily search thousands of technical books, find code samples, download chapters, and access technical information whenever and wherever you need it.

To gain 45-day Safari Enabled access to this book:

- Go to http://www.informit.com/onlineedition
- Complete the brief registration form
- Enter the coupon code YQAN-87SC-8H2X-72BU-8IDT

If you have difficulty registering on Safari Bookshelf or accessing the online edition, please email customer-service@safaribooksonline.com.

Associate Publisher
Greg Wiegand

Acquisitions Editor
Michelle Newcomb

Development Editor
Laura Norman

Managing Editor
Gina Kanouse

Project Editor
Betsy Harris

Technical Editor
Vince Averello

Copy Editor
Andy Beaster

Indexer
Erika Millen

Publishing Coordinator
Cindy Teeters

Book Designer
Anne Jones

Senior Compositor
Gloria Schurick

ABOUT THE AUTHOR

Michael Miller is a successful and prolific author with a reputation for practical advice, technical accuracy, and an unerring empathy for the needs of his readers.

Mr. Miller has written more than 80 best-selling books over the past two decades. His books for Que include *Absolute Beginner's Guide to Computer Basics*, *Absolute Beginner's Guide to eBay*, *How Microsoft Windows Vista Works*, *Your First Notebook PC*, and *Photopedia: The Ultimate Digital Photography Resource*. He is known for his casual, easy-to-read writing style and his practical, real-world advice—as well as his ability to explain a wide variety of complex topics to an everyday audience.

You can email Mr. Miller directly at easycomputer@molehillgroup.com. His website is located at www.molehillgroup.com.

DEDICATION

To Sherry—life can always be easier.

ACKNOWLEDGMENTS

Thanks to the usual suspects at Que, including but not limited to Greg Wiegand, Michelle Newcomb, Laura Norman, Betsy Harris, Andy Beaster, and technical editor Vince Averello.

TELL US WHAT YOU THINK!

As the reader of this book, *you* are our most important critic and commentator. We value your opinion and want to know what we're doing right, what we could do better, what areas you'd like to see us publish in, and any other words of wisdom you're willing to pass our way.

As an associate publisher for Que, I welcome your comments. You can email or write me directly to let me know what you did or didn't like about this book—as well as what we can do to make our books stronger.

Please note that I cannot help you with technical problems related to the topic of this book. We do have a User Services group, however, where I will forward specific technical questions related to the book.

When you write, please be sure to include this book's title and author as well as your name, email address, and phone number. I will carefully review your comments and share them with the author and editors who worked on the book.

Email: feedback@quepublishing.com

Mail: Greg Wiegand
Que Publishing
800 East 96th Street
Indianapolis, IN 46240 USA

READER SERVICES

Visit our website and register this book at informit.com/register for convenient access to any updates, downloads, or errata that might be available for this book.

IT'S AS EASY AS 1-2-3

Each part of this book is made up of a series of short, instructional lessons, designed to help you understand basic information.

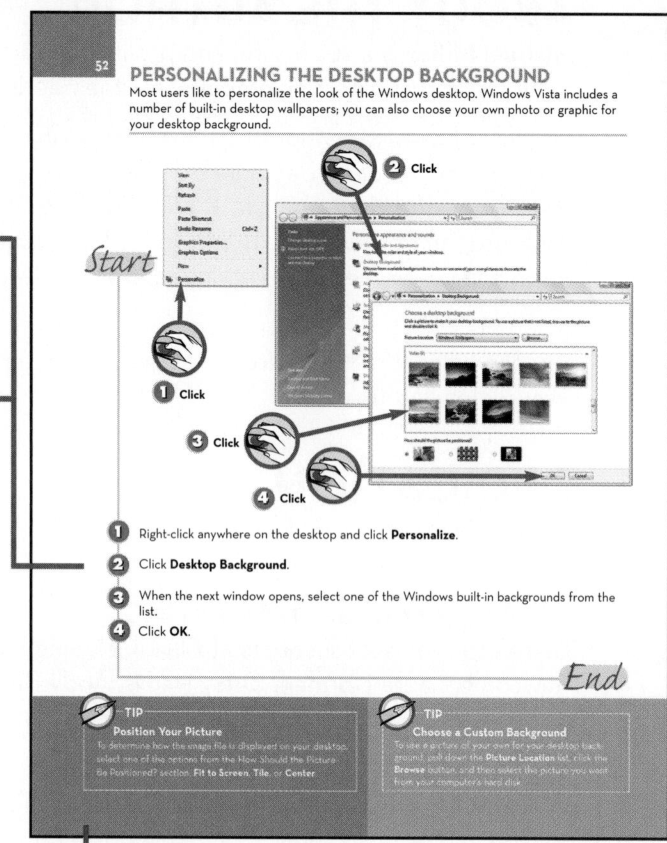

52

PERSONALIZING THE DESKTOP BACKGROUND

Most users like to personalize the look of the Windows desktop. Windows Vista includes a number of built-in desktop wallpapers; you can also choose your own photo or graphic for your desktop background.

1. Right-click anywhere on the desktop and click **Personalize**.
2. Click **Desktop Background**.
3. When the next window opens, select one of the Windows built-in backgrounds from the list.
4. Click **OK**.

End

TIP
Position Your Picture
To determine how the image file is displayed on your desktop, select one of the options from the How Should the Picture Be Positioned? section: **Fit to Screen**, **Tile**, or **Center**.

TIP
Choose a Custom Background
To use a picture of your own for your desktop background, pull down the **Picture Location** list, click the **Browse** button, and then select the picture you want from your computer's hard disk.

1. Each step is fully illustrated to show you how it looks onscreen.
2. Each task includes a series of quick, easy steps designed to guide you through the procedure.
3. Items that you select or click in menus, dialog boxes, tabs, and windows are shown in **bold**.

Tips, notes, and cautions give you a heads-up for any extra information you may need while working through the task.

How to Drag:
Point to the starting place or object. Hold down the mouse button (right or left per instructions), move the mouse to the new location, then release the button.

Click

Click:
Click the left mouse button once.

Click & Type:
Click once where indicated and begin typing to enter your text or data.

Selection:
Highlights the area onscreen discussed in the step or task.

Double-click:
Click the left mouse button twice in rapid succession.

Right-click:
Click the right mouse button once.

Pointer Arrow:
Highlights an item on the screen you need to point to or focus on in the step or task.

INTRODUCTION TO *EASY COMPUTER BASICS, WINDOWS VISTA EDITION*

Computers don't have to be scary or difficult. Computers can be easy—if you know what to do.

That's where this book comes in. *Easy Computer Basics, Windows Vista Edition* is an illustrated, step-by-step guide to setting up and using your new computer. You'll learn how computers work, how to connect all the pieces and parts together, and how to start using them. All you have to do is look at the pictures and follow the instructions. Pretty easy.

After you learn the basics, I'll show you how to do lots of useful stuff with your new PC. You'll learn how to use Windows Vista to copy and delete files, use Microsoft Word to write letters and memos, use Windows Mail to send and receive email messages, and use Internet Explorer to search for information on the Internet. We'll even cover some fun stuff, including listening to music and working with digital photographs.

If you're worried about how to keep your PC up and running, we'll cover some basic system maintenance, too. And, just to be safe, I'll show you how to protect your computer when you're online—against viruses, spam, spyware, and computer attacks. It's not hard to do.

To help you find the information you need, I've organized *Easy Computer Basics, Windows Vista Edition* into 13 parts.

Part 1, "Understanding How Your Computer Works," describes all the pieces and parts of a typical computer system. Read this section to find out all about hard drives, keyboards, sound cards, and the like.

Part 2, "Setting Up and Using a Desktop PC," shows you how to connect together all the pieces and parts of a typical desktop PC and get your new computer system up and running.

Part 3, "Setting Up and Using a Notebook PC," covers the basics of using a notebook PC—which, as you might suspect, are somewhat different from using a desktop model.

Part 4, "Using Microsoft Windows Vista," introduces the backbone of your entire system—the Microsoft Windows Vista operating system—including how it works and how to use it.

Part 5, "Working with Files and Folders," shows you how to manage all the computer files you create—by moving, copying, renaming, and deleting them.

Part 6, "Using Microsoft Word," shows you how to use Microsoft's popular word processor to create letters and other documents.

Part 7, "Connecting to the Internet," is all about getting online and doing stuff when you get there. You'll learn how to set up a new Internet connection, connect to public Wi-Fi hotspots, surf the Web, send and receive emails, and use instant messaging programs. You'll even learn how to search for information on the Internet, view YouTube videos, shop online, and bid on eBay auctions!

Part 8, "Setting Up a Wireless Home Network," helps you connect all the computers in your house into a wireless network and share a broadband Internet connection.

Part 9, "Playing Music and Movies," shows you how to download and play digital music files, how to listen to CDs on your PC, how to burn your own audio CDs, how to copy songs from your PC to your Apple iPod, and how to watch DVDs on your computer screen.

Part 10, "Working with Digital Photos," helps you connect a digital camera to your PC and edit your digital photos using Vista's Windows Photo Gallery.

Part 11, "Adding New Devices to Your System," shows you how to upgrade your computer system with new internal and external peripherals.

Part 12, "Protecting Your Computer," is all about stopping spam, viruses, spyware, and the like.

Part 13, "Taking Care of Your Computer," shows you how to keep your PC running smoothly, how to back up your important data, and how to recover from serious crashes. And that's not all. At the back of the book you'll find a glossary of common computer terms—so you can understand what all the techie types are talking about.

So, is using a computer really this easy? You bet—just follow the simple step-by-step instructions, and you'll be computing like a pro!

part 1

UNDERSTANDING HOW YOUR COMPUTER WORKS

Chances are you're reading this book because you have a new computer. At this point you might not be totally sure what it is you've gotten yourself into. Just what is this mess of boxes and cables—how does it all go together, and how does it work?

We'll start by looking at the physical components of your system—the stuff we call computer *hardware*. A lot of different pieces and parts make up a typical computer system. You should note, however, that no two computer systems are identical because you can always add new components to your system—or disconnect other pieces you don't have any use for.

THE PARTS OF YOUR COMPUTER SYSTEM

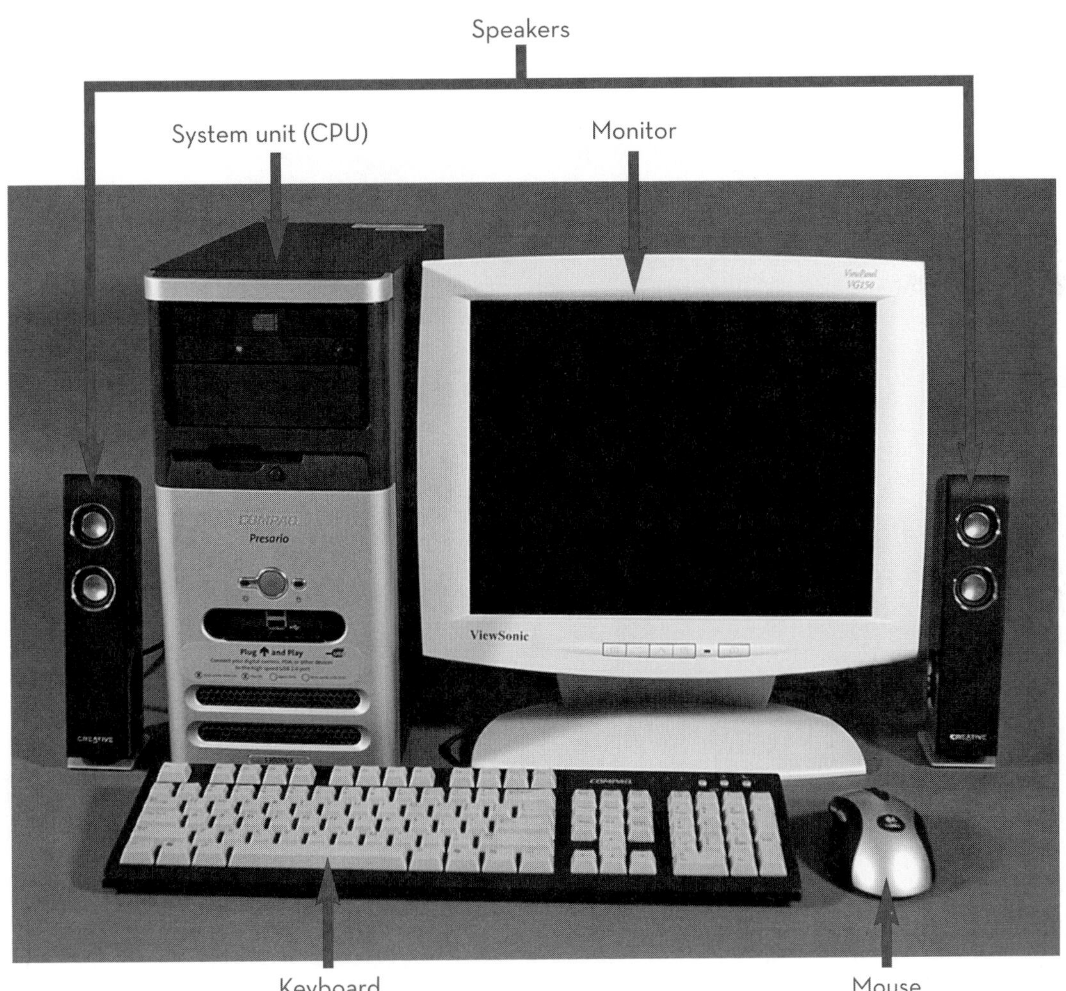

GETTING TO KNOW YOUR SYSTEM UNIT

The system unit is the most important piece of hardware in your computer system. It houses your computer's brain, disk drives, and many other components—which makes it the "mother ship" of your system.

Start

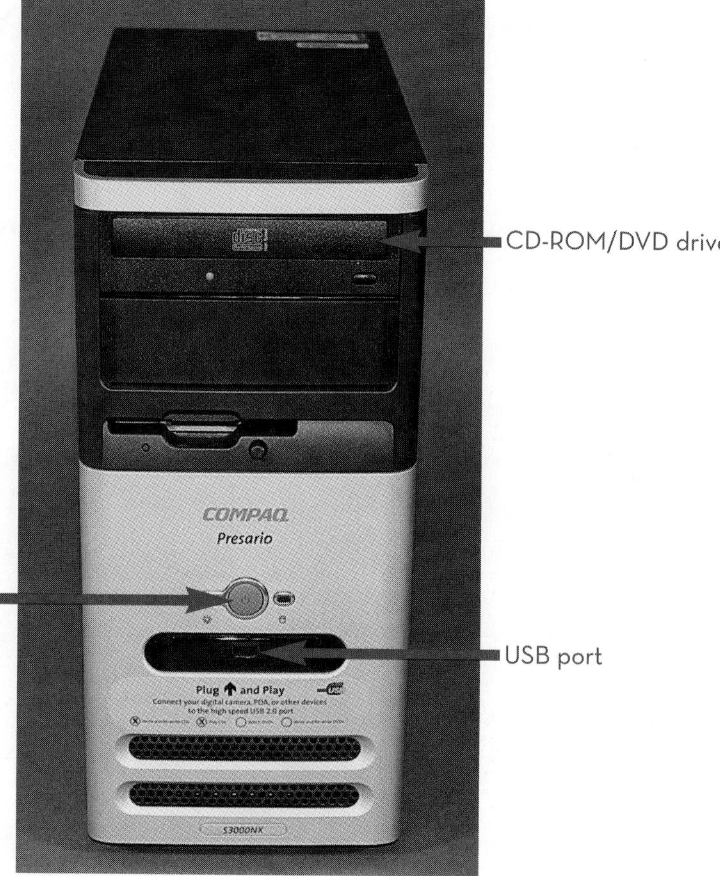

Continued

NOTE

Desktops and Laptops

A *laptop* or *notebook* computer differs from a desktop unit in that it combines all the various elements (except for a printer) into a single case. Learn more in Part 3, "Setting Up and Using a Notebook PC."

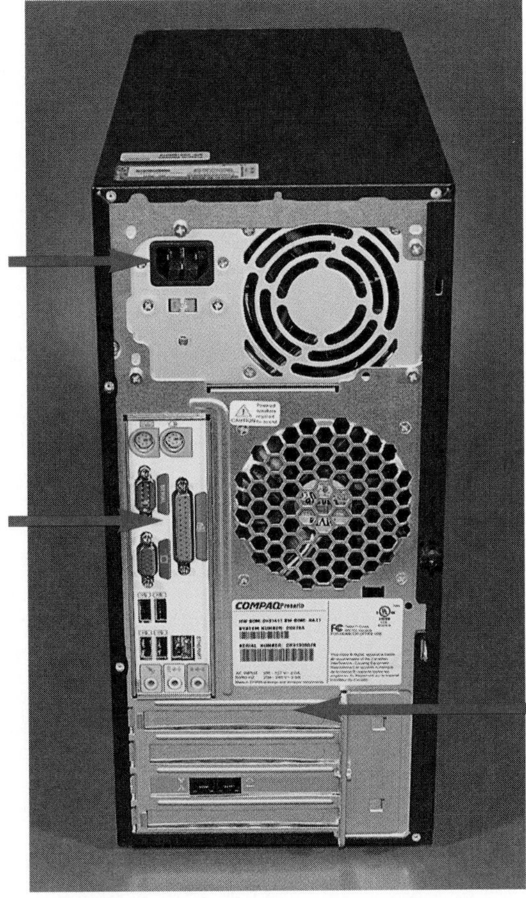

End

NOTE

Front and Back

The front of the system unit is where you insert CDs, DVDs, and other types of storage media. The back of the system unit is where all the other parts of your computer system connect.

NOTE

Connecting Ports

Because every component you plug into your system unit has its own unique type of connector, you end up with an assortment of different jacks—called *ports* in the computer world.

INSIDE THE CASE

Of all the components inside your system unit, the most important is the *motherboard*, which hosts your microprocessor, memory chips, and other components. This motherboard also contains several slots, into which you can plug additional *boards* (also called *cards*) that perform specific functions.

Power supply

Drive bays

Start

Motherboard

Card slots

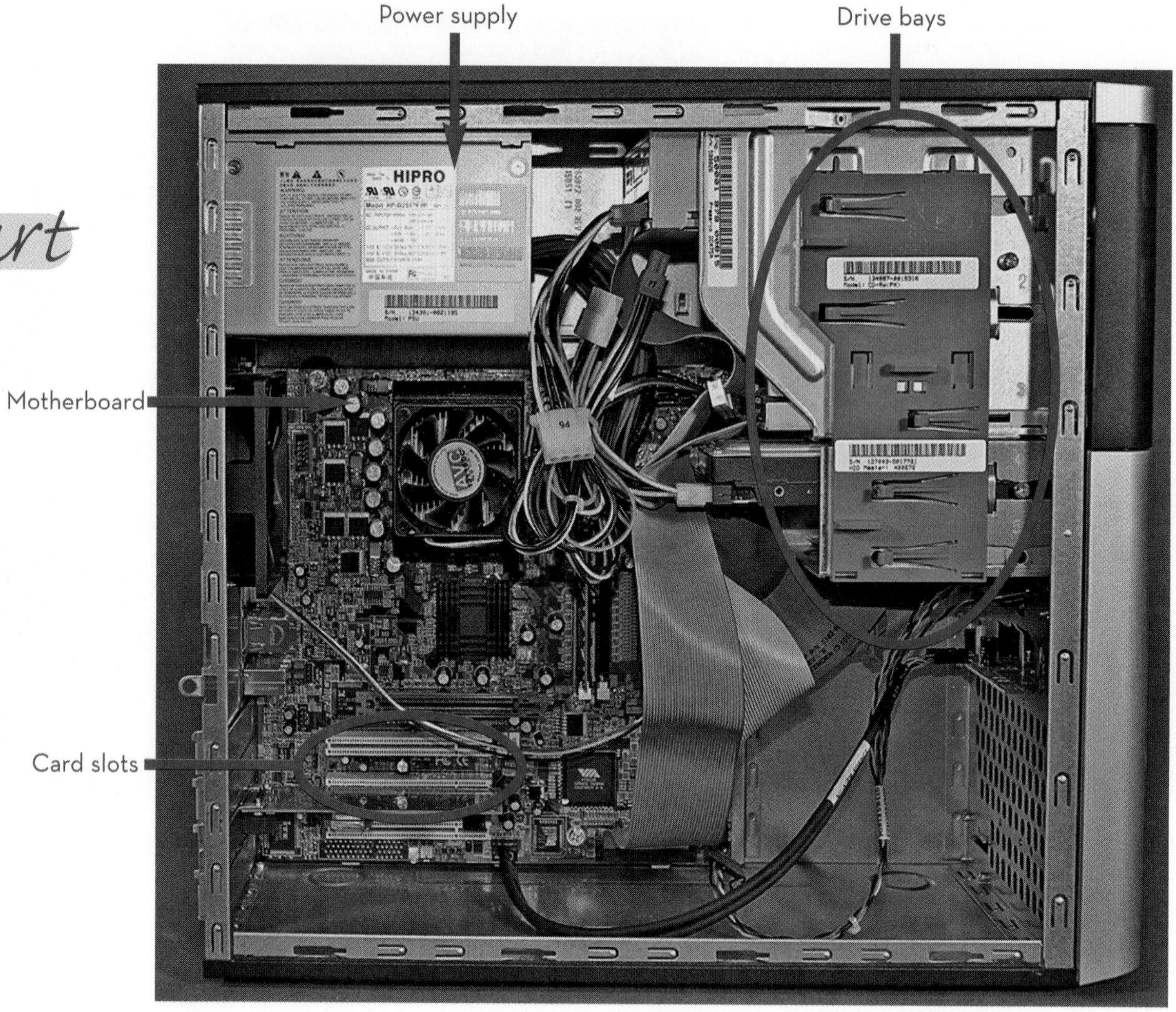

End

TIP

Open the Case

To remove your system unit's case, make sure the unit is unplugged; then loosen the big screws or thumbscrews on either the side or back of the case. You should then be able to either slide off the entire case or pop open the top or back.

HARD DISK DRIVES: LONG-TERM STORAGE

The hard disk drive inside your system unit stores all your important data—up to 400GB or more, depending on your computer. A hard disk consists of metallic platters that store data magnetically. Special read/write heads realign magnetic particles on the platters, much like a recording head records data onto magnetic recording tape.

Start

Hard disk bay

End

TIP

Formatting the Drive

Before data can be stored on a hard disk, the disk must first be *formatted*. When you format a hard disk, your computer prepares each track and sector of the disk to accept and store data magnetically. (Most new hard disks, such as the one in your new PC, come preformatted.)

CD AND DVD DRIVES

Computer or data CDs and DVDs look just like the compact discs and movie DVDs you play on your home audio/video system. Data is encoded in microscopic pits below the disc's surface and is read from the disc via a drive that uses a consumer-grade laser. The laser beam follows the tracks of the disc and reads the pits, translating the data into a form your computer can understand.

Start

Disc tray

End

NOTE

DVD Versus CD

Most new PCs come with combination CD/DVD drives. The advantage of a data DVD over a data CD is that a DVD disc can hold much more data—4.7GB versus 700MB for a typical CD. In addition, most DVD drives play full-length DVD movies, which turns your PC into a mini movie machine.

KEYBOARD

A computer keyboard looks and functions just like a typewriter keyboard, except that computer keyboards have a few more keys (for navigation and special program functions). When you press a key on your keyboard, it sends an electronic signal to your system unit that tells your machine what you want it to do.

Start

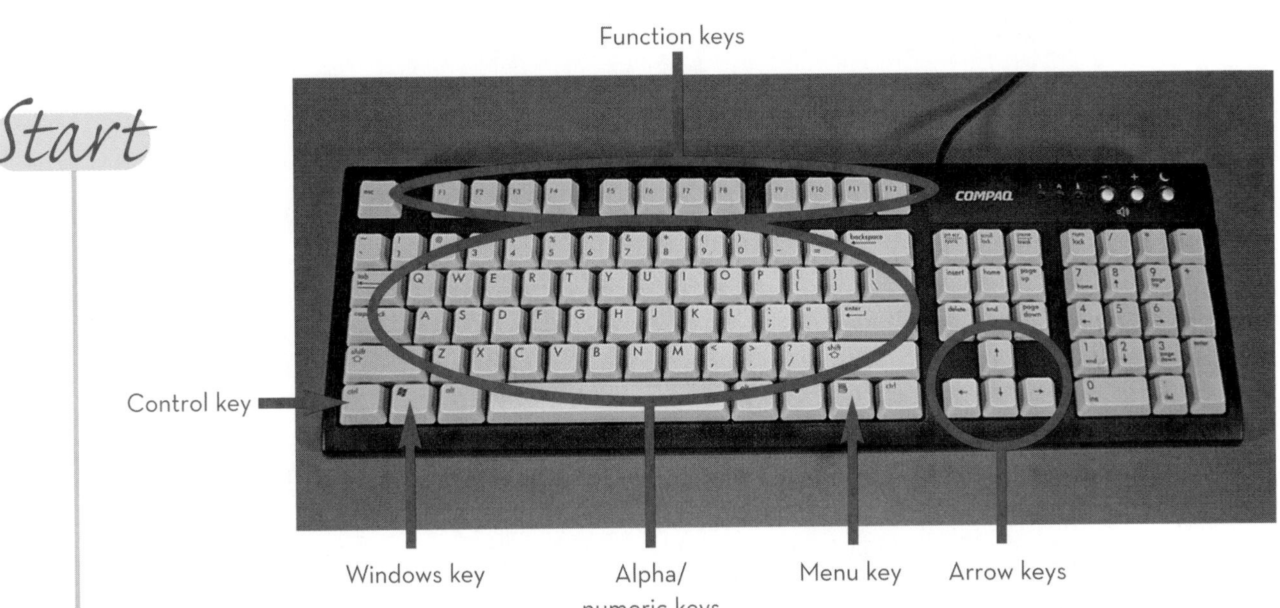

End

TIP

Wireless Keyboards

If you want to cut the cord, consider a wireless keyboard or mouse. These wireless devices work via radio frequency signals and let you work several feet away from your system unit, with no cables necessary.

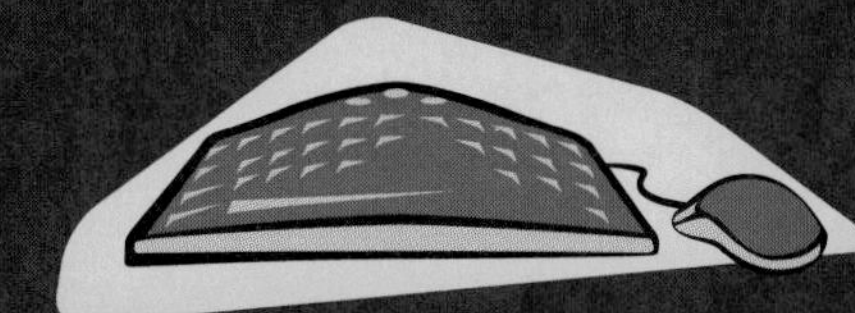

MOUSE

A *mouse* is a small, handheld input device for your computer. When you move the mouse along a flat surface, an onscreen pointer (called a *cursor*) moves in response. When you click (press and release) a mouse button, this motion initiates an action in your program.

Start

End

TIP

Mouse Alternatives

A mouse is just one type of input device you can hook up to your PC. You can also control your computer with trackballs, joysticks, game controllers, and pen pads.

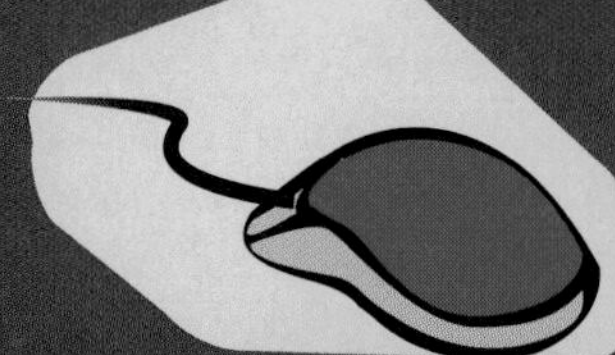

SOUND CARDS AND SPEAKERS

Most computers today come with separate right and left speakers, sometimes accompanied by a subwoofer for better bass. All speaker systems are driven by a sound card or chipset installed inside the system unit.

Start

End

NOTE

Surround Sound

So-called 5.1 surround sound speaker systems come with five satellite speakers (three front and two rear) and the ".1" subwoofer—great for listening to movie soundtracks or playing explosive-laden videogames.

VIDEO CARDS AND MONITORS

Your computer electronically transmits words and pictures to your monitor. These images are created by a *video card* installed inside your system unit. Settings in Windows tell the video card and the monitor how to work together to display the images you see on the screen.

Start

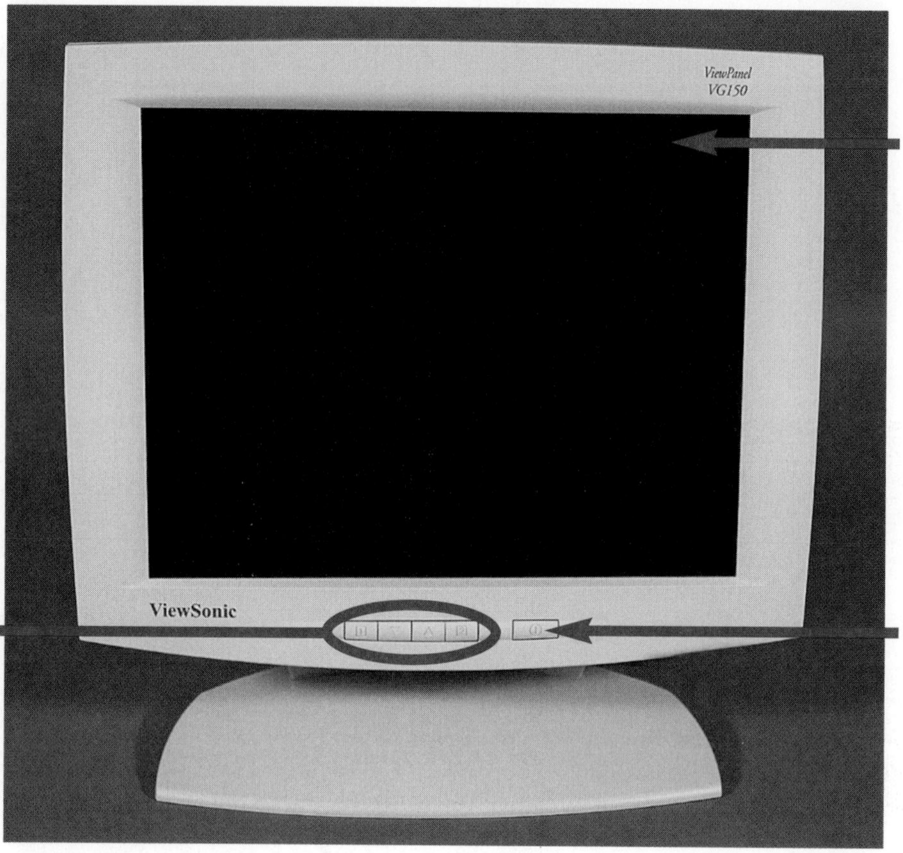

LCD screen

Adjustment buttons

On/Off button

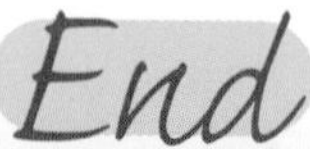

NOTE

CRT Versus LCD

Some lower-priced computer systems use traditional cathode ray tube (CRT) monitors. Newer flat-screen monitors use an LCD display instead, which takes up less desk space.

PRINTERS

To create a hard copy of your work, you must add a printer to your system. The two most common types are *laser* printers and *inkjet* printers. Laser printers work much like copy machines, applying toner (powdered ink) to paper using a small laser. Inkjet printers shoot jets of ink onto the paper's surface to create the printed image.

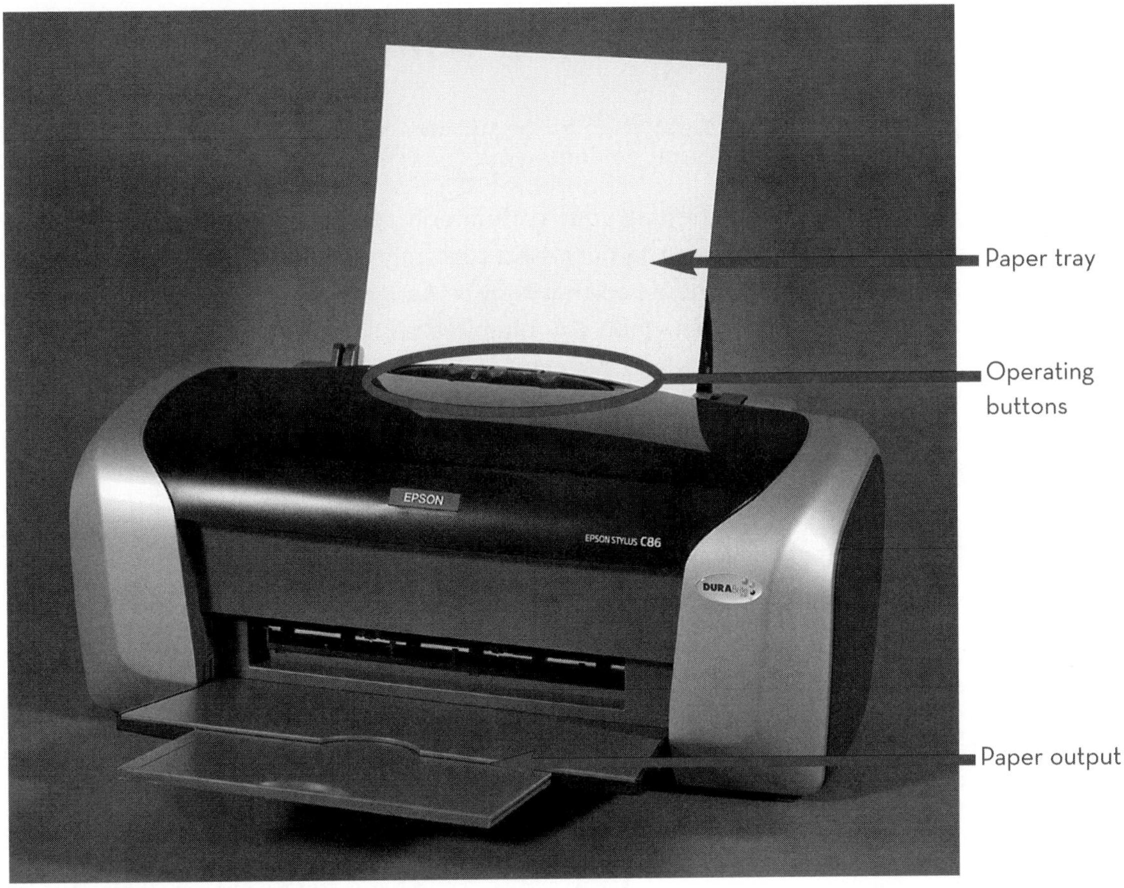

Start

Paper tray

Operating buttons

Paper output

End

—TIP

Black and White Versus Color

Black-and-white printers are faster than color printers and better if you're printing memos, letters, and other single-color documents. Color printers are essential if you want to print pictures taken with a digital camera.

part 2

SETTING UP AND USING A DESKTOP PC

If you're using a desktop PC, it's time to get connected. This involves plugging in all the external devices—your monitor, speakers, keyboard, and such.

Start by positioning your system unit so you easily can access all the connections on the back, and carefully run the cables from each of the other components so that they're hanging freely at the rear of the system unit. And remember, when you plug in a cable, you should make sure that it's *firmly* connected—both to the system unit and to the specific piece of hardware. Loose cables can cause all sorts of weird problems, so be sure they're plugged in really well.

TYPICAL CONNECTIONS

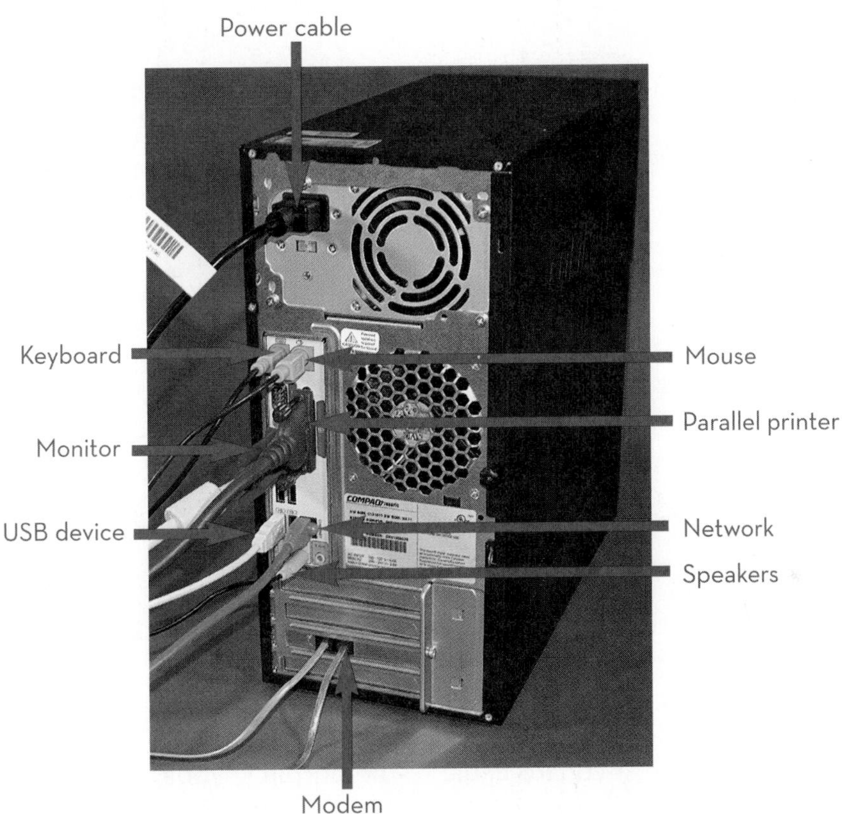

CONNECTING THE MOUSE AND KEYBOARD

The first items you connect should be your mouse and keyboard. Most mice connect to a dedicated mouse port on your system unit. Most keyboards connect to a similar dedicated keyboard port on your system unit. Know, however, that many new mice and keyboards also connect via USB ports, so you should use whatever connection is appropriate.

Start

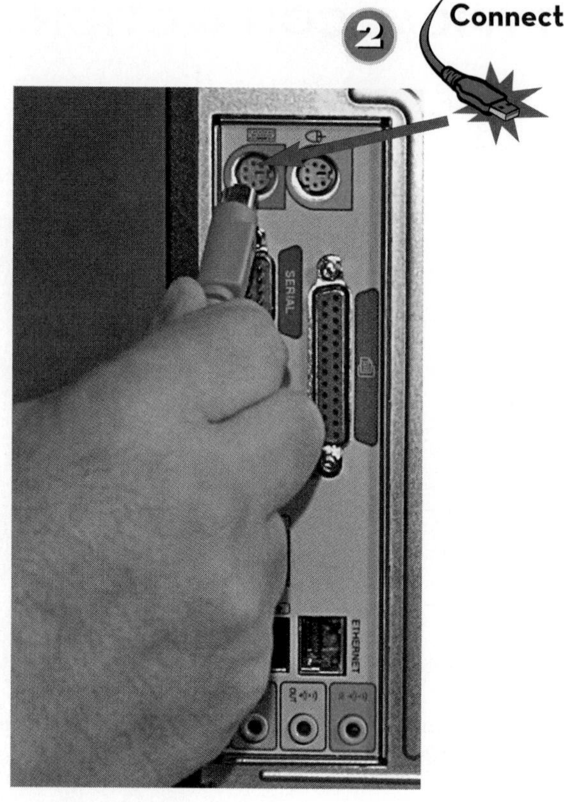

1. Connect the green mouse cable to the green mouse port on the back of your system unit.
2. Connect the purple keyboard cable to the purple keyboard port on the back of your system unit.

End

—TIP—

Connect by Color

Most PC manufacturers color-code the cables and connectors to make the connection even easier—just plug the blue cable into the blue connector and so on.

CONNECTING THE MONITOR

You have to connect your video monitor to your system unit and then connect it to a power source. Do not turn on the monitor until you're ready to power on your entire system.

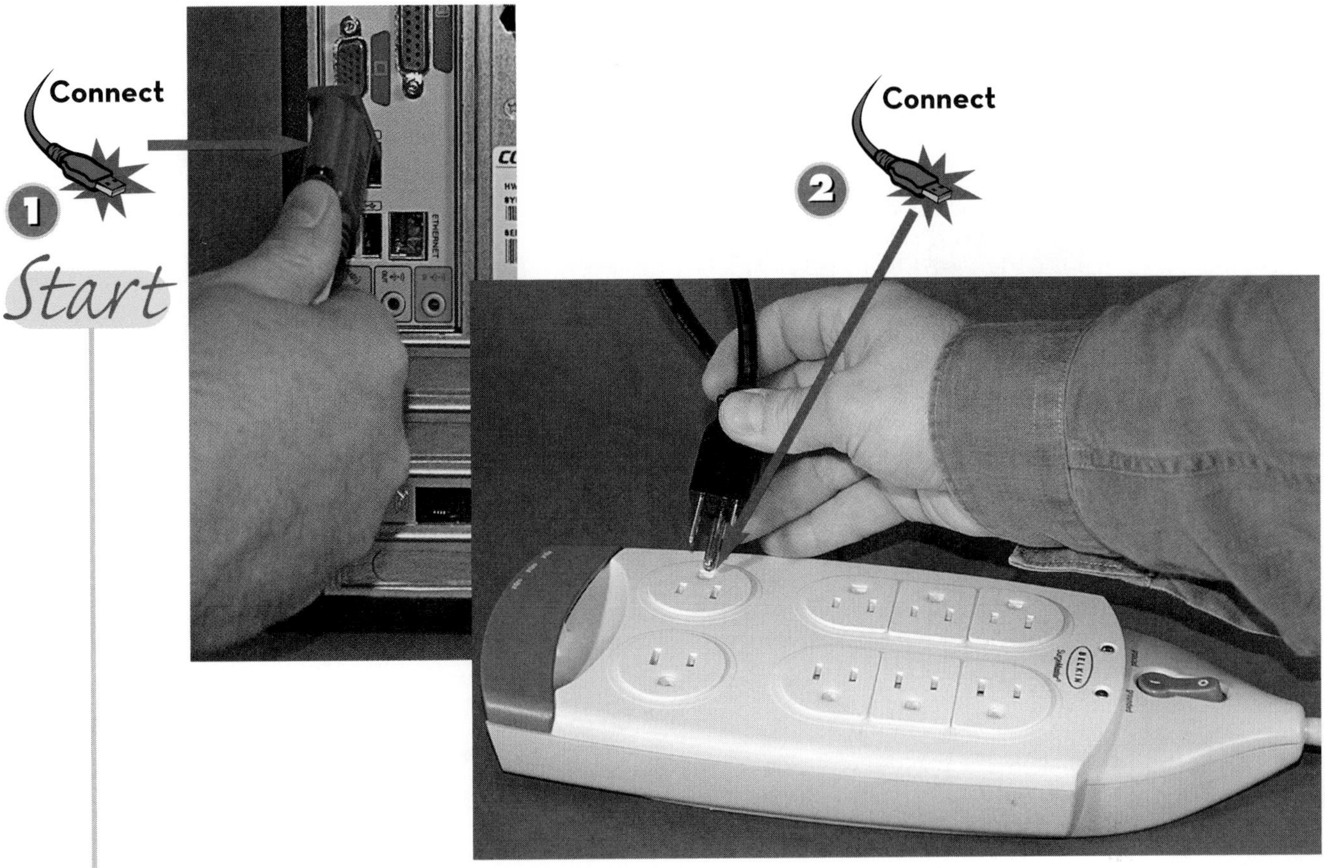

Connect

1

Start

Connect

2

1 Connect the blue monitor cable to the blue monitor port on the back of your system unit.

2 Connect the monitor's power cable to a power outlet.

End

TIP

Digital Connections

Some newer LCD monitors use a digital DVI connection instead of the older VGA-type connection. If you have a choice, a DVI connection delivers a crisper picture than the older analog connection—although a DVI cable is a bit more expensive than a VGA cable.

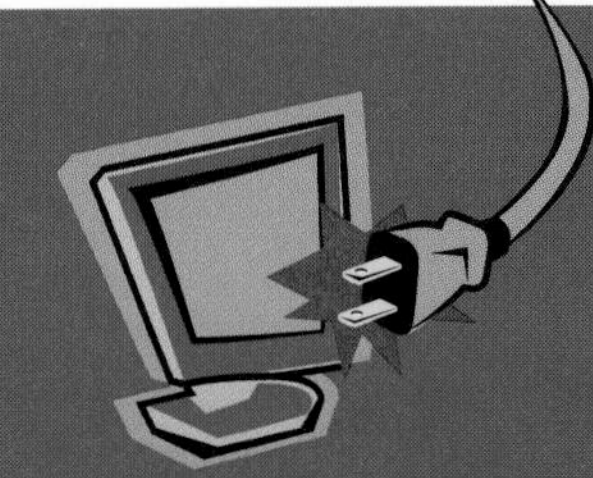

CONNECTING THE AUDIO SYSTEM

To connect your audio system, connect the phono jack from your speaker system to the audio out or sound out connector on your system unit. You'll also have to connect your left and right speakers together—and connect them to your subwoofer, if you have one.

Start

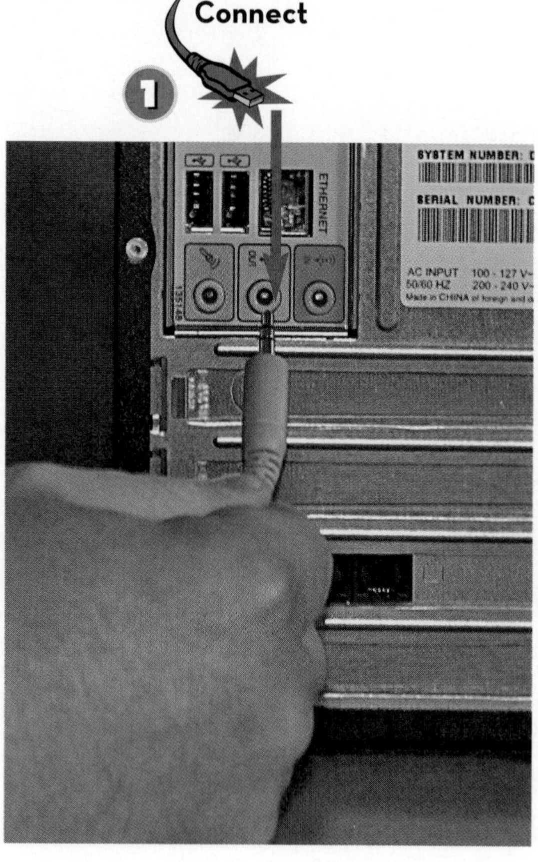

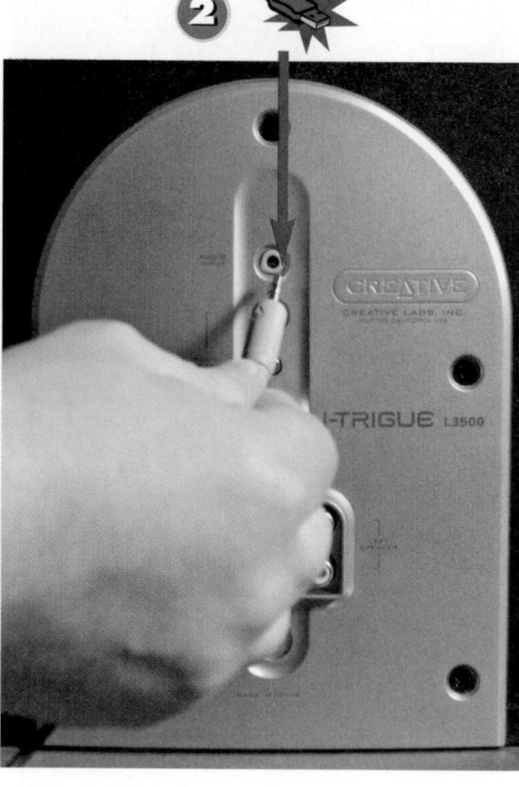

1. Connect one end of the green phono cable to the audio out or sound out connector on your system unit.
2. Connect the other end of this green cable to your subwoofer or main speaker.

Continued

TIP

Your Connection Might Vary

Not all speaker systems connect the same way. Many surround systems use a separate box with various controls (like volume) that connects to both your PC and speakers. Make sure you read your manufacturer's instructions before you connect your speaker system.

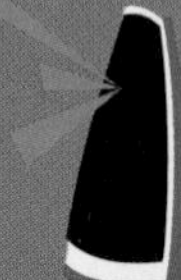
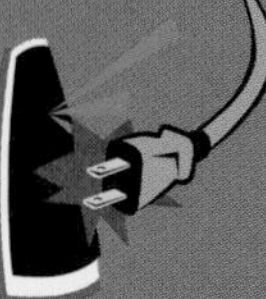

Connect

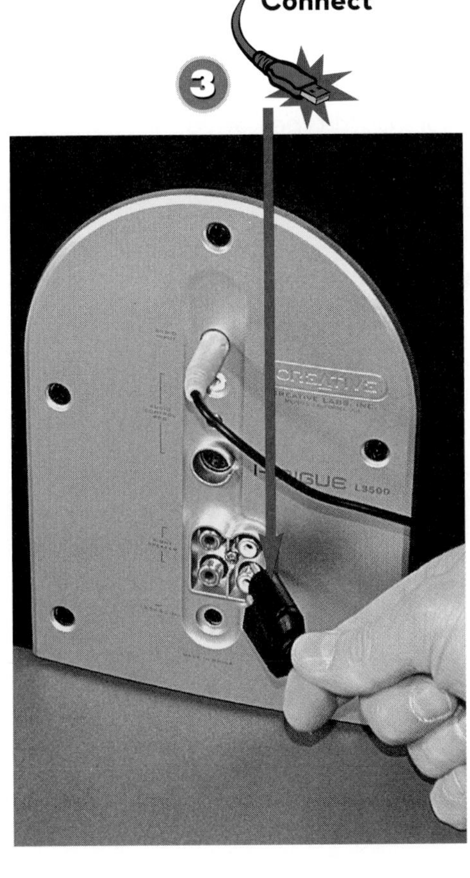

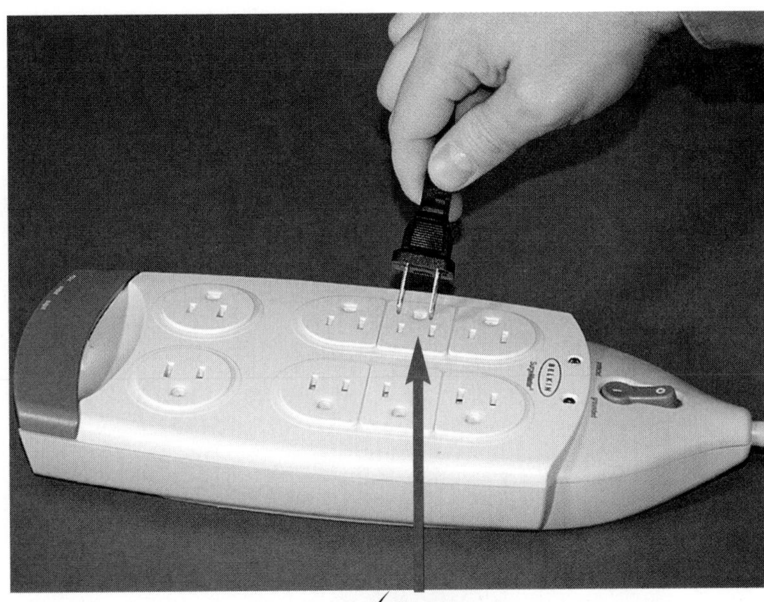

Connect

3. Connect your left and right speakers to your subwoofer, or to each other, as per the manufacturer's instructions.
4. Connect the power cable on your main speaker to a power source.

End

NOTE

Powered Speakers

Your PC doesn't include an audio power amplifier, so your computer speakers must be self-powered. This is why they must be connected to a power source to work.

TIP

Digital Speaker Systems

Some high-end speaker systems use a digital audio connector instead of the traditional analog audio out jack. If you have a digital speaker system, follow the manufacturer's instructions.

CONNECTING A BROADBAND MODEM

Most homes today have broadband Internet access, via either cable or DSL. Cable broadband is piped by your cable company through your normal cable connection; DSL is piped by your telephone company over your telephone connection. Both types of connections feed into a broadband modem, which then connects to your computer via USB or Ethernet.

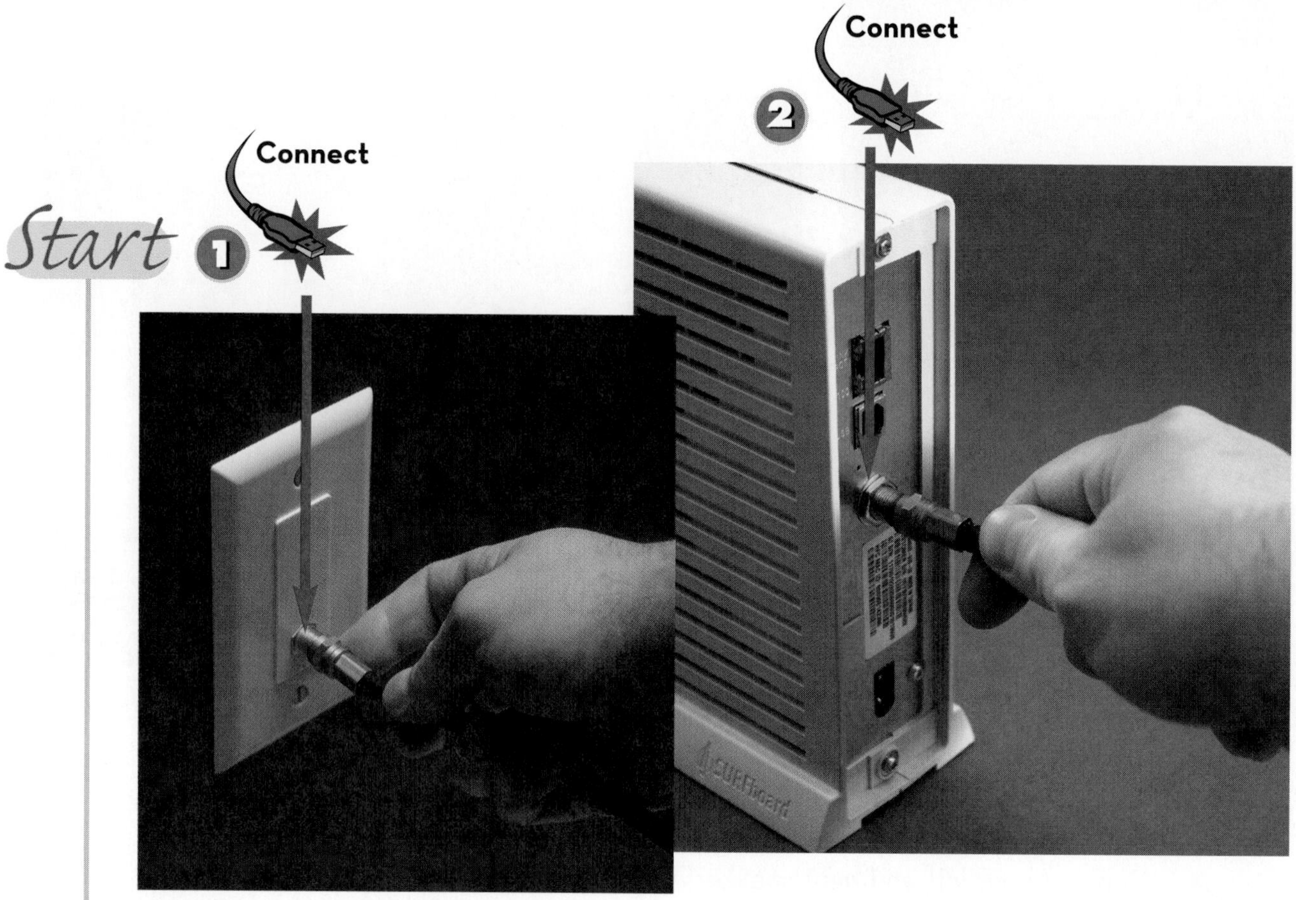

Start

1. Connect one end of the supplied cable to the cable outlet on a nearby wall. (If you have a DSL modem, connect the supplied cable to a nearby telephone outlet, instead.)
2. Connect the other end of the supplied cable to the input jack on the back of your broadband modem.

Continued

TIP

Your Connection Might Vary

Not all cable and DSL Internet connections are the same— especially if you're sharing the connection via a wireless network router. Consult your Internet provider for specific installation instructions.

TIP

Split the Signal

You may need to insert a splitter between your cable or phone connection and your modem. The splitter lets you connect both a television set or telephone and your modem to the same wall jack.

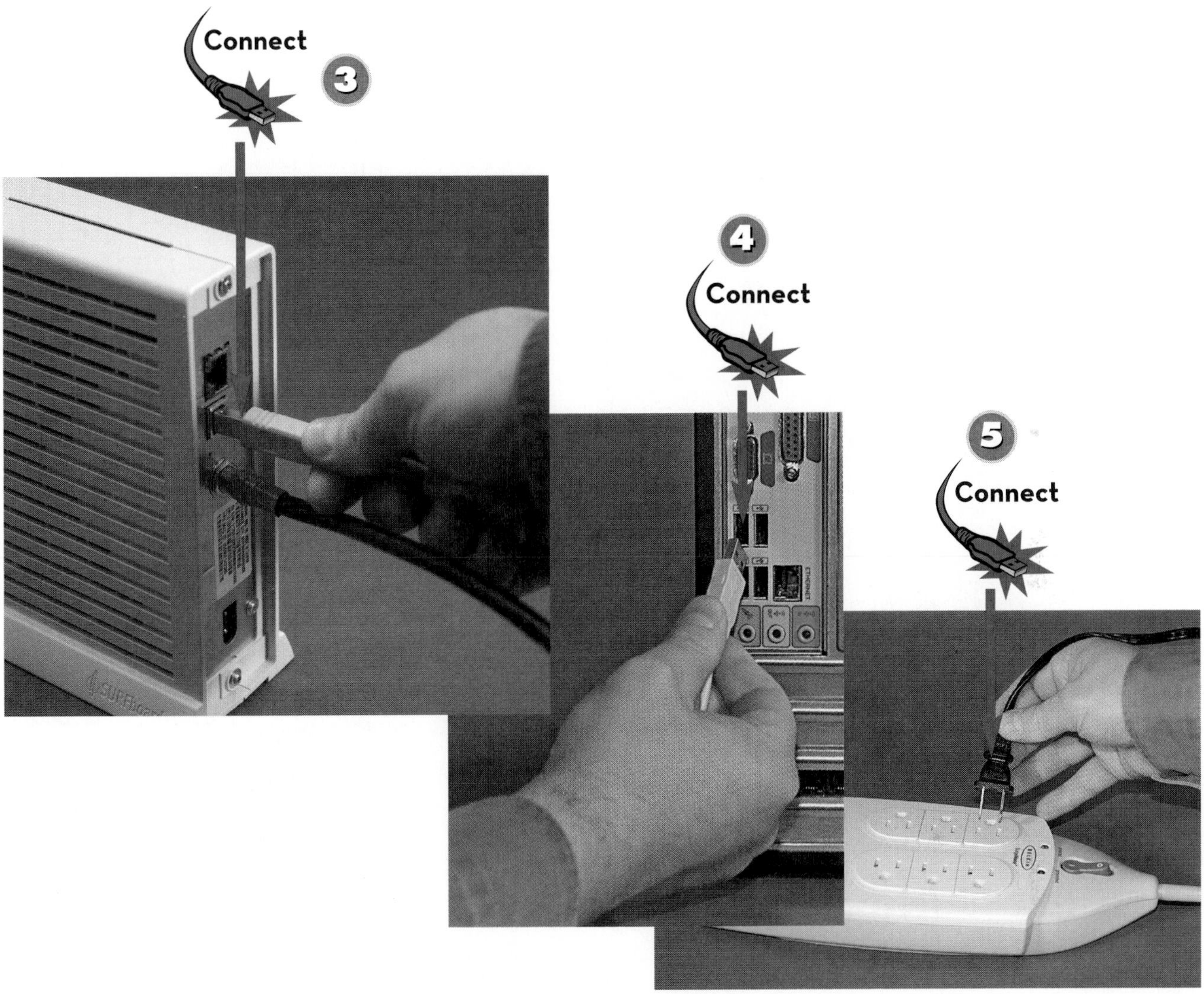

3. Connect one end of a USB cable to the USB "out" port on the back of the broadband modem.
4. Connect the other end of the USB cable to an open USB port on your computer's system unit.
5. Connect the power cable on your broadband modem to a power source. The modem should now turn on.

End

NOTE

USB Versus Ethernet

Some broadband modems can connect via either USB or Ethernet. To connect a single PC to the modem, use the USB connection. To connect the modem to a wireless network router, use the Ethernet connection.

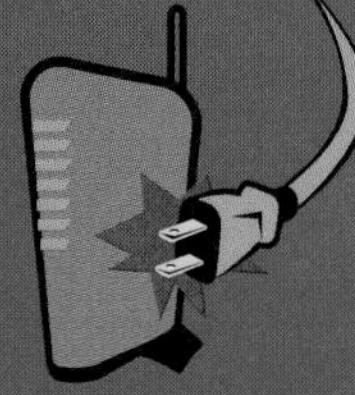

CONNECTING A PRINTER

Most printers connect via an easy-to-use USB cable. This type of connection is easier to configure than the parallel connection found on older printers.

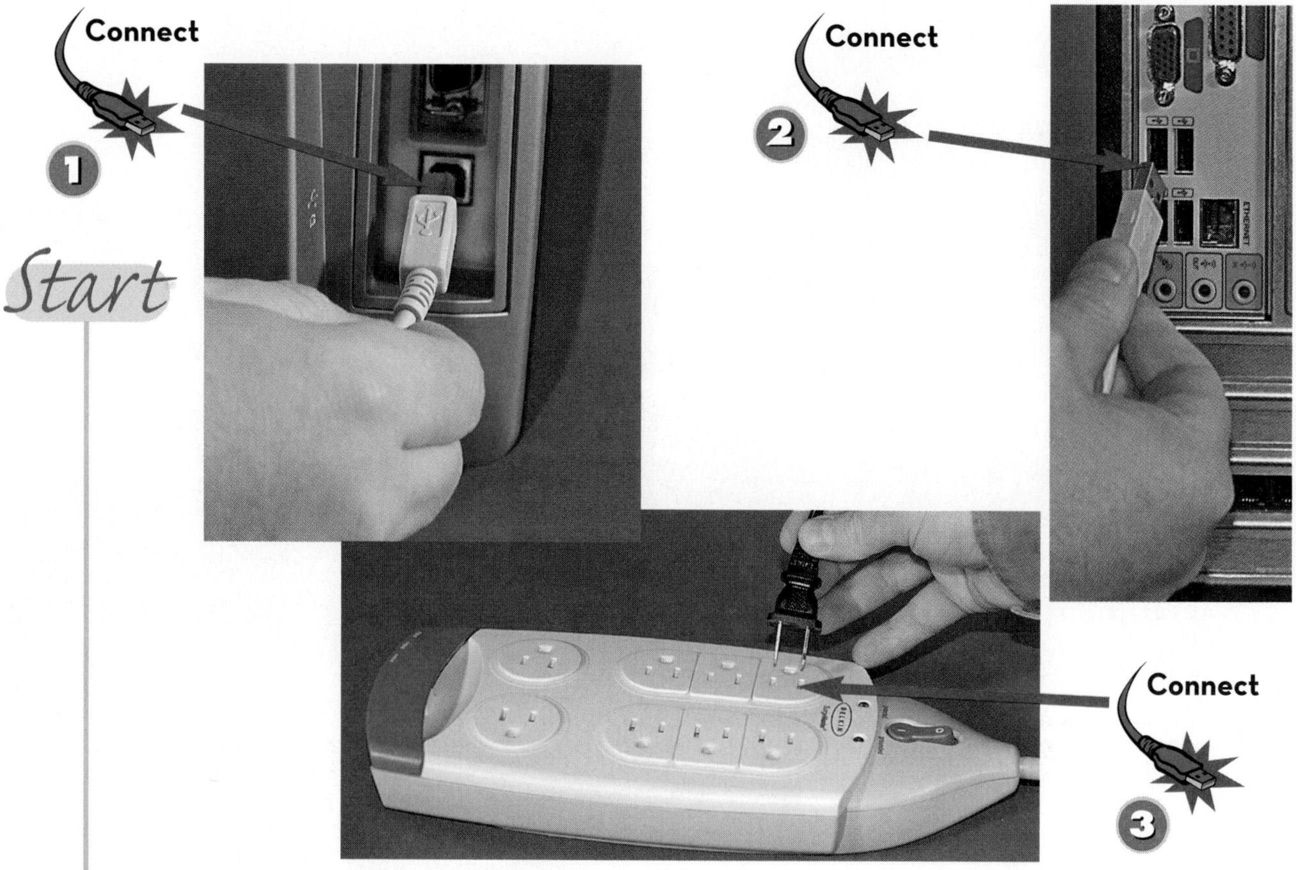

Connect

1

Connect

2

Connect

3

Start

1 Connect one end of a USB cable to the matching USB port on your printer.

2 Connect the other end of the USB cable to a USB port on the back of your system unit.

3 Connect the printer's power cable to a power outlet.

End

TIP

Advantages of USB

Because they can be connected without powering down your PC, USB printers can be moved between computers more easily than printers that use the older parallel connection. In addition, USB cables are a lot thinner than parallel cables, so if your space is tight, this is the way to go.

CONNECTING THE SYSTEM POWER CABLE

When all the other parts of your computer system are connected, you can then connect your system unit to a power source. Just make sure the power source is turned off before you connect!

Start

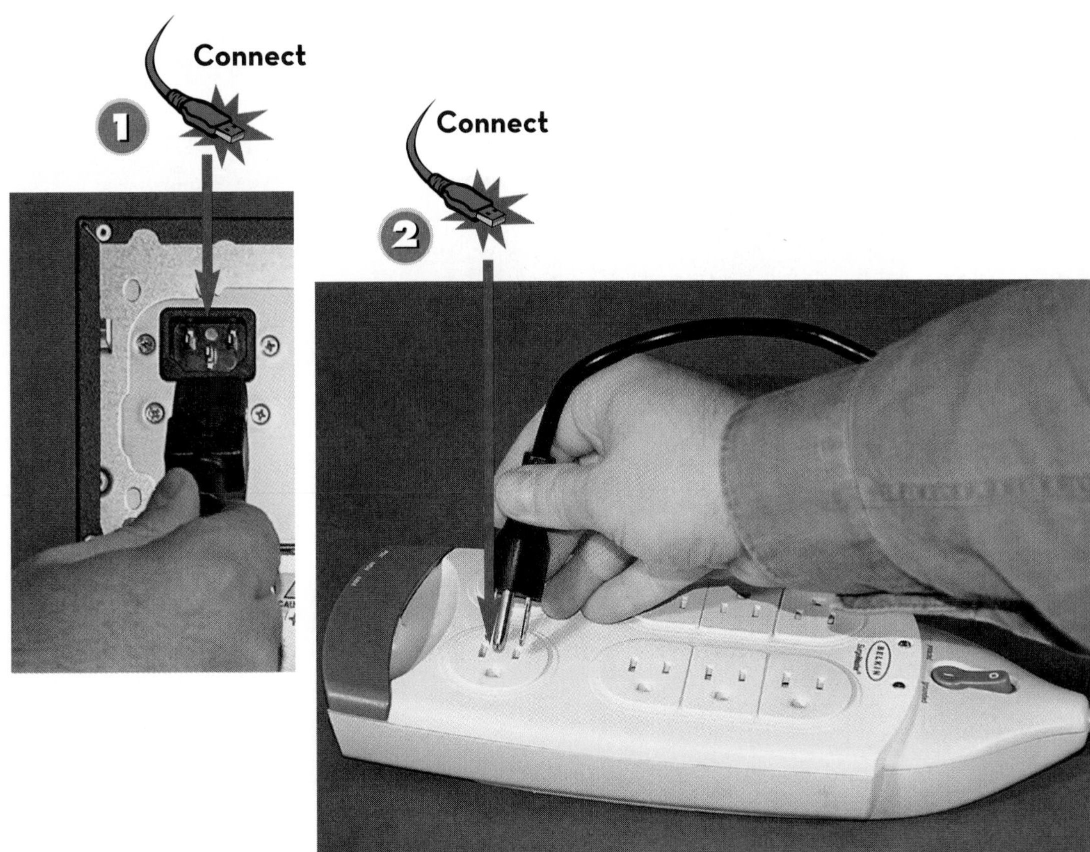

1 Connect one end of the power cable to the cable connector on the back of your system unit.

2 Connect the other end of the power cable to a power source.

End

TIP

Use a Surge Suppressor

For extra protection, connect the power cable on your system unit to a surge suppressor rather than directly into an electrical outlet. This will protect your PC from power-line surges that could damage its delicate internal parts.

POWERING ON

Now that you have everything connected, sit back and rest for a minute. Next up is the big step—turning it all on!

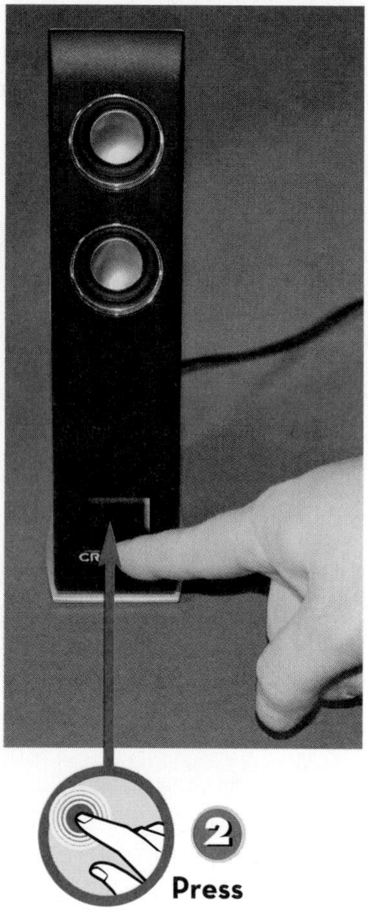

Press

Press

Start

1. Turn on your monitor.
2. Turn on your speaker system—but make sure the speaker volume knob is turned down (toward the left).

Continued

NOTE

Booting Up

Technical types call the procedure of starting up a computer *booting* or *booting up* the system. Restarting a system (turning it off and then back on) is called *rebooting*.

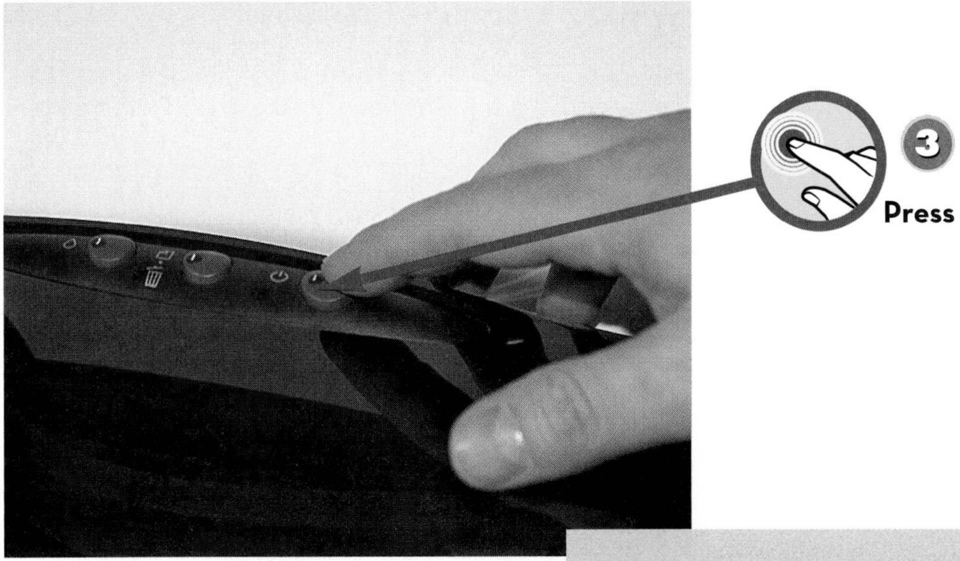

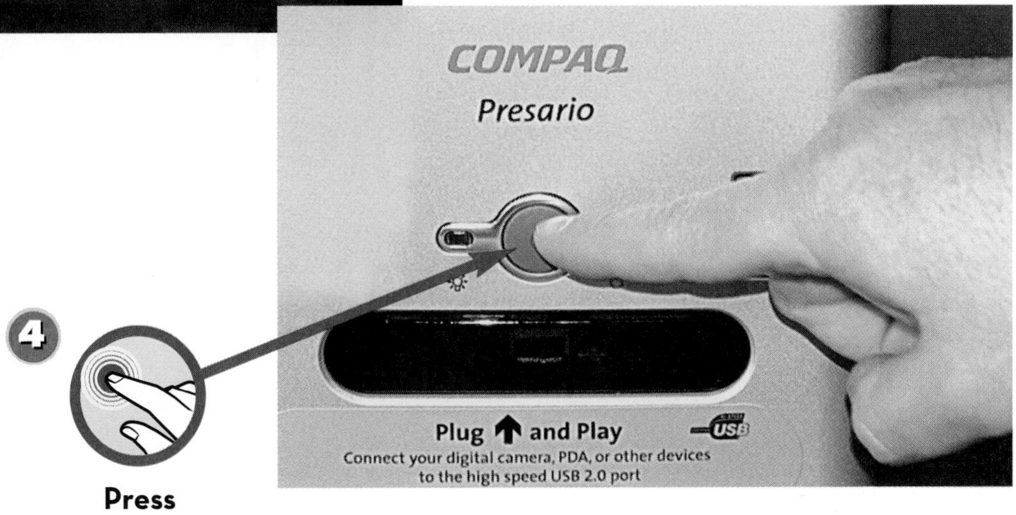

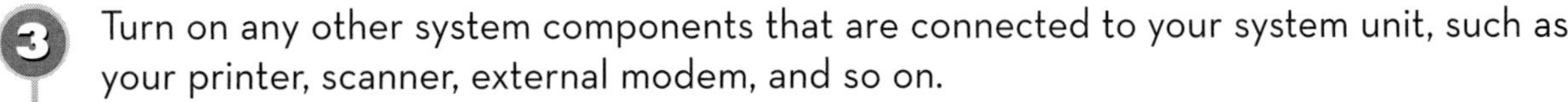

3. Turn on any other system components that are connected to your system unit, such as your printer, scanner, external modem, and so on.
4. Turn on your system unit.

End

CAUTION

Go in Order

Your system unit is the *last* thing you turn on. That's because when it powers on, it has to sense the other components of your system—which it can do only if the other components are plugged in and turned on.

TIP

Starting Up for the First Time

The first time you start your new PC, you're asked to perform some basic setup operations, including activating and registering Windows and configuring your system for your personal use.

LOGGING ON TO WINDOWS VISTA

Windows Vista launches automatically as your computer starts up. After you get past the Windows Welcome screen, you're taken directly to the Windows desktop and your system is ready to run.

Start

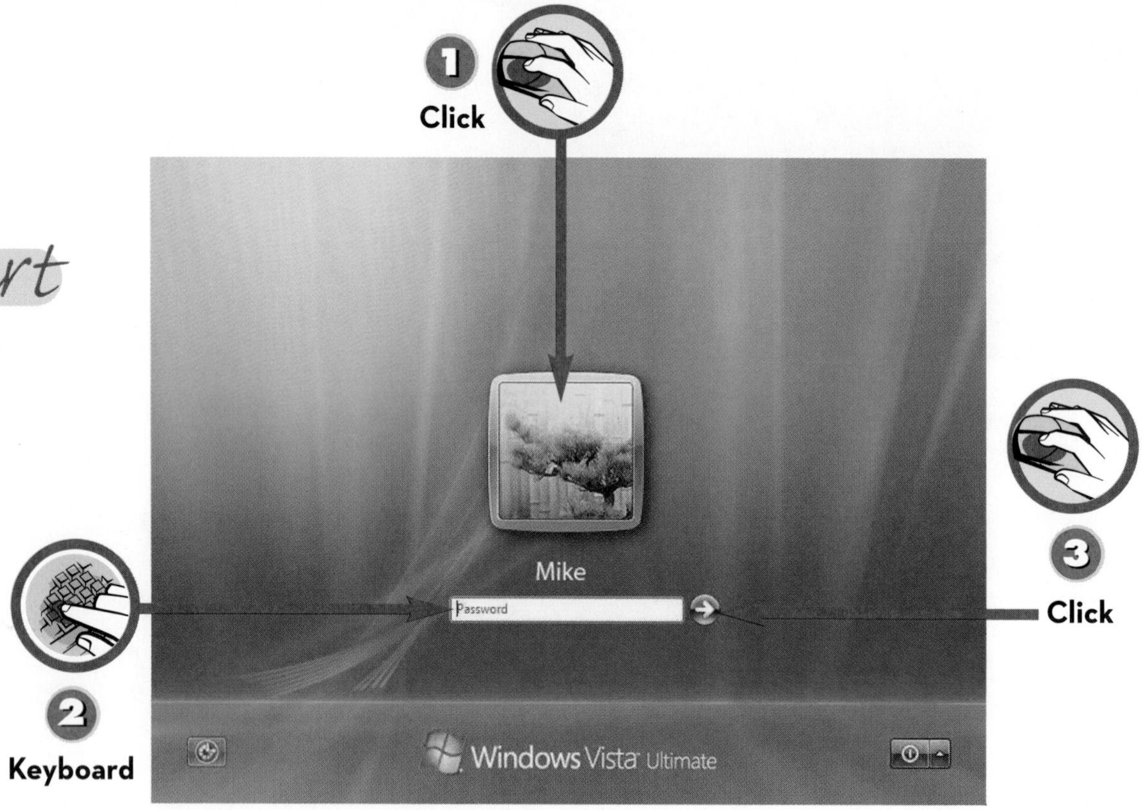

Click

Mike

Password

Click

Keyboard

Windows Vista Ultimate

1. When the Windows Welcome screen appears, click your username or picture.
2. Enter your password (if necessary).
3. Press the **Enter** key on your keyboard or click the green right-arrow button.

End

TIP

Single-User Systems

If you have only a single user on your PC and that user doesn't have a password assigned, Windows moves past the Welcome screen with no action necessary on your part.

SHUTTING DOWN

When you want to turn off your computer, you do it through Windows. In fact, you don't want to turn off your computer any other way—you *always* want to turn things off through the official Windows procedure.

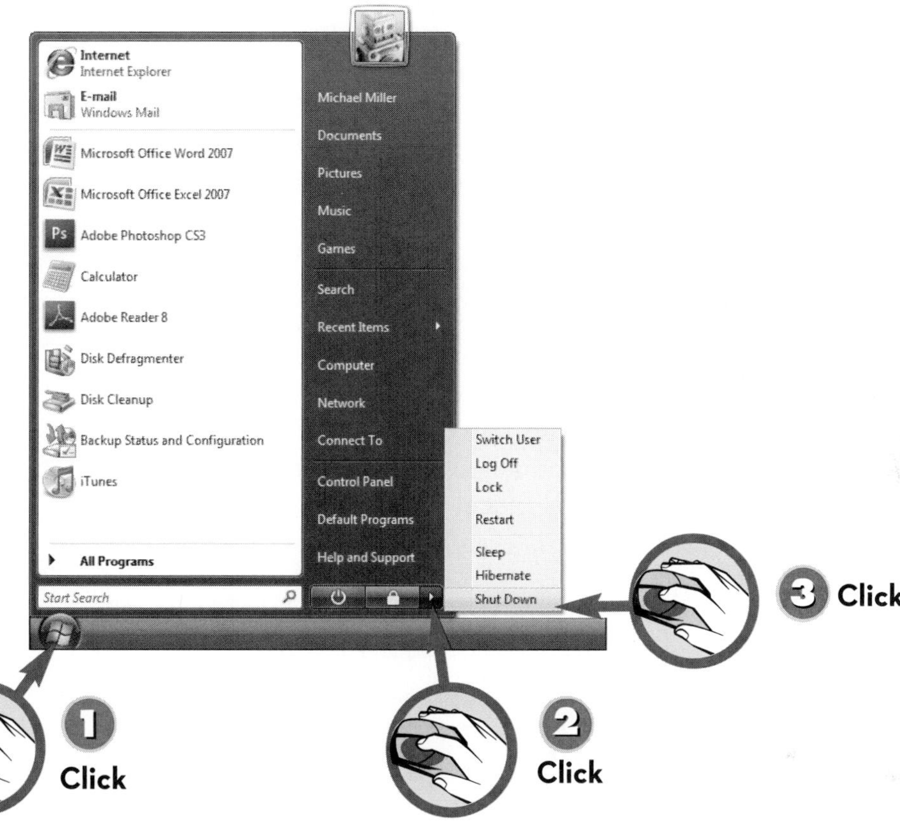

1. Click the **Start** button to display the Start menu.
2. Click the right arrow (at the bottom right) to display the pop-up menu.
3. Click **Shut Down**.

CAUTION

Always Use Windows to Shut Down

Do *not* turn off your computer without shutting down Windows. You could lose data and settings that are temporarily stored in your system's memory.

TIP

Sleep Mode

You might think you turn off your computer by clicking the "off" button on the Start menu, but this merely puts Windows Vista into Sleep mode; your computer's hardware is still running in a low-power state, ready to start up quickly when you turn it on again. To fully power down your system, you need to go through the extra step of selecting Shut Down from the pop-up menu.

SETTING UP AND USING A NOTEBOOK PC

Setting up a notebook PC is different from setting up a desktop PC. In most instances, it's a lot easier; most of the external devices on a desktop PC (monitor, keyboard, mouse, and so on) are built into a notebook, so there's less to connect. And, for those few external devices you do have to connect, almost all of them connect via USB.

The other thing that's different about using a notebook PC is operating on battery power. Yes, you can plug the notebook into a power outlet and use it that way, but you can also unplug the cord and run on the internal battery. This makes a notebook PC truly portable—which is one of the reasons you bought it in the first place!

NOTEBOOK CONNECTIONS

CONNECTING THE POWER CABLE

Most notebook PCs use a unique cable to connect to AC power. The end that connects to your notebook uses a mini power adapter; the end that connects to the wall outlet is a normal AC connector. In between is a brick-like power supply that manages the power connection.

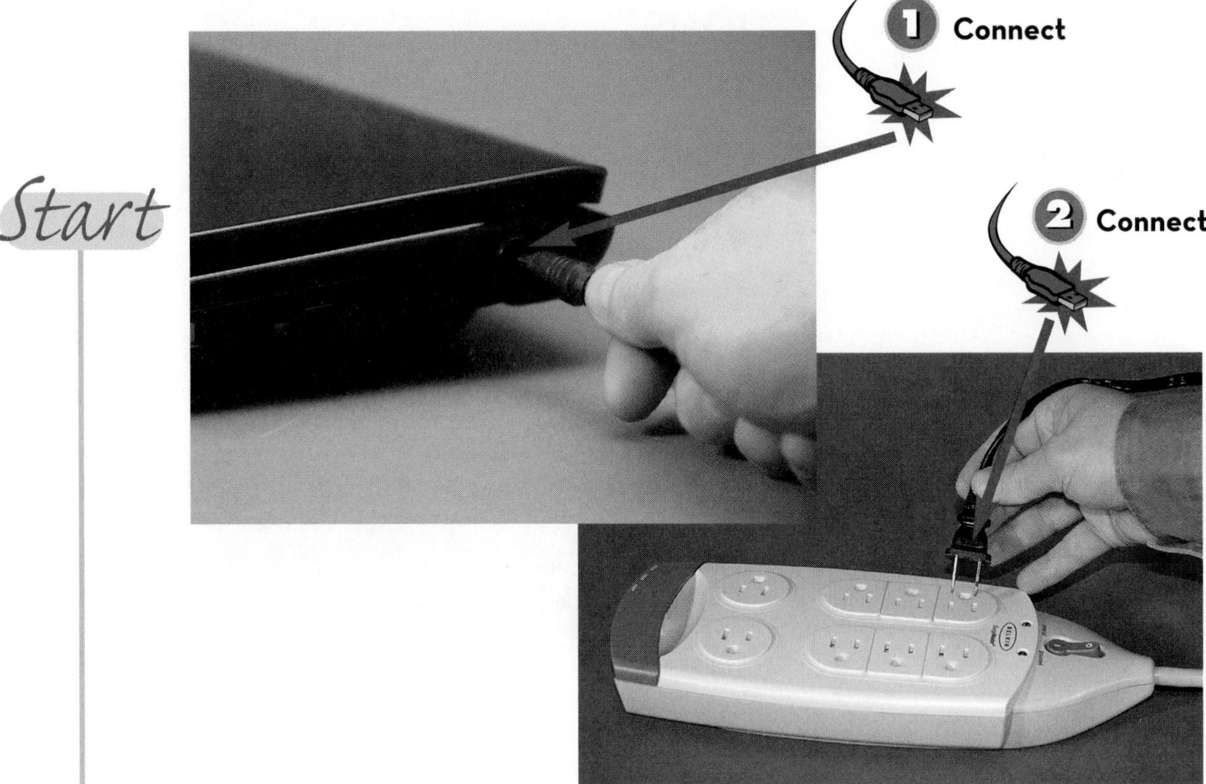

1. Connect one end of the power cable to the power connector on the side or back of your notebook PC.
2. Connect the other end of the power cable to a power source.

End

TIP

Power Supplies

In a desktop PC, the power supply is built into the system unit. To minimize the size and weight of a notebook PC, the power supply is kept external as part of the power cable assembly.

CONNECTING A PRINTER

Any USB printer can connect directly to a notebook PC. Just connect a USB cable between the two, and you're ready to start printing!

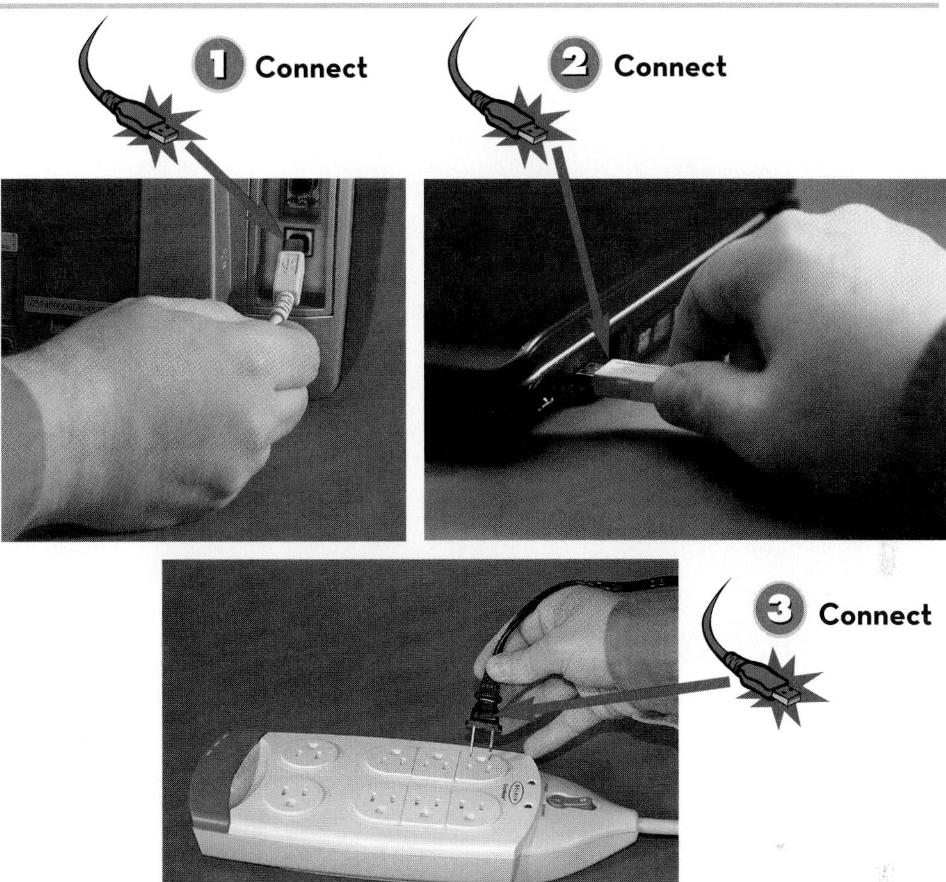

Start

1. Connect one end of a USB cable to the matching USB port on your printer.
2. Connect the other end of the USB cable to a USB port on the side of your notebook PC.
3. Connect the printer's power cable to a power outlet.

End

NOTE

Recognizing the Printer

The first time you connect a printer to your notebook PC, Windows should automatically install it on your system. (You might also need to run the printer's installation CD.) The next time you connect the printer, Windows should recognize the printer and activate it without the need to reinstall it again.

CONNECTING A BROADBAND MODEM

If your notebook PC is your home's main PC, you can connect it directly to a broadband modem to connect to the Internet. The easiest way to connect is via USB; most broadband modems feature a USB connector.

Start

1 Connect

2 Connect

1. Connect one end of the supplied cable to the cable outlet on a nearby wall. (If you have a DSL modem, connect the supplied cable to a nearby telephone outlet, instead.)
2. Connect the other end of the supplied cable to the input jack on the back of your broadband modem.

Continued

NOTE

Connecting via Wireless

If you prefer not to anchor yourself to a wired Internet connection, you can connect your broadband modem to a wireless network router and then connect your notebook PC wirelessly. Learn more in Part 8, "Setting Up a Wireless Home Network."

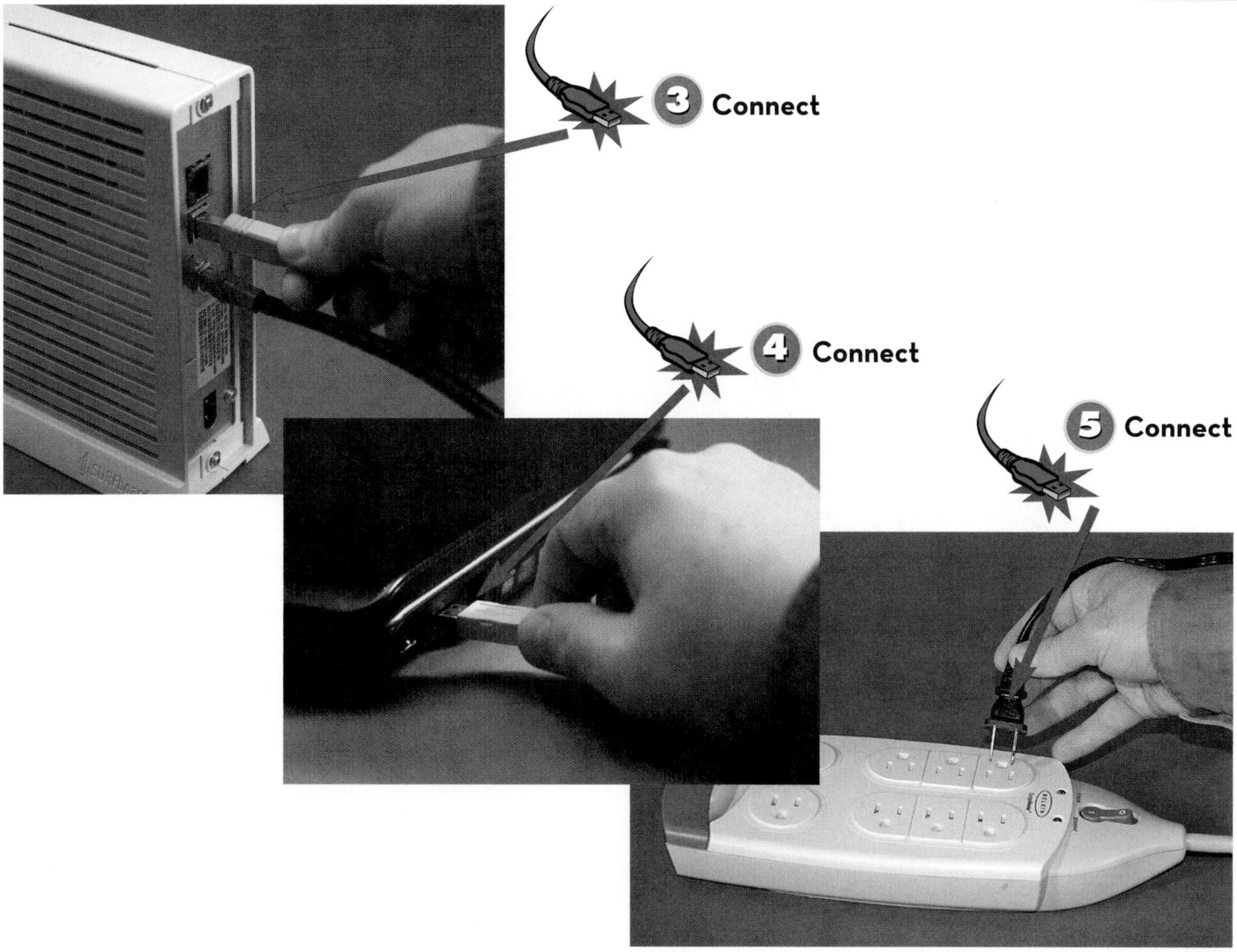

3 Connect

4 Connect

5 Connect

3. Connect one end of a USB cable to the USB "out" port on the back of the broadband modem.
4. Connect the other end of the USB cable to an open USB port on your notebook PC.
5. Connect the power cable on your broadband modem to a power source. The modem should now turn on.

End

NOTE

Wired or Wireless?

One advantage of a notebook PC is the fact that you can use it from any room in your house. For this reason, many users prefer a wireless Internet connection, which requires you to connect your broadband modem to a wireless home network. On the other hand, a direct wired connection from your modem to your notebook is an easier connection, with no network to set up.

POWERING ON

Turning on a notebook PC is as easy as opening the case and pressing the power button. Just wait a minute or two for Windows to start!

Start

1 Open

2 Press

1. Open your notebook's case so that you can see the screen and access the keyboard.
2. Press your notebook's "power on" button until the notebook comes to life.

End

NOTE

Turning On Automatically

Some manufacturers configure their notebooks to turn on automatically when the case is opened. If your notebook is so configured, you don't even have to press the power button to turn it on.

USING SLEEP MODE

You don't always want to completely shut down your notebook; the full power-down (and subsequent power-up) process is time consuming. For that reason, Windows Vista includes a special Sleep mode that stores your current programs and documents in memory while it puts your notebook into a low-power type of hibernation. When you wake your computer from Sleep mode, it quickly resumes full-power operation, with your programs and documents already onscreen.

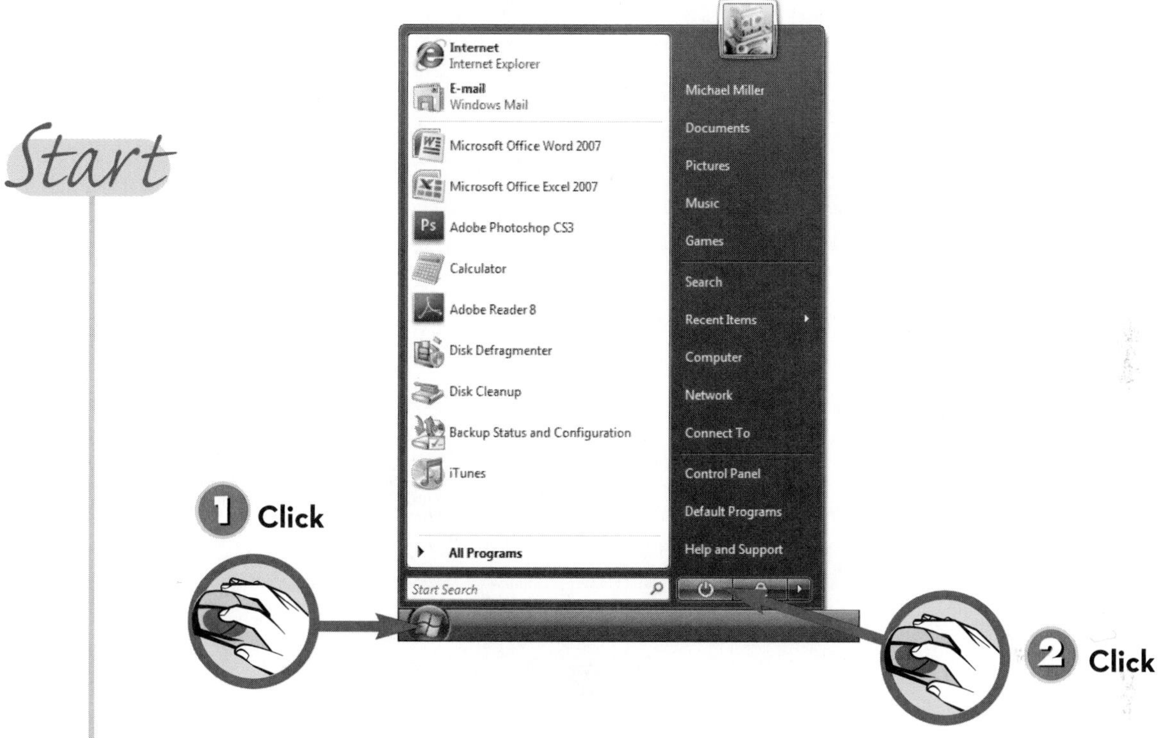

1. Click the **Start** button to display the Start menu.
2. Click the **power** button.

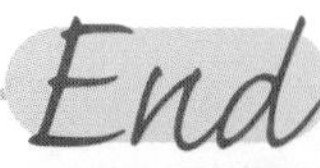

TIP

Other Ways to Sleep

Some manufacturers configure their notebooks to enter Sleep mode if you press the power button or just close the notebook case. Consult your PC's instruction manual to see what happens when you perform either of these operations.

NOTE

Waking Up from Sleep Mode

When your notebook is in Sleep mode, you can wake it up (resume full-power operation) by opening the case and pressing the power button.

SHUTTING DOWN

Sleep mode is great for quick on/off situations. But when your computer is going to go unused for longer periods of time, you want to completely power off your notebook—which you do via the Windows Start menu.

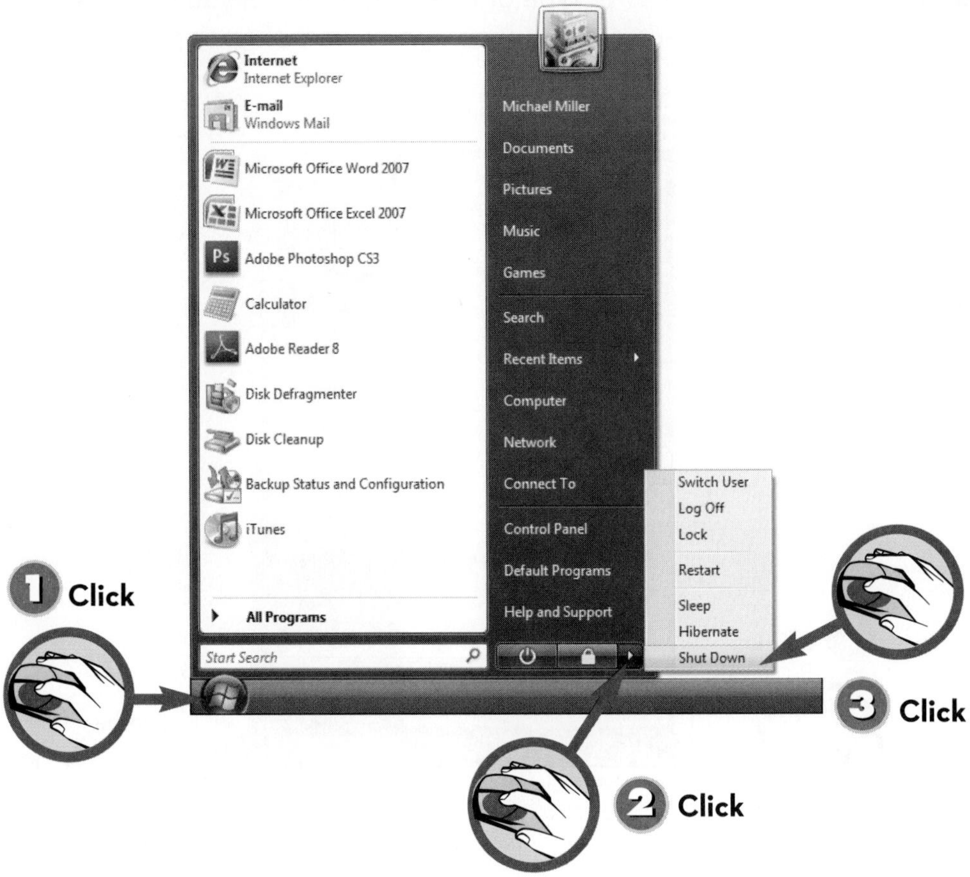

1. Click the **Start** button to display the Start menu.
2. Click the right arrow (at the bottom right) to display the pop-up menu.
3. Click **Shut Down**.

TIP

Sleep Versus Power Off

Remember, clicking the power button on the Start menu doesn't power down your computer; this button activates Sleep mode. To fully power down your system, you need to go through the extra step of selecting Shut Down from the pop-up menu.

RUNNING ON BATTERIES

Most notebook batteries last for two hours or more before you need to plug into a power outlet and recharge. The battery icon in the Windows Taskbar notification area (system tray) tells you how much battery power is left—and lets you select an alternate power plan.

Start

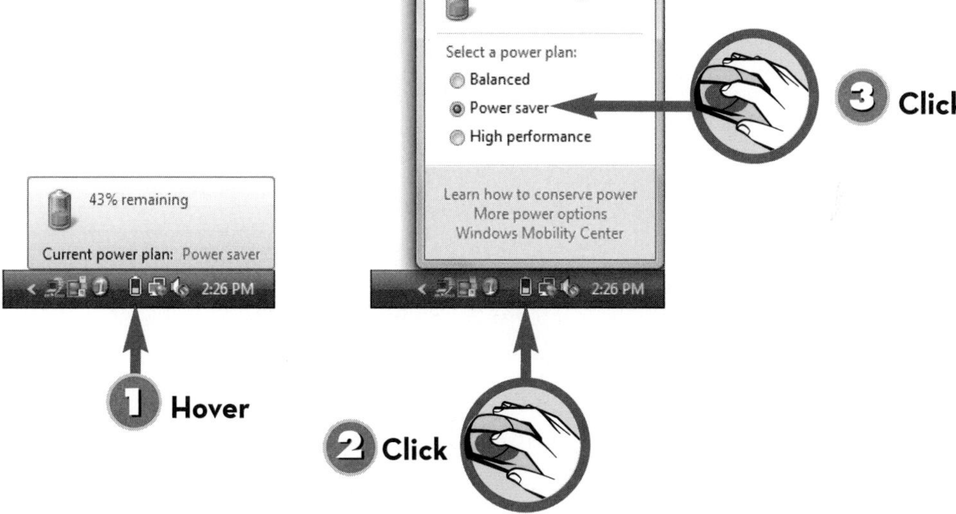

1. To view the remaining battery life, hover your cursor over the battery icon.
2. To select a different power plan, click the battery icon.
3. Select a new power plan from the pop-up menu.

End

NOTE

Power Plans

A *power plan* combines different power-saving features to help you get more life out of each battery charge. For example, the Power Saver plan reduces screen brightness, turns off the display after three minutes of inactivity, and puts the computer to sleep if you haven't used it in 15 minutes.

part

USING MICROSOFT WINDOWS VISTA

Microsoft Windows Vista is a piece of software called an *operating system*. An operating system does what its name implies—it operates your computer system, working in the background every time you turn on your PC.

Equally important, Windows is what you see when you first turn on your computer, after everything turns on and boots up. The *desktop* that fills your screen is part of Windows, as is the Taskbar at the bottom of the screen and the big menu that pops up when you click the Start button.

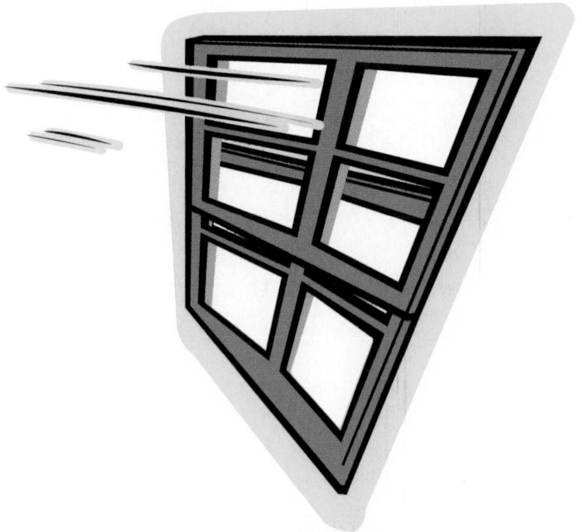

EXPLORING THE WINDOWS VISTA DESKTOP

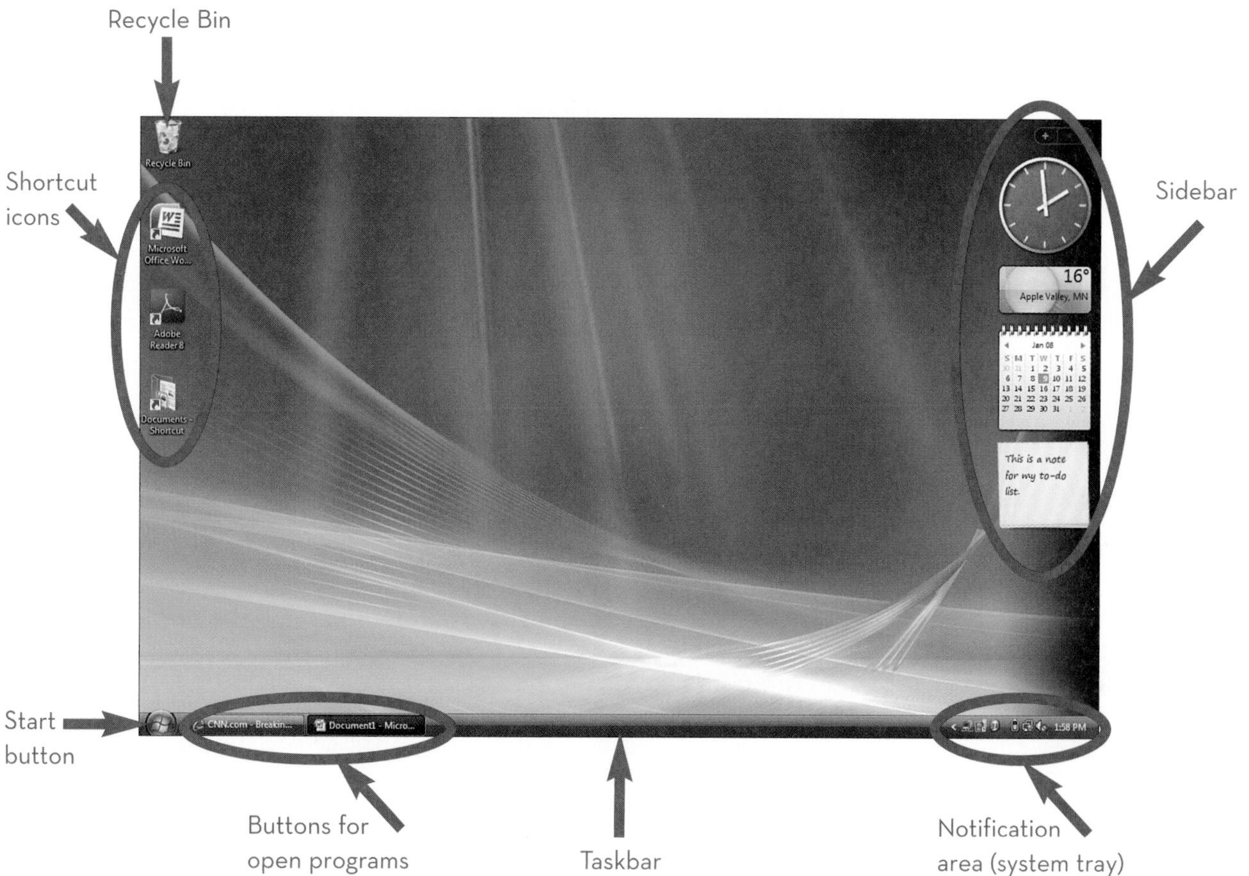

USING THE MOUSE

To use Windows efficiently, you must master a few simple operations, all of which you perform with your mouse. Most mouse operations include pointing and clicking. Normal clicking uses the left mouse button; however, some operations require that you click the right mouse button, instead.

Start

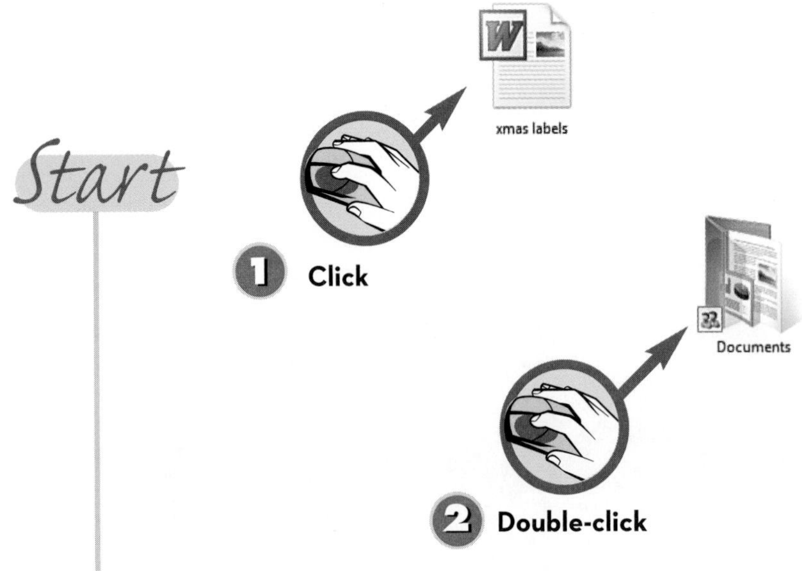

1 To single-click, position the cursor over the onscreen item and click the left mouse button.

2 To double-click, position the cursor over the onscreen item and click the left mouse button twice in rapid succession.

Continued

TIP

Click to Select

Pointing and clicking is an effective way to select icons, menu items, directories, and files.

TIP

Hovering

Another common mouse operation is *hovering*, where you hold the cursor over an onscreen item without pressing either of the mouse buttons. For example, when you hover your cursor over an icon or menu item, Windows displays a *ToolTip* that tells you a little about the selected item.

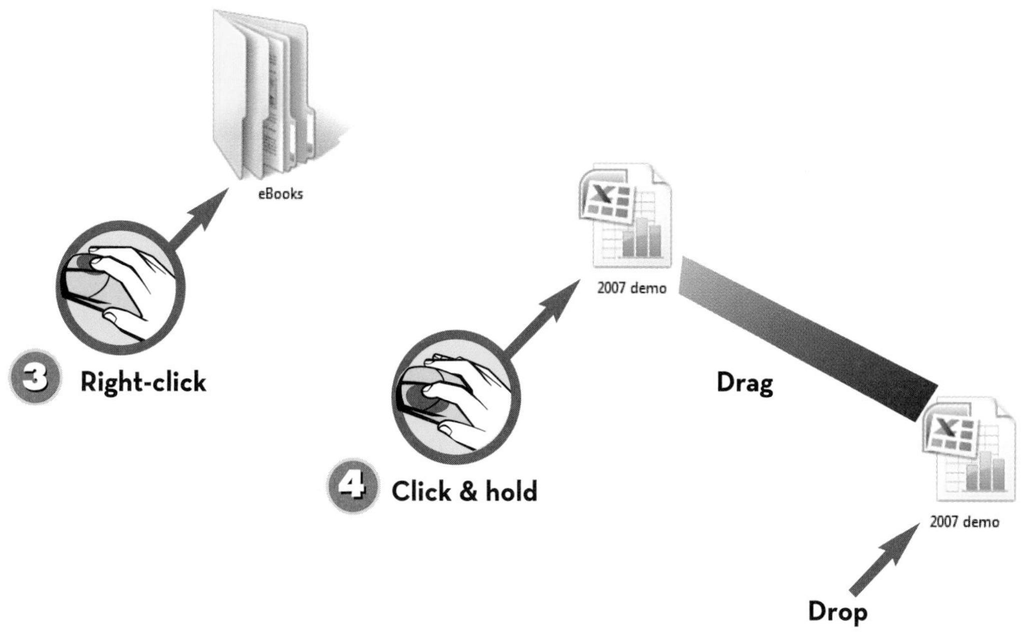

3 To right-click, position the cursor over the onscreen item and then click the *right* mouse button.

4 To drag and drop an item from one location to another, position the cursor over the item, click and hold the left mouse button, drag the item to a new position, and then release the mouse button.

End

TIP

Pop-Up Menus

Many items in Windows feature a context-sensitive pop-up menu. You access this menu by right-clicking the item. (When in doubt, right-click the item and see what pops up!)

TIP

Moving Files

You can use dragging and dropping to move files from one folder to another or to delete files by dragging them onto the Recycle Bin icon.

SCROLLING A WINDOW

Many windows contain more information than can be displayed in the window at once. When you have a long document or web page, only the first part of the document or page is displayed in the window. To view the rest of the document or page, you have to scroll down through the window, using the various parts of the scrollbar.

1. Click the **up arrow** on the window's scrollbar to scroll up one line at a time.
2. Click the **down arrow** on the window's scrollbar to scroll down one line at a time.

End

TIP

Other Ways to Scroll

To move to a specific place in a long document, use your mouse to grab the scrollbox (also called a slider) and drag it to a new position. You can also click the scrollbar between the scrollbox and the end arrow, which scrolls you one screen at a time.

MAXIMIZING, MINIMIZING, AND CLOSING A WINDOW

After you've opened a window, you can maximize it to display full-screen. You can also minimize it so that it disappears from the desktop and resides as a button on the Windows Taskbar, and you can close it completely.

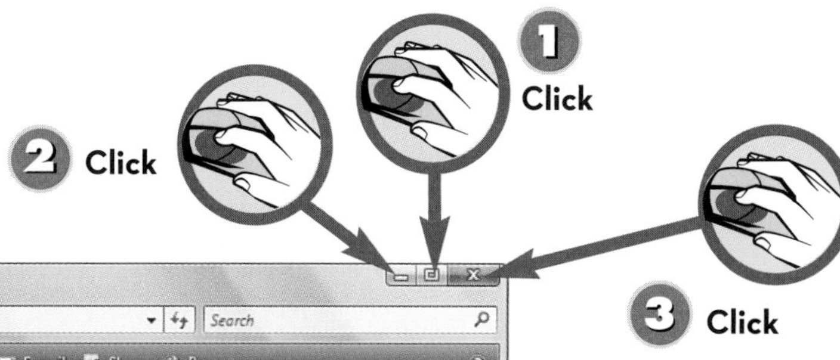

Start

1. To maximize the window, click the **Maximize** button.
2. To minimize the window, click the **Minimize** button.
3. To close the window completely, click the **Close** button.

End

TIP

Restoring a Window

If a window is already maximized, the Maximize button changes to a Restore Down button. When you click the Restore Down button, the window resumes its previous (premaximized) dimensions.

USING THE WINDOWS START MENU

All the software programs and utilities on your computer are accessed via the Windows Start menu, which consists of two columns of icons. Your most frequently used programs are listed in the left column; basic Windows utilities and folders are listed in the right column. To open a specific program or folder, just click the menu icon.

Start

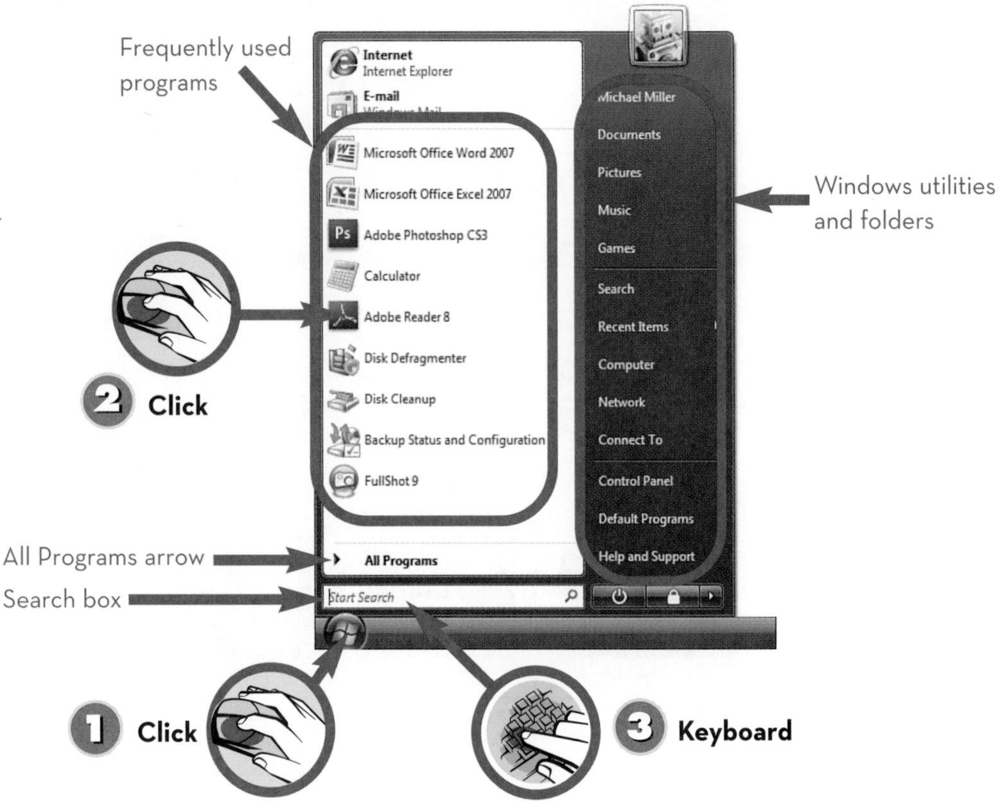

Frequently used programs

Windows utilities and folders

2 Click

All Programs arrow

Search box

1 Click

3 Keyboard

1. Click the round **Start** button to open the Start menu.
2. Click any menu item to launch a program or open a folder.
3. Alternately, you can enter a program name into the **Search** box to search for that program.

End

OPENING A PROGRAM

To view all the programs installed on your PC, open the Start menu and click the All Programs arrow. This displays a new menu called the Programs menu. From here, you can access various programs, organized by type and title or manufacturer.

Start

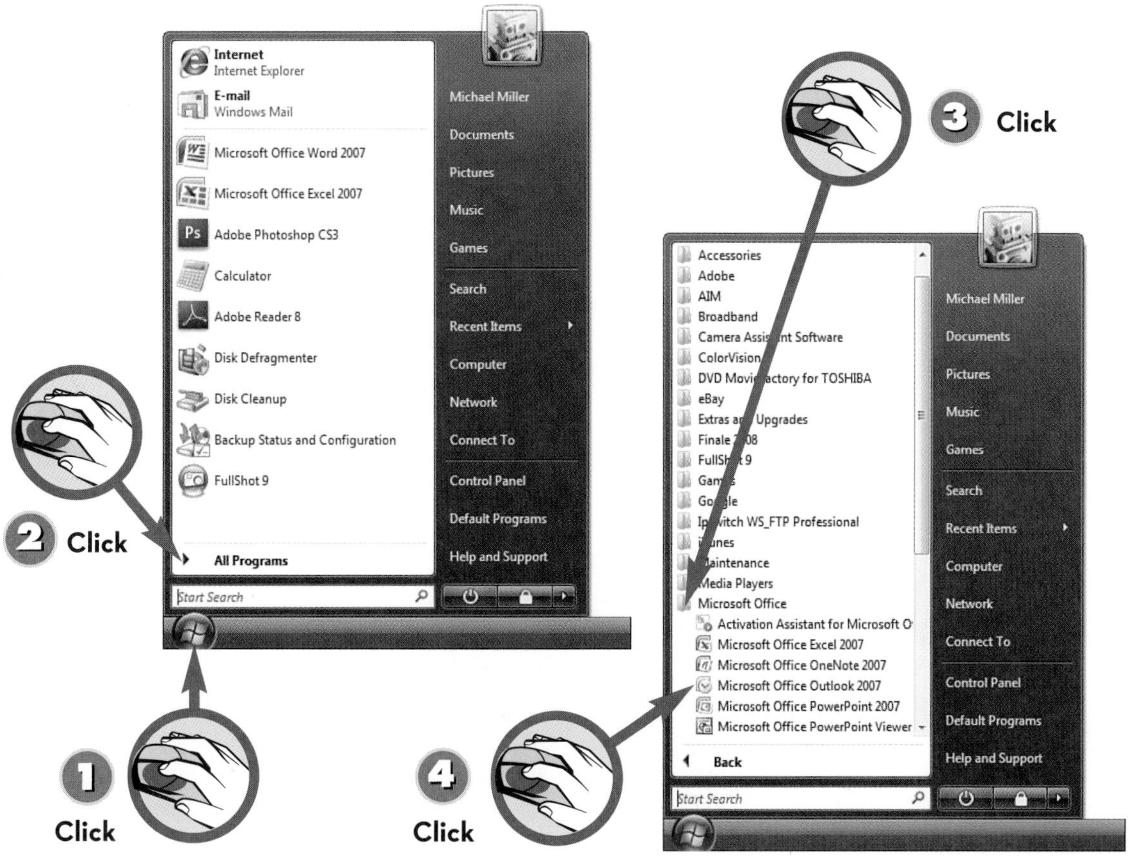

1. Click the **Start** button to display the Start menu.
2. Click the **All Programs** icon to display the Programs menu.
3. Click any folder to expand that item and show its contents.
4. Click the icon for the program you want to launch.

End

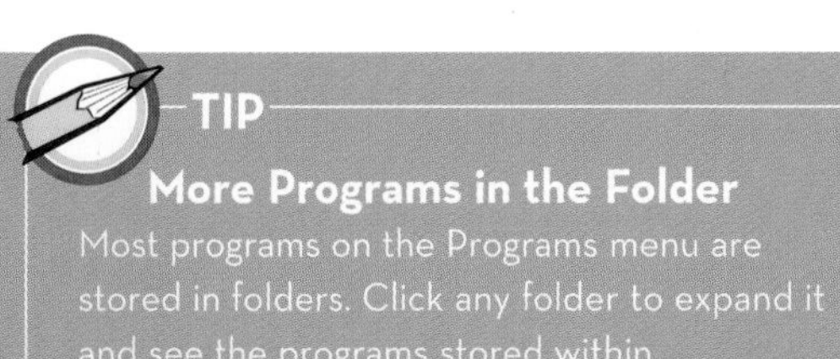

TIP

More Programs in the Folder

Most programs on the Programs menu are stored in folders. Click any folder to expand it and see the programs stored within.

SWITCHING BETWEEN PROGRAMS

After you've launched a few programs, you can easily switch between one open program and another by using one of two different keyboard shortcuts. The Windows Flip method (Alt + Tab) displays icons of all open programs; the Flip 3D method (Windows + Tab) displays a three-dimensional stack of your open programs.

1 Alt + Tab

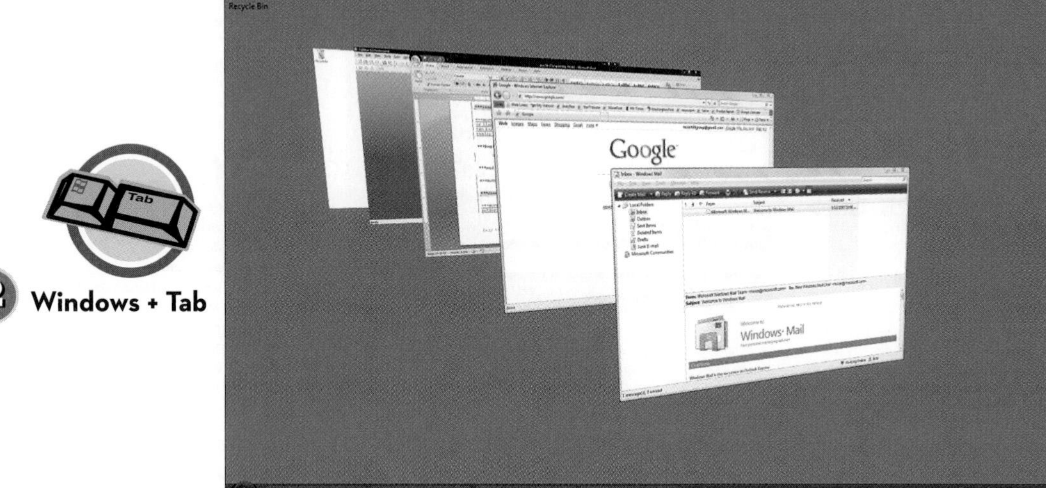

2 Windows + Tab

1. To display thumbnails of all open programs, press **Alt + Tab**; repeat to cycle through and select a program.
2. To display a 3D stack of all open programs, press **Windows + Tab**; repeat to cycle through and select a program.

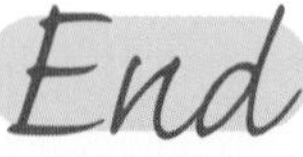

TIP

Button Switching

When a program or document is open, a button for that item appears in the Windows Taskbar. You can quickly switch to any program or document by clicking that item's Taskbar button.

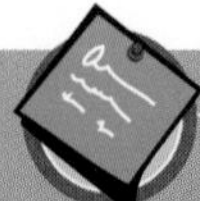

NOTE

Flip 3D

The Flip 3D feature is not available in the Home Basic version of Windows Vista or if your hardware isn't capable of running Vista's Aero interface.

USING MENUS

Most Windows programs and utilities use a set of pull-down menus to store all the commands and operations you can perform. The menus are aligned across the top of the window, just below the title bar, in what is called a menu bar. You open (or pull down) a menu by clicking the menu's name; you select a menu item by clicking it with your mouse.

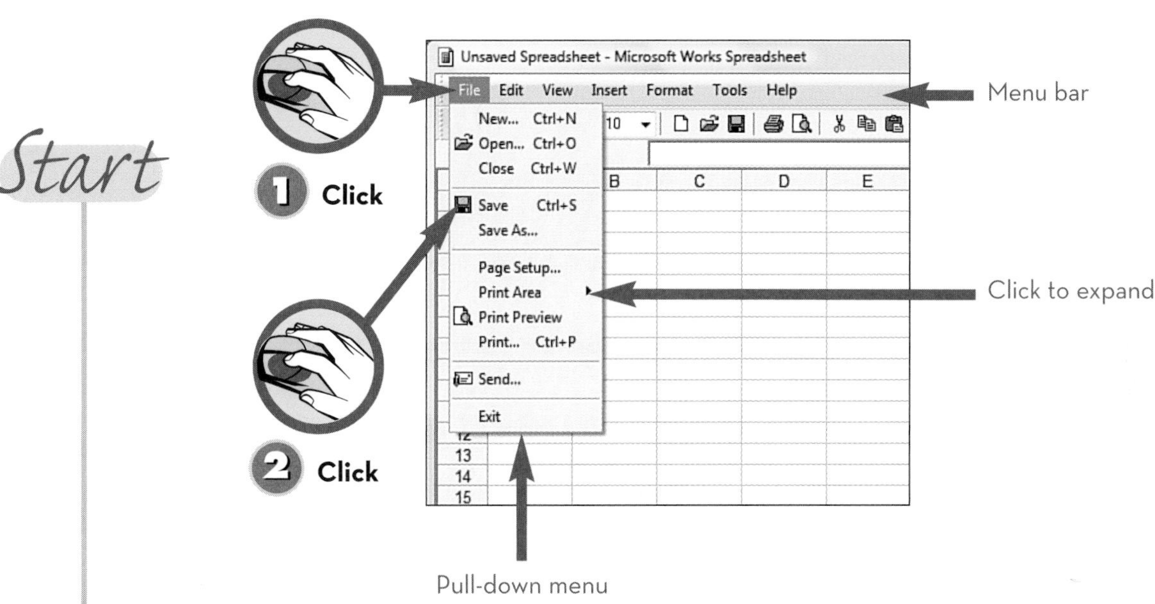

1. Click the menu's name to pull down the menu.
2. Click the menu item to select it.

End

TIP

Not All Items Are Available

If an item in a menu, toolbar, or dialog box is dimmed (or grayed), that means it isn't available for the current task.

USING TOOLBARS AND RIBBONS

Some Windows programs put the most frequently used operations on one or more *toolbars* or *ribbons*, typically located just below the menu bar. A toolbar looks like a row of buttons, each with a small picture (called an *icon*) and maybe a bit of text. You activate the associated command or operation by clicking the button with your mouse.

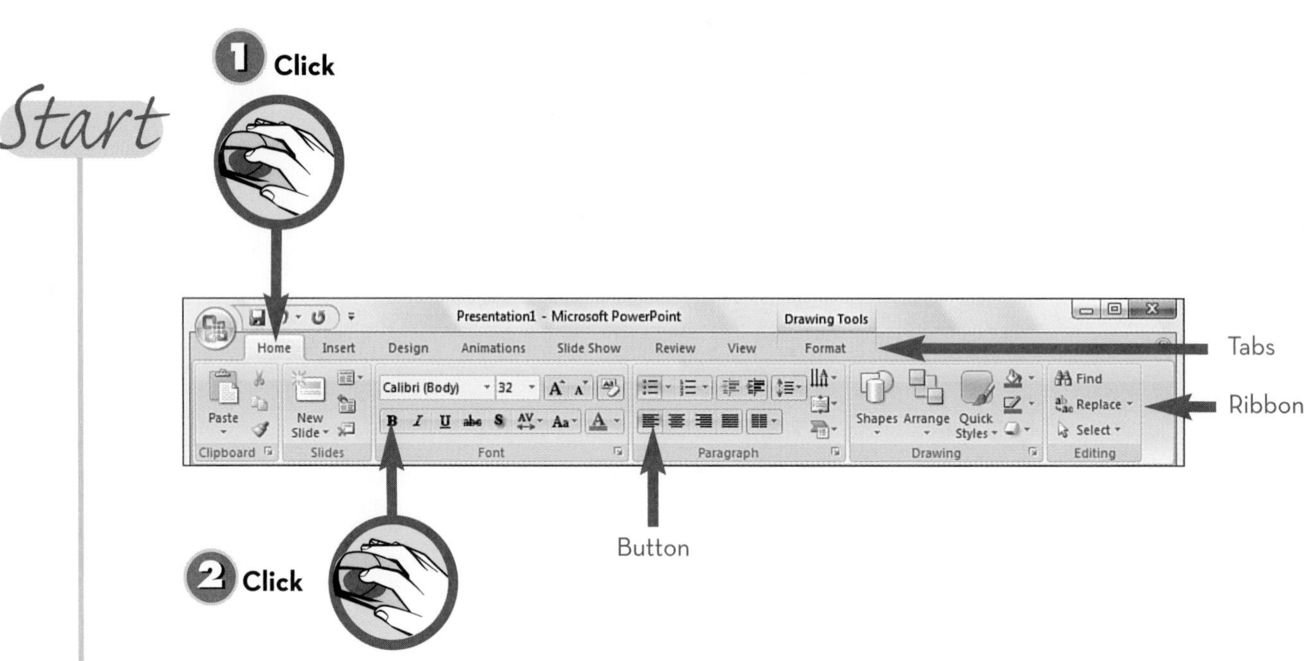

1. Click a tab to select that particular ribbon.
2. Click a ribbon/toolbar button to select that operation.

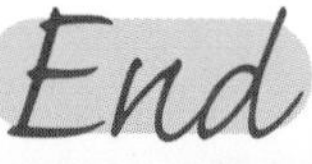

TIP

Long Toolbars

If the toolbar is too long to display fully on your screen, you'll see a right arrow at the far-right side of the toolbar. Click this arrow to display the buttons that aren't currently visible.

NOTE

Ribbons

The ribbon interface is available only in some newer applications, such as Microsoft Office 2007. Older applications use the traditional toolbar interface.

MANAGING PC RESOURCES WITH COMPUTER EXPLORER

TheWindows Computer Explorer folder lets you access each major component of your system and perform basic maintenance functions. For example, you can use Computer Explorer to "open" the contents of your hard disk and then copy, move, and delete individual files.

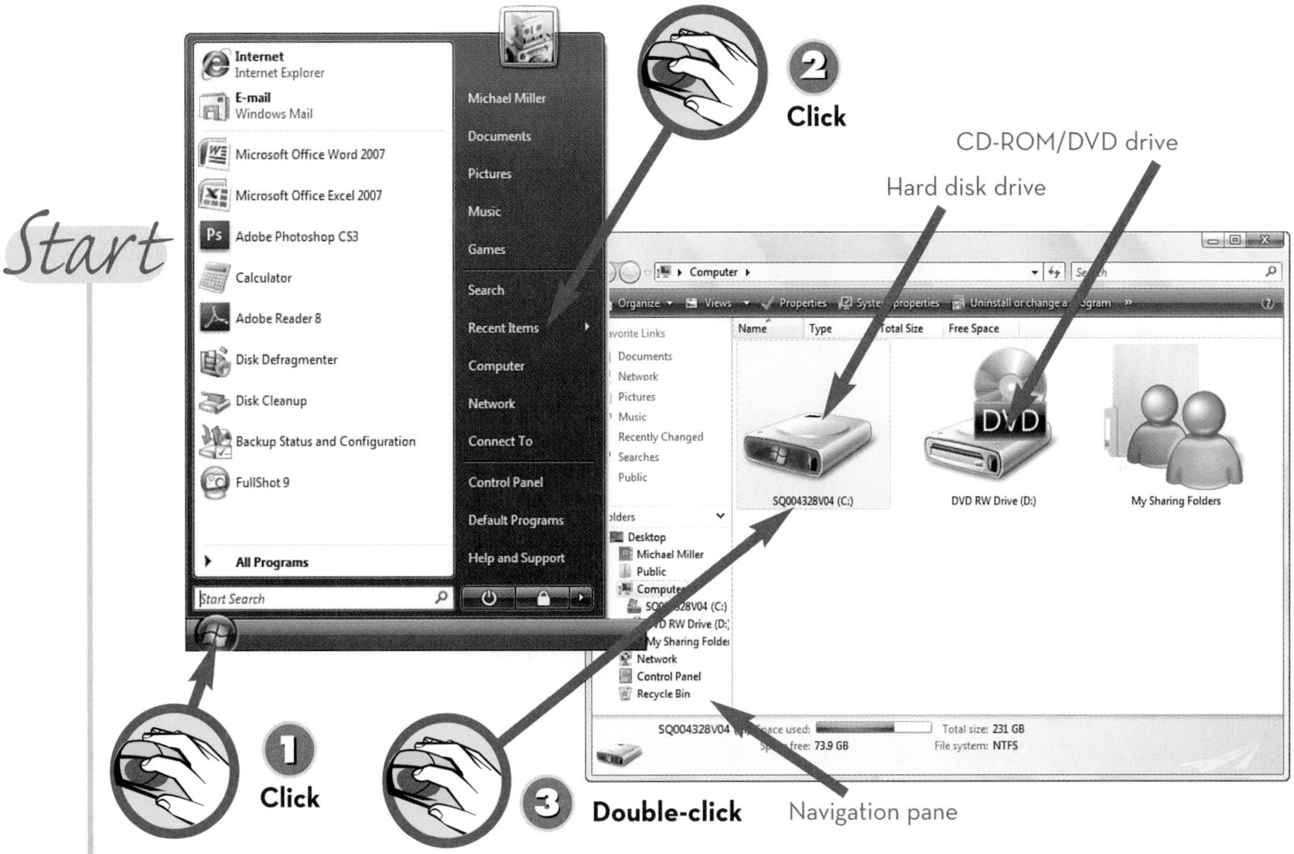

1. Click the **Start** button to display the Start menu.
2. Click **Computer**.
3. Double-click any icon to view its contents.

End

TIP

View Drive Contents

To view the contents of a specific drive, double-click the drive's icon. You'll see a list of folders and files located on that drive; to view the contents of any folder, double-click the icon for that folder.

TIP

Explore the Navigation Pane

Every folder in Windows Vista features a Navigation pane on the left side of the window that contains a list of Favorite Links and a "tree" view of all the drives, folders, and subfolders on your computer. Click any item to view its contents in the main folder window.

MANAGING WINDOWS WITH THE CONTROL PANEL

The Windows Control Panel is used to manage most (but not all) of the Windows configuration settings. The Control Panel contains links to individual utilities that let you adjust and configure various system properties.

Start

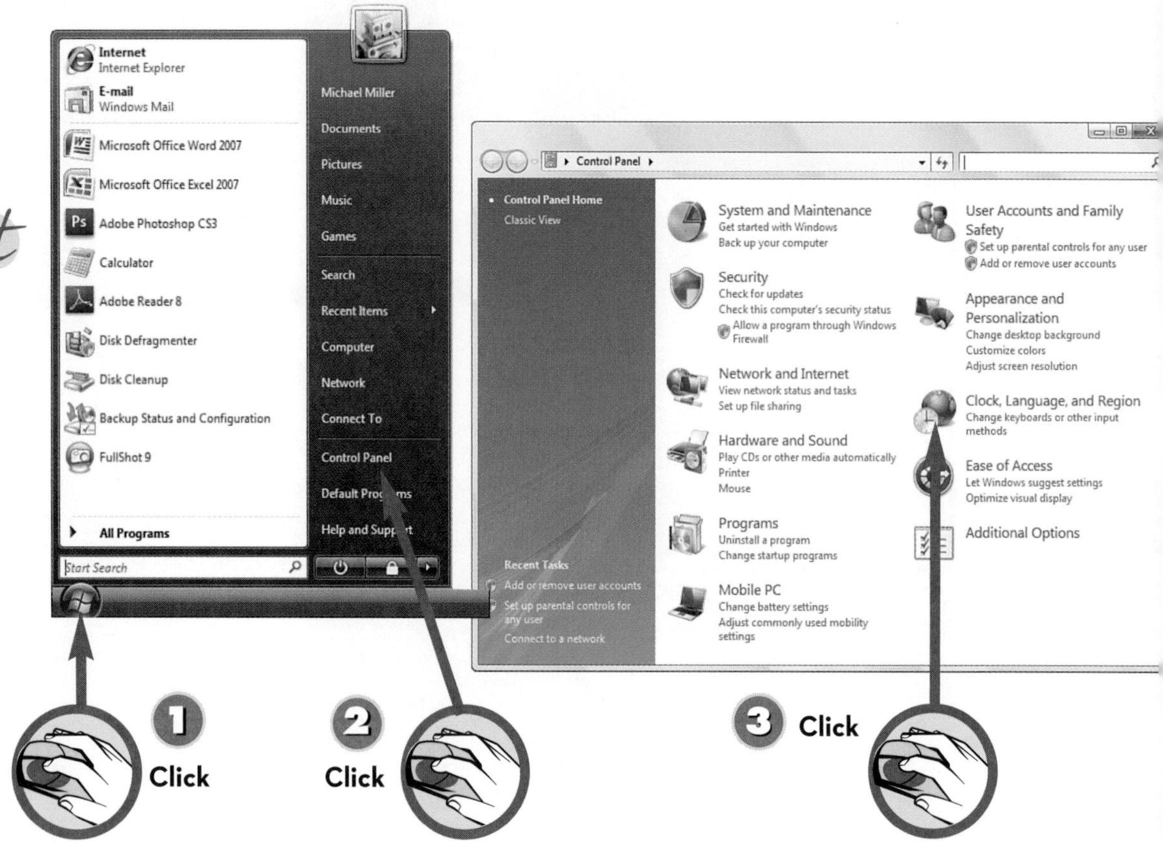

1 Click 2 Click 3 Click

1. Click the **Start** button to display the Start menu.
2. Click **Control Panel** to open the Control Panel.
3. Click the link for the category you want to configure.

Continued

TIP

Control Panel Categories

Individual settings within the Control Panel are organized by major category—System and Maintenance, Security, Network and Internet, and so on. You first have to select a specific category to access all its related settings.

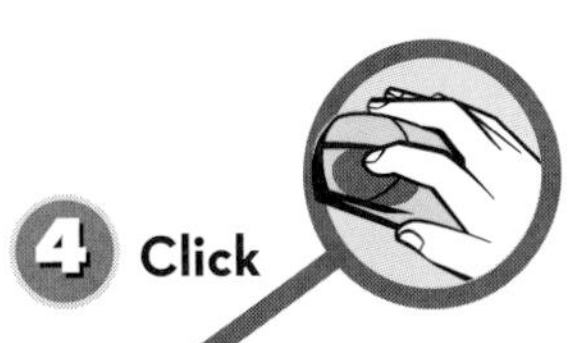

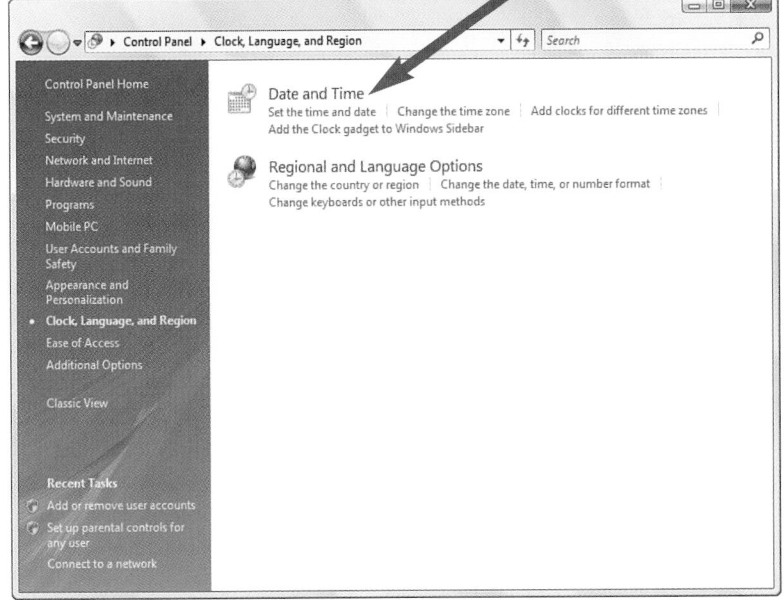

4. Click the task you want to perform.
5. Configure the settings for that task using the selected utility's dialog box.

End

TIP

Configuring Individual Settings

When you open a configuration utility, you'll see a dialog box for that particular item. You can then change the individual settings within that dialog box; click the **OK** button to register your new settings.

PERSONALIZING THE DESKTOP BACKGROUND

Most users like to personalize the look of the Windows desktop. Windows Vista includes a number of built-in desktop wallpapers; you can also choose your own photo or graphic for your desktop background.

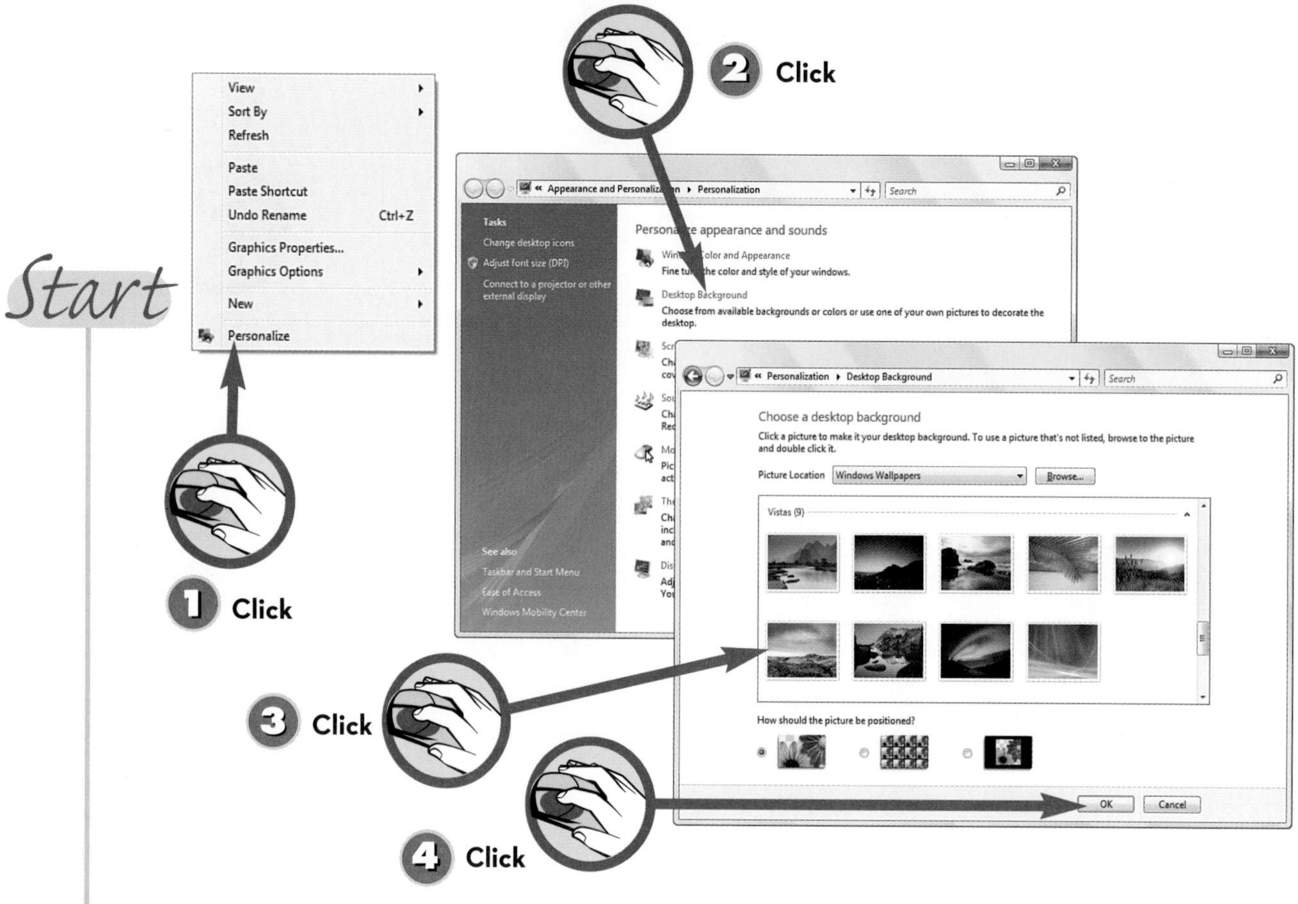

1. Right-click anywhere on the desktop and click **Personalize**.
2. Click **Desktop Background**.
3. When the next window opens, select one of the Windows built-in backgrounds from the list.
4. Click **OK**.

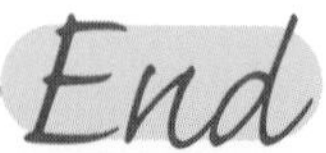

TIP

Position Your Picture

To determine how the image file is displayed on your desktop, select one of the options from the How Should the Picture Be Positioned? section: **Fit to Screen**, **Tile**, or **Center**.

TIP

Choose a Custom Background

To use a picture of your own for your desktop background, pull down the **Picture Location** list, click the **Browse** button, and then select the picture you want from your computer's hard disk.

CHANGING THE COLOR SCHEME

The default Windows Vista desktop uses a predefined combination of colors and transparencies. If you don't like the way this looks, you can choose from several other predefined schemes.

Start

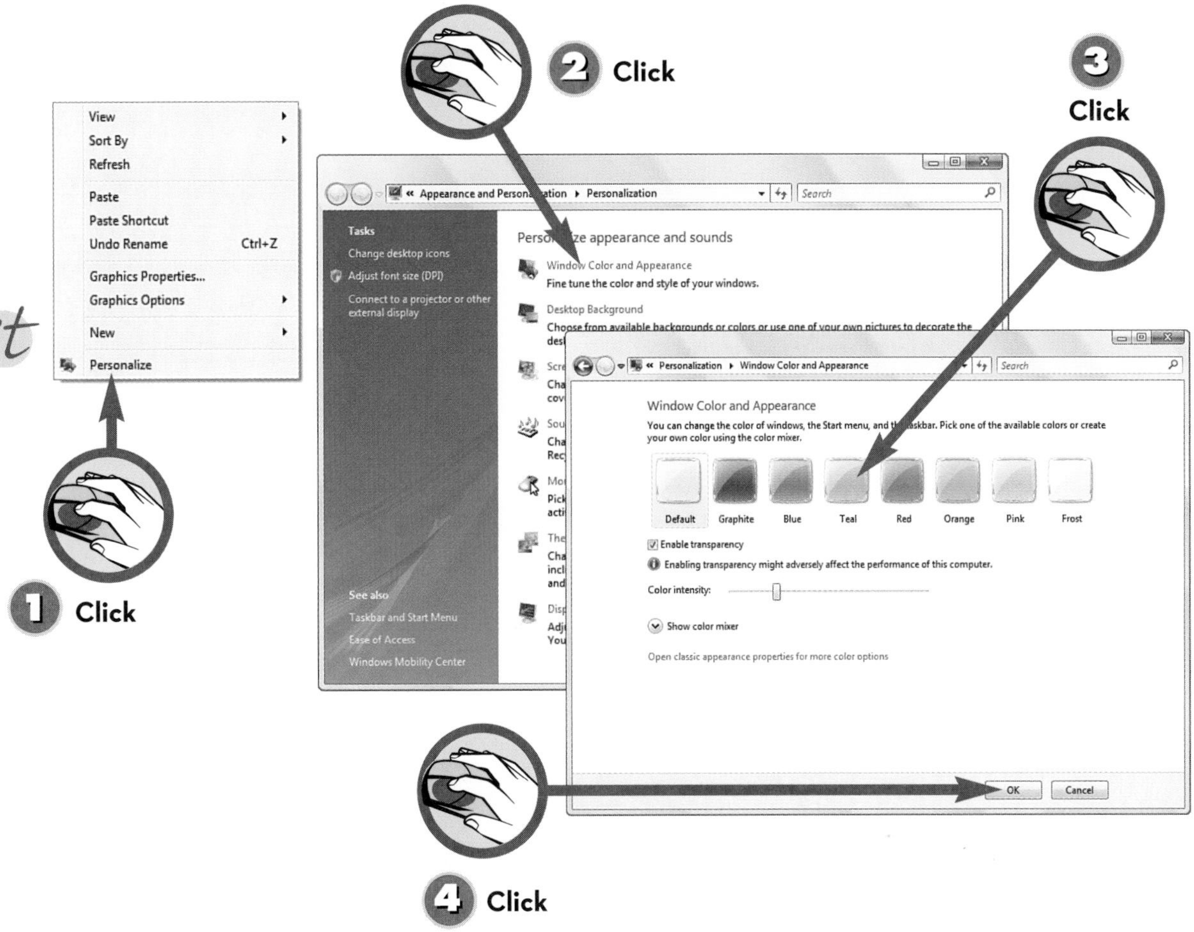

1 Click

2 Click

3 Click

4 Click

1. Right-click anywhere on the desktop and click **Personalize**.
2. Click **Window Color and Appearance**.
3. Click any of the default color schemes.
4. Click **OK**.

End

TIP

Change the Transparency

To change the amount of transparency in Vista's windows and dialog boxes, adjust the Color Intensity slider. Or, to turn off the transparency, uncheck the Enable Transparency option.

USING A SCREENSAVER

Screensavers display moving designs on your computer screen when you haven't typed or moved the mouse for a while. This prevents static images from burning into your screen and provides some small degree of entertainment if you're bored at your desk.

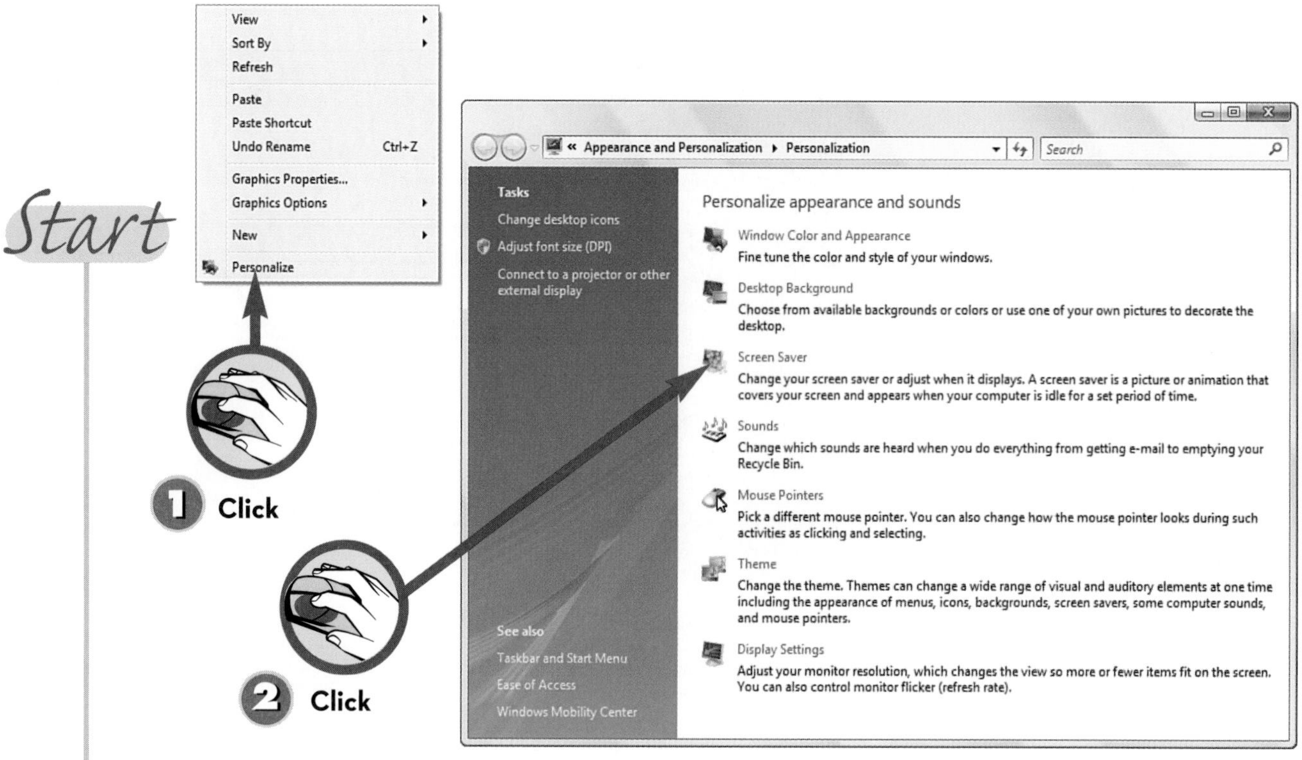

Start

1 Click

2 Click

1. Right-click anywhere on the desktop and click **Personalize**.
2. Click **Screen Saver**.

Continued

NOTE

Default Screensavers

Windows Vista's default screensavers include 3D Text, Aurora, Blank (nothing onscreen), Bubbles, Mystify, Photos, Ribbons, Windows Energy, and Windows Log.

TIP

Photo Slideshow

The Photos screensaver turns your computer screen into a slideshow of your favorite pictures. It's like your computer has been turned into a digital photo frame!

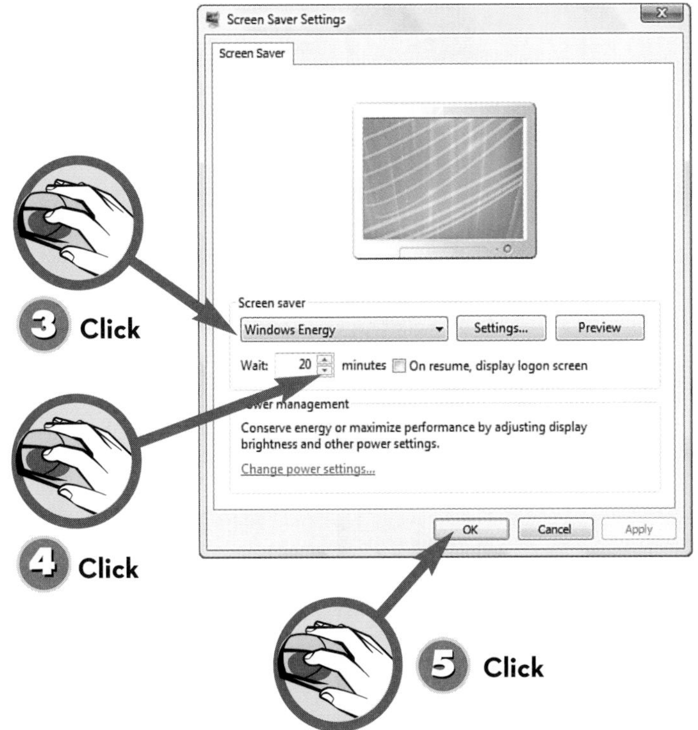

3. Select a screensaver from the **Screen Saver** drop-down list.
4. Select the number of minutes you want the screen to be idle before the screensaver activates.
5. Click **OK** when you're done.

End

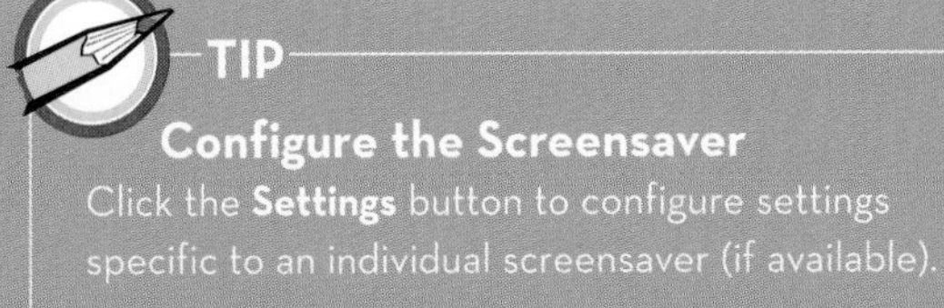

TIP

Configure the Screensaver

Click the **Settings** button to configure settings specific to an individual screensaver (if available).

USING THE WINDOWS SIDEBAR

New to Windows Vista is the Sidebar, a collection of small utilities called *gadgets*. The Sidebar is docked on the right side of the screen; you can add or delete different gadgets from the Sidebar.

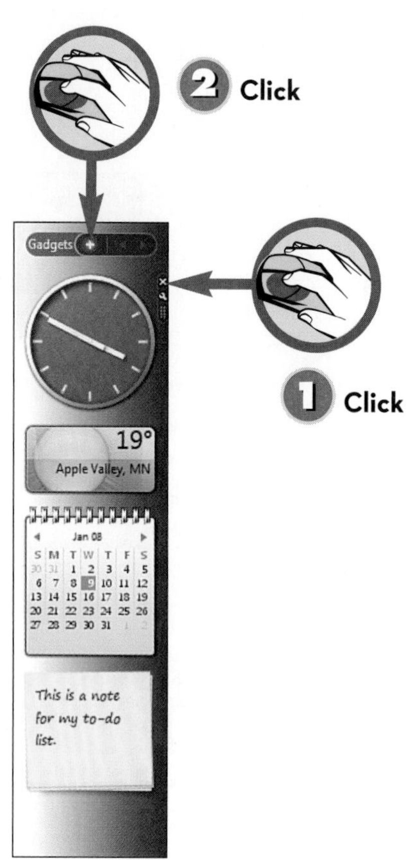

1. To delete a gadget from the Sidebar, hover over the gadget and then click the **X**.
2. To add a new gadget, click the + button at the top of the Sidebar.

Continued

TIP

Configuring Gadgets

To configure a gadget, hover over the gadget, click the wrench button, then select **Options**.

TIP

Closing the Sidebar

To close the Sidebar, right-click anywhere on the Sidebar and select **Close Sidebar**.

3 Double-click

4 Click

5 Click

3. Double-click a gadget to add it to the Sidebar.
4. To view more gadgets, click **Get More Gadgets Online**.
5. Select a category, then click the **Download** button under the gadget you want to add.

End

TIP

Gadgets on the Desktop

You can undock gadgets from the Sidebar and display them directly on the Windows Vista desktop. Just drag the gadget from the Sidebar to the desktop.

SETTING UP ADDITIONAL USERS

If you have multiple people using your PC, you should assign each user in your household his or her own password-protected user account. Anyone trying to access another user's account and files without the password will then be denied access.

Start

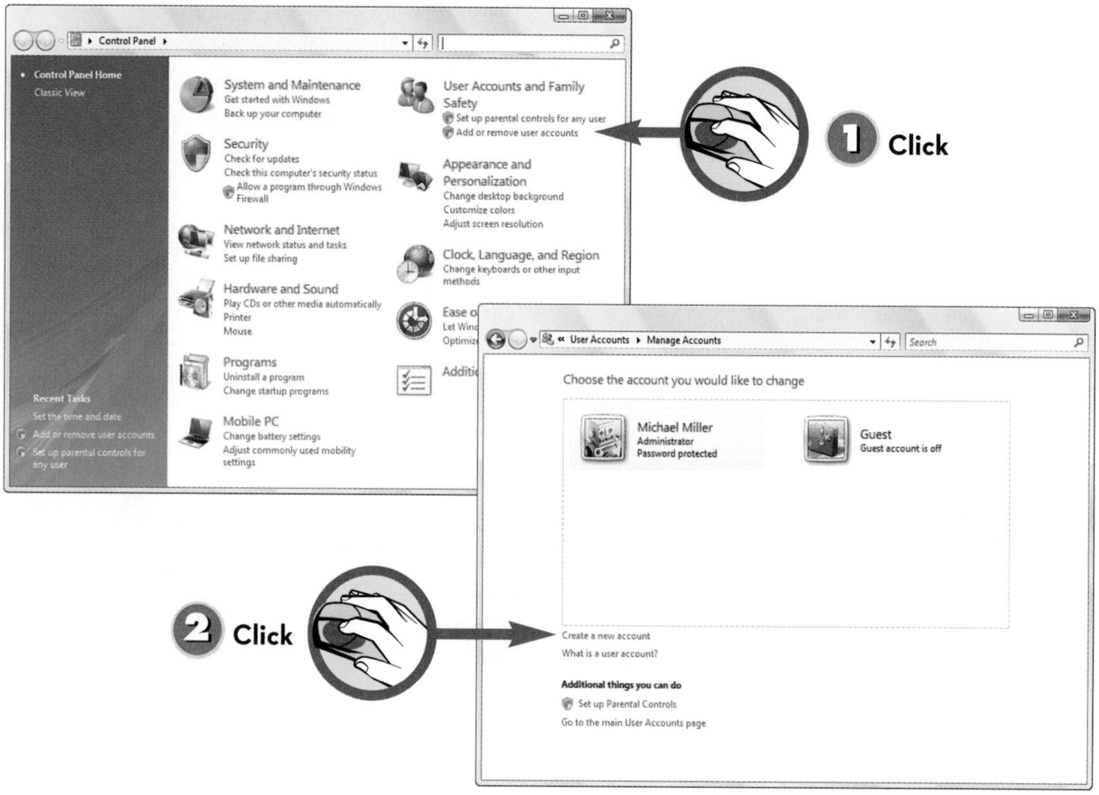

1 Click

2 Click

1. From the Windows Control Panel, click **Add or Remove User Accounts**.
2. Click **Create a New Account**.

Continued

CAUTION

User Account Control

When you try to create a new user account, Windows displays a dialog box asking for your permission to continue. This is part of the User Account Control safety feature; click the **Continue** button to confirm.

TIP

Different Users

You can create two types of user accounts—Standard User or Administrator. You should set yourself up as an administrator because only this account can make system-wide changes to your PC.

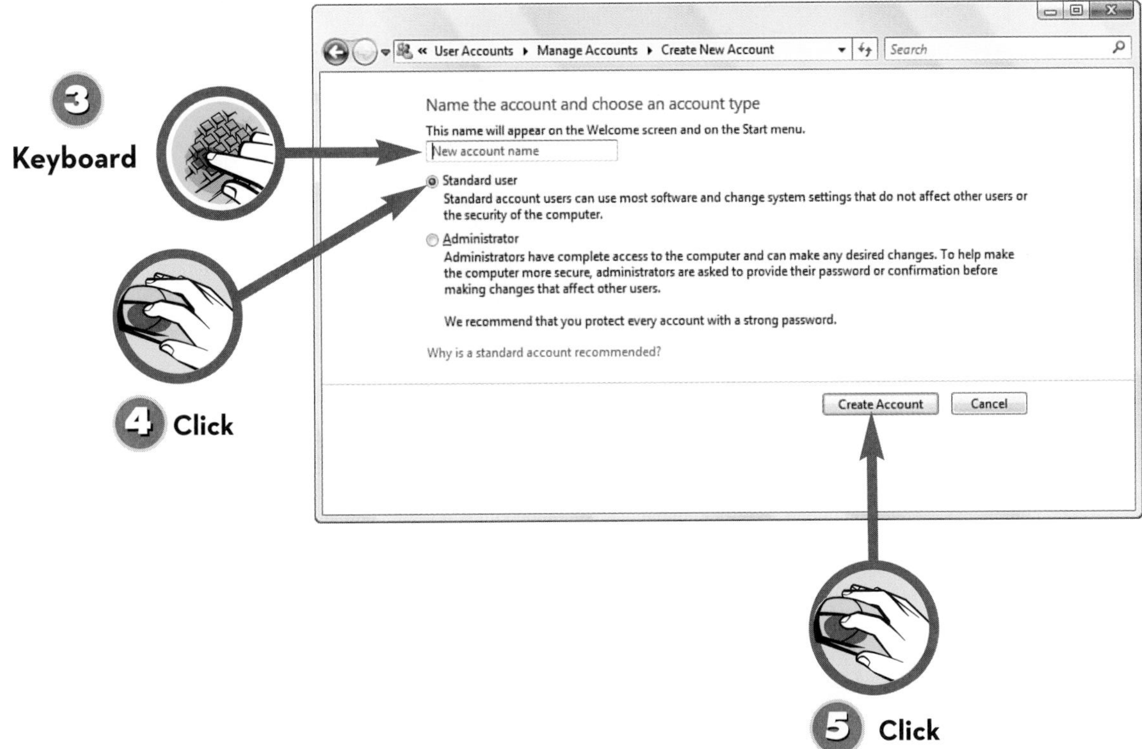

3. Enter a name for the account.
4. Select the type of account to create, **Standard User** or **Administrator**.
5. Click the **Create Account** button. Windows Vista now creates the new account and randomly assigns a picture that will appear next to the username.

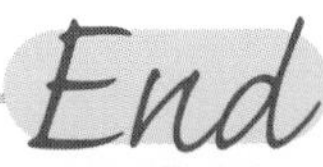

TIP

Change Your Picture

You can change an account picture by returning to the Manage Accounts window, selecting the account, and then selecting the **Change the Picture** option.

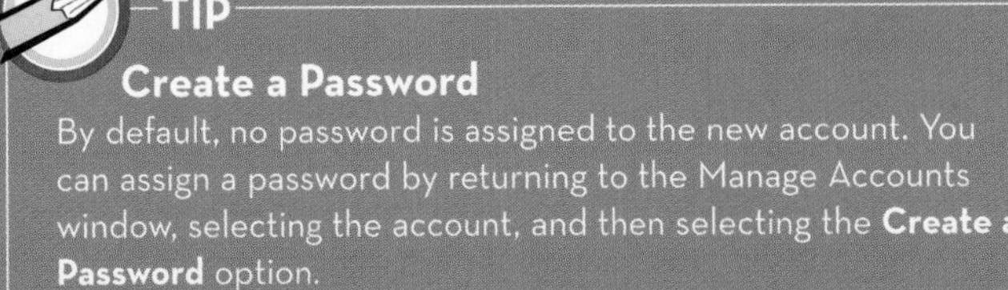

TIP

Create a Password

By default, no password is assigned to the new account. You can assign a password by returning to the Manage Accounts window, selecting the account, and then selecting the **Create a Password** option.

GETTING HELP IN WINDOWS

When you can't figure out how to perform a particular task, it's time to ask for help. In Windows Vista, this is done through the Windows Help and Support Center.

Start

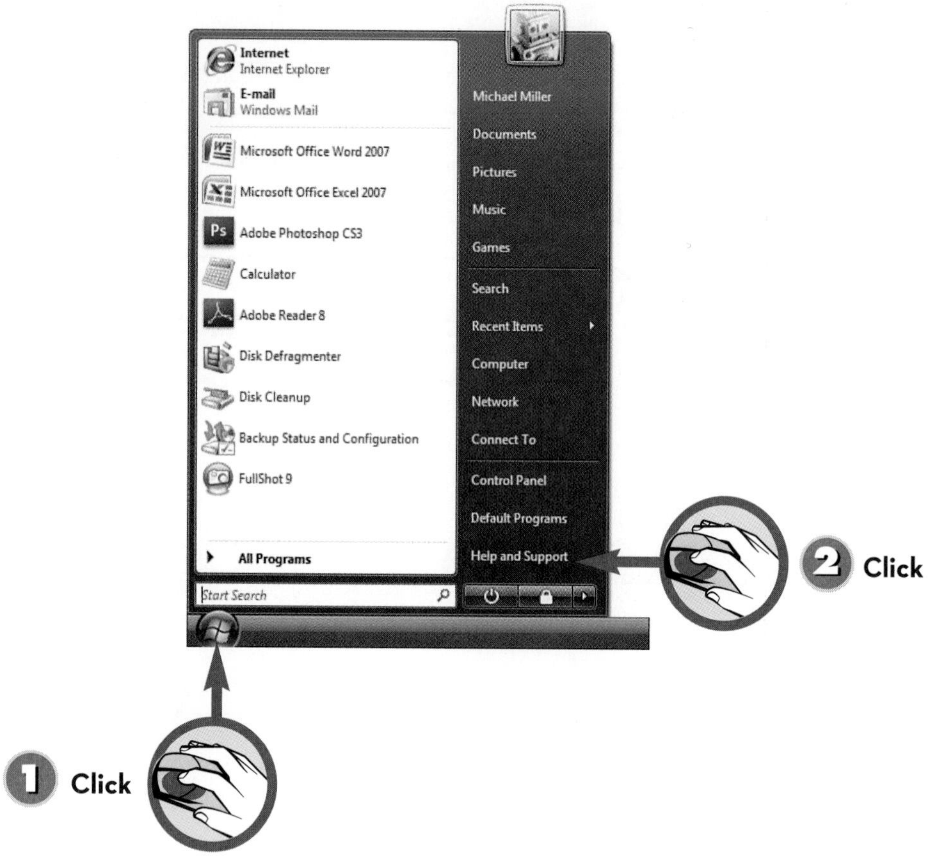

1. Click the **Start** button to display the Start menu.
2. Click **Help and Support**.

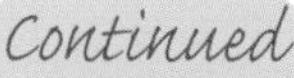

TIP

Other Help Options

Microsoft provides other options in the Help and Support window, including Windows Basics, Security and Maintenance, Windows Online Help, Troubleshooting, and What's New.

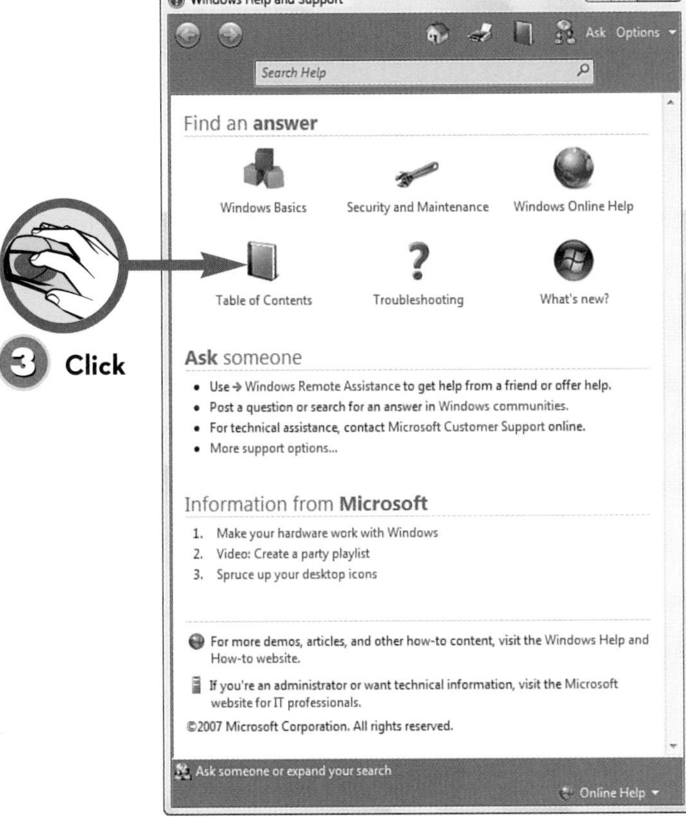

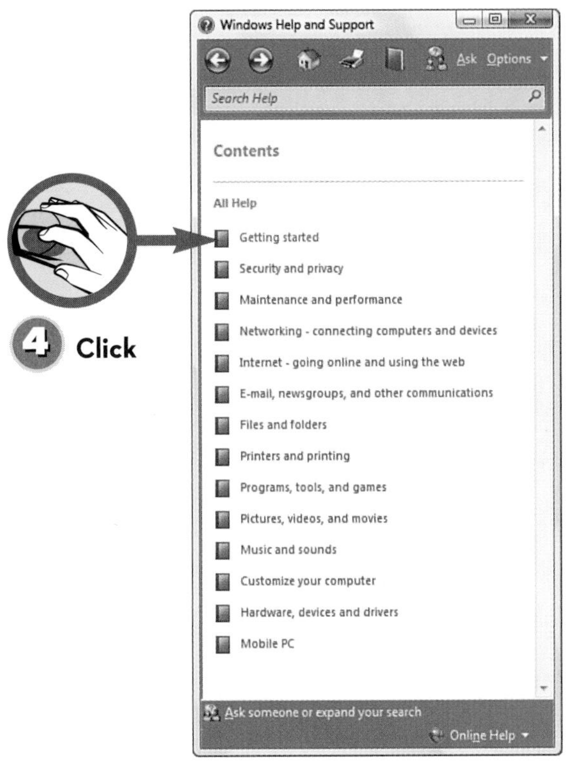

3. Click the **Table of Contents** icon to display a list of help topics.
4. Click a topic to display information about that topic.

End

TIP

Search for Help

You can also use the Search Help box to search for specific help topics. If you're connected to the Internet, Windows will search Microsoft's online Knowledge Base for more answers.

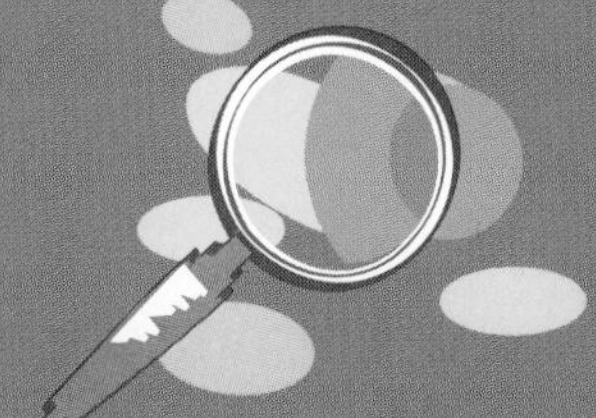

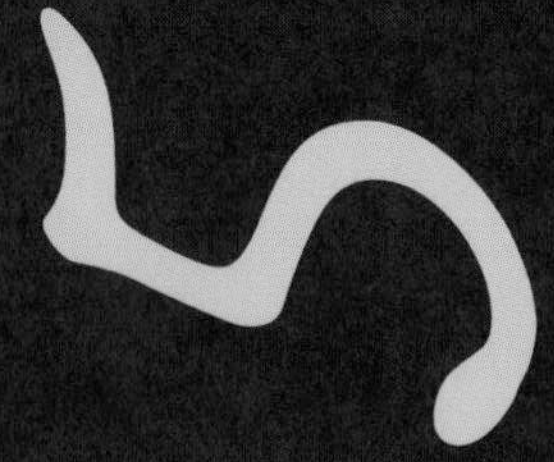

part 5

WORKING WITH FILES AND FOLDERS

All the data for documents and programs on your computer are stored in electronic files. These files are then arranged into a series of folders and subfolders—just as you'd arrange paper files in a series of file folders in a filing cabinet.

In Windows Vista you can use either the Documents Explorer or Computer Explorer (both accessible from the Windows Start menu) to view and manage the folders and files on your system. Both of these tools work similarly and enable you to customize the way they display their contents.

The Documents Explorer contains not only individual files, but also other folders—called *subfolders*—that themselves contain other files. Most of the file-related operations you'll want to undertake are accessible directly from the folder's Organize menu.

THE DOCUMENTS EXPLORER

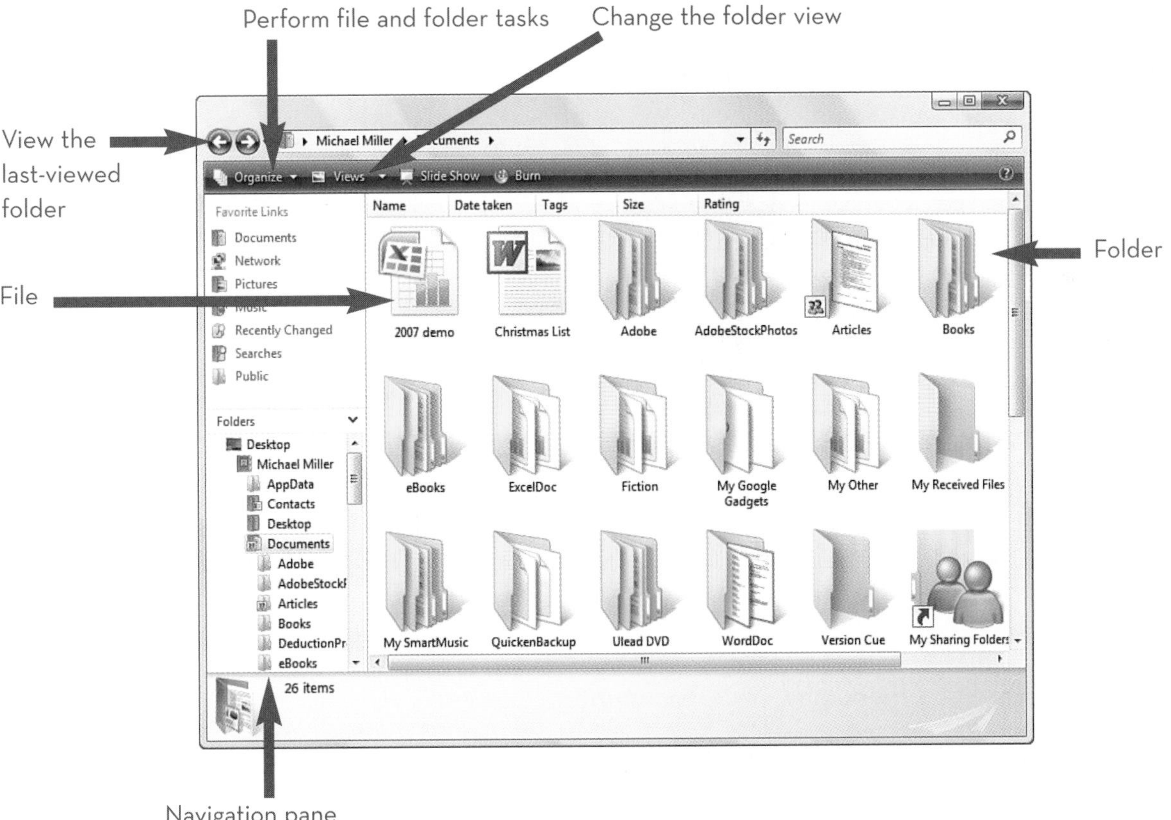

CHANGING THE WAY FILES ARE DISPLAYED

You can choose to view the contents of a folder in a variety of ways. The icon views are nice in that they show a small thumbnail preview of any selected file.

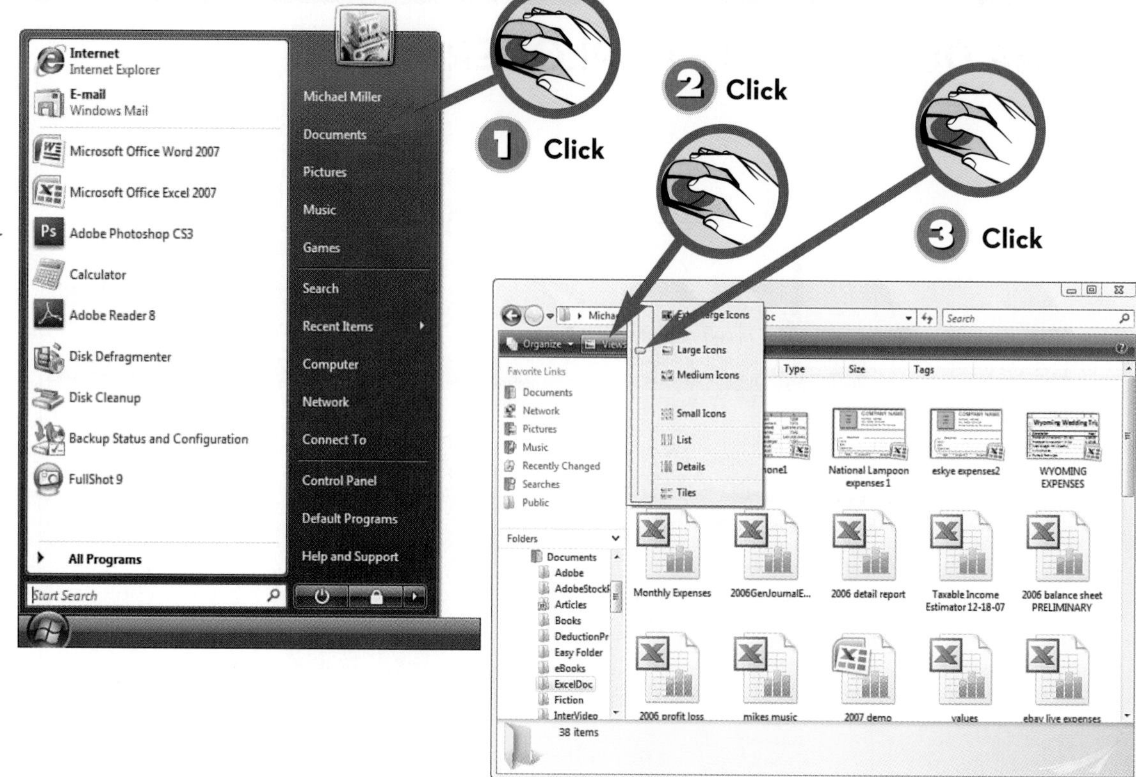

1. Open the **Start** menu and click **Documents**.
2. Double-click any folder to view the folder's contents; then click the down arrow next to the **Views** button on the toolbar.
3. Move the slider to select from the **Tiles, Details, List, Small Icons, Medium Icons, Large Icons**, and **Extra Large Icons** views.

End

TIP

Which View Is Best?

Any of the larger icon views are best for working with graphics files. Details view is best if you're looking for files by date or size.

SORTING FILES AND FOLDERS

When viewing files in the Documents Explorer, you can sort your files and folders in a number of ways. To view your files in alphabetical order, choose to sort by Name. To see all similar files grouped together, choose to sort by Type. To sort your files by the date and time they were last edited, select Date Modified.

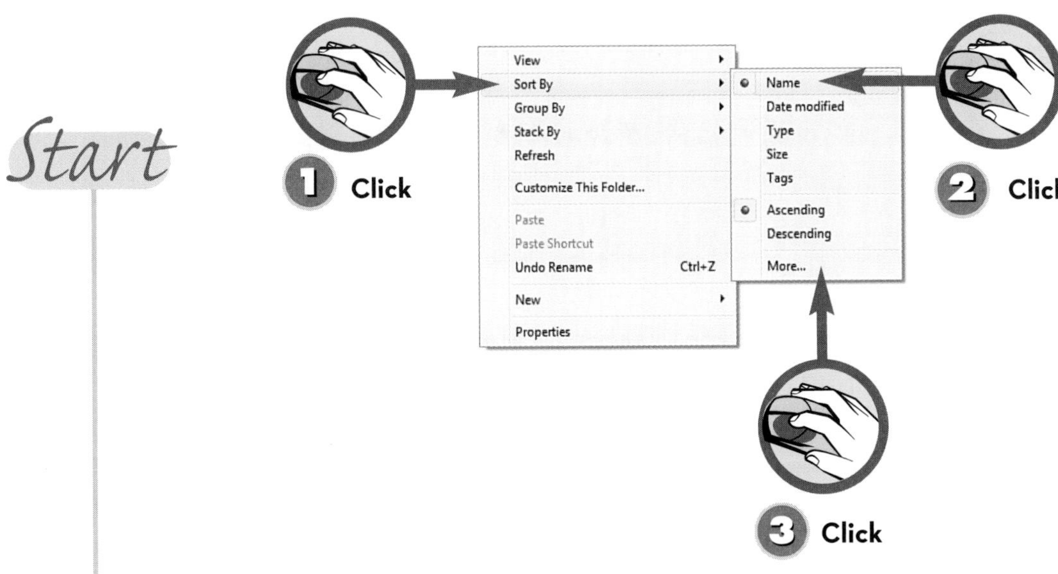

1. Right-click any open space within the Documents Explorer and select **Sort By**.
2. Choose to sort by **Name**, **Date Modified**, **Type**, **Size,** or **Tags.**
3. To view more sorting options, click **More**.

End

—TIP—

More Sorting Options

When you opt to view More sorting options, you can sort by dozens of different parameters, all of which change based on what type of file you're viewing. For example, if you're viewing music files, you can sort by Album, Artists, Bit Rate, Composers, Genre, and the like.

NAVIGATING FOLDERS

You can navigate through the folders and subfolders in Windows Explorer in several different ways.

Start

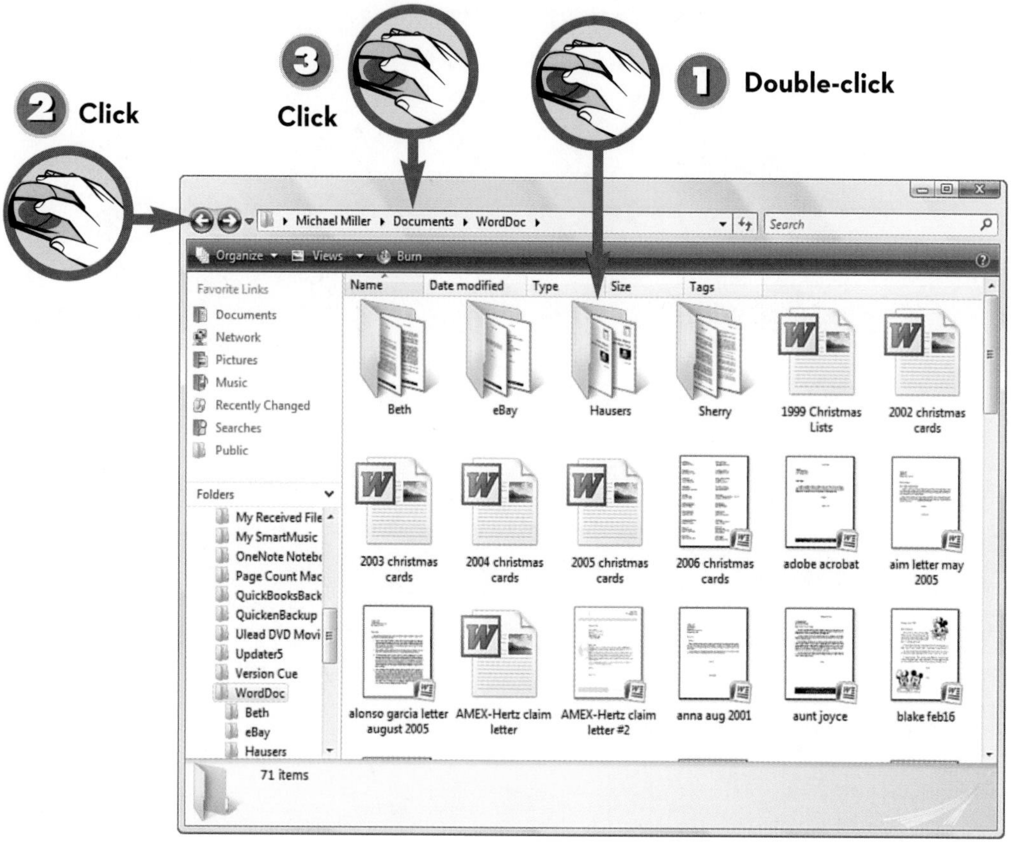

2 Click

3 Click

1 Double-click

1 To view the contents of a disk or folder, double-click an icon.

2 To move back to the disk or folder previously selected, click the **Back** button on the toolbar.

3 To move up the hierarchy of folders and subfolders to the next highest item, click that item in the address box at the top of the window.

End

TIP

Moving Forward

If you've moved back through multiple disks or folders, you can move forward to the next folder by clicking the **Forward** button.

TIP

Breadcrumbs

The list of folders and subfolders in the Explorer address box present a "breadcrumb" approach to navigation. You can view even earlier folders by clicking the left arrow next to the folder icon in the address box; this displays a pull-down menu of recently visited and most popular items.

NAVIGATING WITH THE NAVIGATION PANE

Another way to navigate your files and folders is to use the Navigation pane. This pane, on the left side of the Explorer window, displays both favorite links and a hierarchical folder tree.

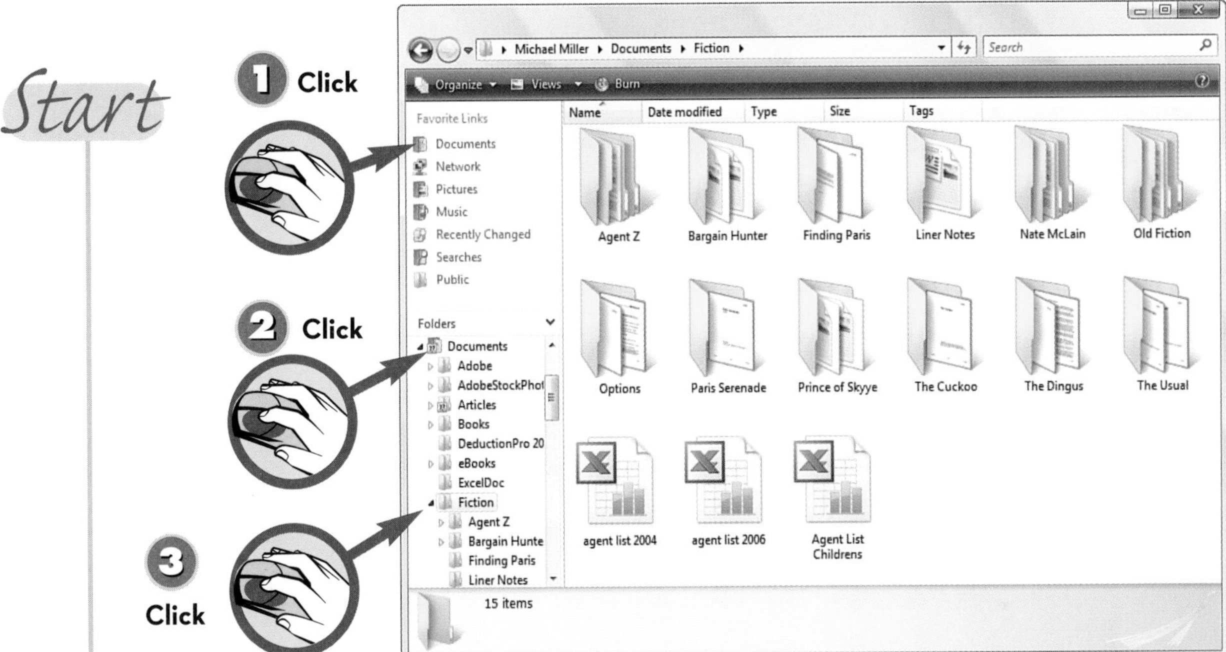

1. Click an icon in the **Favorite Links** section to open the contents of the selected item.
2. Click the arrow icon next to a folder in the **Folders** section to display all the subfolders it contains.
3. Click a folder to display its contents in the main Explorer window.

End

NOTE

Favorite Links

Windows Vista's Favorite Links include the following actual and virtual folders: Documents, Pictures, Music, Recently Changed, Searches, and Public.

CREATING A NEW FOLDER

The more files you create, the harder it is to organize and find things on your hard disk. When the number of files you have becomes unmanageable, you need to create more folders—and subfolders—to better categorize your files.

Start

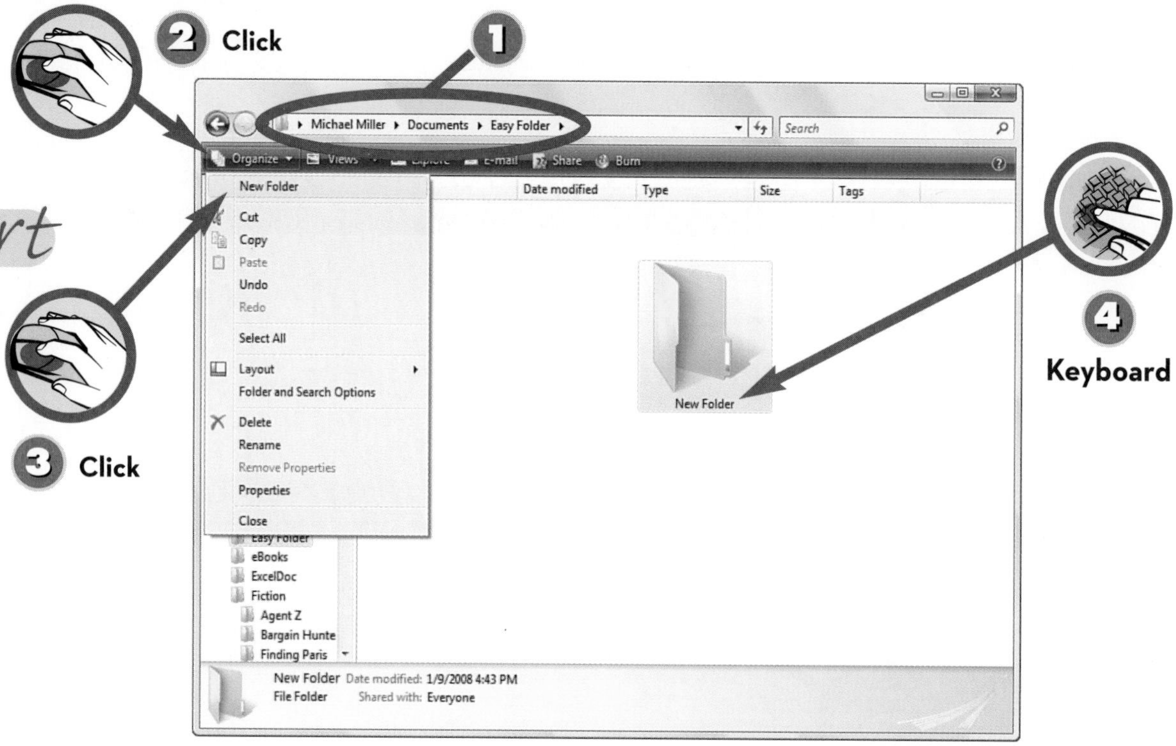

1. Navigate to the drive or folder where you want to place the new folder.
2. Click the **Organize** button.
3. Click **New Folder** from the pull-down menu.
4. A new, empty folder now appears with the filename **New Folder** highlighted. Type a name for your folder and press **Enter**.

End

CAUTION

Illegal Characters

Folder names and filenames can include up to 255 characters—including many special characters. You *can't*, however, use the following "illegal" characters: \ / : * ? " < > |.

RENAMING A FILE OR FOLDER

When you create a new file or folder, it helps to give it a name that describes its contents. Sometimes, however, you might need to change a file's name. Fortunately, Windows makes renaming an item relatively easy.

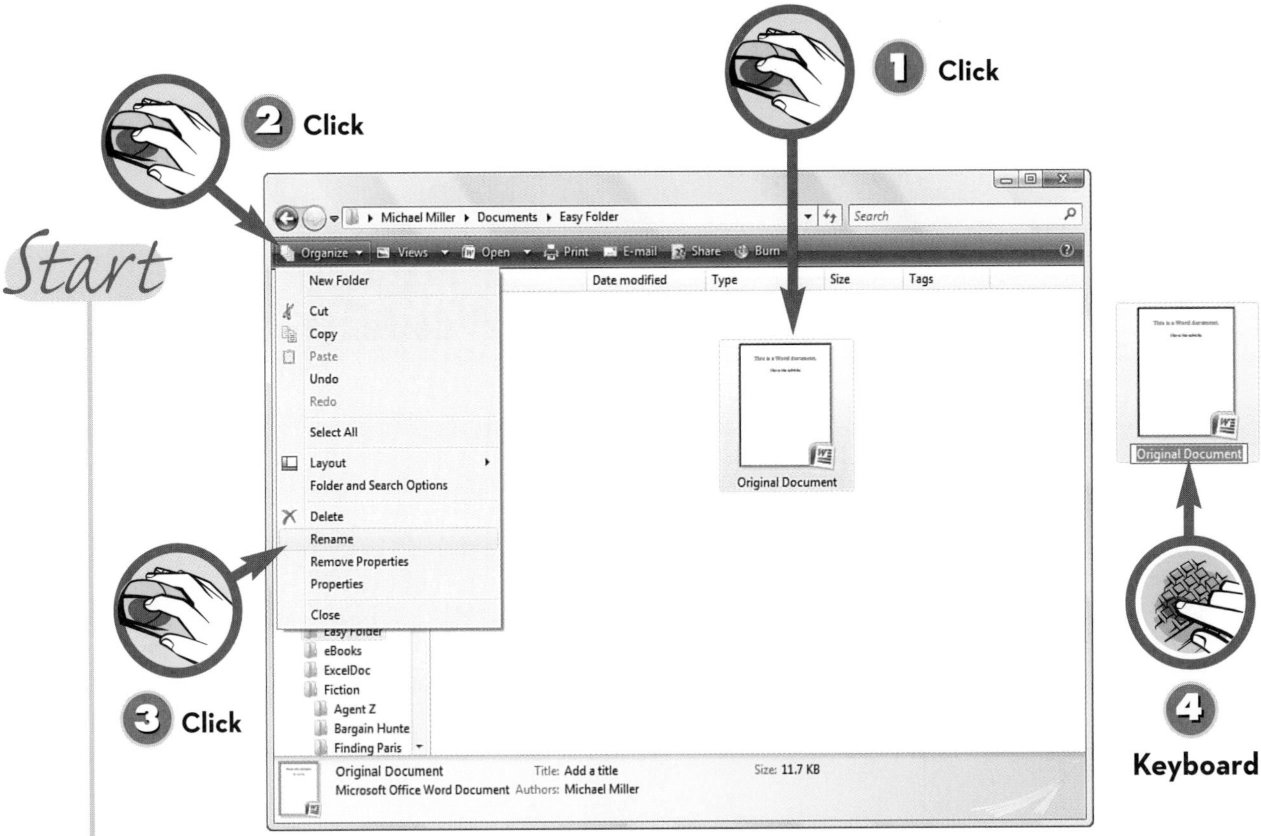

1 Click

2 Click

Start

3 Click

4 Keyboard

1. Click the file or folder you want to rename.
2. Click the **Organize** button.
3. Click **Rename**; this highlights the filename.
4. Type a new name for your folder (which overwrites the current name), and press **Enter**.

End

CAUTION

Don't Change the Extension

The one part of the filename you should never change is the extension—the part that comes after the "dot" if you choose to show file extensions. Try to change the extension, and Windows will warn you that you're doing something wrong.

TIP

Keyboard Shortcut

You can also rename a file by selecting the file and pressing **F2** on your computer keyboard. This highlights the filename and readies it for editing.

COPYING A FILE OR FOLDER

There are many ways to copy a file in Windows Vista. The easiest method is to use Copy and Paste commands on the Organize menu.

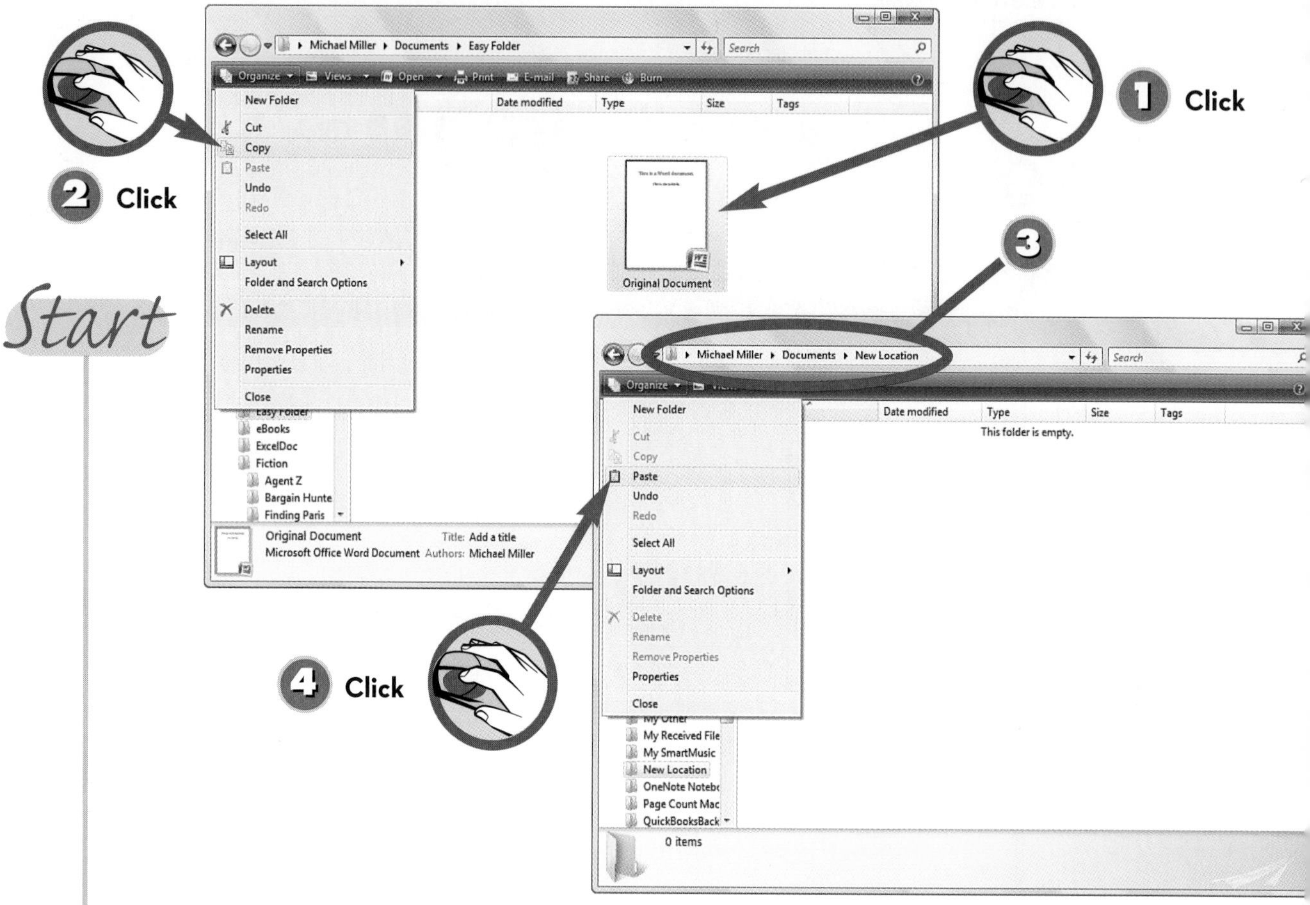

Start

1 Click

2 Click

3

4 Click

1. Click the item you want to copy.
2. Click the **Organize** button and then click **Copy**.
3. Navigate to and select the new location for the item.
4. Click the **Organize** button and then click **Paste.**

End

TIP

Copy to a New Folder

If you want to copy the item to a new folder, pull down the Organize menu and click **New Folder** before you click the Paste button.

MOVING A FILE OR FOLDER

Moving a file (or folder) is different from copying it. Moving cuts the item from its previous location and pastes it into a new location. Copying leaves the original item where it was *and* creates a copy of the item elsewhere.

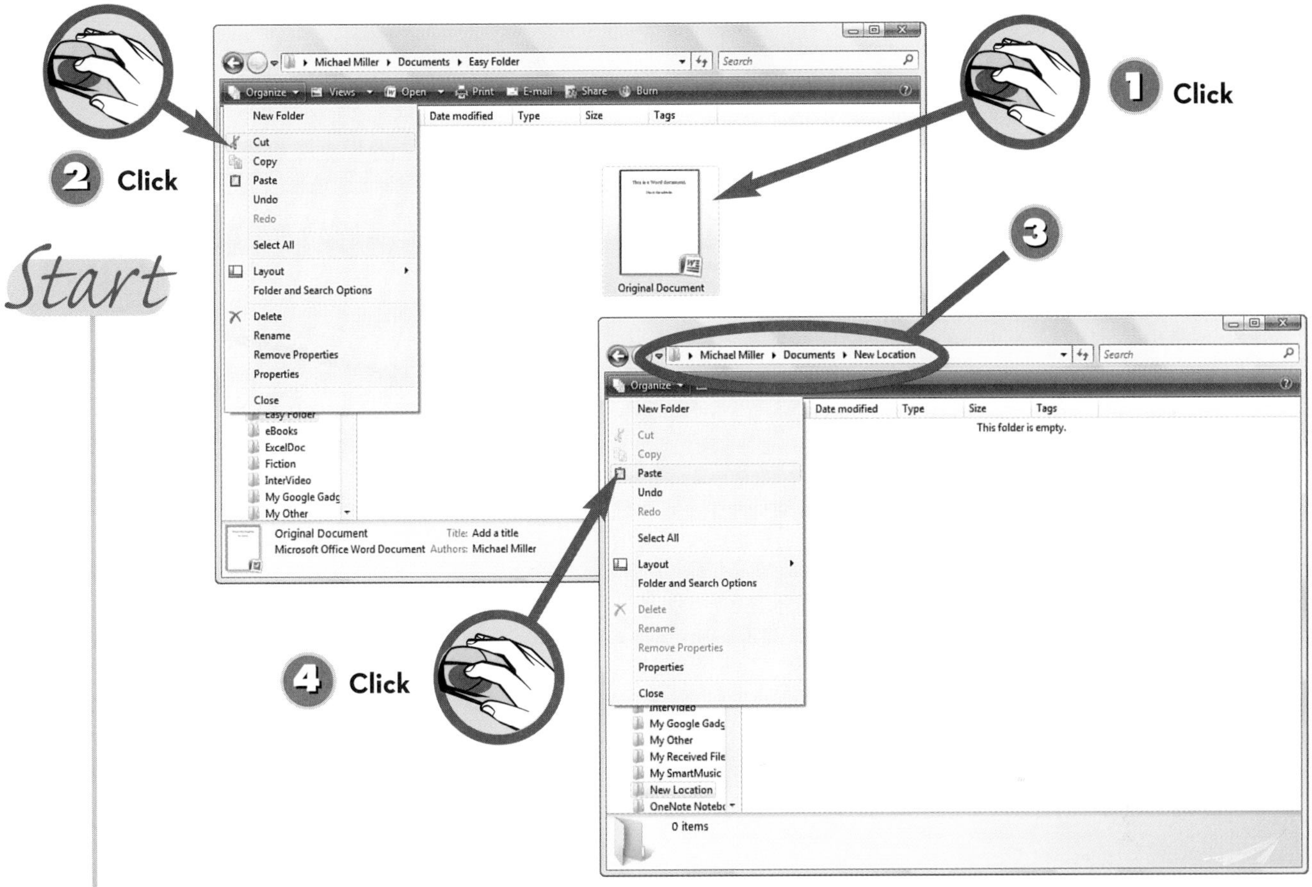

Start

1. Click the item you want to move.
2. Click the **Organize** button and click **Cut**.
3. Navigate to and select the new location for the item.
4. Click the **Organize** button and click **Paste**.

End

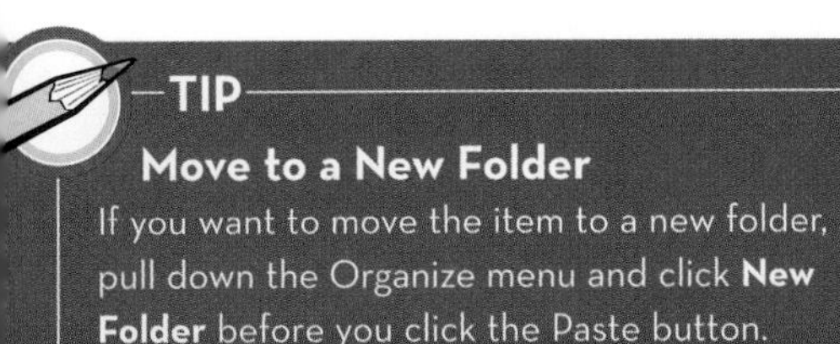

TIP

Move to a New Folder

If you want to move the item to a new folder, pull down the Organize menu and click **New Folder** before you click the Paste button.

DELETING A FILE OR FOLDER

Keeping too many files eats up too much hard disk space—which is a bad thing. Because you don't want to waste disk space, you should periodically delete those files (and folders) you no longer need. When you delete a file, you send it to the Windows Recycle Bin, which is kind of a trash can for deleted files.

Start

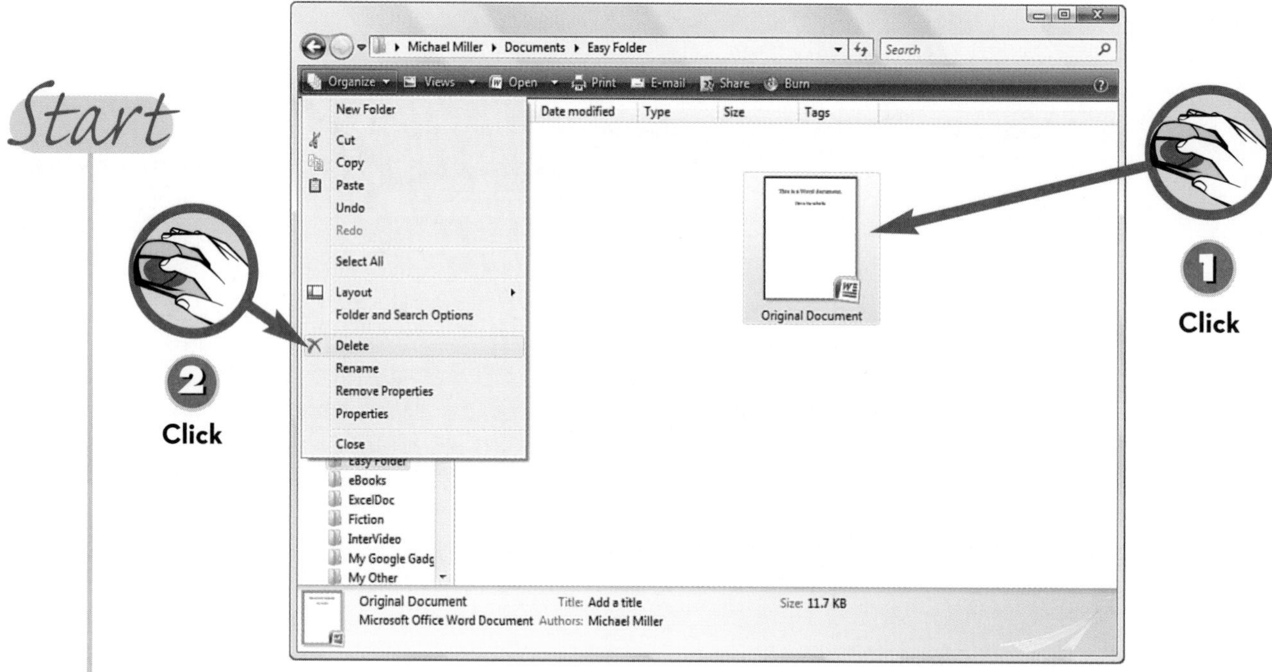

1. Click the file you want to delete.
2. Click the **Organize** button and click **Delete**.

End

—TIP—

Other Ways to Delete

You can also delete a file by dragging it from the folder window onto the Recycle Bin icon on the desktop, or by highlighting it and pressing the **Delete** key on your computer keyboard.

RESTORING DELETED FILES

Have you ever accidentally deleted the wrong file? If so, you're in luck. Windows stores the files you delete in the Recycle Bin, which is actually a special folder on your hard disk. For a short period of time, you can "undelete" files from the Recycle Bin back to their original locations.

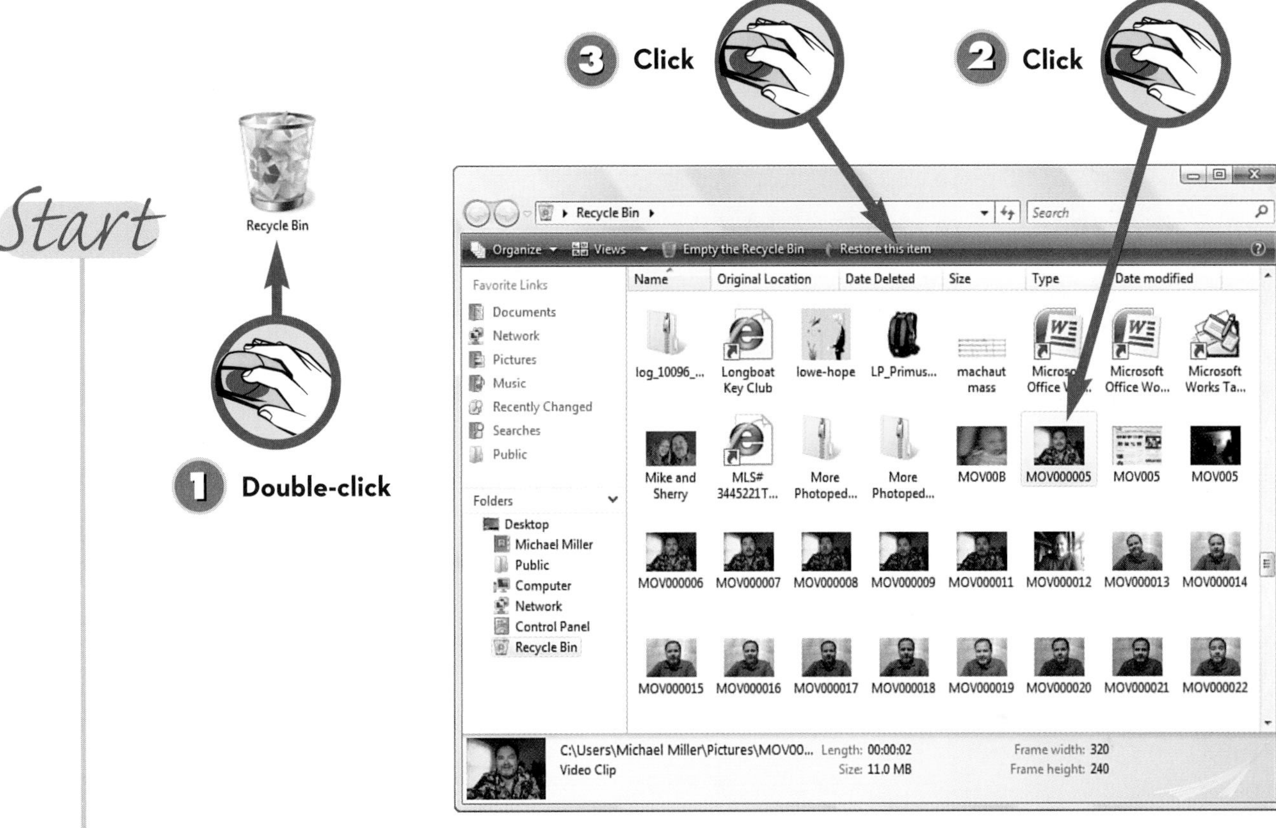

1. Double-click the **Recycle Bin** icon on your desktop to open the Recycle Bin folder.
2. Click the file you want to restore.
3. Click the **Restore This Item** button.

End

EMPTYING THE RECYCLE BIN

By default, the deleted files in the Recycle Bin can occupy 4GB plus 5% of your hard disk space. When you've deleted enough files to exceed this limit, the oldest files in the Recycle Bin are automatically and permanently deleted from your hard disk. You can also manually empty the Recycle Bin and thus free up some hard disk space.

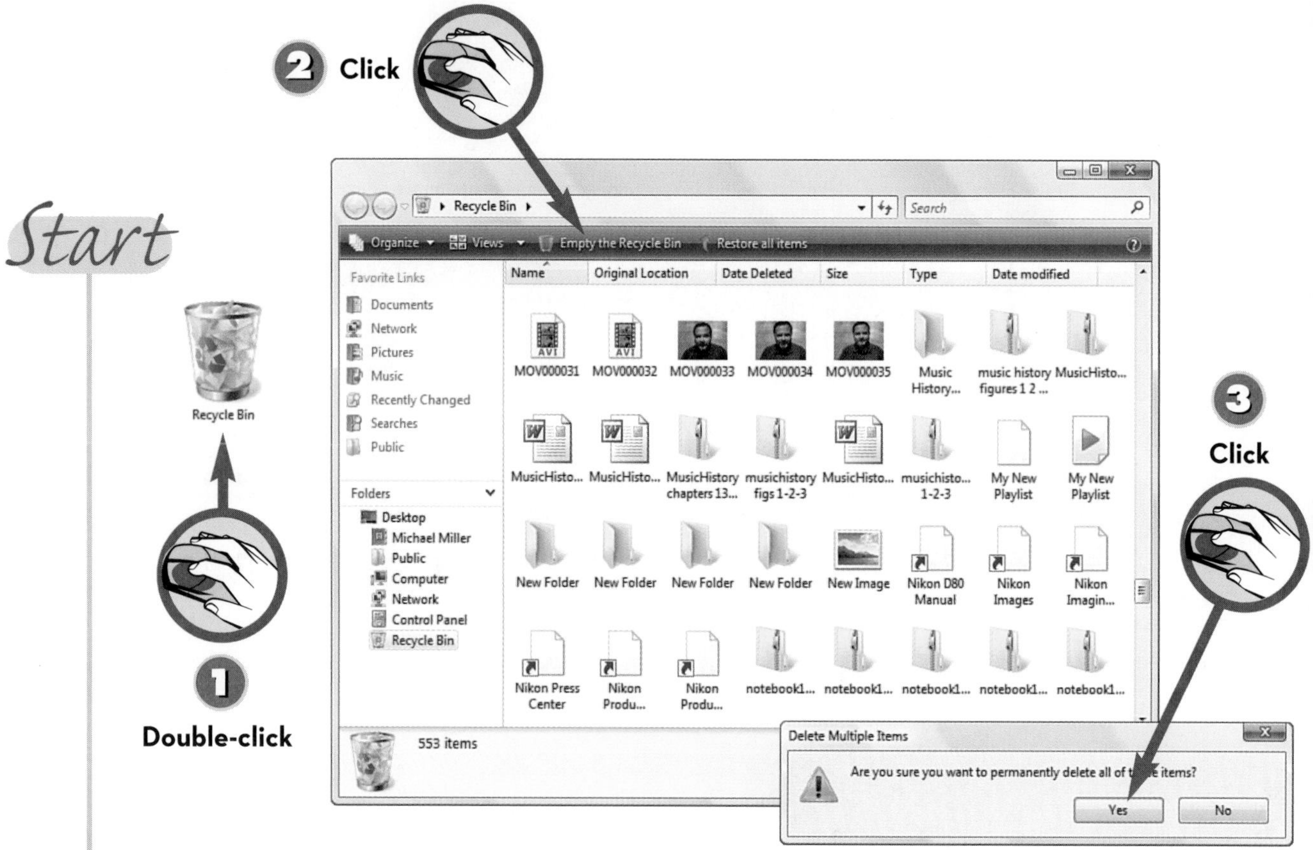

Start

1 Double-click

2 Click

3 Click

End

1. Double-click the **Recycle Bin** icon on your desktop to open the Recycle Bin folder.
2. Click the **Empty the Recycle Bin** button.
3. When the Delete Multiple Items dialog box appears, click **Yes** to completely erase the files.

TIP

Fast Empty

You can also empty the Recycle Bin by right-clicking its icon on the Windows desktop and selecting **Empty Recycle Bin** from the pop-up menu.

COMPRESSING A FILE

Really big files can be difficult to copy or share. Fortunately, Windows Vista lets you create compressed folders, which take big files and compress them down in size (called a "zipped" file). After the file has been transferred, you can then uncompress the file back to its original state.

Start

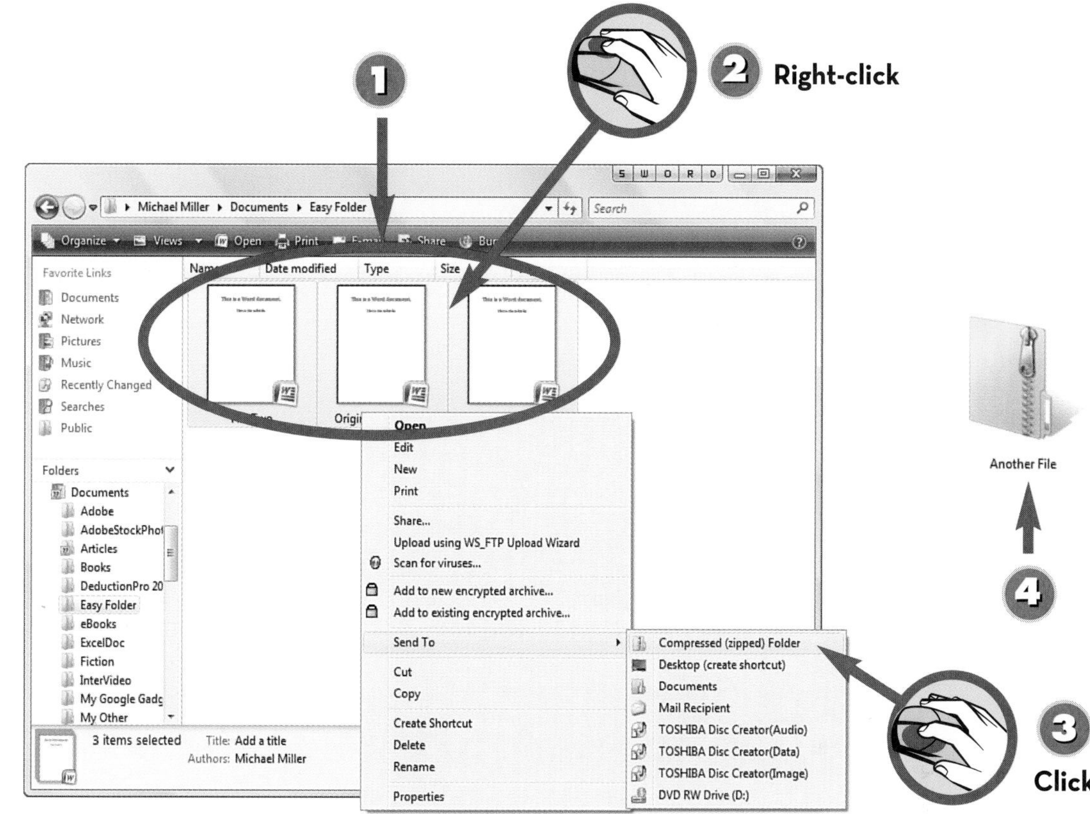

1. Select the file(s) you want to compress. (To select more than one file, hold down the **Ctrl** key when clicking.)
2. Right-click the selected file(s) to display the pop-up menu.
3. Select **Send To**, **Compressed (Zipped) Folder**.
4. Windows creates a new zipped folder in this same folder that contains copies of the selected files.

NOTE

Zip Files

The compressed folder is actually a file with a **.zip** extension, so it can be used with other compression/decompression programs, such as WinZip.

EXTRACTING FILES FROM A COMPRESSED FOLDER

The process of decompressing a file is actually an extraction process. That's because you extract the original file(s) from the compressed folder. In Windows Vista, this process is eased by the use of the Extraction Wizard.

Start

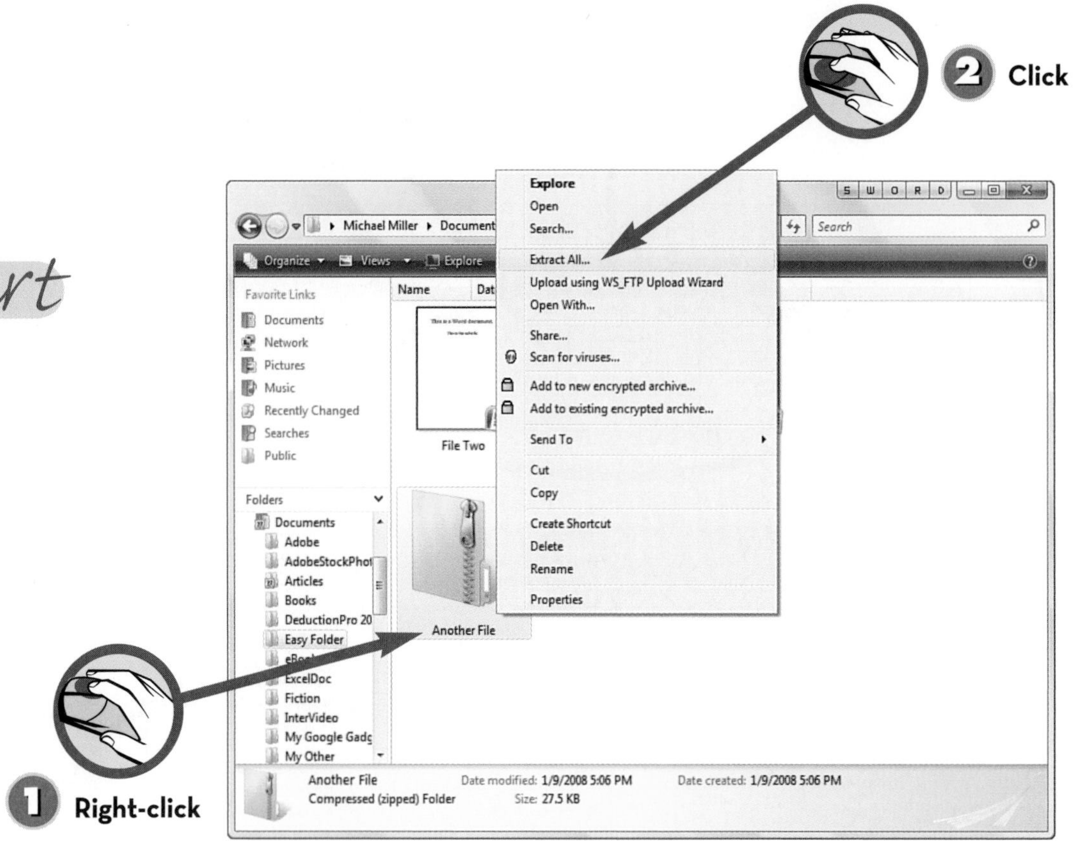

2 Click

1 Right-click

1 Right-click the compressed folder to display the pop-up menu.

2 Click **Extract All**.

Continued

TIP

Extracted Folder

By default, compressed files are extracted to a new folder with the same name. You can change this, however, to extract to any folder you like.

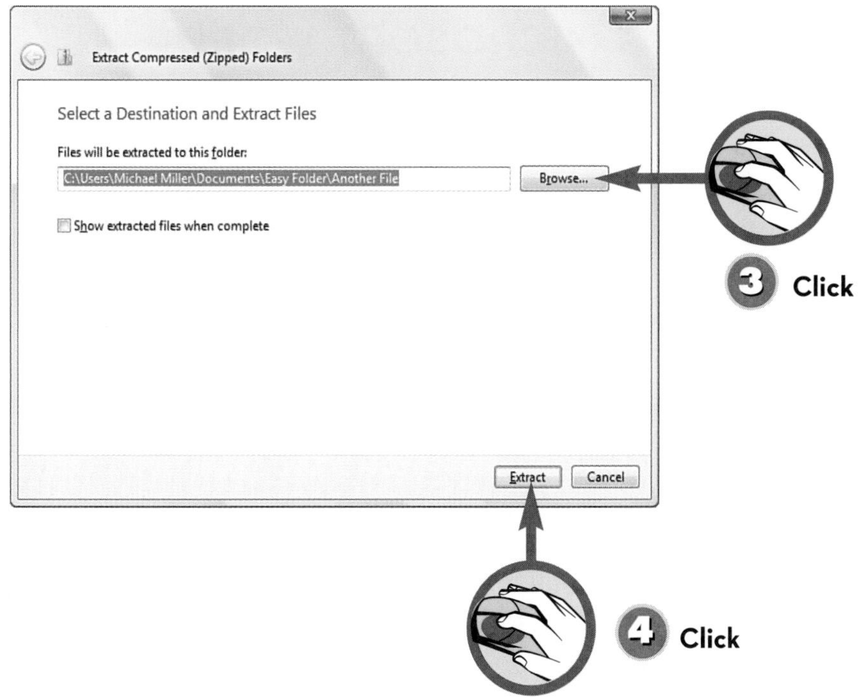

3. Click **Browse** to select the folder to which you want to extract the files.
4. Click the **Extract** button. Windows now extracts the files to the location you selected.

End

TIP

Zipper Icon

Compressed folders are distinguished by the little zipper on the folder icon.

USING MICROSOFT WORD

When you want to write a letter, fire off a quick memo, create a fancy report, or publish a newsletter, you use a type of software program called a *word processor*. For most computer users, Microsoft Word is the word processing program of choice. Word is a full-featured word processor, and it's included on many new PCs and as part of the Microsoft Office suite and some versions of Microsoft Works. You can use Word for all your writing needs—from basic letters to fancy newsletters, and everything in between.

You start Word either from the Windows Start menu (by selecting Start, All Programs, Microsoft Office, Microsoft Office Word 2007) or, if you're using Microsoft Works, from the Works Task Launcher. When Word launches, a blank document appears in the Word workspace. Word can display your document in one of five views: Print Layout, Full Screen Reading, Web Layout, Outline, and Draft. You select a view by using the View buttons at the bottom left of the Word window or by making a selection from the View ribbon.

THE WORD 2007 WORKSPACE

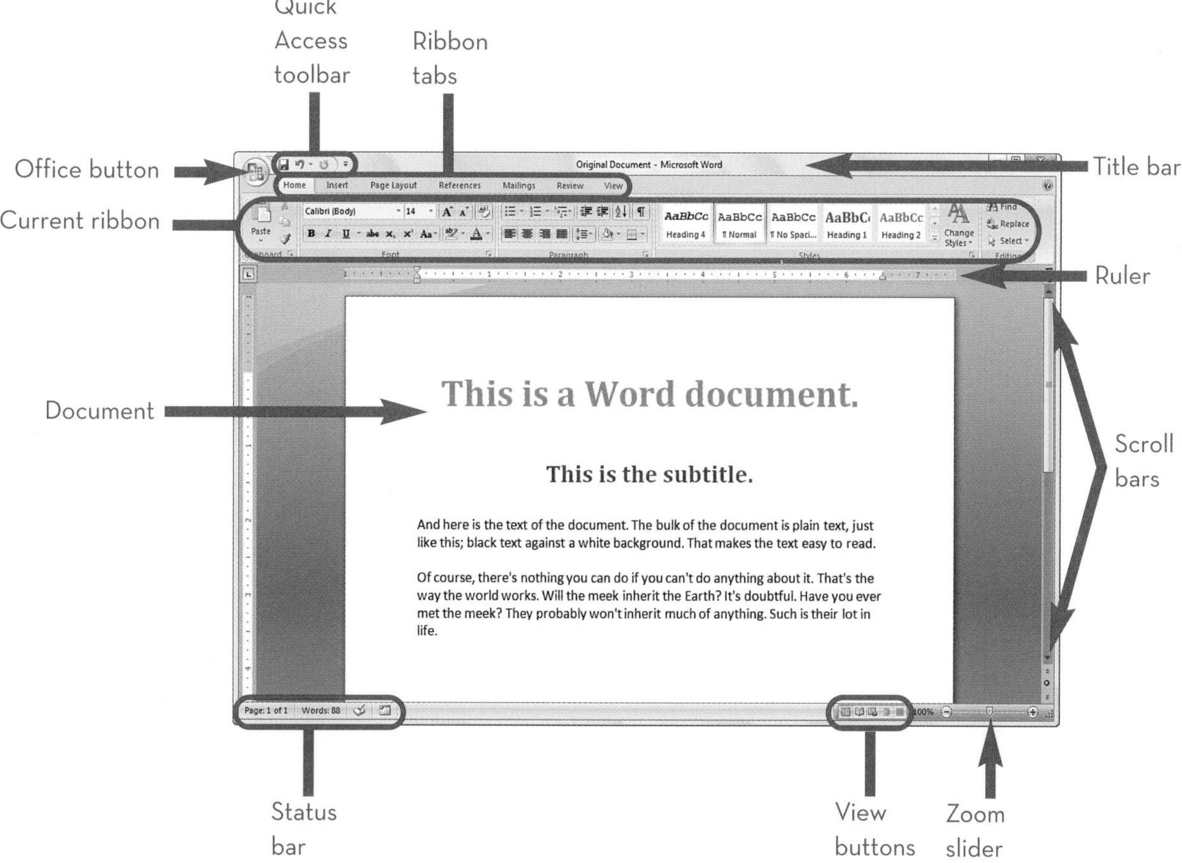

NAVIGATING WORD 2007

Microsoft Word 2007 introduced a new interface that uses toolbar-like ribbons in place of the traditional menu bar and toolbar. Each ribbon contains buttons and controls for specific operations; for example, the Page Layout ribbon contains controls for Margins, Columns, Indent, Spacing, and the like.

Start

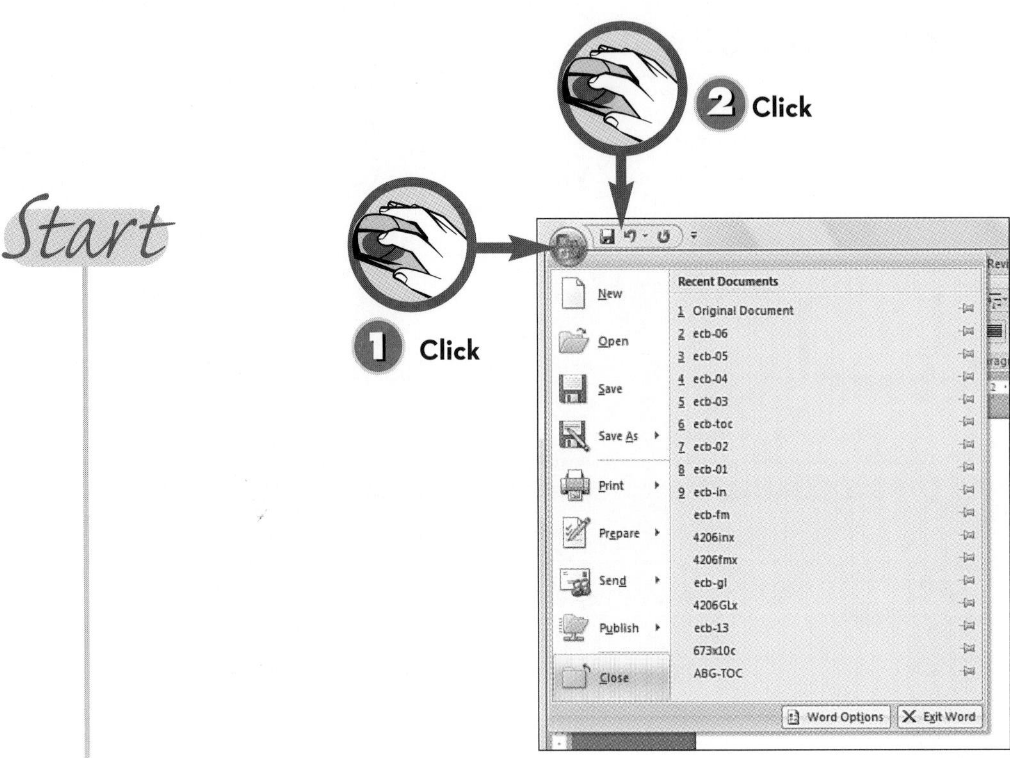

1. Click the **Office** button to access a pull-down menu with common operations and recently-used files.
2. Click any icon on the **Quick Access** toolbar to perform common operations, such as Save and Undo.

Continued

NOTE

Microsoft Word 2007

This section covers the latest version of Microsoft Word—Word 2007, included in Microsoft Office 2007. If you have a previous version of Word, consult the program's Help file for information on how to perform common operations.

NOTE

Upgrading from Previous Versions

If you're used to previous versions of Word, the new version, Word 2007, takes a little getting used to. But once you've figured out what's where, the ribbon-based interface is a lot easier to use.

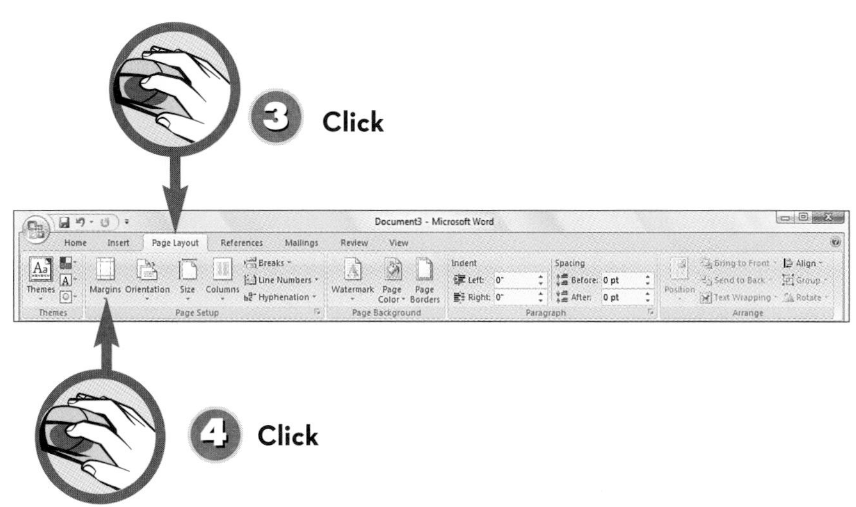

3 Click any tab to display the related ribbon.

4 Click a button or control on the ribbon to perform the given operation.

End

TIP

Context-Sensitive Ribbons

Some ribbons appear automatically when you perform a specific task. For example, if you insert a picture and then select that picture, a new Format ribbon tab (not otherwise visible) will appear, with controls for formatting the selected picture.

TIP

Customize the Quick Access Toolbar

You can add icons to the Quick Access toolbar by clicking the down arrow to the right of the toolbar and checking the items you want to add.

CREATING A NEW DOCUMENT

Any new Word document you create is based on what Word calls a template. A template combines selected styles and document settings—and, in some cases, prewritten text or calculated fields—to create the building blocks for a specific type of document. You use templates to give yourself a head start on specific types of documents.

Start

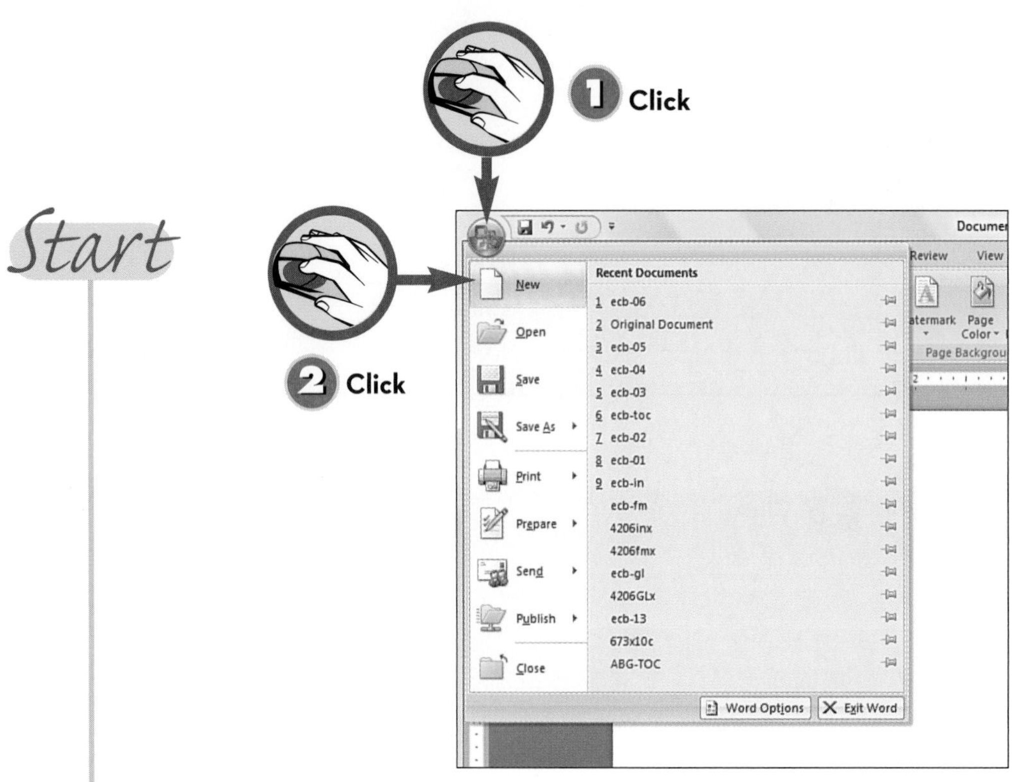

1. Click the **Office** button.
2. Select **New** from the pull-down menu.

Continued

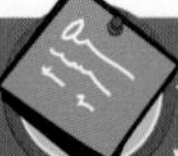

NOTE

Working with Documents

Anything you create with Word—a letter, memo, newsletter, and so on—is called a *document*. A document is nothing more than a computer file that can be copied, moved, deleted, or edited from within Word.

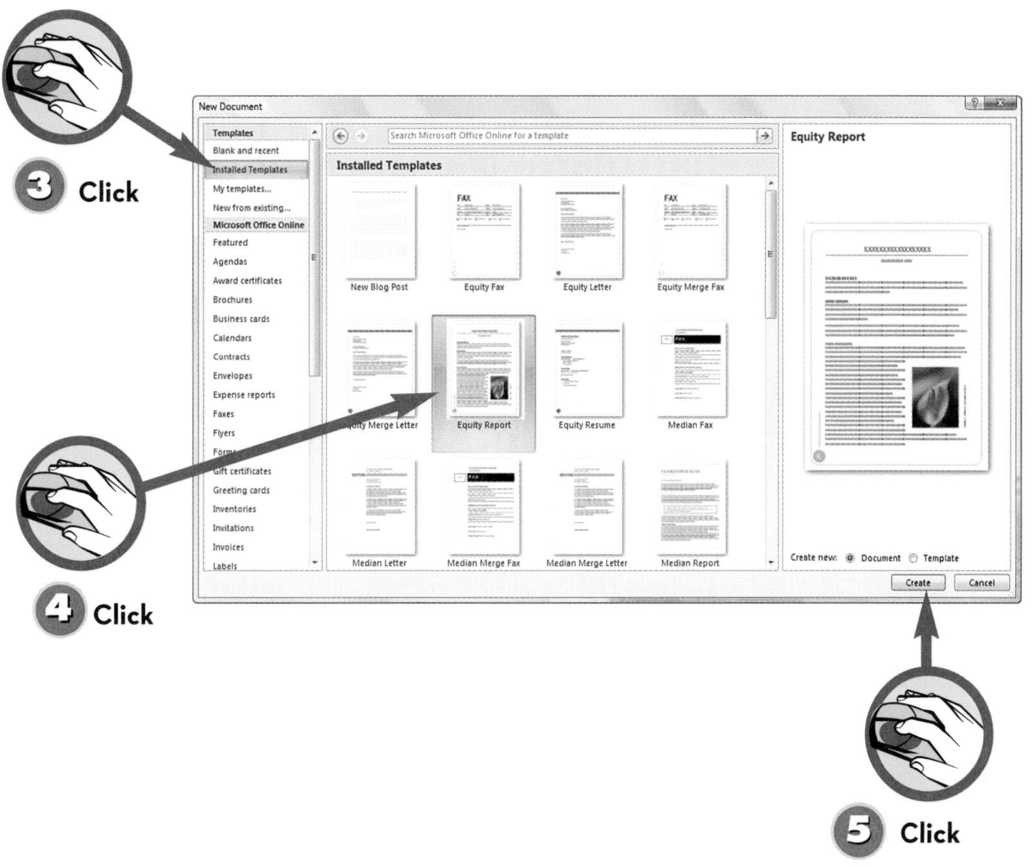

3. Click the type of template you want to create from the list on the left.
4. Click the icon for the template you want.
5. Click the **Create** button to create a new document based on this template.

End

NOTE

Downloading Templates

If you choose to download a template from Microsoft Office Online, you'll need to be connected to the Internet. These templates are free to download for your personal use.

SAVING A DOCUMENT

Every document you create that you want to keep must be saved to a new file. The first time you save a file, you have to specify a filename and location.

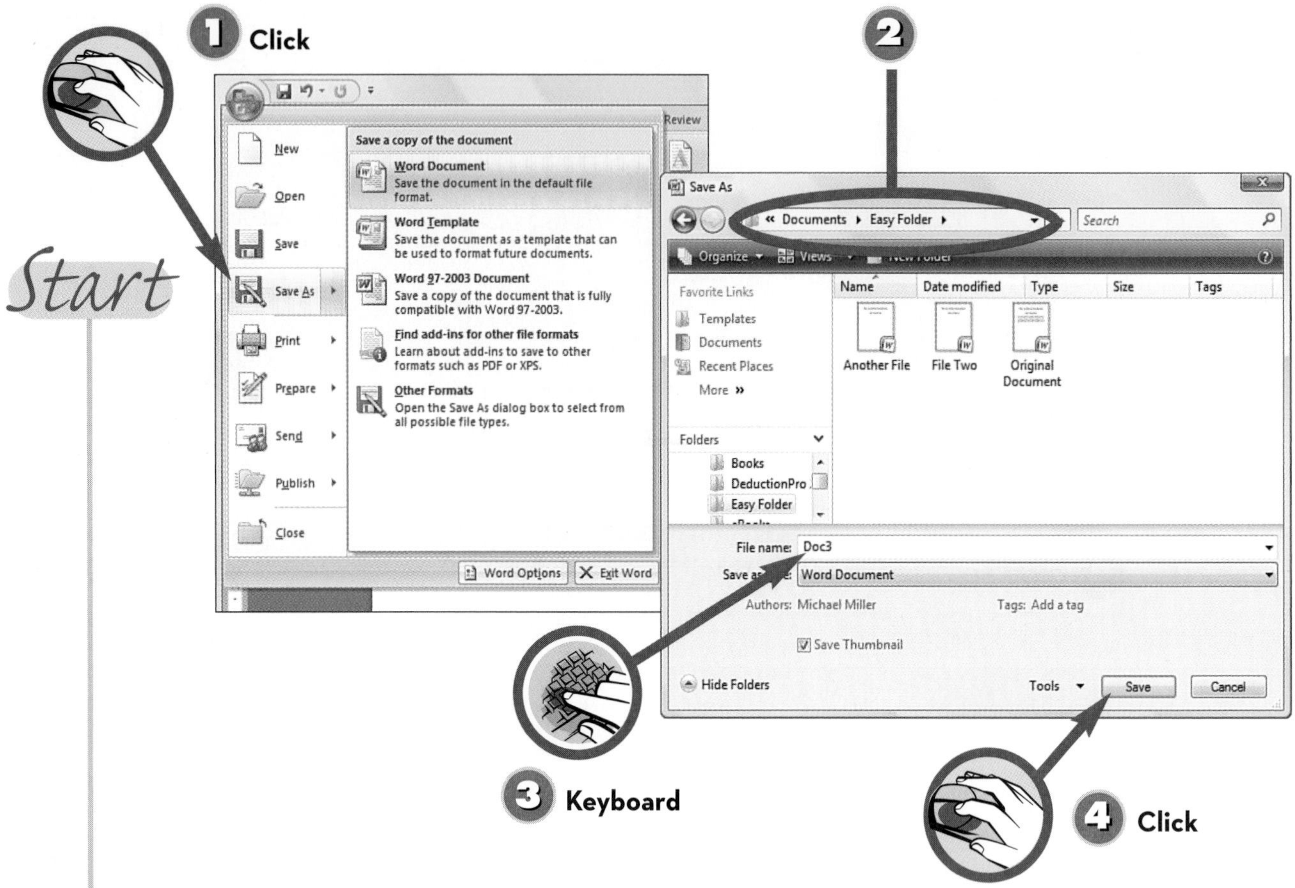

Start

1 Click

2

3 Keyboard

4 Click

1. Click the **Office** button and click **Save As, Word Document**.
2. Navigate to the folder where you want to save the file.
3. Enter a name for the new file.
4. Click the **Save** button.

End

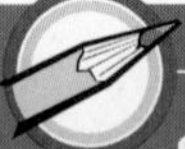

TIP

Saving Again

After you've saved a file once, you don't need to go through the whole Save As routine again. To "fast save" an existing file, click the **Save** button on Word's Quick Access toolbar—or pull down the **Office** menu and select **Save**.

TIP

Compatibility

Saving your new document as a Word Document saves the file in the new file format used exclusively by Word 2007. If you want your document to be compatible with older versions of Word, save it as a Word 97-2003 document instead.

OPENING AN EXISTING DOCUMENT

After you've created a document, you can reopen it at any time for additional editing.

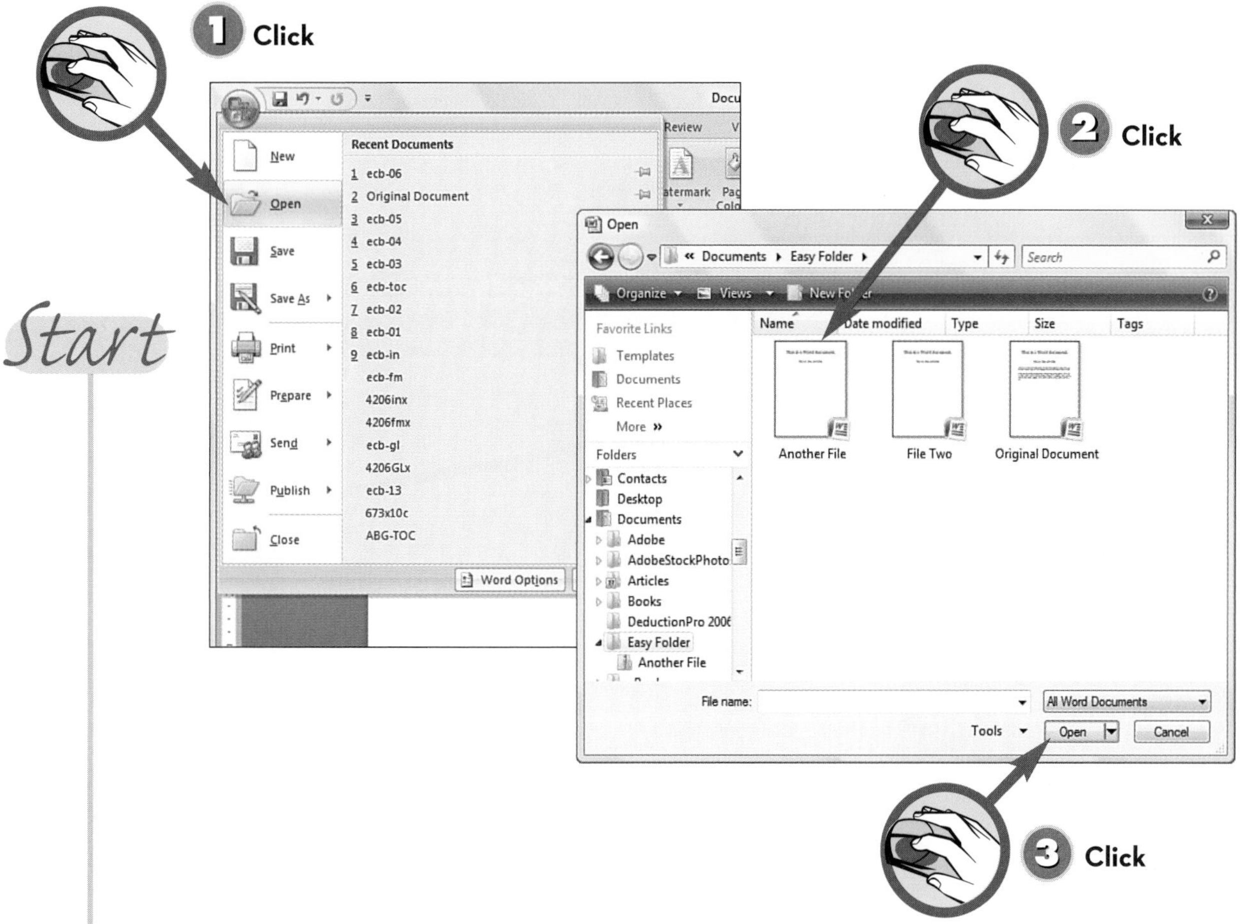

1. Click the **Office** button and then click **Open**.
2. Navigate to and select the file you want to open.
3. Click **Open**.

TIP

Easy Opening

You can also open a document by double-clicking the file icon from within the Open dialog box.

ENTERING TEXT

You enter text in a Word document at the insertion point, which appears onscreen as a blinking cursor. When you start typing on your keyboard, the new text is added at the insertion point.

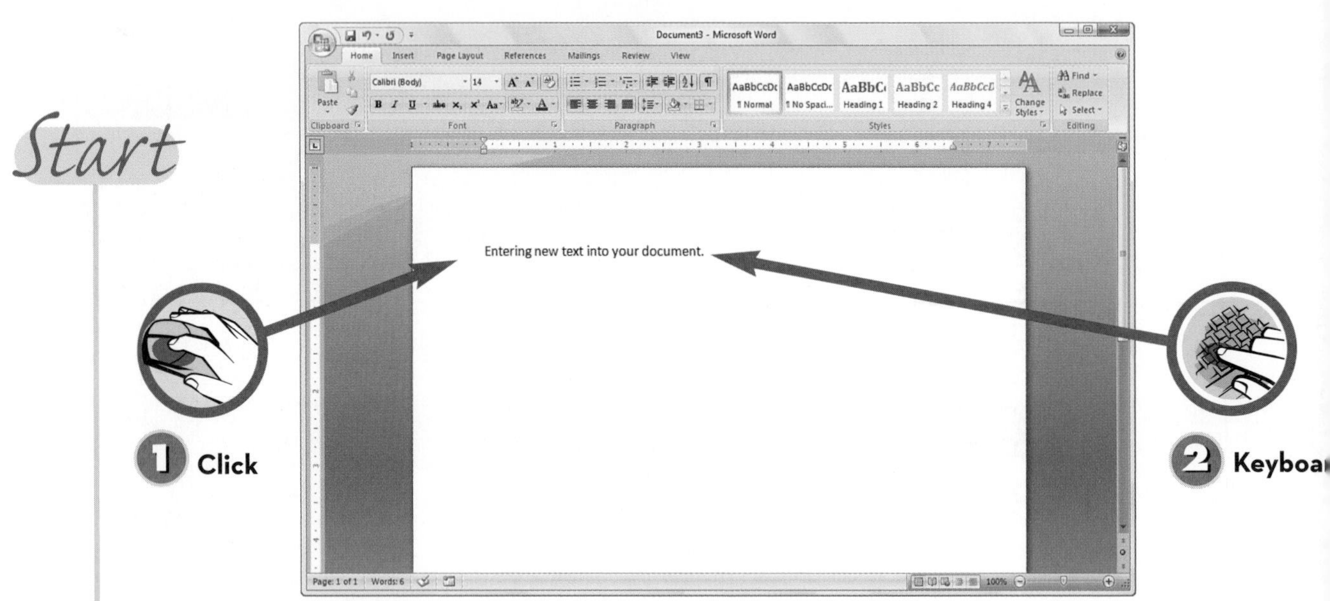

1. Within your document, click where you want to enter the new text.
2. Type the text.

End

TIP

Move the Insertion Point

You move the insertion point with your mouse by clicking a new position in your text. You move the insertion point with your keyboard by using your keyboard's arrow keys.

CUTTING/COPYING AND PASTING TEXT

Word lets you cut, copy, and paste text—or graphics—to and from anywhere in your document or between documents. Use your mouse to select the text you want to edit and then select the appropriate command from the Home ribbon.

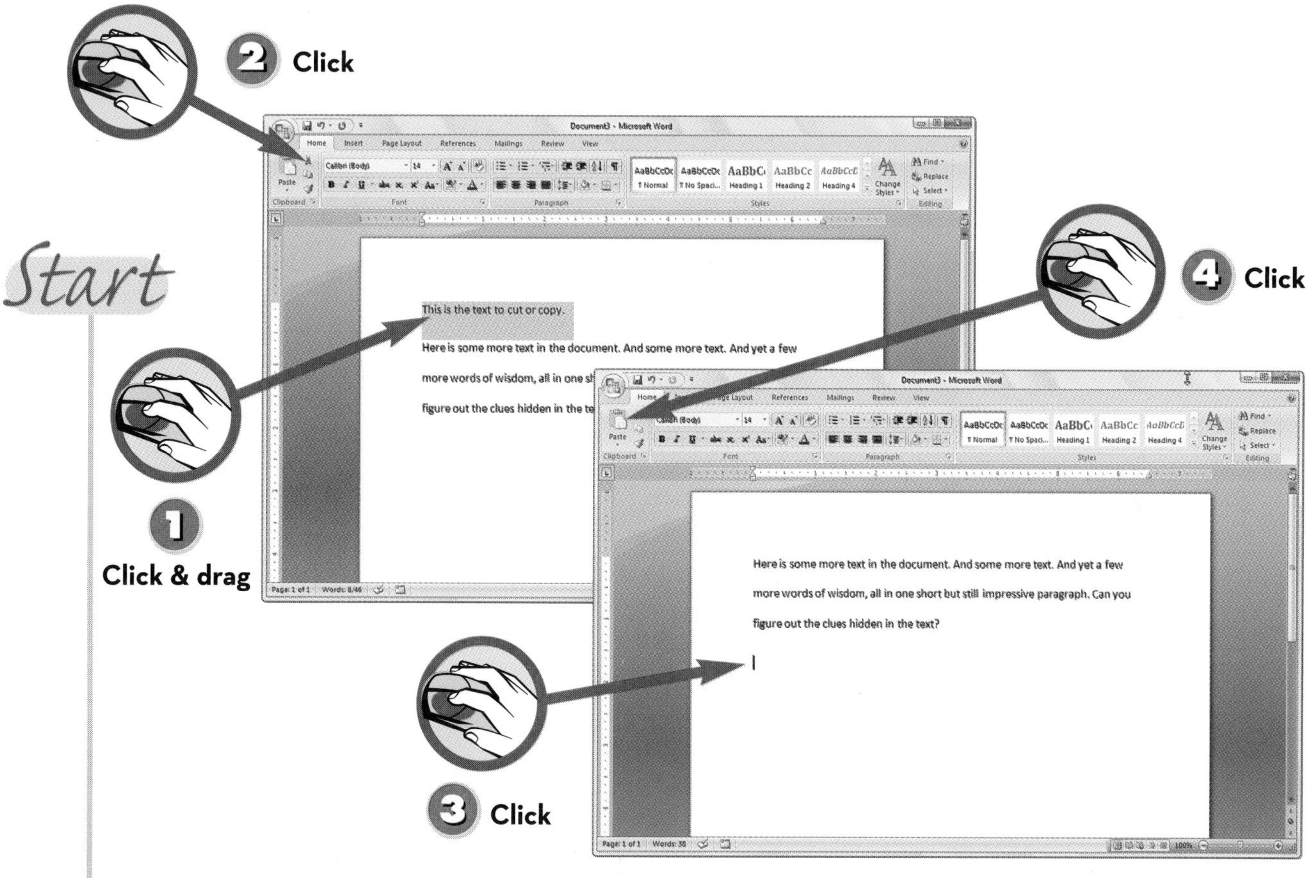

Start

2 Click

4 Click

1 Click & drag

3 Click

1. Click and drag the cursor to select the text you want to copy or cut.
2. From the Home ribbon, click **Copy** to copy the text or **Cut** to cut the text.
3. Within the document, click where you want to paste the cut or copied text.
4. From the Home ribbon, click **Paste**.

TIP

Keyboard Shortcuts

You also can select text using your keyboard; use the Shift key—in combination with other keys—to highlight blocks of text. For example, Shift+Left arrow selects one character to the left.

NOTE

Cut Versus Copy

Cutting text removes the text from the original location and then pastes it into a new location. Copying text leaves the text in the original location and pastes a copy of it into a new location—essentially duplicating the text.

FORMATTING TEXT

After your text is entered and edited, you can use Word's numerous formatting options to add some pizzazz to your document.

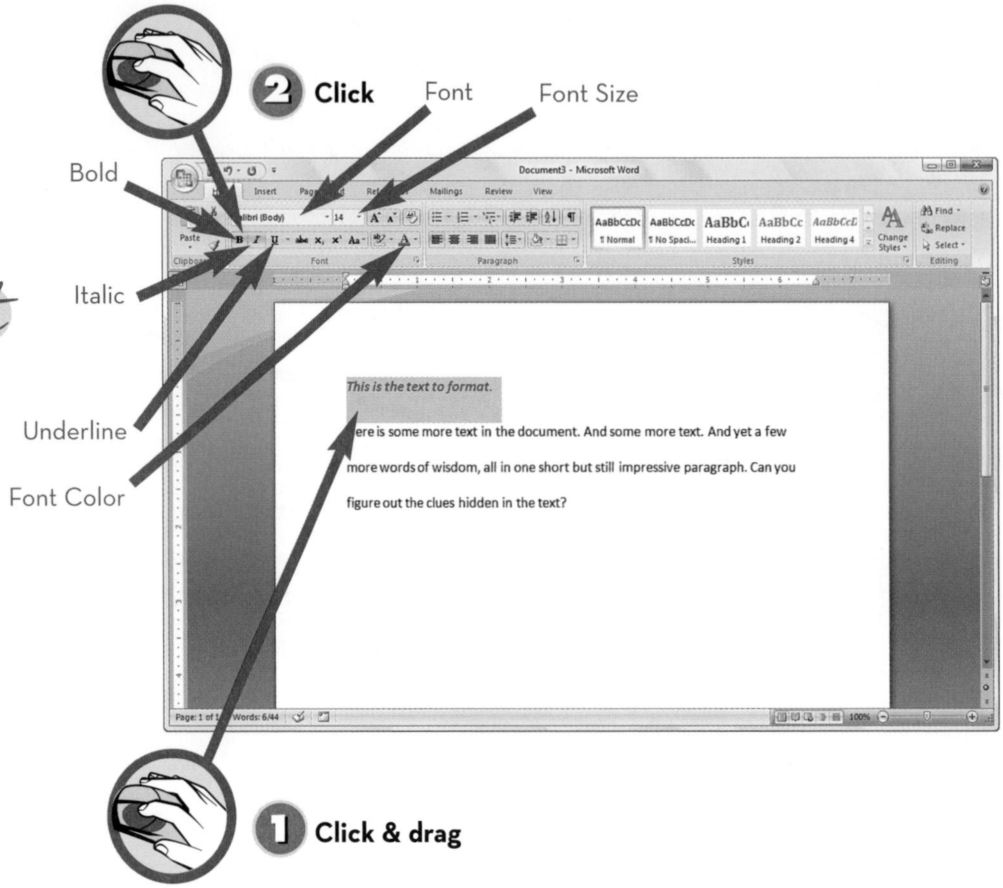

2 Click
Font
Font Size
Bold
Italic
Underline
Font Color

Start

1 Click & drag

1. Click and drag the cursor over the text you want to edit.
2. Click the desired button in the Font section of the Home ribbon—**Font**, **Font Size**, **Bold**, **Italic**, **Underline**, or **Font Color**.

Continued

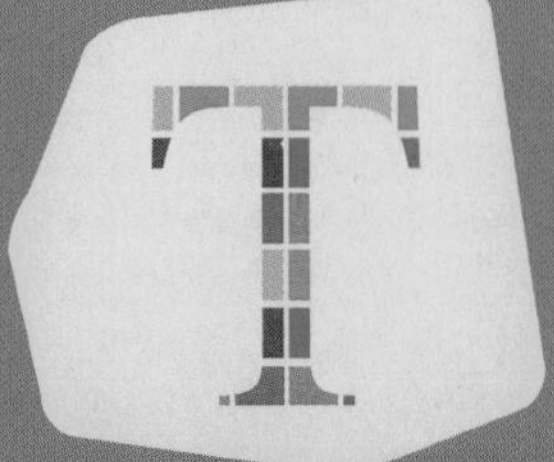

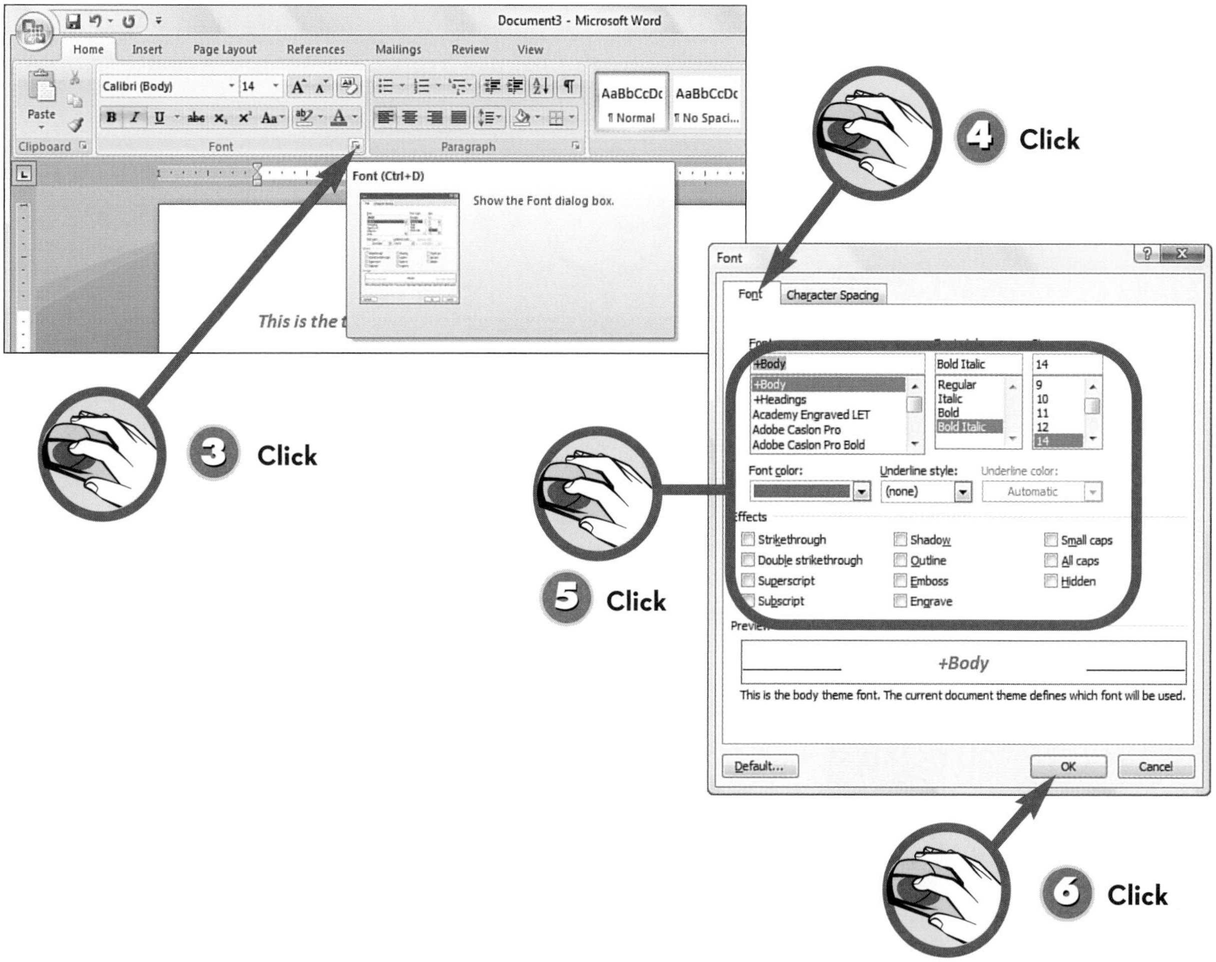

3 For additional formatting options, click the right arrow on the bottom right of the Font section of the Home ribbon; this displays the Font dialog box.

4 Click the **Font** tab.

5 Select the type of formatting you want.

6 Click **OK** when done.

End

TIP

See Your Formatting

It's easiest to format text when you're working in Print Layout view because this displays your document as it will look when printed. To switch to this view, pull down the **View** menu and select **Print Layout**.

FORMATTING PARAGRAPHS

When you're creating a complex document, you need to format more than just a few words here and there. To format complete paragraphs, use Word's Paragraph formatting options on the Home ribbon.

2 Click

Start

1 Click

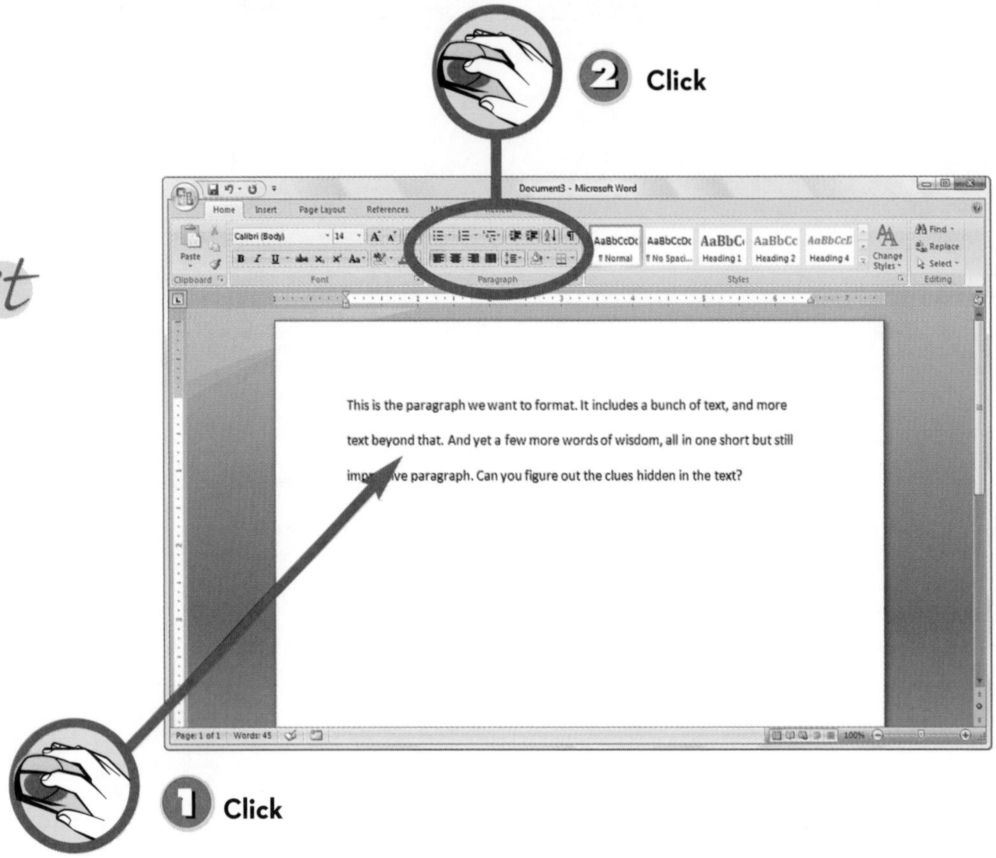

1. Click anywhere within the paragraph you want to format.
2. Click the desired button in the Paragraph section of the Home ribbon—including **Bullets, Numbering, Decrease Indent, Increase Indent, Line Spacing**, or any of the four **Align Text** options.

Continued

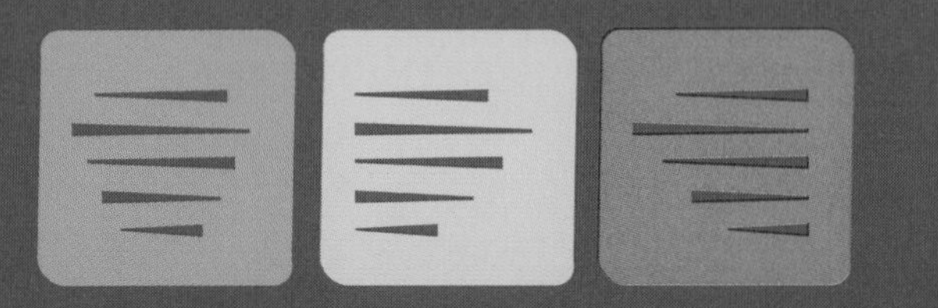

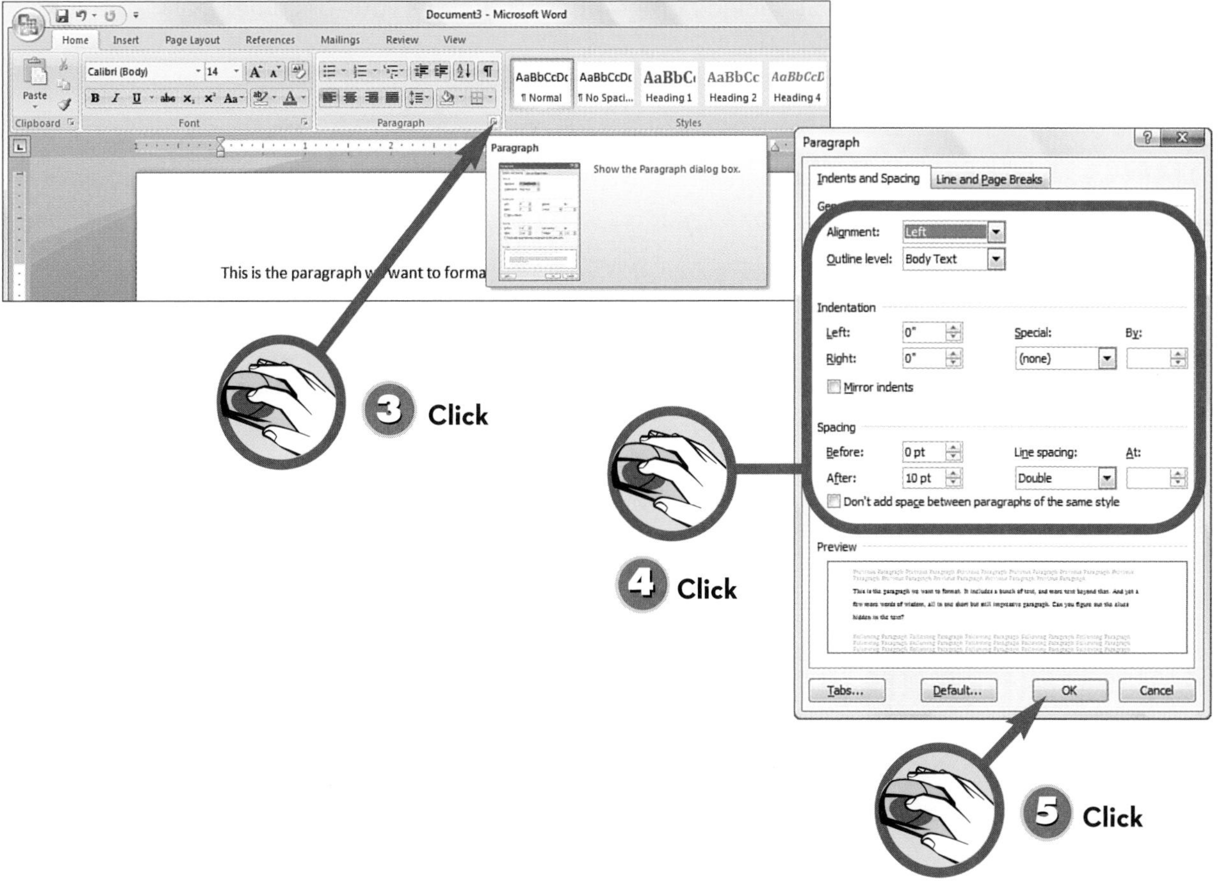

3 For additional paragraph formatting options, click the right arrow at the bottom right of the Paragraph section of the Home ribbon; this displays the Paragraph dialog box.

4 Select the necessary options to adjust how the entire paragraph appears, including indentation, line spacing, and alignment.

5 Click **OK** when done.

End

TIP

Line and Page Breaks

Click the Line and Page Breaks tab in the Paragraph dialog box to add a page break before the current paragraph, keep lines together, and configure widow/orphan control.

APPLYING STYLES

If you have a preferred paragraph formatting you use repeatedly, you don't have to format each paragraph individually. Instead, you can assign all your formatting to a paragraph style and then assign that style to specific paragraphs throughout your document.

Start

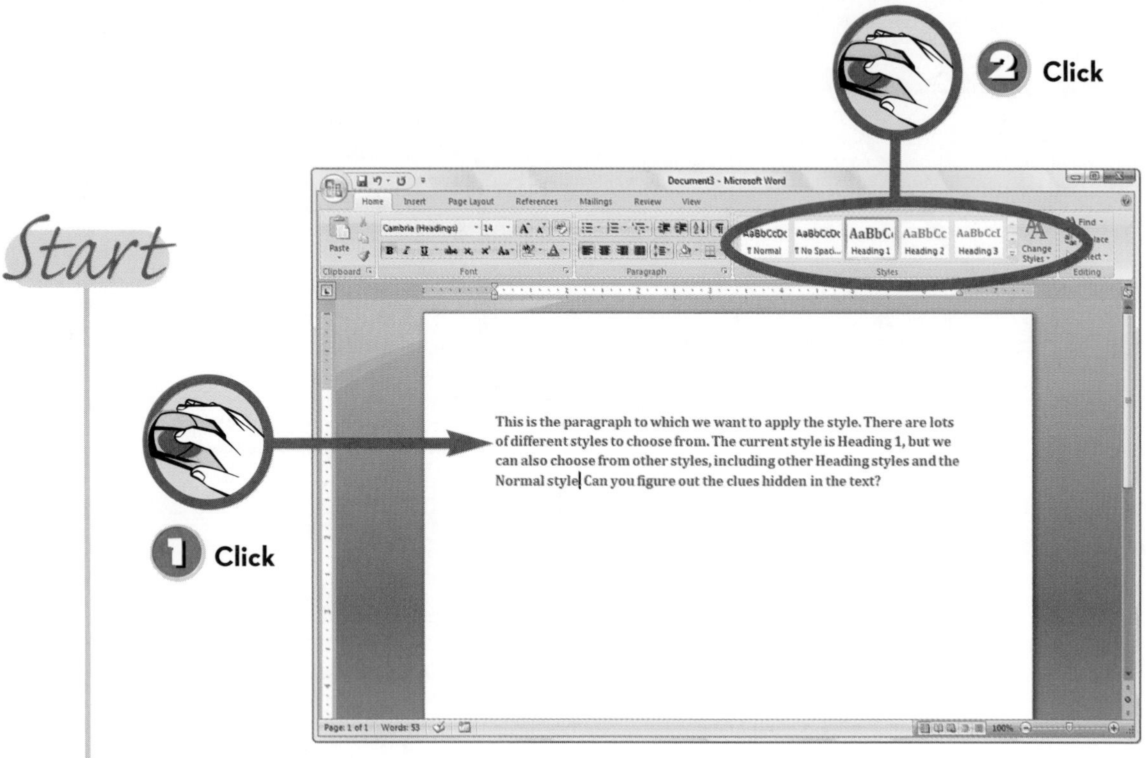

1. Click anywhere within the paragraph to which you want to apply the style.
2. Select a paragraph style from the Styles section of the Home ribbon.

Continued

NOTE

Style Elements

Styles include formatting for fonts, paragraphs, tabs, borders, numbering, and more.

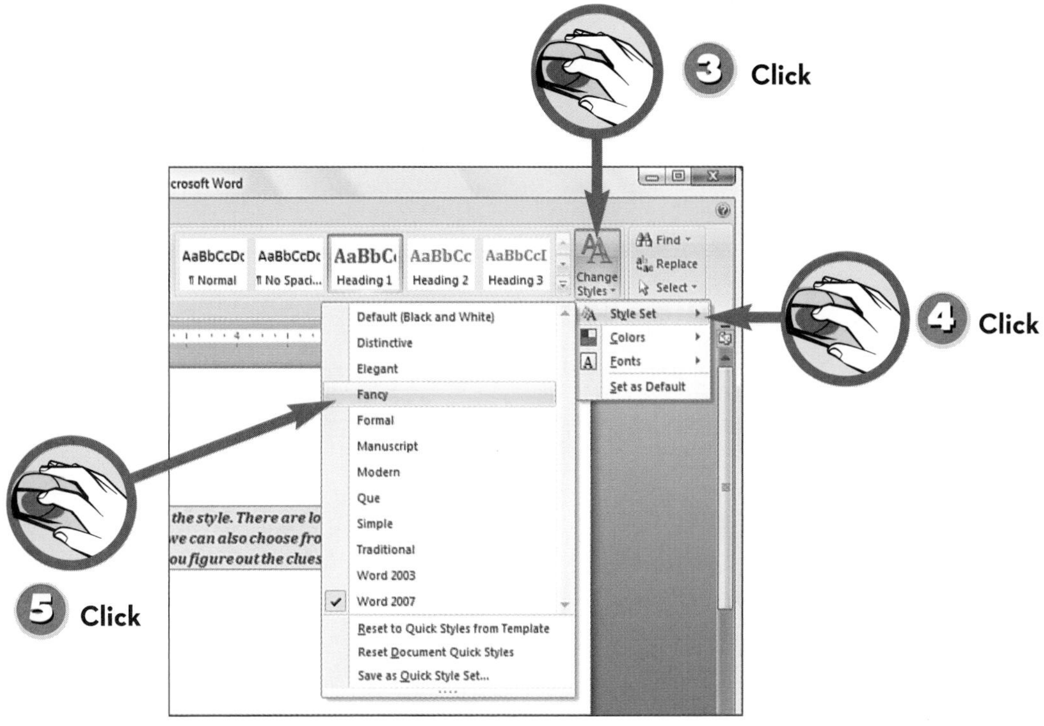

3. To change the entire look of your document, switch style sets by clicking the **Change Styles** button on the Home ribbon.
4. Click **Style Set**.
5. Select a new style set from the list.

End

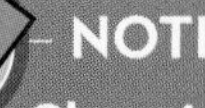

NOTE

Changing Style Sets

Word 2007 includes several different style sets, each of which has its own distinct look.

CHECKING YOUR SPELLING

If you're not a great speller, you'll appreciate Word's automatic spell checking. You can see it right onscreen; just deliberately misspell a word, and you'll see a squiggly red line under the misspelling. That's Word telling you you've made a spelling error!

Start

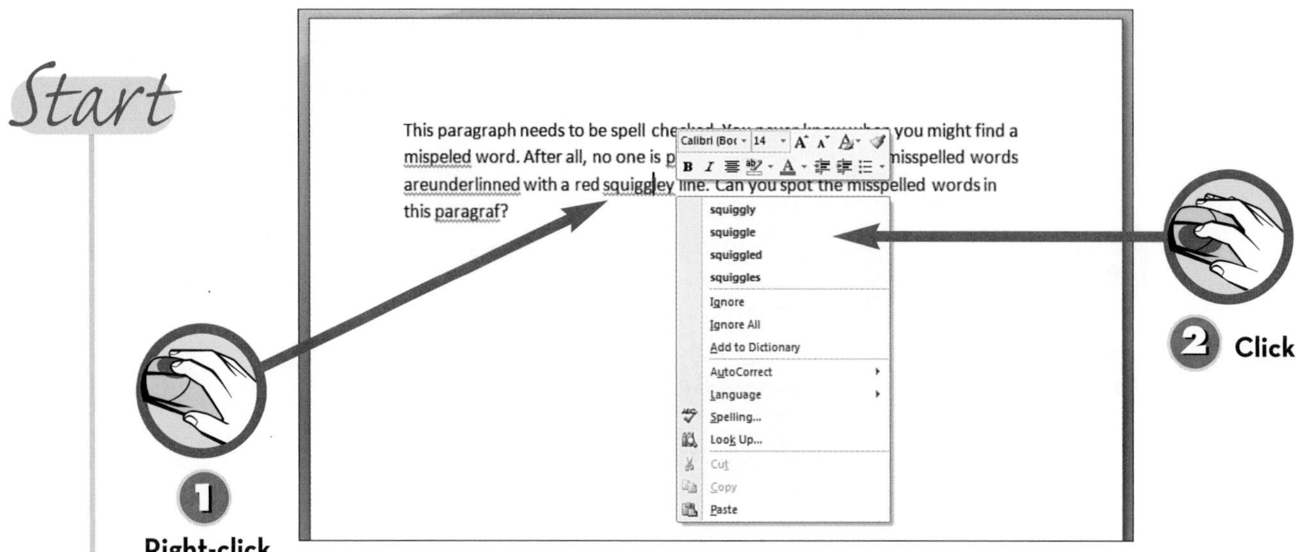

1. Position your cursor over a misspelled word and right-click with your mouse.
2. Choose a replacement word from the list.

End

TIP

Add New Words

If Word doesn't recognize a legitimate word and marks it as misspelled, you can add it to the spelling dictionary by selecting Add to Dictionary from the pop-up menu.

PRINTING A DOCUMENT

When you've finished editing your document, you can instruct Word to send a copy to your printer. When you want to print multiple copies, print only selected pages, or print to a different (nondefault) printer, use Word's Print dialog box.

Start

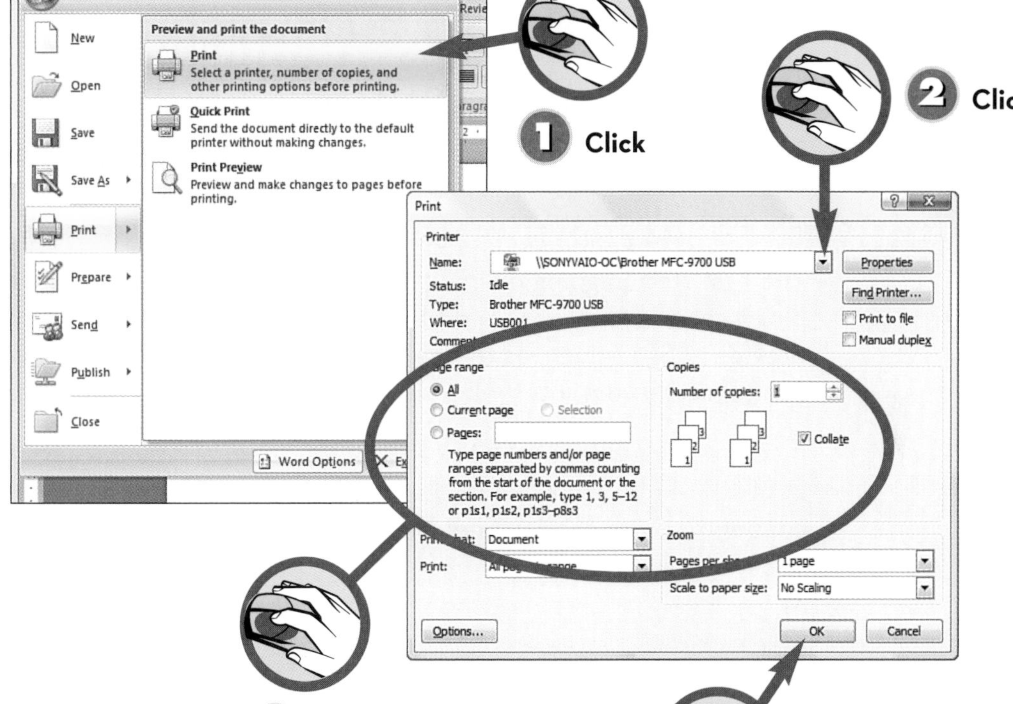

1. Click the **Office** button and then click **Print, Print.**
2. Pull down the name list and select your printer.
3. Select which part(s) of your document to print and how many copies you want.
4. Click the **OK** button to print the document.

End

TIP

Quick Print

The fastest way to print a document is with Word's quick print option. You activate a quick print by opening the **Office** menu and selecting **Print, Quick Print**. This bypasses the Print dialog box and all other configuration options.

part 7

CONNECTING TO THE INTERNET

It used to be that most people bought personal computers to do work—word processing, spreadsheets, databases, that sort of thing. But today, most people also buy PCs to access the Internet—to send and receive email, surf the Web, and chat with other users.

The first step in going online is establishing a connection between your computer and the Internet. To do this, you have to sign up with an Internet service provider (ISP), which, as the name implies, provides your computer with a connection to the Internet.

If you're using your notebook PC on the road, all you have to do is look for a public Wi-Fi hotspot. Your notebook connects to the hotspot, which then connects you to the Internet, simple as pie.

INTERNET EXPLORER

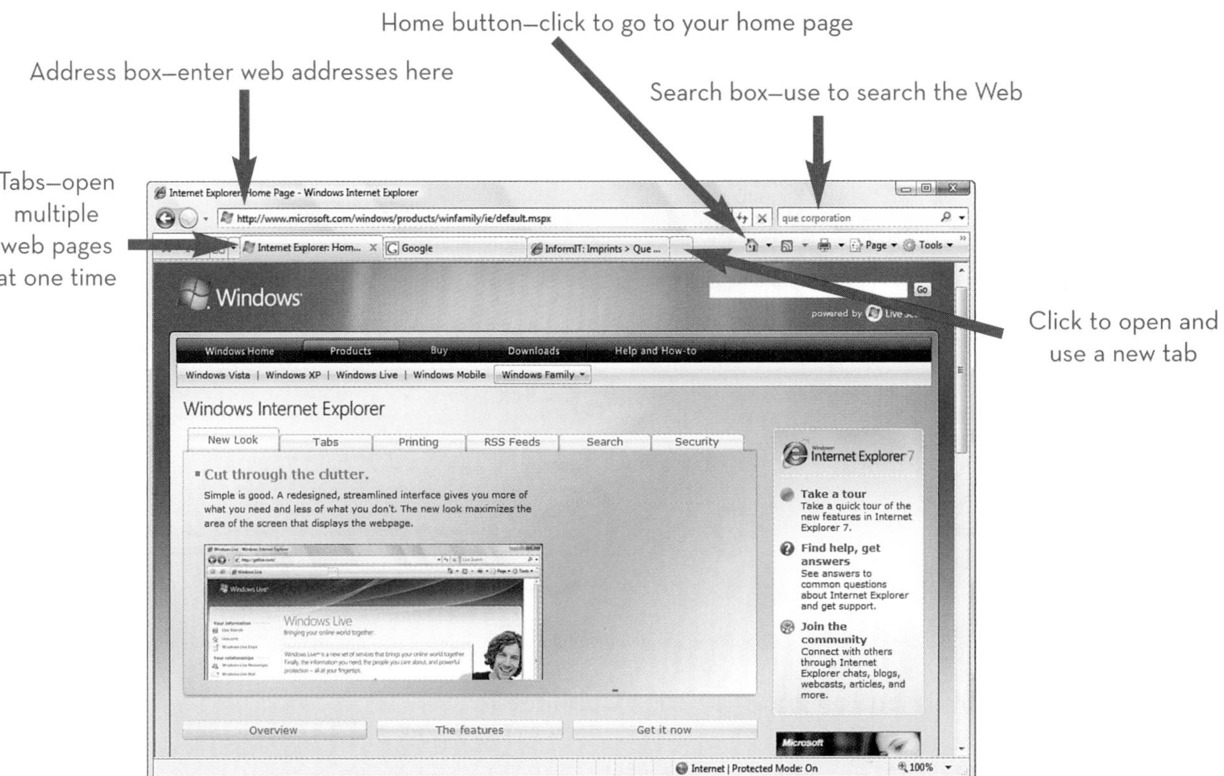

SETTING UP A NEW HOME INTERNET CONNECTION

After you sign up for your home Internet service, you need to configure your computer to work with your ISP. Windows Vista makes this simple; just connect your broadband modem (cable or DSL) to your computer and then perform a few simple steps.

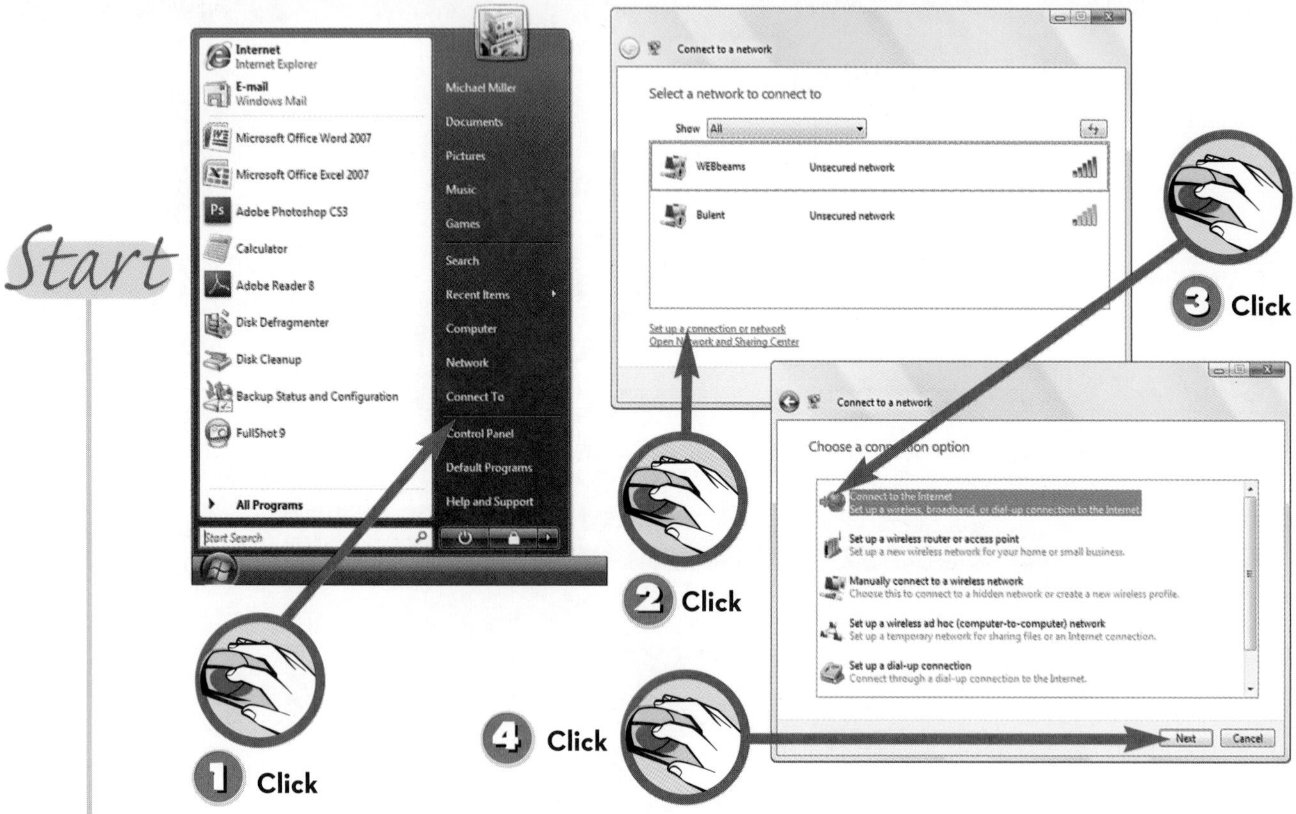

Start

1 Click

2 Click

3 Click

4 Click

1. Click the **Start** button and then click **Connect To**.
2. Click **Set Up a Connection or Network**.
3. Click **Connect to the Internet**.
4. Click **Next**.

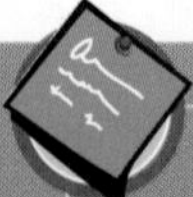

NOTE

Dial-Up Connections

These instructions cover connecting to a broadband (cable or DSL) Internet connection. If you're connecting via a slower dial-up connection, consult your ISP for setup instructions.

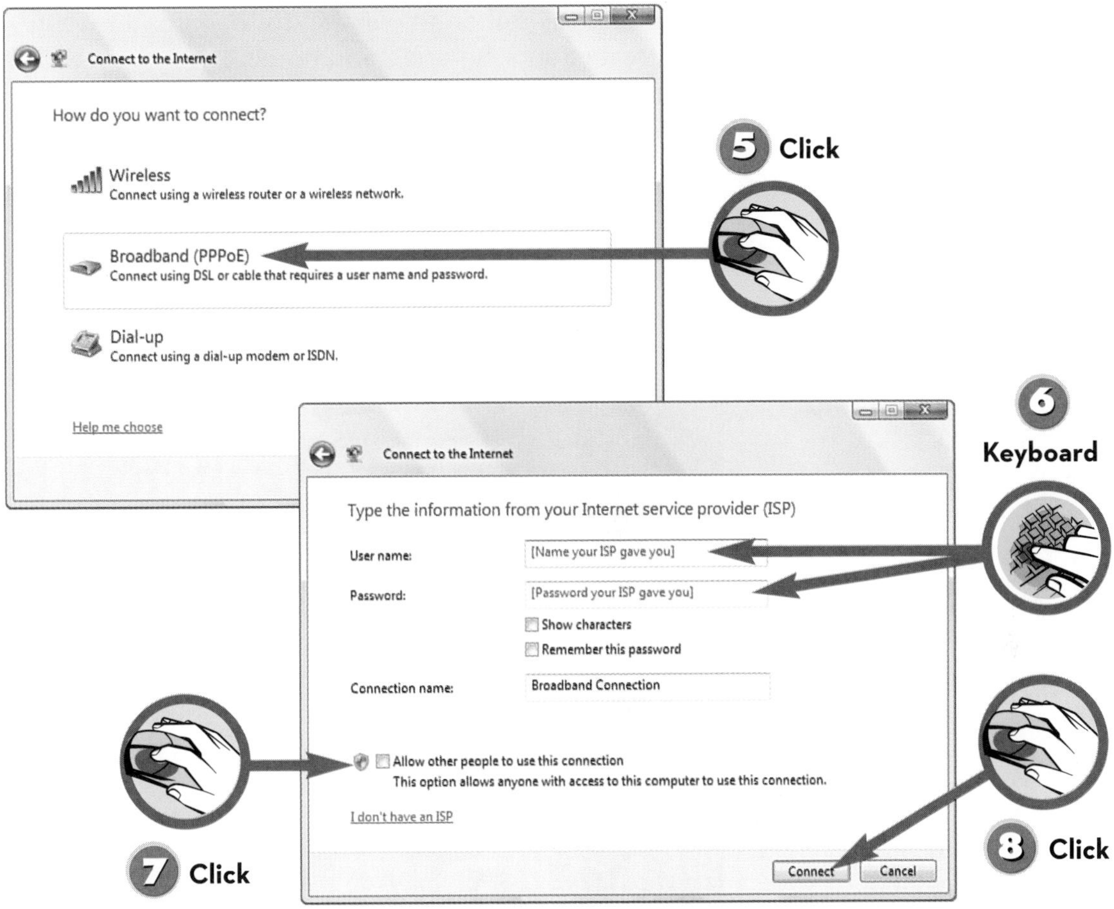

5. Click **Broadband**.
6. If your ISP provided a user name and password, enter that information now. (Most broadband connections do not require this information.)
7. If you want other users of your computer to use this Internet connection, check **Allow Other People to Use This Connection**.
8. Click **Connect**.

End

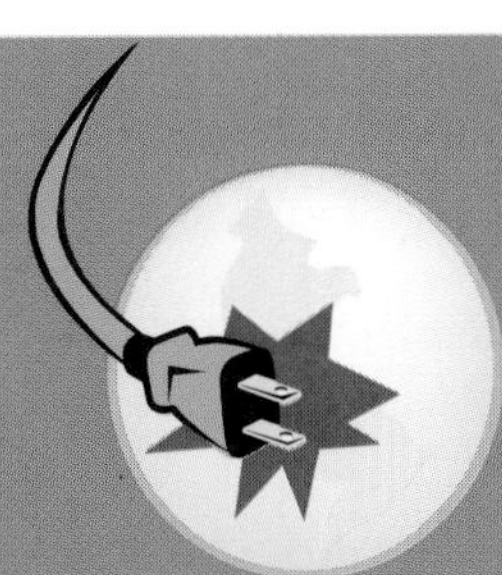

CONNECTING TO AN INTERNET WI-FI HOTSPOT

If you have a notebook PC, you have the option to connect to the Internet when you're out and about. Many coffeehouses, restaurants, libraries, and hotels offer wireless Wi-Fi Internet service, either free or for an hourly or daily fee. Assuming that your notebook has a built-in Wi-Fi adapter (and it probably does), connecting to a public Wi-Fi hotspot is a snap.

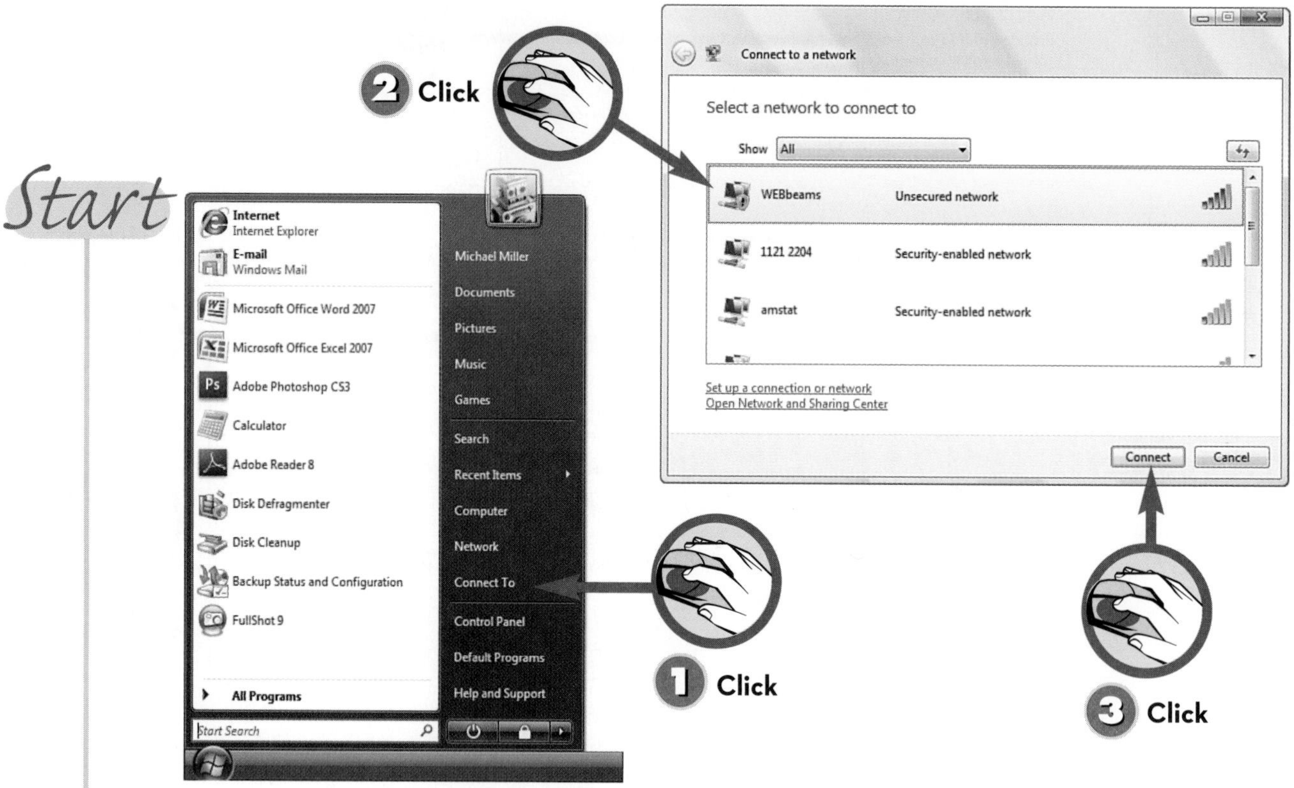

1. Click the **Start** button and then click **Connect To**.
2. The Connect to a Network window should now list all available Wi-Fi networks. Click the network you wish to connect to.
3. Click **Connect**.

Continued

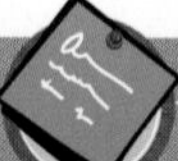

NOTE

Finding the Wi-Fi Signal

When you're near a Wi-Fi hotspot, your PC should automatically pick up the Wi-Fi signal. Just make sure that your Wi-Fi adapter is turned on (some notebooks have a switch for this, either on the front or on the side of the unit), and then look for a wireless connection icon in the Windows system tray or notification area.

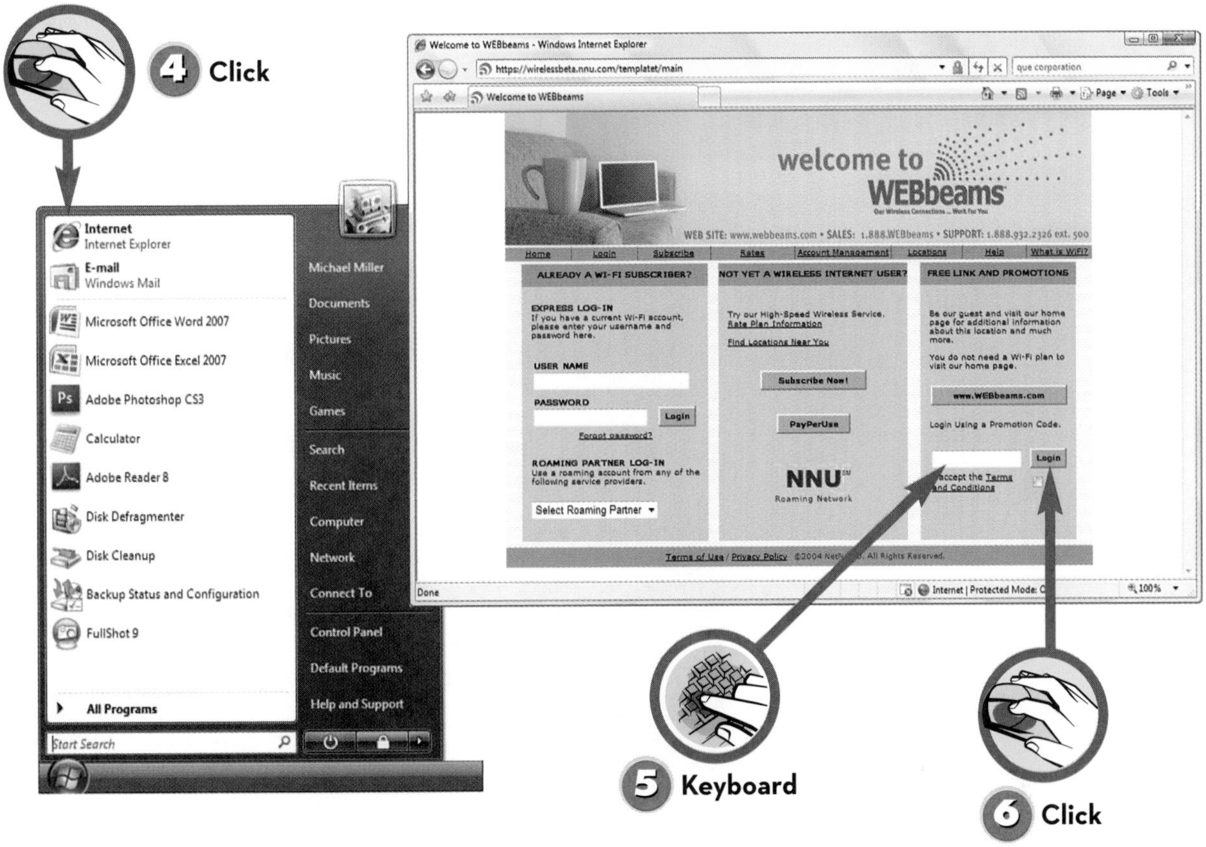

4 Click

5 Keyboard

6 Click

4 Click the Start menu and click **Internet** to launch the Internet Explorer Web browser.

5 Some hotspots will ask for your user name or passcode, or require a credit card for payment. Enter the necessary information.

6 Click the **Login** or **Enter** button to access the hotspot.

End

NOTE

Logging In to the Hotspot

After Windows connects to the selected hotspot, you can log on to the wireless network, which you do by opening Internet Explorer. If the hotspot has free public access, you'll be able to surf normally. If the hotspot requires a password, payment, or other logon procedure, it will intercept the request for your normal home page and instead display its own login page.

SURFING THE WEB WITH INTERNET EXPLORER

Internet Explorer (IE) is a web browser that lets you quickly and easily browse the World Wide Web. When you enter a new web address in the Address box and press Enter (or click the Go button), IE loads the new page. You can also click any link on a web page to go to the new page. Let's demonstrate with a quick tour of the Web.

1 Click

2 Keyboard

Start

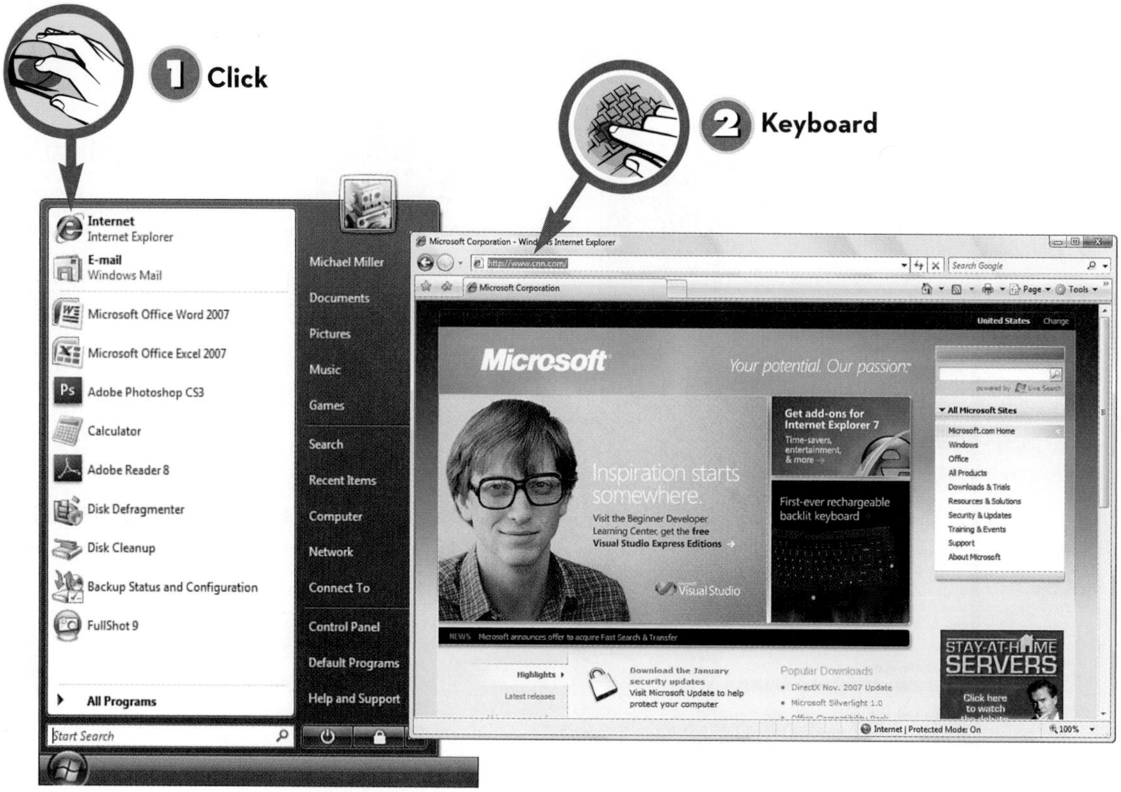

1. Launch Internet Explorer by selecting **Start**, **Internet**.
2. Let's find out what's happening out in the real world by heading over to one of the most popular news sites. Enter **www.cnn.com** in the **Address** box, and then press **Enter**.

Continued

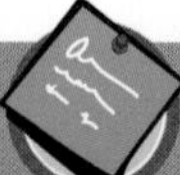

NOTE

Internet Explorer 7

These instructions are written for Internet Explorer 7. If you're using a different version of Internet Explorer, operation may be slightly different.

3 Click

4 Click

3. Click any headline or link to read the complete story.
4. Click the down scroll button to read more of the story.

Continued

TIP

Change IE's Home Page

When you first launch Internet Explorer, it loads your predefined home page. To change Internet Explorer's home page, go to the new page, click the down arrow next to the Home button on the toolbar, select **Add or Change Home Page**, then check **Use This Webpage as Your Only Home Page**, and click **Yes**.

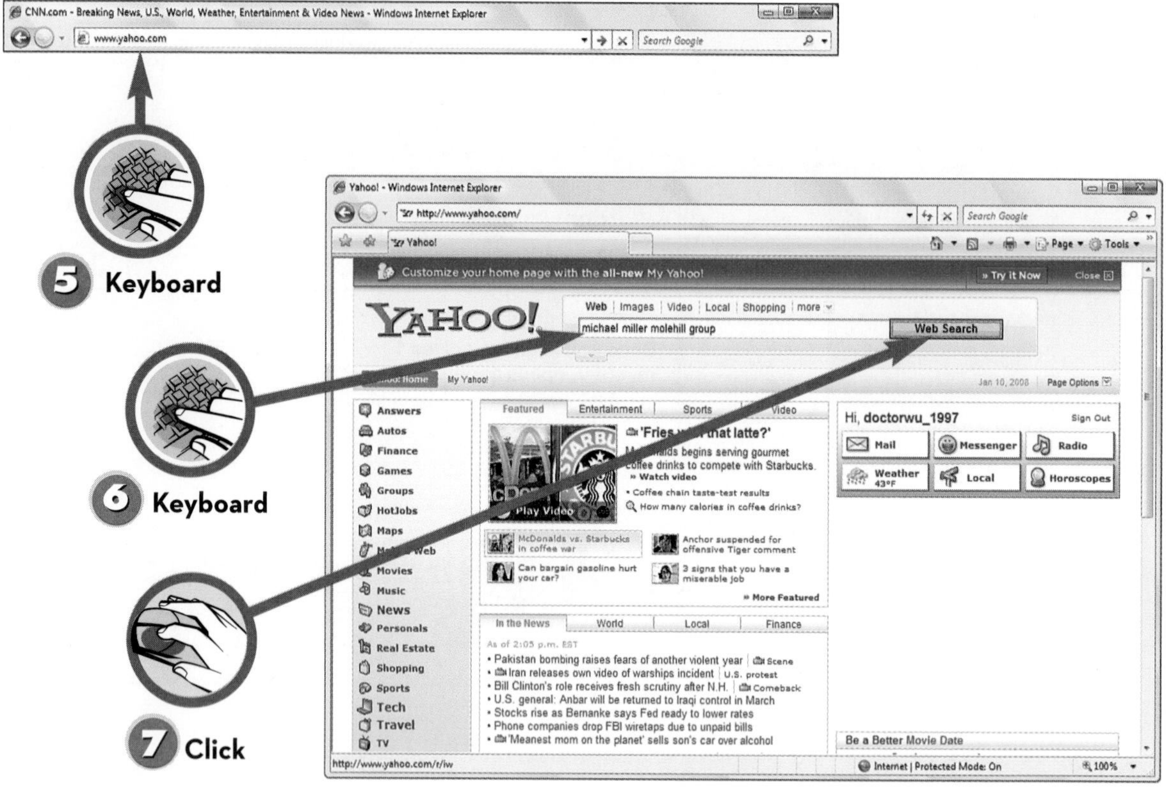

5 Now, let's do a little searching at Yahoo!. Enter **www.yahoo.com** in the **Address** box and press **Enter**.

6 Ready to search? Enter **michael miller molehill group** in the Search box at the top of the page.

7 Click the **Web Search** button to begin the search.

Continued

TIP

Searching the Web

To find a particular page on the Web, you use a search site. These sites, such as Google and Yahoo!, let you enter a query and search for web pages that contain those keywords.

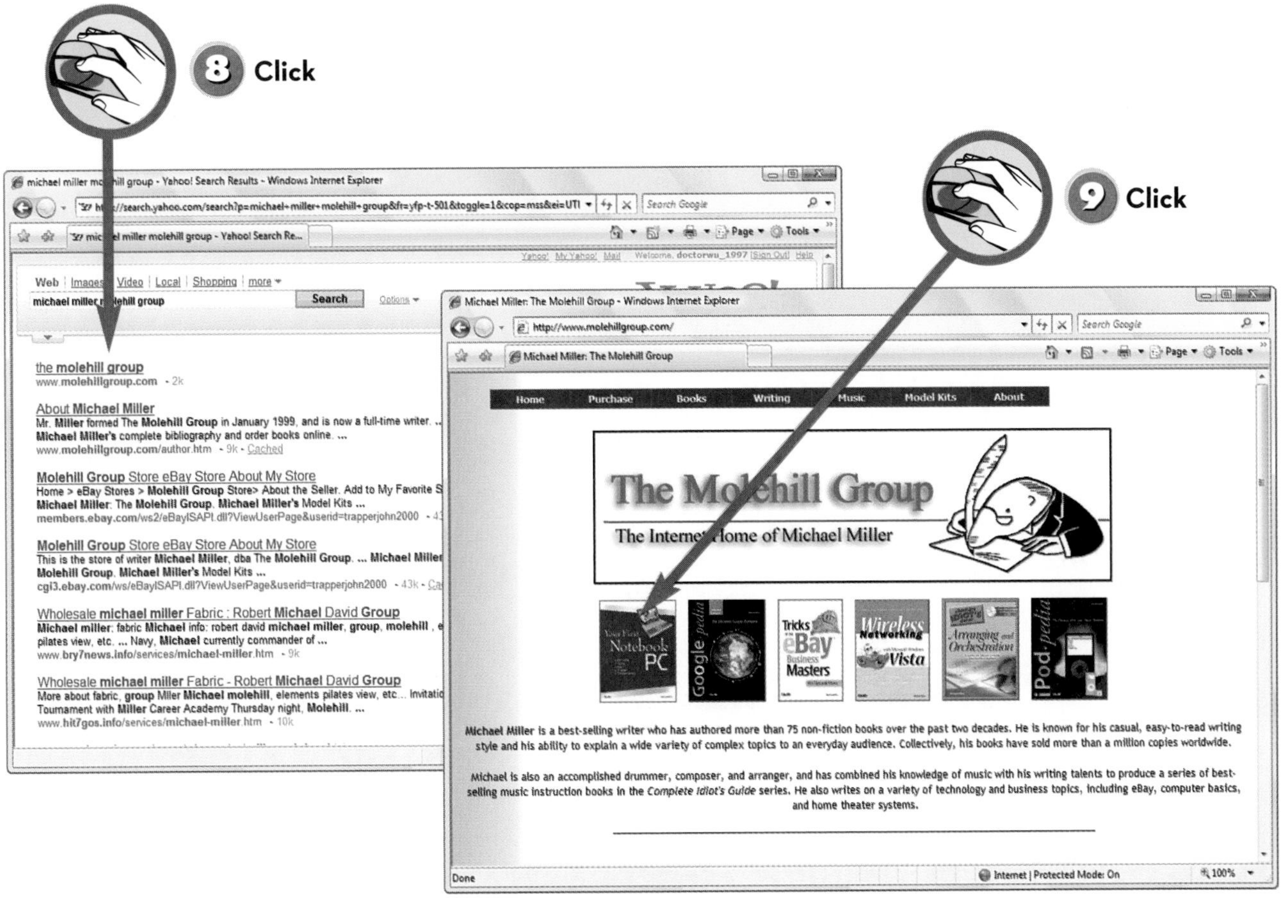

8 Click

9 Click

8 When the search results page appears, find the listing for The Molehill Group (it should be near the top) and click the link.

9 You're now taken to *my* website, The Molehill Group. Click one of the book pictures at the top of the page to read more about that book.

End

TIP

Going Back

To return to the last-viewed web page, click the **Back** button next to the Address box, or press the **Backspace** key on your keyboard. If you've backed up several pages and want to return to the page you were on last, click the **Forward** button.

SAVING YOUR FAVORITE PAGES

When you find a web page you like, you can add it to a list of Favorites within Internet Explorer. This way, you can easily access any of your favorite sites just by selecting them from the list.

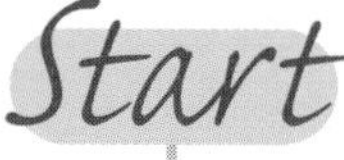

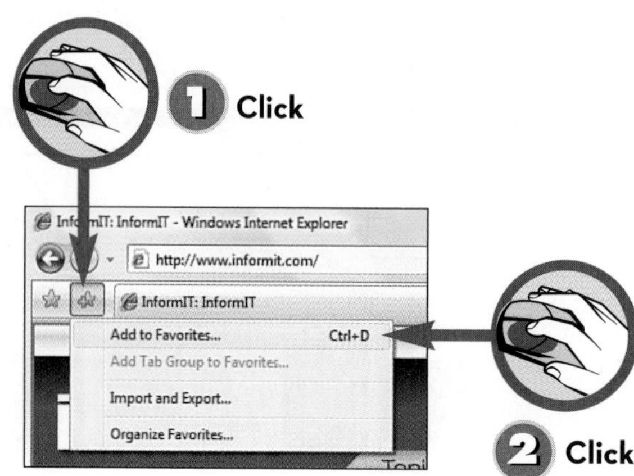

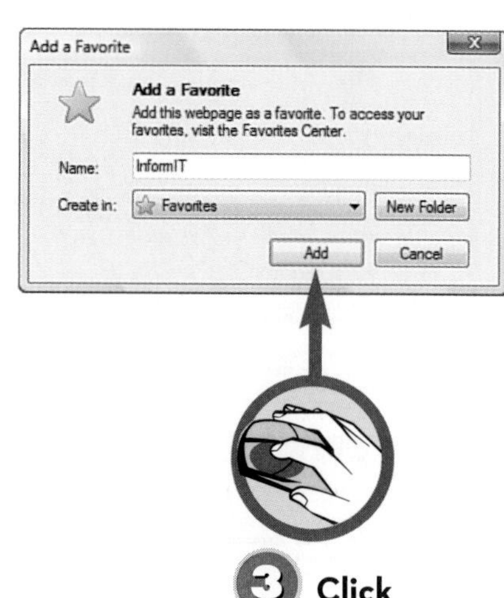

1. Go to the web page you want to add to your Favorites list, then click the **Add to Favorites** button.
2. Click **Add to Favorites**.
3. Confirm the page's name and then click the **Add** button.

End

TIP

Organizing Favorites

You can store your favorite websites in the main Favorites folder or create additional subfolders for different types of Favorites.

RETURNING TO A FAVORITE PAGE

After a web page is saved to your Favorites list, you can return to that page at any time by selecting it from the list—no need to reenter that page's web address.

Start

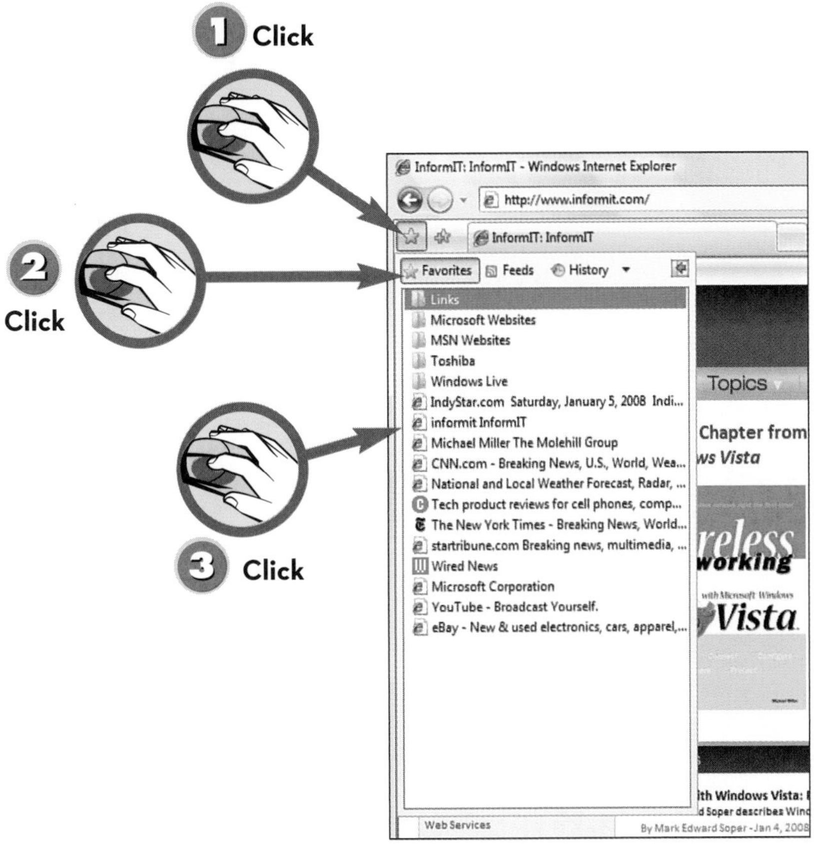

1. Click the **Favorites Center** button on the toolbar.
2. Click the **Favorites** button to display the Favorites list.
3. Click a favorite page, and IE goes to that page.

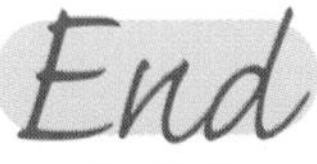

TIP

Hide the Favorites Pane

Click the **Favorites** button again to hide the Favorites pane.

REVISITING HISTORY

Internet Explorer keeps track of web pages you've recently visited so you can easily revisit them without having to reenter the web page address.

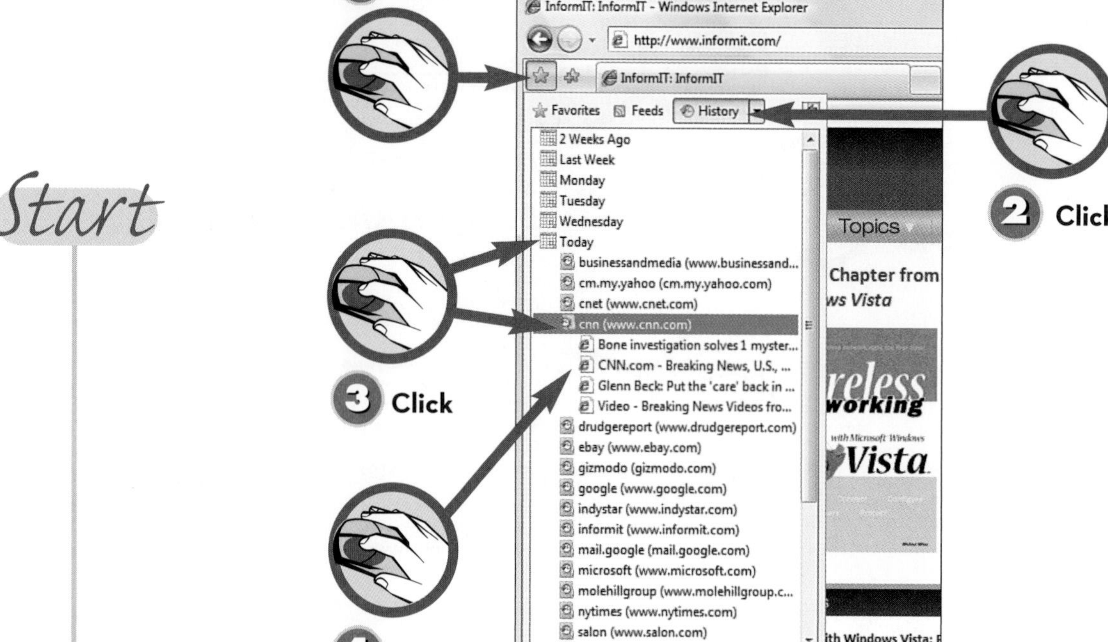

1. Click the **Favorites Center** button on the toolbar.
2. Click the **History** button to display the History list.
3. Click any folder in the History pane to display the sites you visited that day, and any subfolder to display the pages within that site.
4. Click a specific page to display that page in the right pane.

End

TIP

Recent History

To revisit one of the last half-dozen or so pages viewed in your current session, click the down arrow on the **Back** button. This drops down a menu containing the last nine pages you've visited. Click a page to return to it.

SEARCHING THE WEB WITH GOOGLE

A web search engine lets you search for virtually anything online. The most popular search engine today is Google (www.google.com), which indexes billions of individual web pages. Google is very easy to use and returns extremely accurate results.

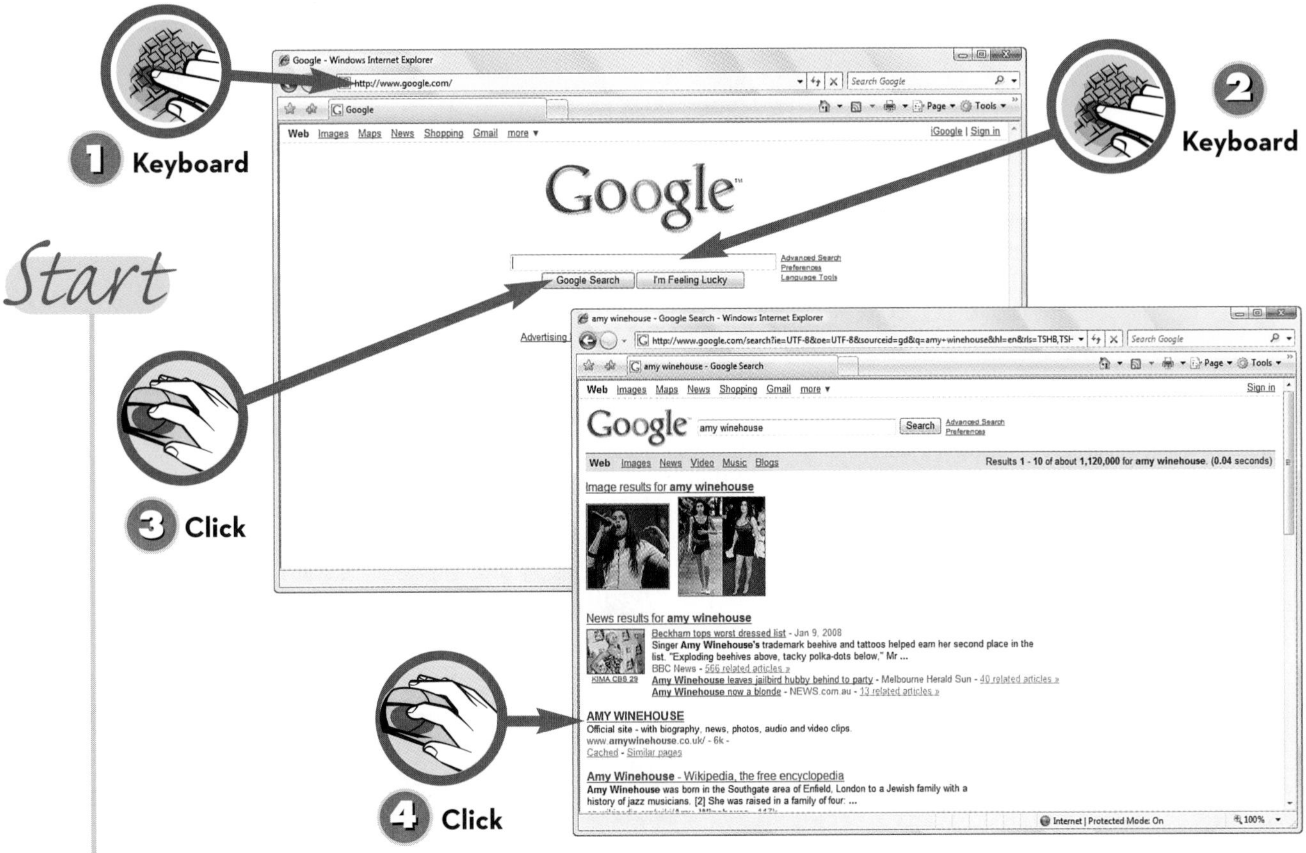

Start

1 Keyboard

2 Keyboard

3 Click

4 Click

1 Go to **www.google.com**.

2 Enter one or more keywords into the search box.

3 Click the **Google Search** button.

4 When the results are displayed, click any page link to view that page.

End

TIP

Advanced Searching

Google also offers a variety of advanced search options to help you fine-tune your search. Just click the **Advanced Search** link and choose the appropriate options.

TIP

Internet Explorer Search Box

You can also search the web from Internet Explorer's Search box, located next to the Address box. To choose a search provider, click the down arrow next to the Search box, select **Find More Providers**, and when the Add Search Providers page appears, click **Google**.

FINDING NEWS AND OTHER INFORMATION ONLINE

The Web is a terrific source for all sorts of news and information. Let's take a quick look at some of the most popular news, weather, and sports sites—the best way to stay informed online!

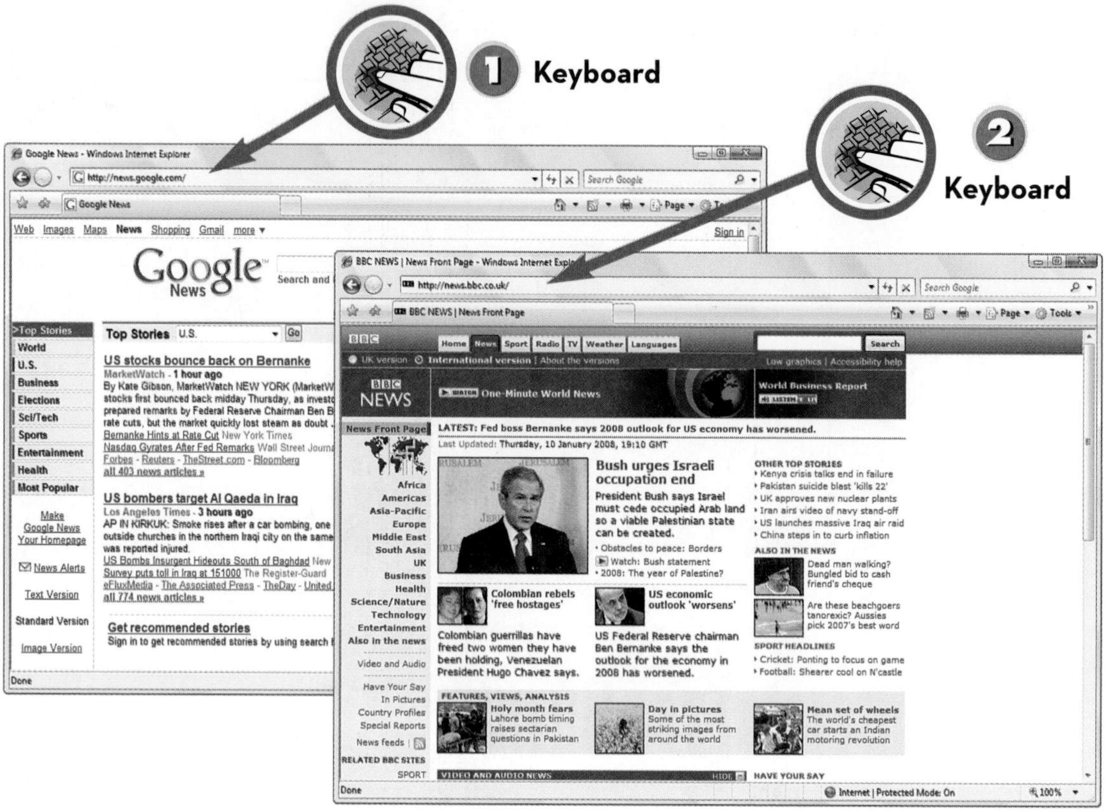

Start

1 Keyboard

2 Keyboard

1. For the top headlines from a variety of sources, go to Google News (news.google.com).
2. For in-depth international news, go to BBC News (news.bbc.co.uk).

Continued

TIP

More News

Other full-service news sites include ABC News (abcnews.go.com), CBSNews.com (www.cbsnews.com), CNN.com (www.cnn.com), and MSNBC (www.msnbc.msn.com).

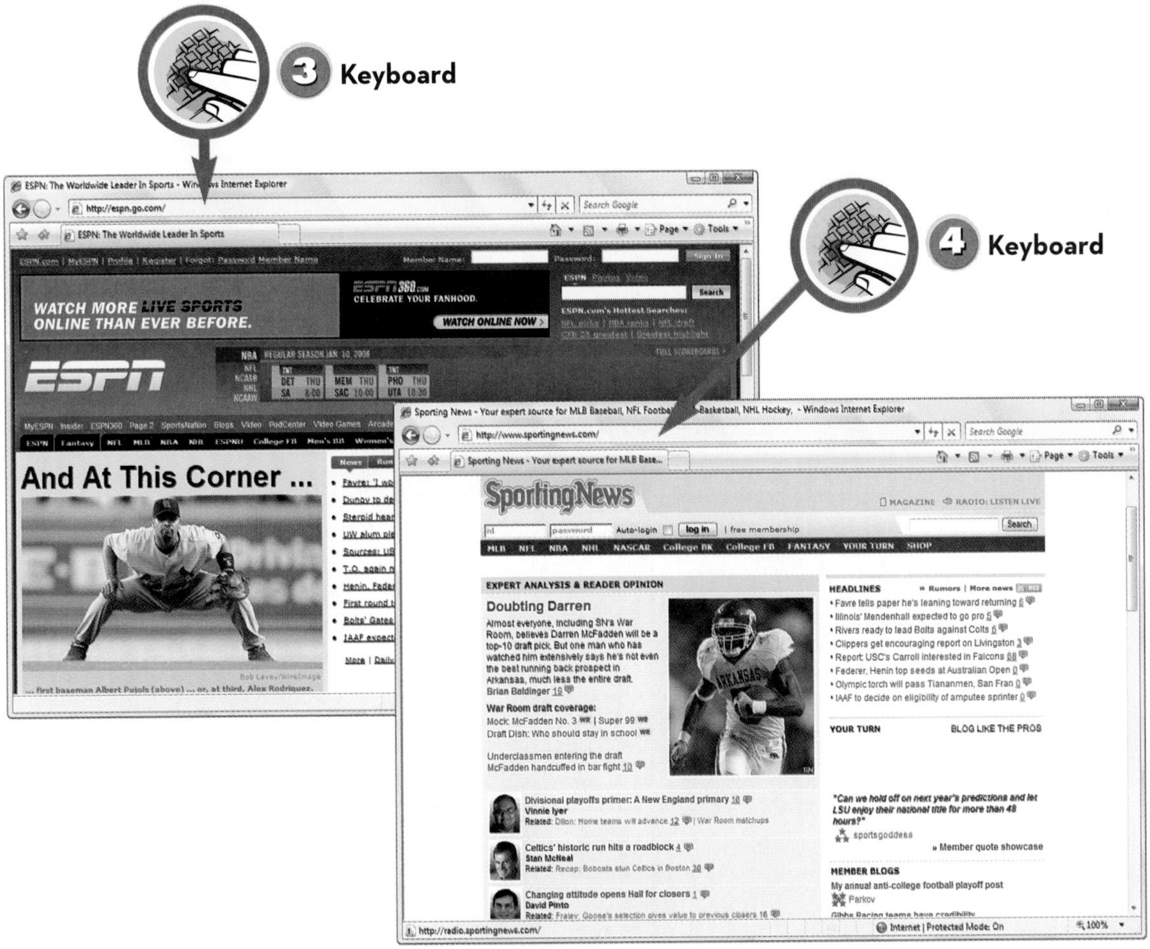

3 Keyboard

4 Keyboard

3 For comprehensive sports coverage, go to ESPN.com (espn.go.com).

4 For additional sports coverage, go to SportingNews.com (www.sportingnews.com).

Continued

Note

Sports on the Web

The best sports sites on the Web resemble the best news sites—they're actually portals to all sorts of content and services, including up-to-the-minute scores, post-game recaps, in-depth reporting, and much more.

TIP

Local Sports

If you follow a particular sports team, check out that team's local newspaper on the Web. Chances are you'll find a lot of in-depth coverage there that you won't find at other sites.

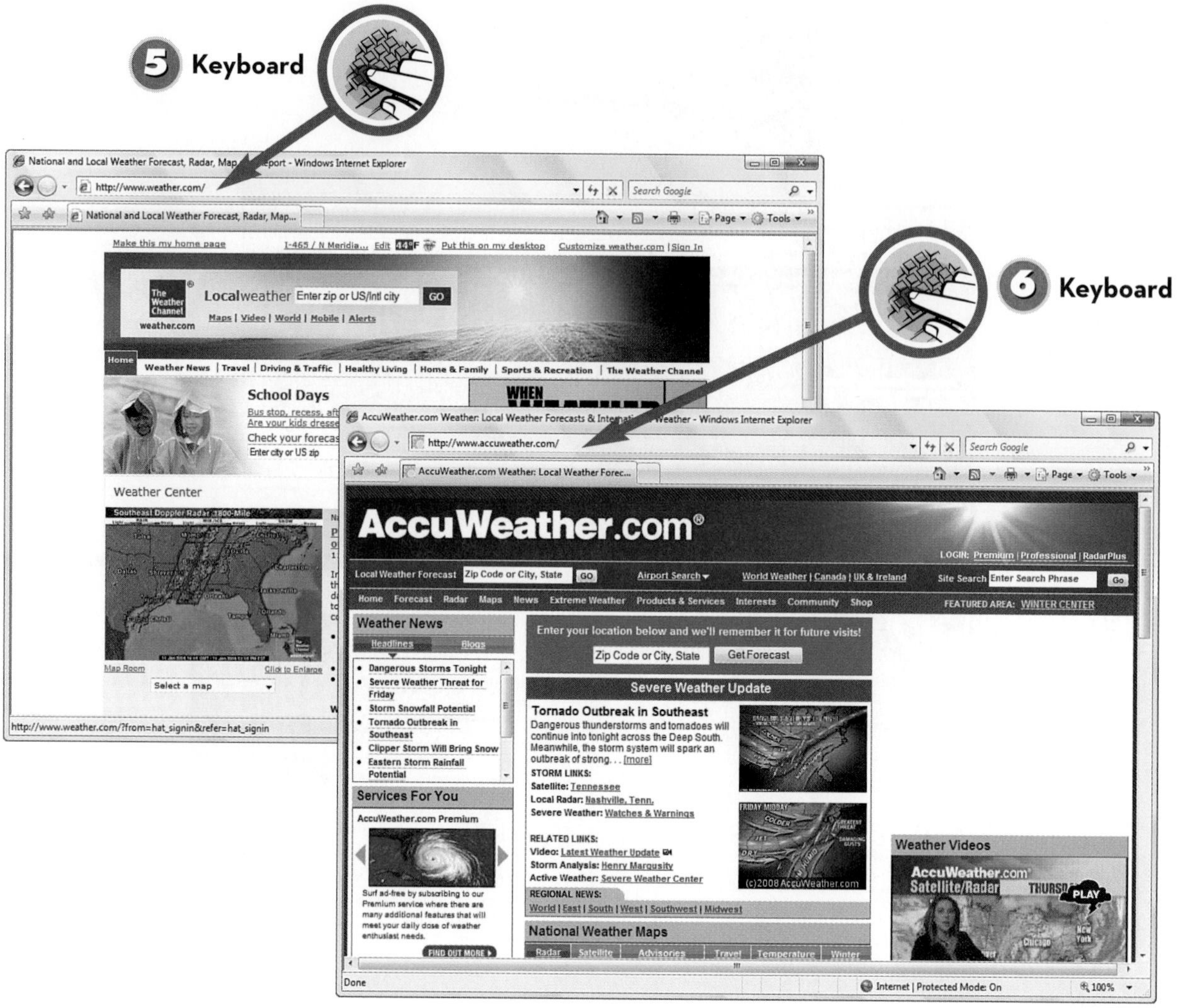

5 Keyboard

6 Keyboard

5 The online site for The Weather Channel is found at www.weather.com.

6 For additional weather forecasts and information, go to AccuWeather.com (www.accuweather.com).

Continued

TIP

Weather on the Web

Weather reports and forecasts are readily available on the Web; most of the major news portals and local websites offer some variety of weather-related services. There are also a number of dedicated weather sites on the Web, all of which offer local and national forecasts, weather radar, satellite maps, and more.

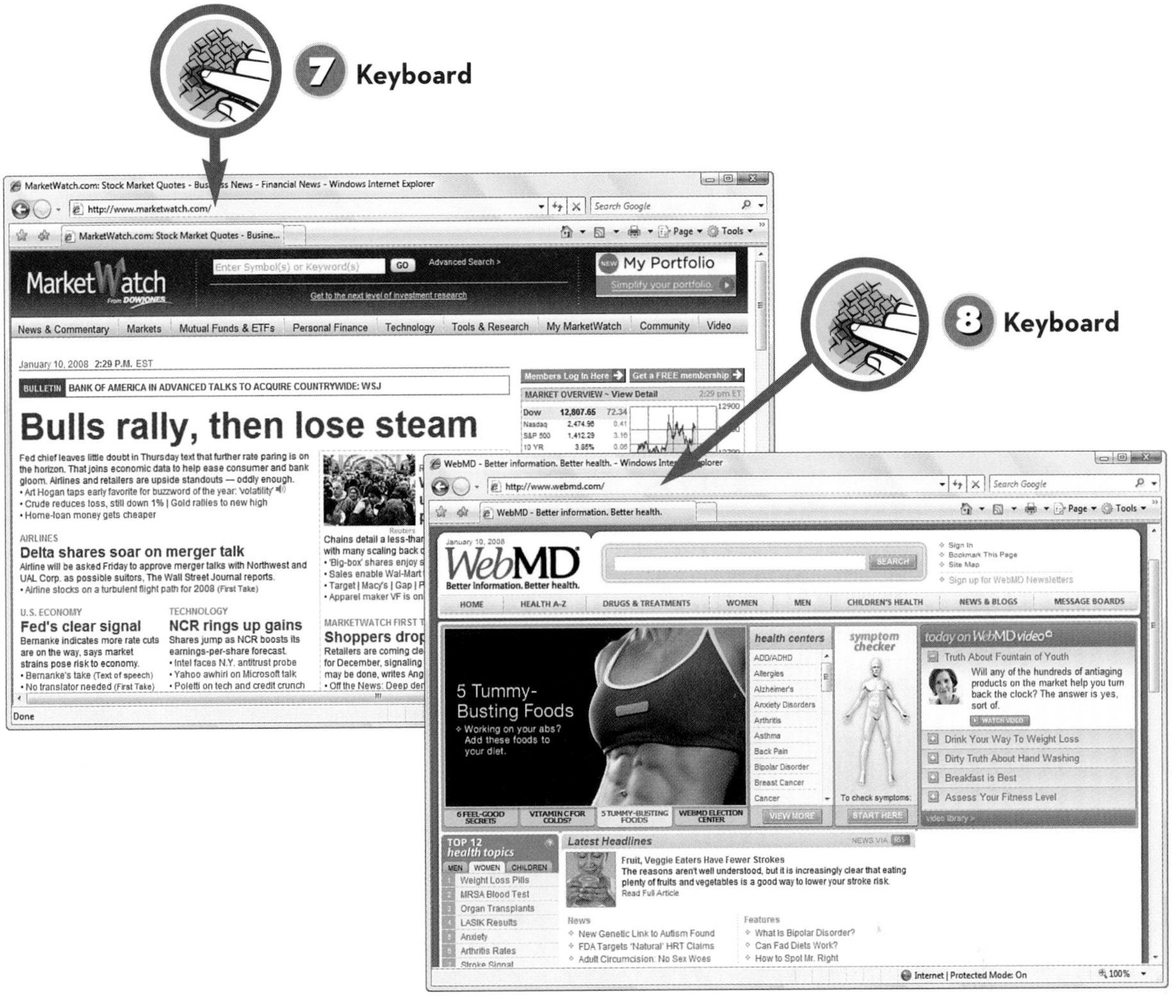

7 Keyboard

8 Keyboard

7 Find in-depth financial information at MarketWatch (www.marketwatch.com).

8 For health and medical information, go to WebMD (www.webmd.com).

End

TIP

More Financial Sites

Other popular financial sites include Motley Fool (www.fool.com), MSN Money (moneycentral.msn.com), and Yahoo! Finance (finance.yahoo.com).

CAUTION

Health Information Online

As useful as online health sites are, they should not and cannot serve as substitutes for a trained medical opinion.

WATCHING WEB VIDEOS ON YOUTUBE

One of the most popular Web activities is watching videos online. The best site for this is YouTube, which is a video-sharing community; users can upload their own videos and watch videos uploaded by other members.

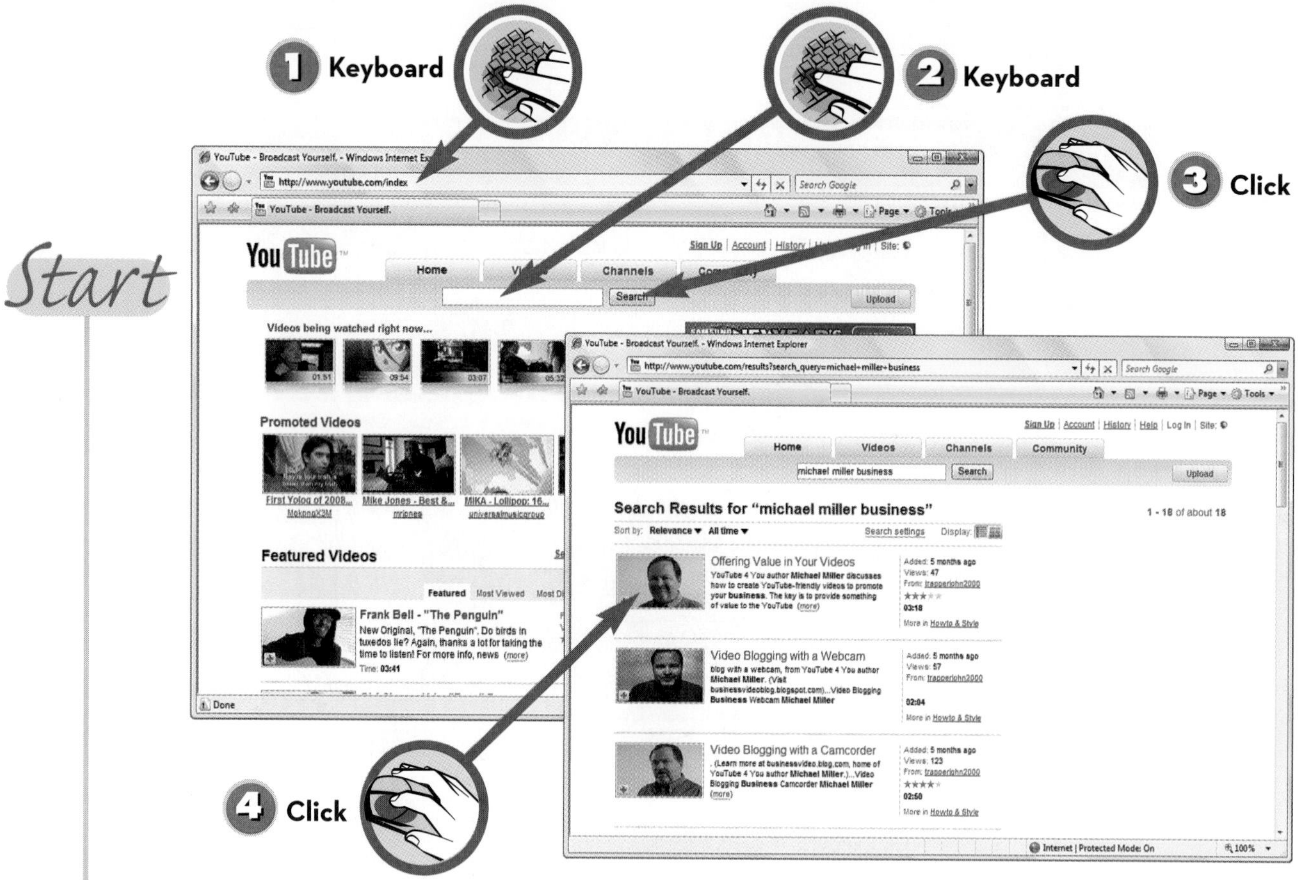

1. Go to **www.youtube.com**.
2. Enter the type of video you're looking for into the **Search** box.
3. Click the **Search** button.
4. When the list of matching videos appears, click the video you want to watch.

Continued

5 When the video page appears, the video begins playing automatically.

6 Click the **Pause** button to pause playback; click the button again to resume playback.

End

TIP

Uploading Your Own YouTube Videos

You can also upload your own videos to YouTube for the entire Web to watch. Just click the **Upload** button on the YouTube home page and follow the onscreen instructions. You'll need to create a YouTube account (it's free), and then you can upload any video you have stored on your computer.

SHOPPING FOR BARGAINS AT SHOPPING.COM

When you're shopping for bargains online, numerous sites let you perform automatic price comparisons. Search for the product you want, and then search for the lowest price—it's that easy. One of the most popular of these shopping comparison sites is Shopping.com (www.shopping.com).

Start

1 Keyboard

2 Click

3 Click

4 Click

1. Go to www.shopping.com.
2. Click a category in the left column.
3. Fine-tune your search by price point, product feature, brand, and other parameters.
4. When you find the product you want, click the **Compare Prices** button.

Continued

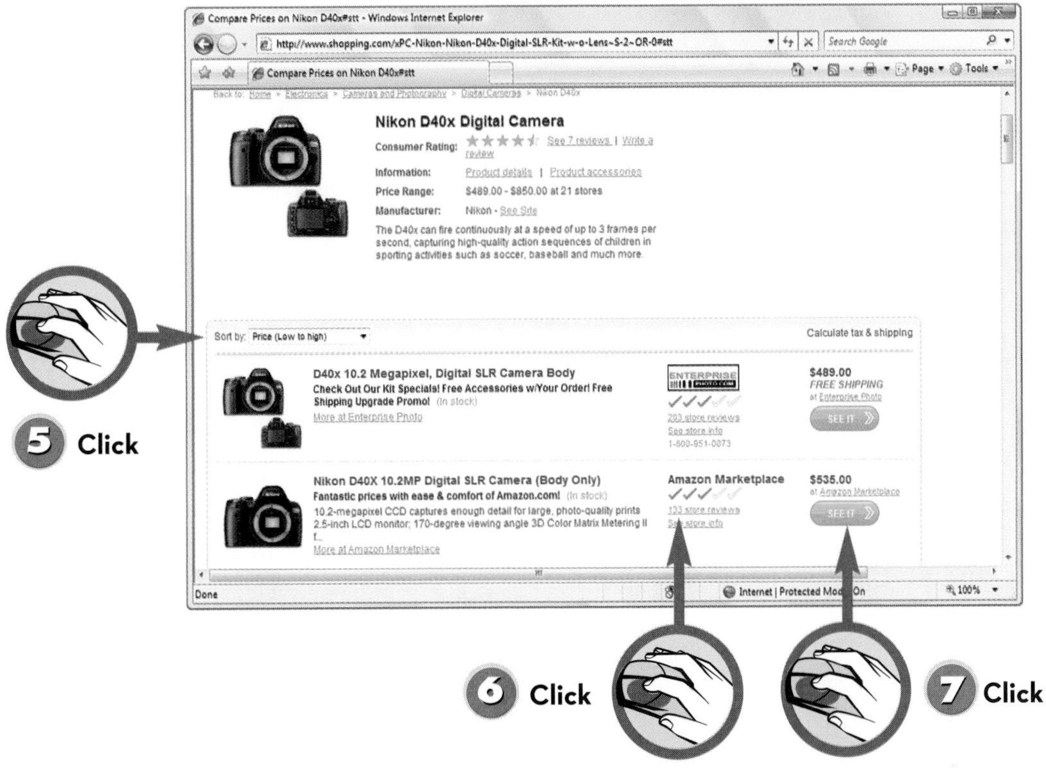

5 Click the **Sort By:** list to sort by price, store name, or store rating.

6 Click a Store Reviews link to find out what other customers think of a particular retailer.

7 Click the **See It** or **Buy It** button to go to a store and make a purchase.

End

TIP

Shipping Costs

Often the merchant with the lowest price also has the highest shipping costs. Enter your ZIP code to calculate the total price for the item, including shipping costs. Base your decision on the total price you'll have to pay.

CAUTION

Merchant Reputation

Some online retailers might be bait-and-switch artists, or offer poor service, or take forever to ship items. Check the retailer ratings and take the time to read the customer reviews—and skip those merchants that rate poorly.

BIDDING FOR ITEMS ON EBAY

Some of the best bargains on the Web come from other consumers selling items via online auction at eBay (www.ebay.com). An eBay auction is a web-based version of a traditional auction. You find an item you'd like to own and then place a bid on the item. Other users also place bids, and at the end of the auction the highest bidder wins.

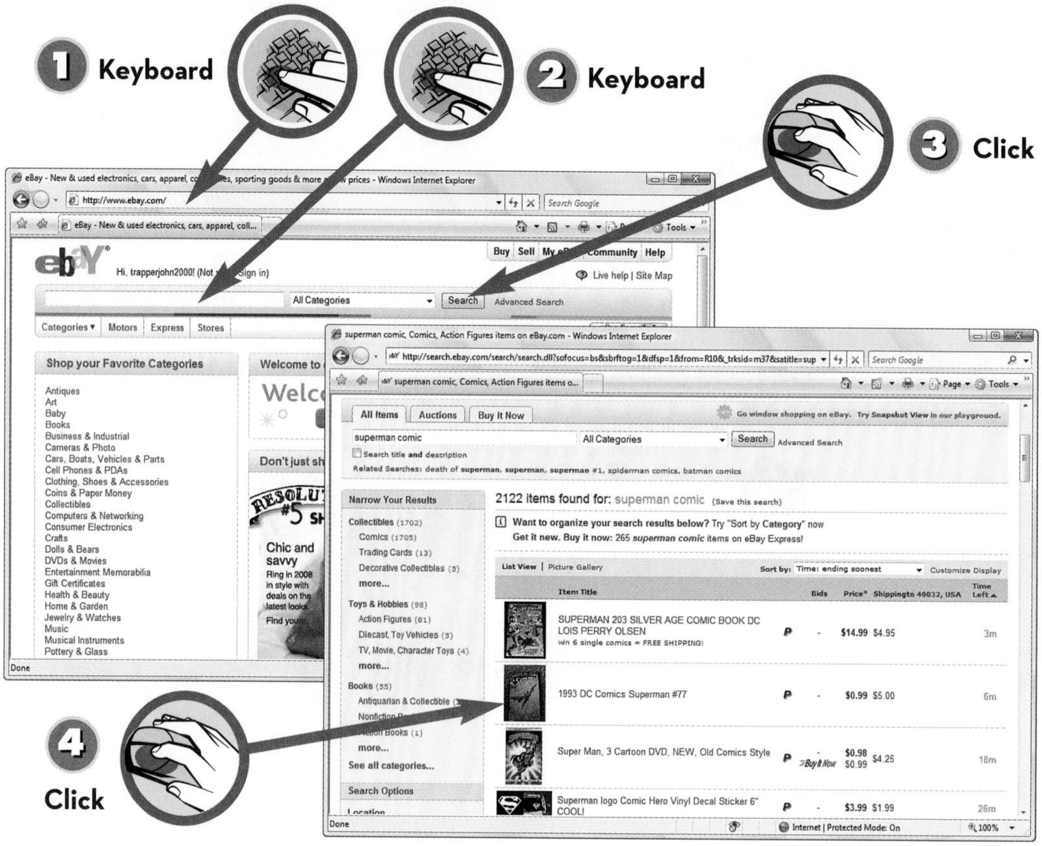

Start

1 Keyboard

2 Keyboard

3 Click

4 Click

1. Go to www.ebay.com.
2. Enter keywords describing the item you're looking for into the **Search** box.
3. Click the **Search** button.
4. When the search results page appears, click the link for the item you're interested in.

Continued

TIP
Learn More About eBay

Learn more about eBay in my companion book, *Absolute Beginner's Guide to eBay*, Fourth Edition (Que, 2008).

TIP
Check the Feedback

Check the feedback rating of the seller and avoid those sellers with low or negative feedback. Click the feedback number to read individual comments from other users.

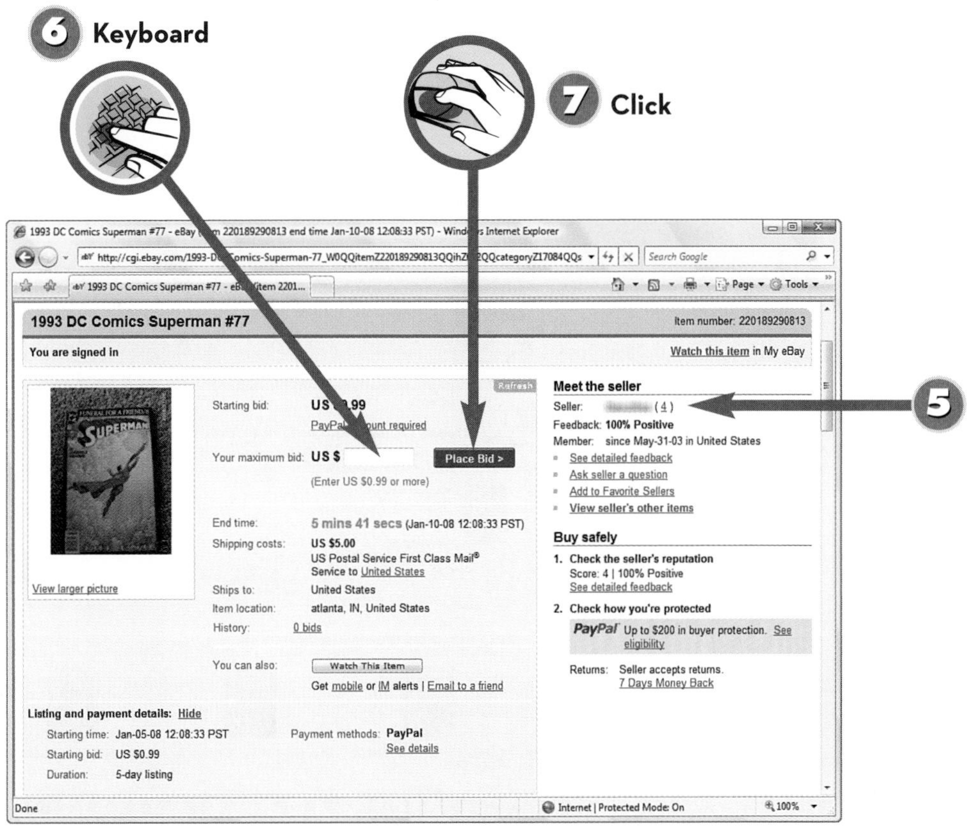

5 Read the description of the item and check out the seller's feedback rating.

6 Enter the maximum amount you're willing to pay into the **Your Maximum Bid** box.

7 Click the **Place Bid** button.

Continued

TIP

Place Your Best Bid

Always bid the highest amount you're willing to pay. eBay's proxy software enters only the minimum bid necessary, without revealing your maximum bid amount. Your bid will be automatically raised when other users bid until it reaches your maximum.

TIP

Buy It Now

Some sellers offer the option of buying the item without bidding, for a fixed price. Look for the Buy It Now option to buy an item immediately!

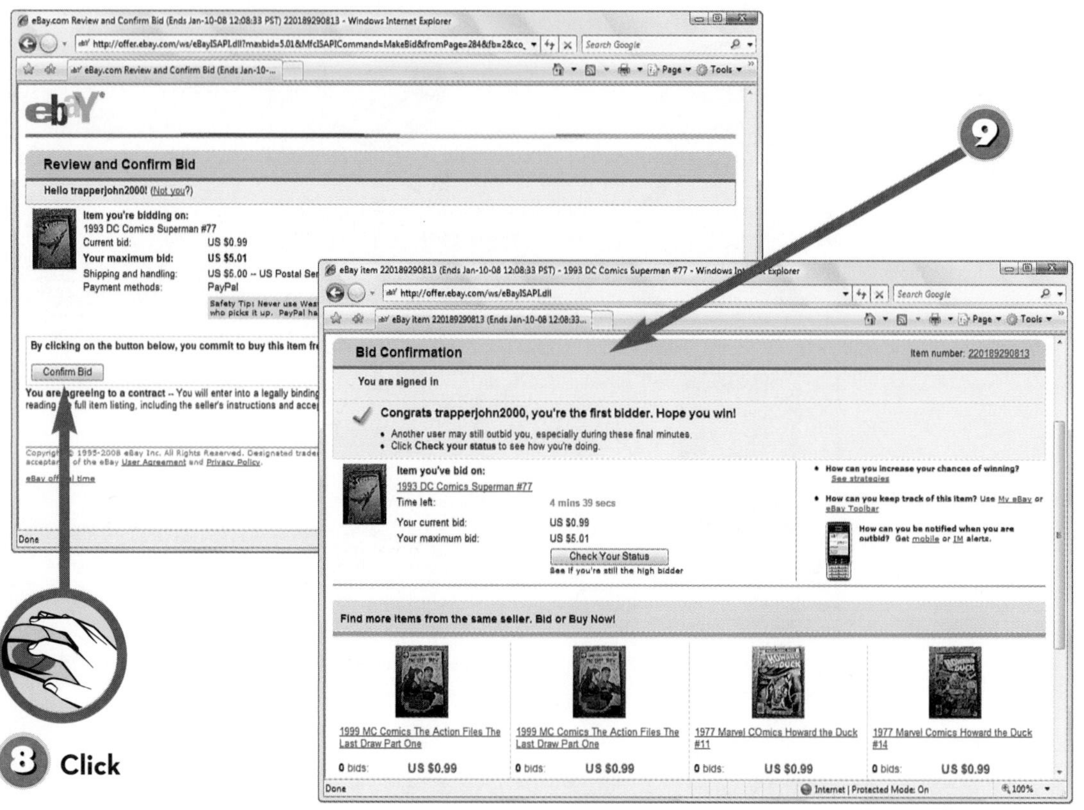

8. When the Review and Confirm Bid page appears, click the **Confirm Bid** button.

9. Your bid is officially entered and the Bid Confirmation page is displayed, which shows your bid status.

Continued

TIP

Outbid? Bid Again!

If you get outbid during the course of the auction, eBay sends you an immediate email informing you of this. You can then return to the item listing bid and make a new, higher bid—or not.

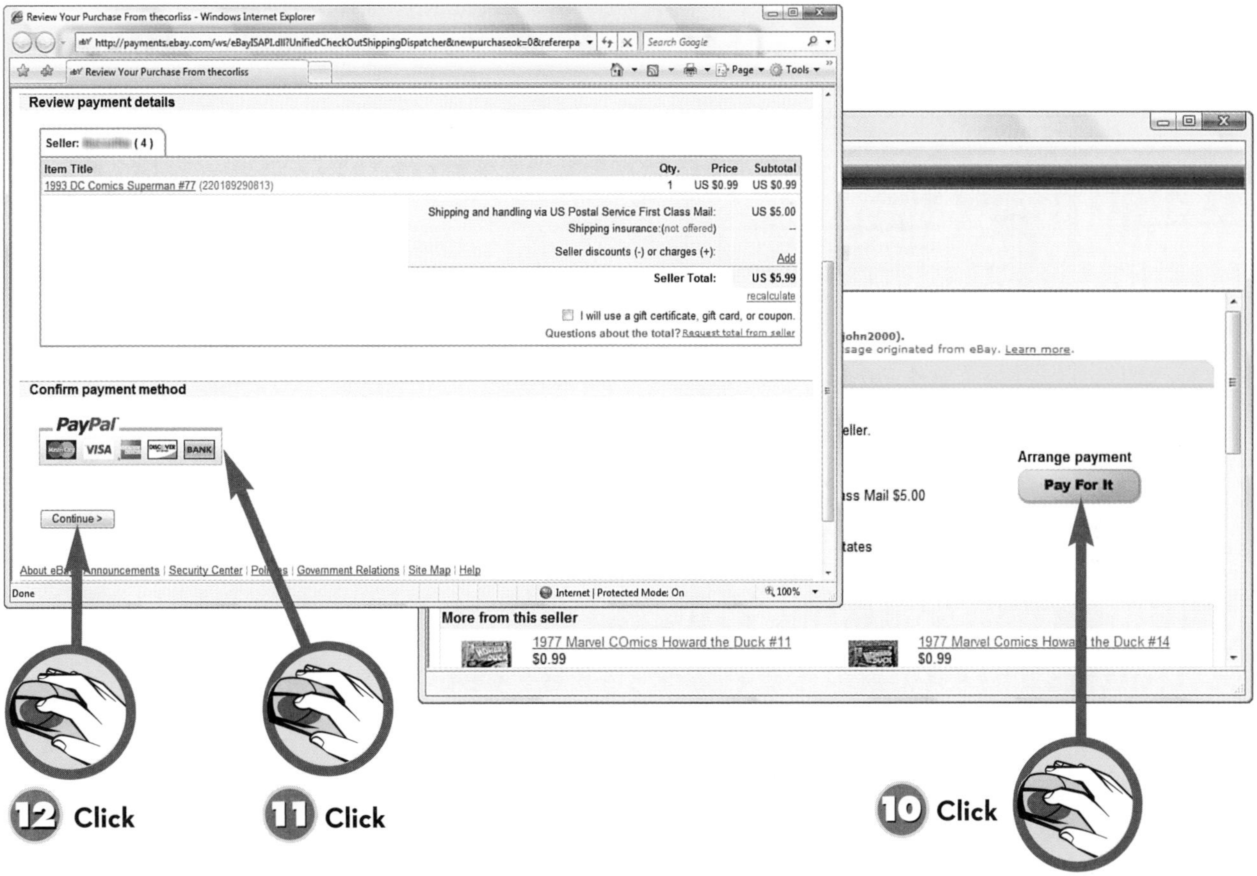

12 Click

11 Click

10 Click

10 If you're the high bidder at the end of the auction period, you win! When you receive the end-of-auction notification email from eBay, click the **Pay For It** button.

11 You're now taken to a Review Your Purchase page on the eBay site. Scroll down to the bottom of the page and confirm or select a payment method.

12 Click the **Continue** button; then follow the onscreen instructions to make your payment and complete your purchase.

End

TIP

Win by Sniping

Experienced buyers don't place their bids until the final seconds of an auction—a process called *sniping*. When you place a high bid at the last second, other bidders don't have a chance to respond, which increases your odds of winning.

Note

Pay with Plastic

If the seller accepts PayPal payments, you can pay for your auction purchase with a credit card. If not, you'll have to send a check or money order via mail.

SETTING UP AN EMAIL ACCOUNT

An email message is like a regular letter, except that it's composed electronically and delivered almost immediately via the Internet. One of the most popular email programs is Windows Mail, which is included as part of Windows Vista. We'll look at how to set up Windows Mail to work with the email account you have with your Internet service provider.

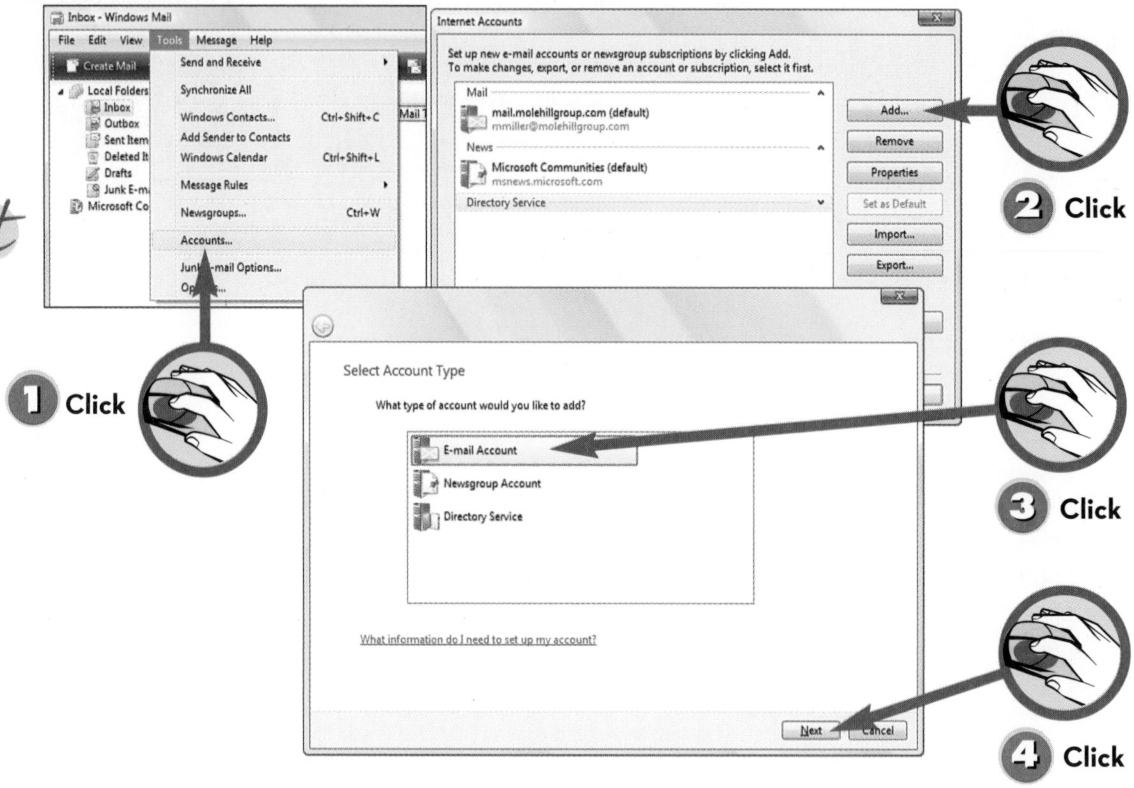

1. From within Windows Mail, pull down the **Tools** menu and select **Accounts**.
2. When the Internet Accounts dialog box appears, click the **Add** button.
3. Click **E-mail Account.**
4. Click **Next**.

Continued

Note

Outlook Express

Windows Mail is the new name for the program that was called Outlook Express in previous versions of Windows.

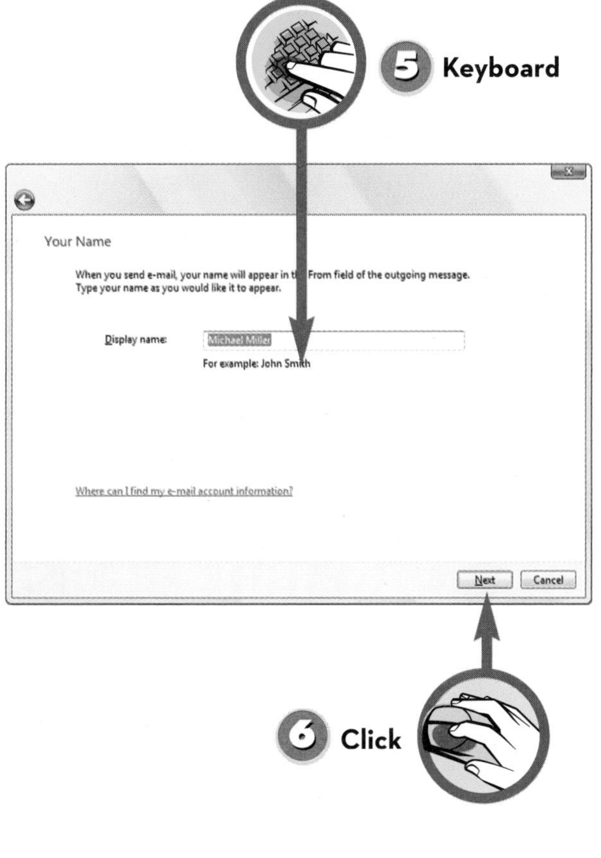

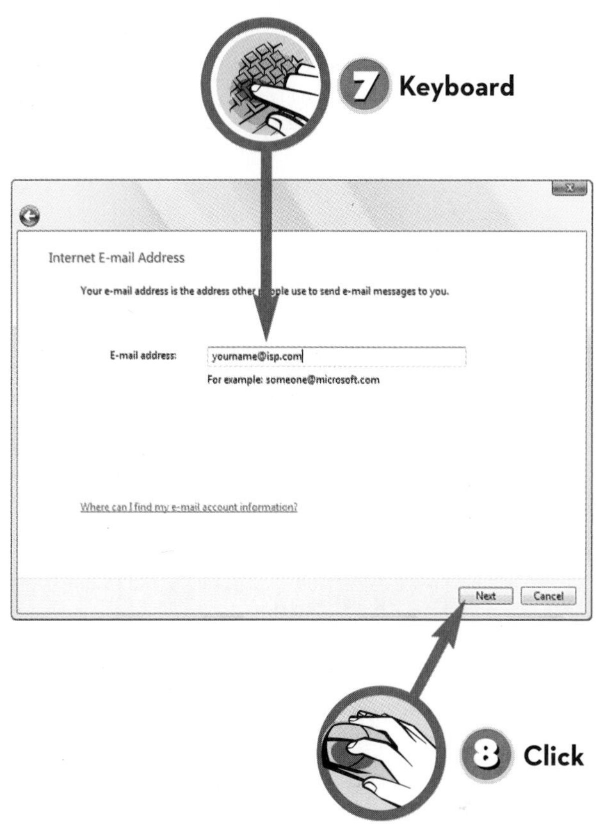

5. Enter your name.
6. Click **Next**.
7. Enter your email address.
8. Click **Next**.

Continued

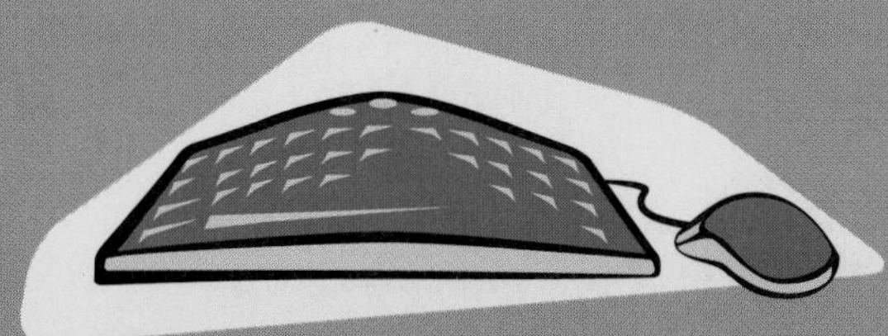

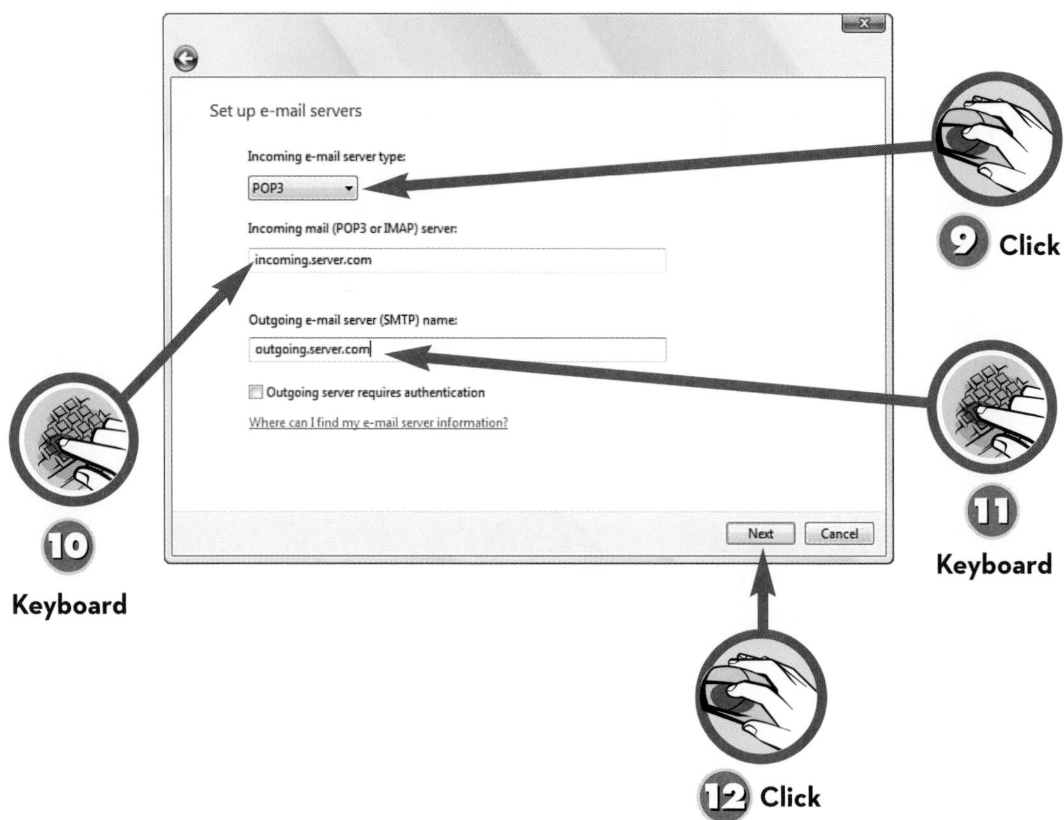

9. Pull down the **Incoming E-mail Server Type:** list and select **POP3**.
10. Enter the name or address for your incoming email server, as provided by your ISP.
11. Enter the name or address for your outgoing mail server, as provided by your ISP.
12. Click **Next**.

Continued

TIP

Server Names

Your Internet service provider should provide you with the server names you need to enter. Some providers might instruct you to use a server type other than POP3.

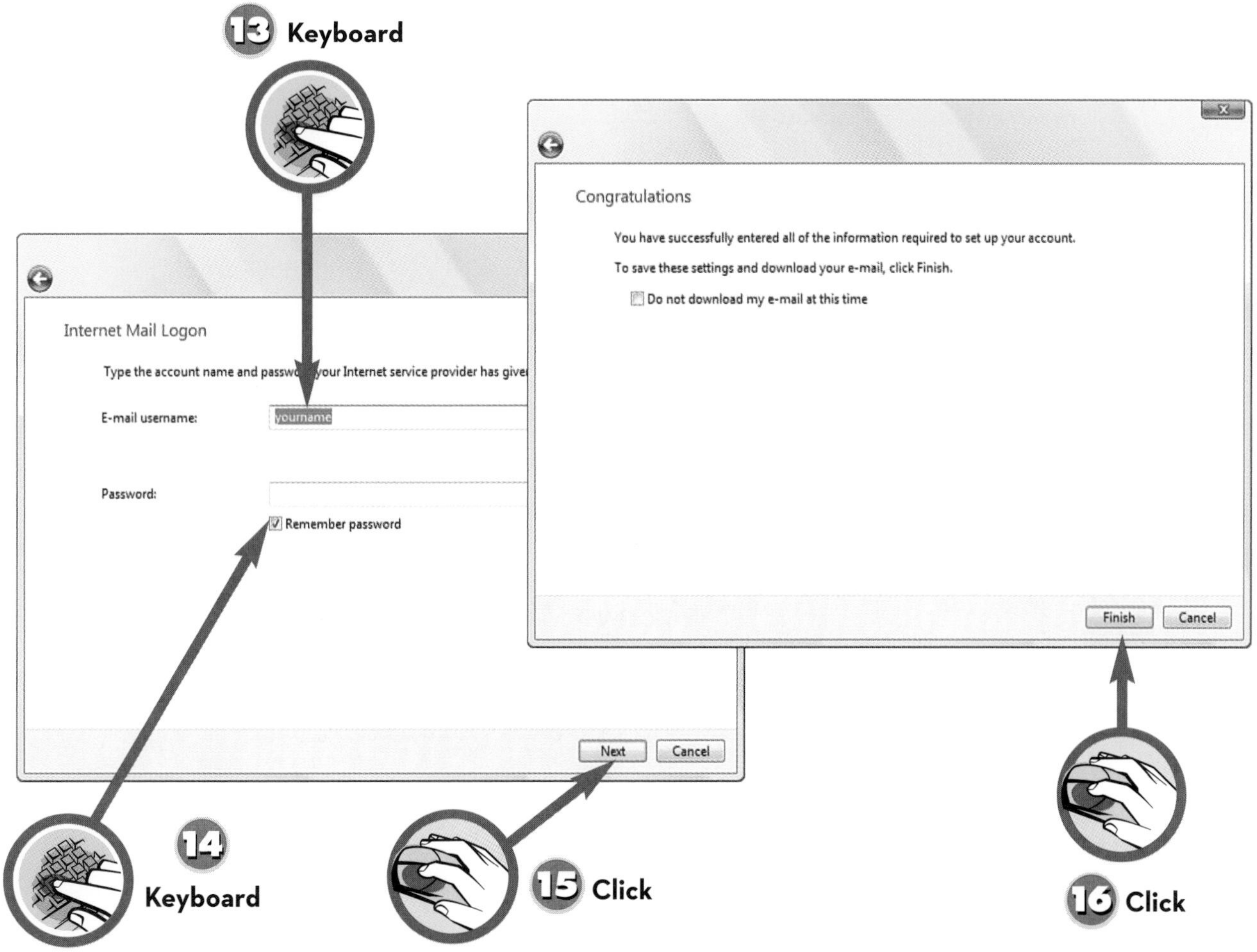

13 Enter your username as provided by your ISP.

14 Enter your password as provided by your ISP.

15 Click **Next**.

16 Click the **Finish** button to finalize your new account.

End

TIP

Remember Your Password

If you want Windows Mail to remember your password so that you don't have to enter it every time you log on, check the **Remember Password** box.

READING AN EMAIL MESSAGE

When you receive new email messages, they're stored in the Windows Mail Inbox. To display all new messages, select the **Inbox** icon from the **Folders** list. All waiting messages now appear in the Message pane.

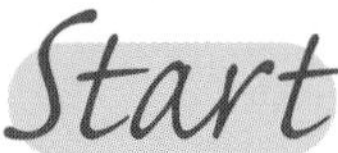

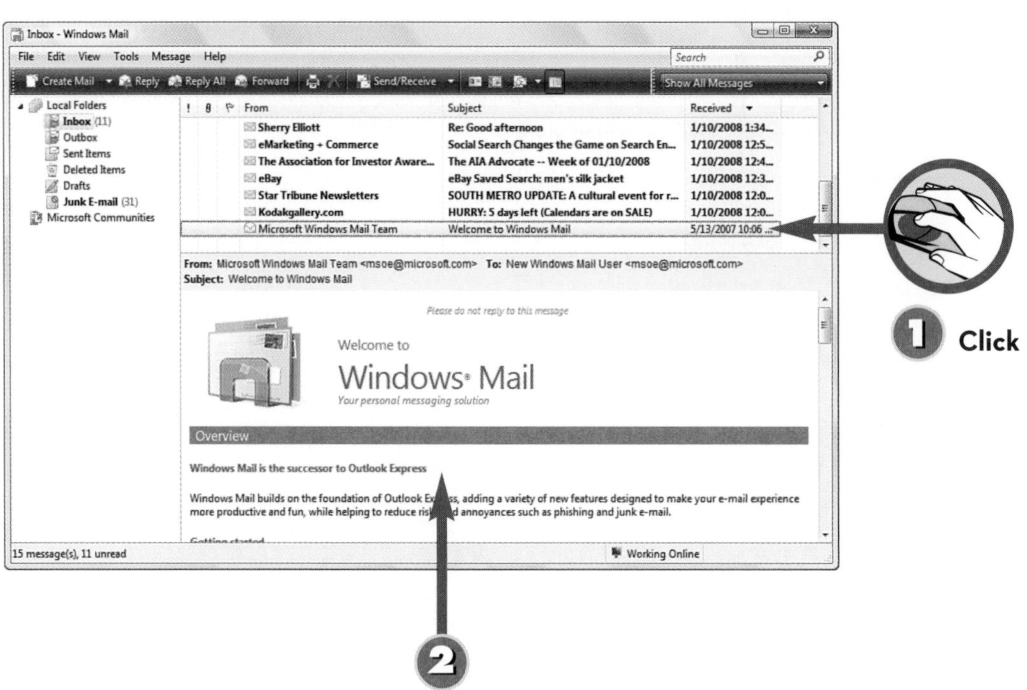

1. Select the header in the Message pane.
2. Scroll through the message in the Preview pane.

End

TIP

Message Window

To view a message in its own window, double-click the message header in the Message pane.

REPLYING TO AN EMAIL MESSAGE

It's easy to reply to any message you receive. And here's a neat trick: All the text from your original message is automatically "quoted" in your reply!

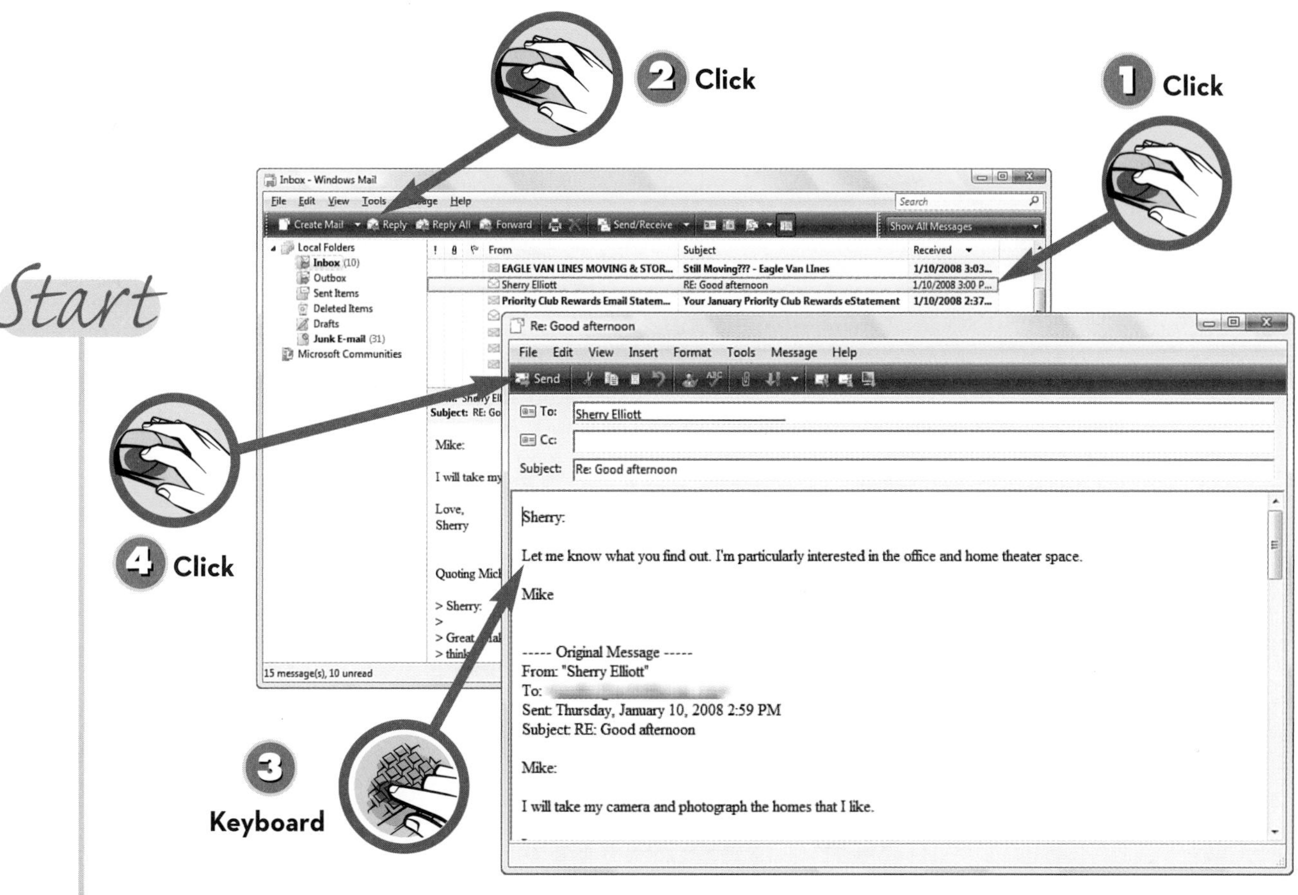

1. Select the message header in the Message pane.
2. Click the **Reply** button on the Windows Mail toolbar.
3. Enter your reply text in the message window.
4. Click the **Send** button to send your reply to the original sender.

End

COMPOSING A NEW EMAIL MESSAGE

Composing a new message is similar to replying to a message. The big difference is that you have to manually enter the recipient's email address.

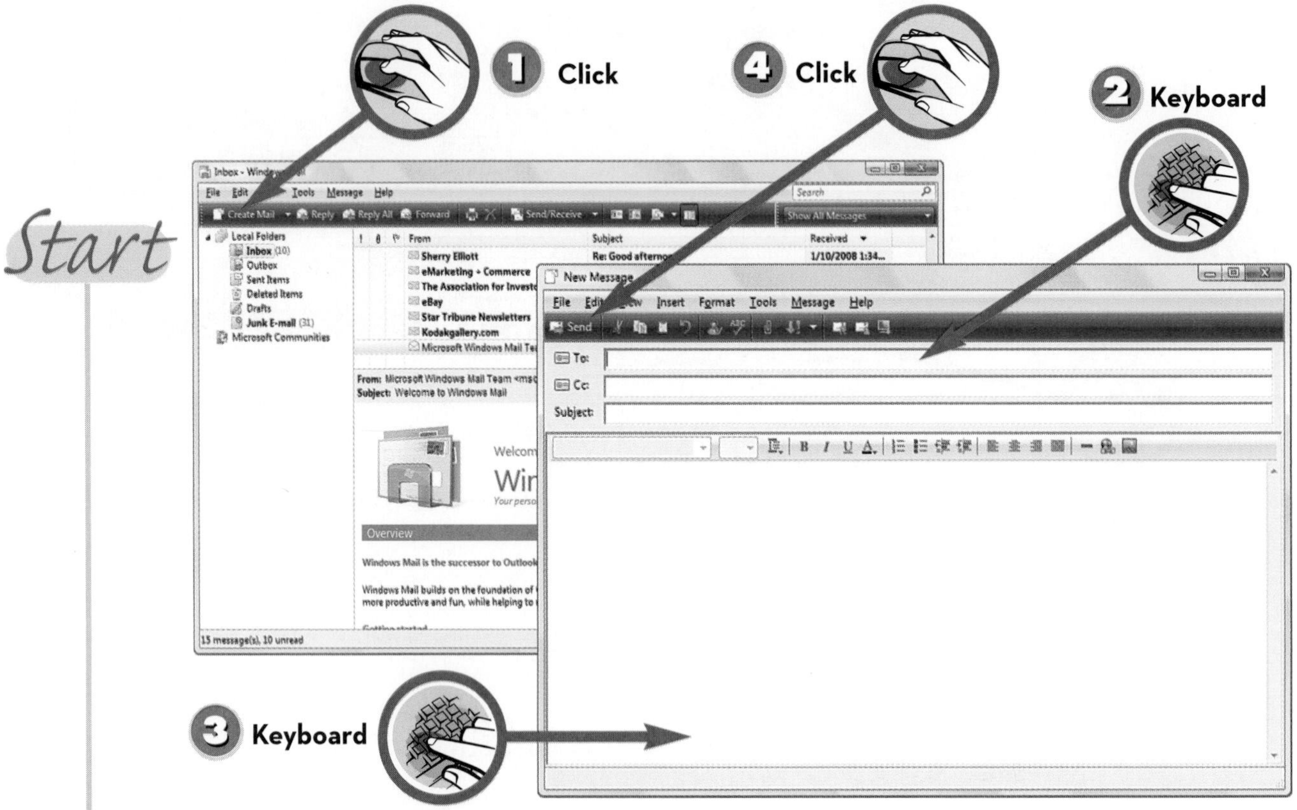

1 Click

4 Click

2 Keyboard

Start

3 Keyboard

1. Click the **Create Mail** button on the Windows Mail toolbar.
2. Enter the email address of the recipient(s) in the **To:** field; enter the address of anyone you want to receive a carbon copy in the **Cc:** box; then enter a subject in the **Subject** box.
3. Move your cursor to the main message area and type your message.
4. When your message is complete, send it to the Outbox by clicking the **Send** button.

End

TIP

Send to Multiple Recipients

You can enter multiple addresses in the To: field, as long as you separate multiple addresses with a semicolon (;), like this: mmiller@molehillgroup.com; gjetson@sprockets.com.

SENDING A FILE VIA EMAIL

The easiest way to share a file with another user is via email, as an *attachment*. To send a file via email, you attach that file to a standard email message. When the message is sent, the file travels along with it; when the message is received, the file is right there, waiting to be opened.

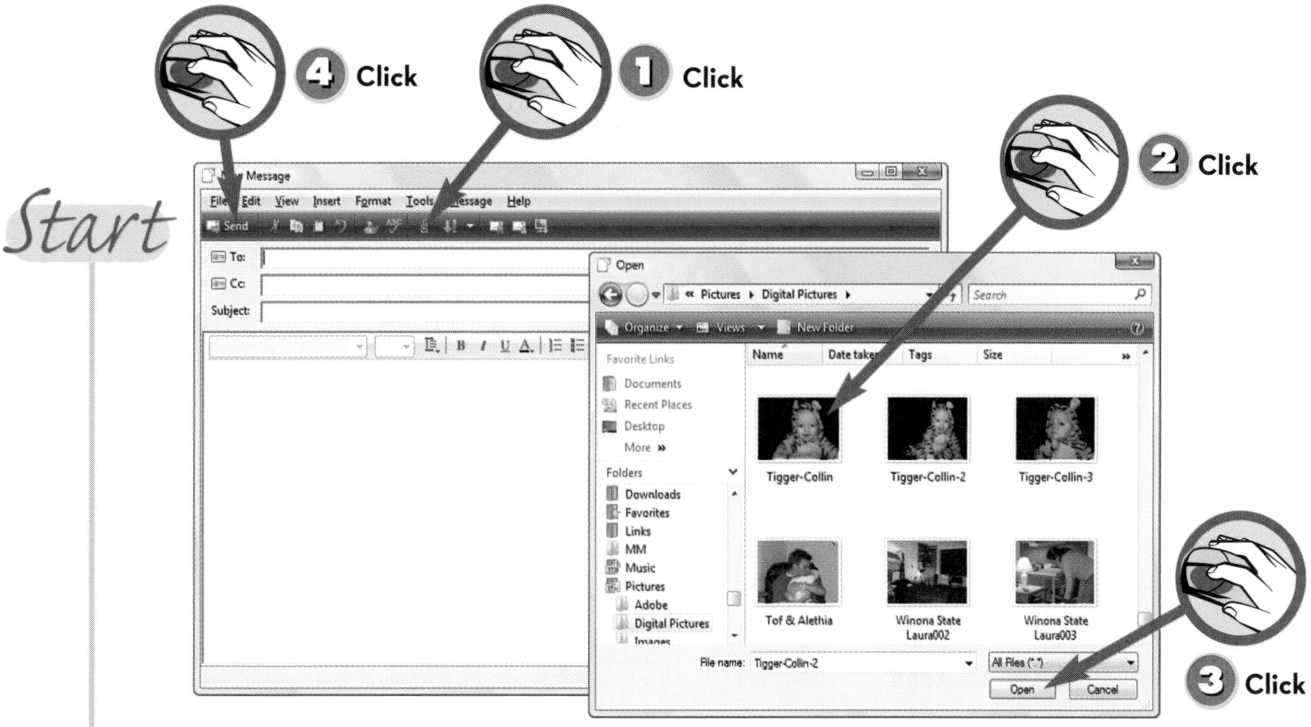

1. Start with a new message and then click the **Attach File to Message** button in the message's toolbar.
2. Navigate to and select the file you want to send.
3. Click **Open**.
4. Send the message as normal by clicking the **Send** button.

CAUTION

Large Files

Be wary of sending extra-large files over the Internet. They can take a long time to upload if you're on a dial-up connection—and just as long for the recipient to download when received.

ADDING CONTACTS IN WINDOWS LIVE MESSENGER

Instant messaging (IM) lets you communicate one on one, in real-time, with your friends, family, and colleagues. One of the most popular IM programs is Windows Live Messenger. But before you can send an instant message to another user, that person has to be on your Messenger contact list.

Start

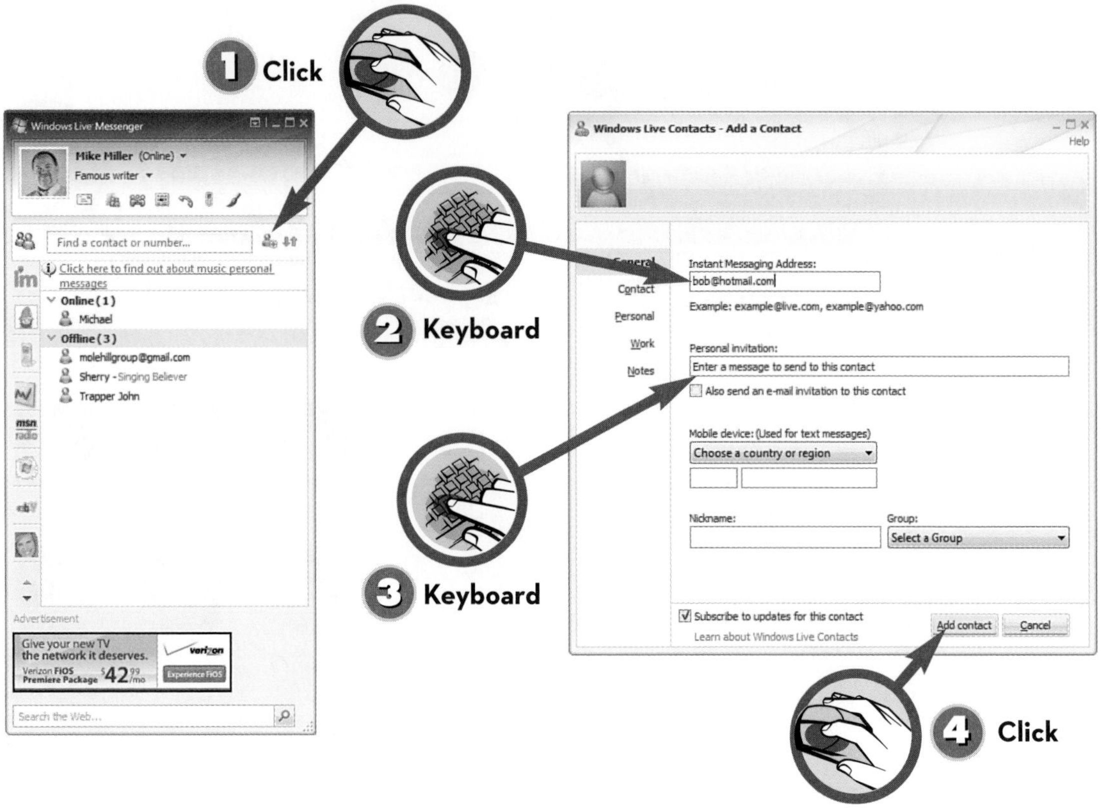

1. Click the **Add a Contact** button.
2. When the Add a Contact Wizard appears, enter the other person's instant message ID or email address.
3. Enter a personal invitation to that person.
4. Click **Add Contact**.

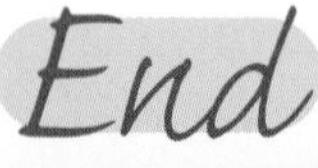

NOTE

Other IM Services

Other popular instant messaging services include AOL Instant Messenger (www.aim.com), Yahoo! Messenger (messenger.yahoo.com), Google Talk (www.google.com/talk/), and ICQ (www.icq.com).

INSTANT MESSAGING WITH WINDOWS LIVE MESSENGER

To send an instant message to another user, both of you have to be online at the same time. If that person is on your contact list, he'll show up as being online in Windows Live Messenger; you'll also appear on his online list.

Start

1 Double-click

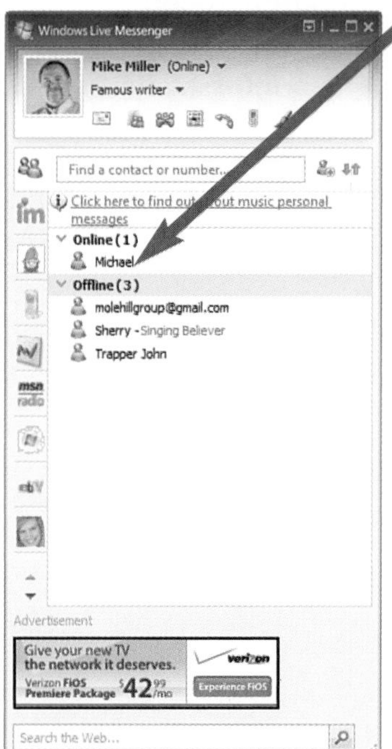

2 Keyboard

3 Click

1. Double-click a name in your contact list to open the Conversation window.
2. Enter your message in the lower part of the window.
3. Click the **Send** button (or press **Enter**).

End

NOTE

Messages in the Window

Your message text appears in your Conversation window—and in the Conversation window of your recipient. Messages sent by your recipient also appear in your Conversation window.

CAUTION

Don't Accept Files

Don't accept any unexpected files sent to you during instant messaging sessions. These files are likely to contain computer viruses, which can damage your computer system.

part

SETTING UP A WIRELESS HOME NETWORK

When you want to connect two or more computers together, you need to create a computer *network*. A network is all about sharing; you can use your network to share files, share peripherals (such as printers), and share a broadband Internet connection.

There are two ways to connect your network—wired or wireless. A wireless network is more convenient (no wires to run), which makes it the network of choice for most home users. Wireless networks use radio frequency (RF) signals to connect one computer to another. The most popular type of wireless network uses the Wi-Fi standard and can transfer data at either 11Mbps (802.11b), 54Mbps (802.11g), or 248Mbps (802.11n).

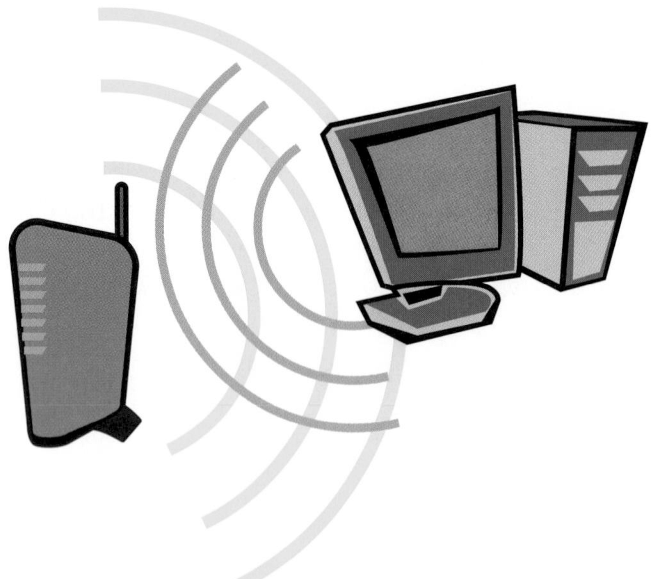

HOW A WIRELESS NETWORK WORKS

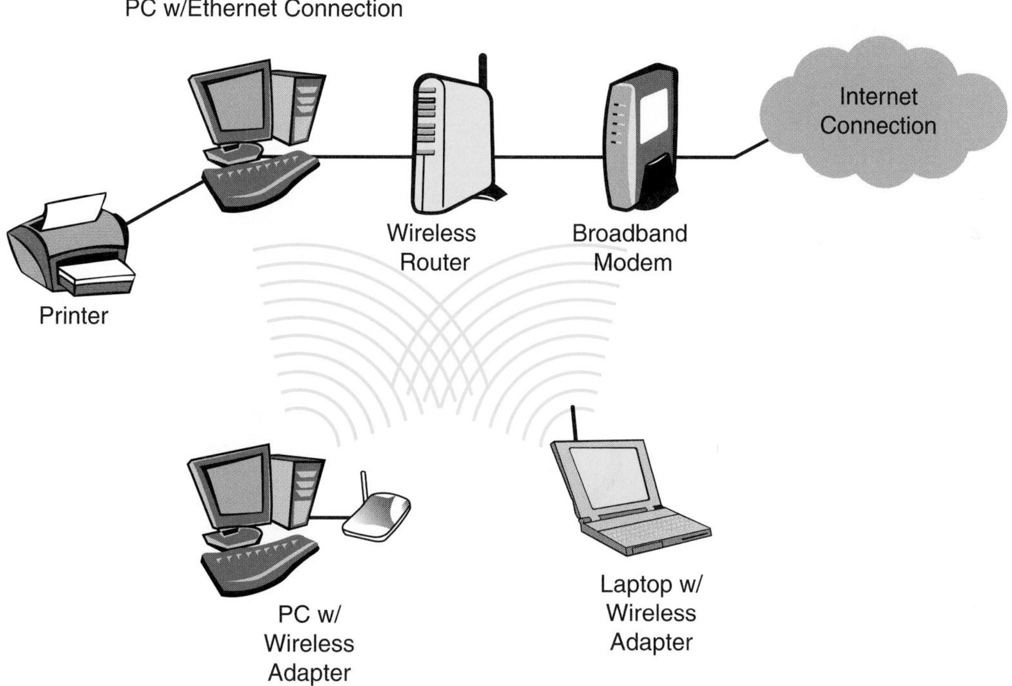

SETTING UP YOUR NETWORK'S MAIN PC

The focal point of your wireless network is the wireless router, sometimes called a *base station* or an *access point*. The wireless PCs on your network must be connected to or contain *wireless adapters*, which function as mini-transmitters/receivers to communicate with the base station.

Start

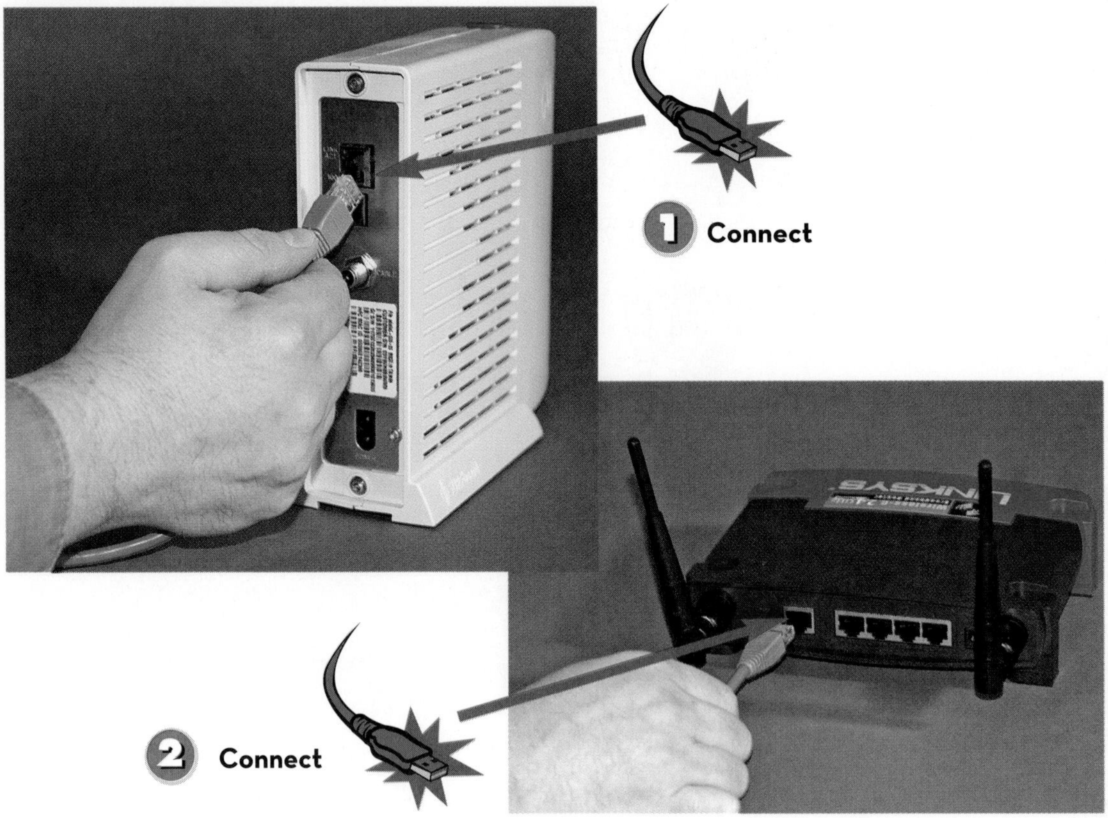

1 Connect

2 Connect

1. Connect one end of an Ethernet cable to the Ethernet port on your broadband modem.
2. Connect the other end of the Ethernet cable to one of the Ethernet ports on your wireless router.

Continued

TIP

Internet Port

Most routers have a dedicated input for your broadband modem, sometimes labeled "Internet."

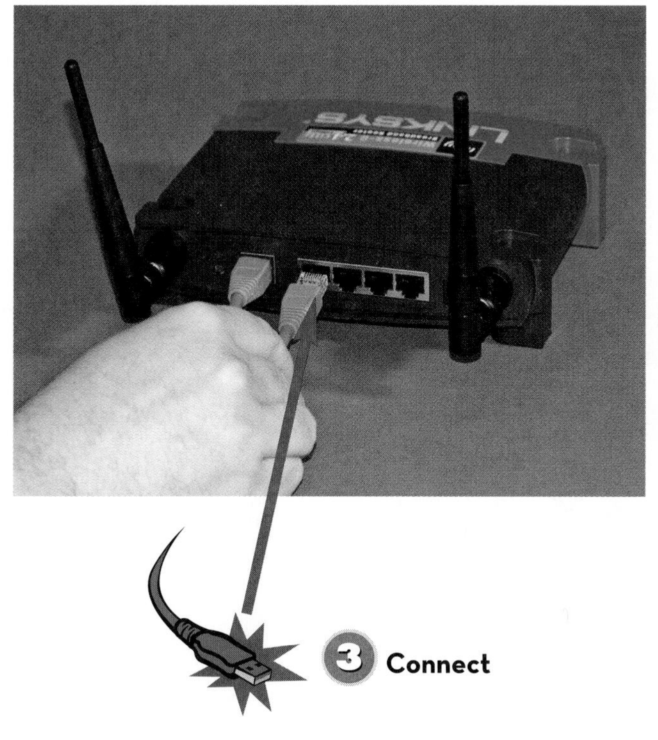

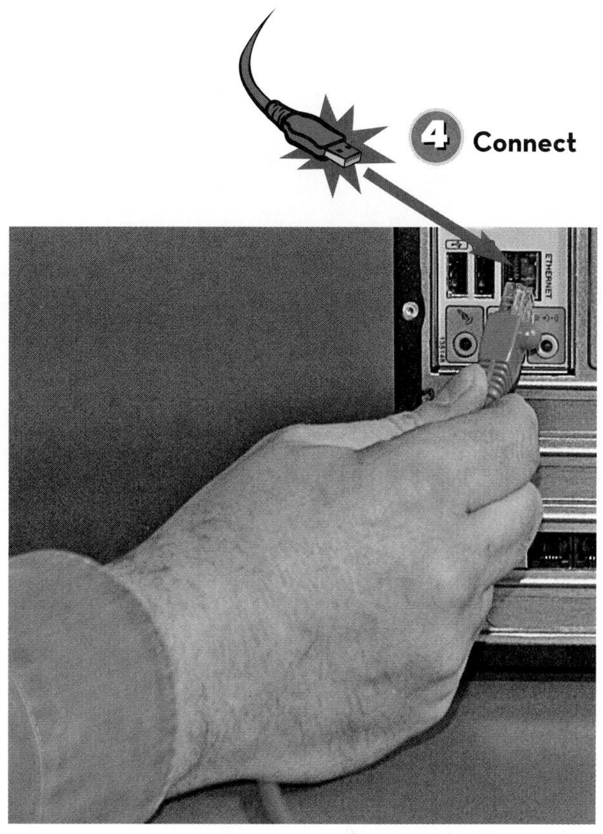

3. Connect one end of an Ethernet cable to another Ethernet port on your wireless router.
4. Connect the other end of the Ethernet cable to the Ethernet port on your main PC.

Continued

NOTE

Ethernet Connections

Your main PC connects to the wireless router via an Ethernet cable. If your main PC doesn't have a built-in Ethernet port, you'll need to install an internal network interface card or an external Ethernet adapter via USB.

NOTE

Wi-Fi Networks

Wi-Fi is short for *wireless fidelity*. Learn more about the Wi-Fi standard at the Wi-Fi Alliance website (www.wi-fi.org). This website also lets you search for public Wi-Fi hotspots near you.

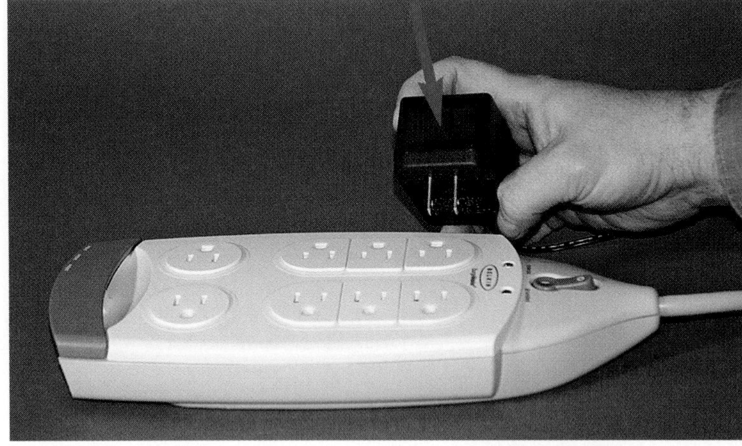

5. Connect your wireless router to a power source and, if it has a power switch, turn it on.

6. On your main PC, click the **Start** button and click **Connect To**.

Continued

TIP

Wired and Wireless Connections

Most wireless routers include four or more wired Ethernet connectors in addition to wireless capabilities.

TIP

Broadband Routers

Some ISPs provide broadband modems that include built-in wireless routers. If you have one of these, you don't need to buy a separate router.

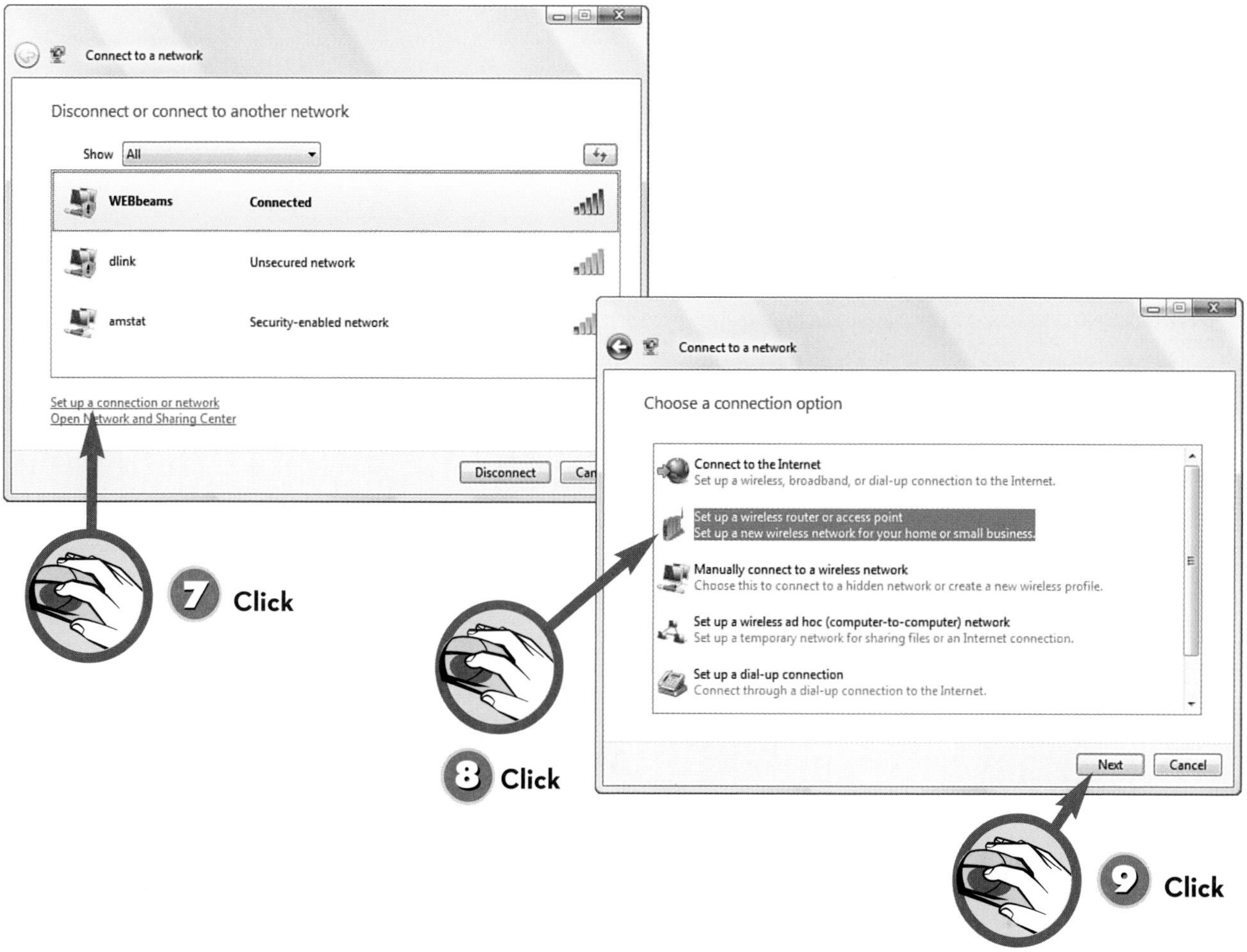

7 Click **Set Up a Connection or Network.**

8 Click **Set Up a Wireless Router or Access Point**.

9 Click **Next**.

Continued

TIP

Installation Software

Many wireless routers come with their own installation software. You should run this software before—or, in some cases, instead of—running the Windows configuration utility.

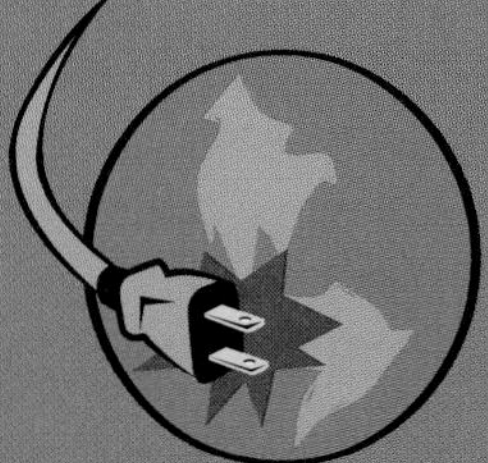

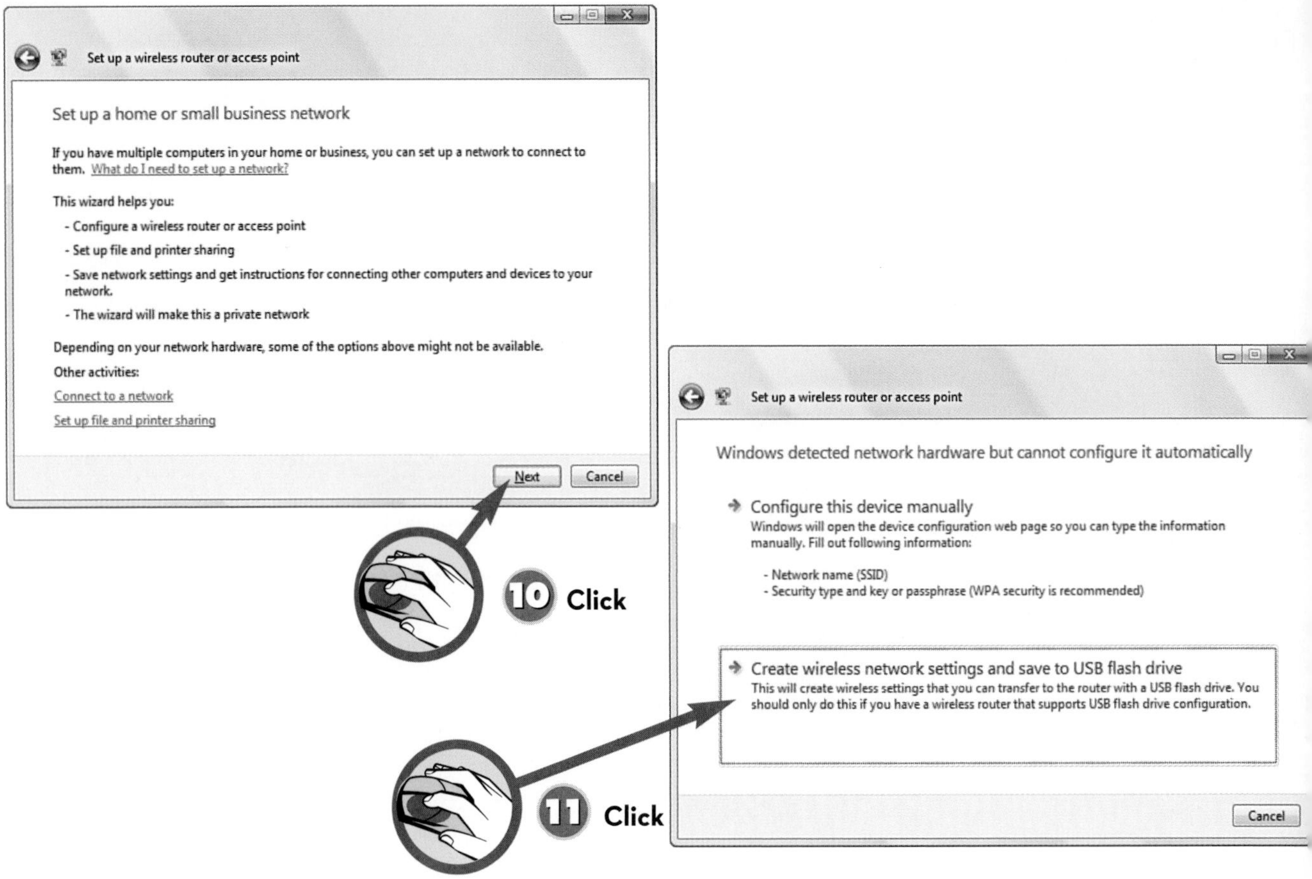

Set up a wireless router or access point

Set up a home or small business network

If you have multiple computers in your home or business, you can set up a network to connect to them. What do I need to set up a network?

This wizard helps you:

- Configure a wireless router or access point
- Set up file and printer sharing
- Save network settings and get instructions for connecting other computers and devices to your network.
- The wizard will make this a private network

Depending on your network hardware, some of the options above might not be available.

Other activities:

Connect to a network

Set up file and printer sharing

Next Cancel

10 Click

Set up a wireless router or access point

Windows detected network hardware but cannot configure it automatically

Configure this device manually
Windows will open the device configuration web page so you can type the information manually. Fill out following information:

- Network name (SSID)
- Security type and key or passphrase (WPA security is recommended)

Create wireless network settings and save to USB flash drive
This will create wireless settings that you can transfer to the router with a USB flash drive. You should only do this if you have a wireless router that supports USB flash drive configuration.

Cancel

11 Click

10 Click **Next**.

11 If Windows can configure your router automatically, it will do so now. If it can't, click **Create Wireless Network Settings and Save to USB Flash Drive**.

Continued

NOTE

Measuring Network Speed

How quickly data is transferred across a network is measured in megabits per second (Mbps). The bigger the Mbps number, the faster the network—and faster is always better than slower.

TIP

Wireless Security

To keep outsiders from tapping into your wireless network, you need to enable wireless security for the network. This adds an encrypted key to your wireless connection; no other computer can access your network without this key.

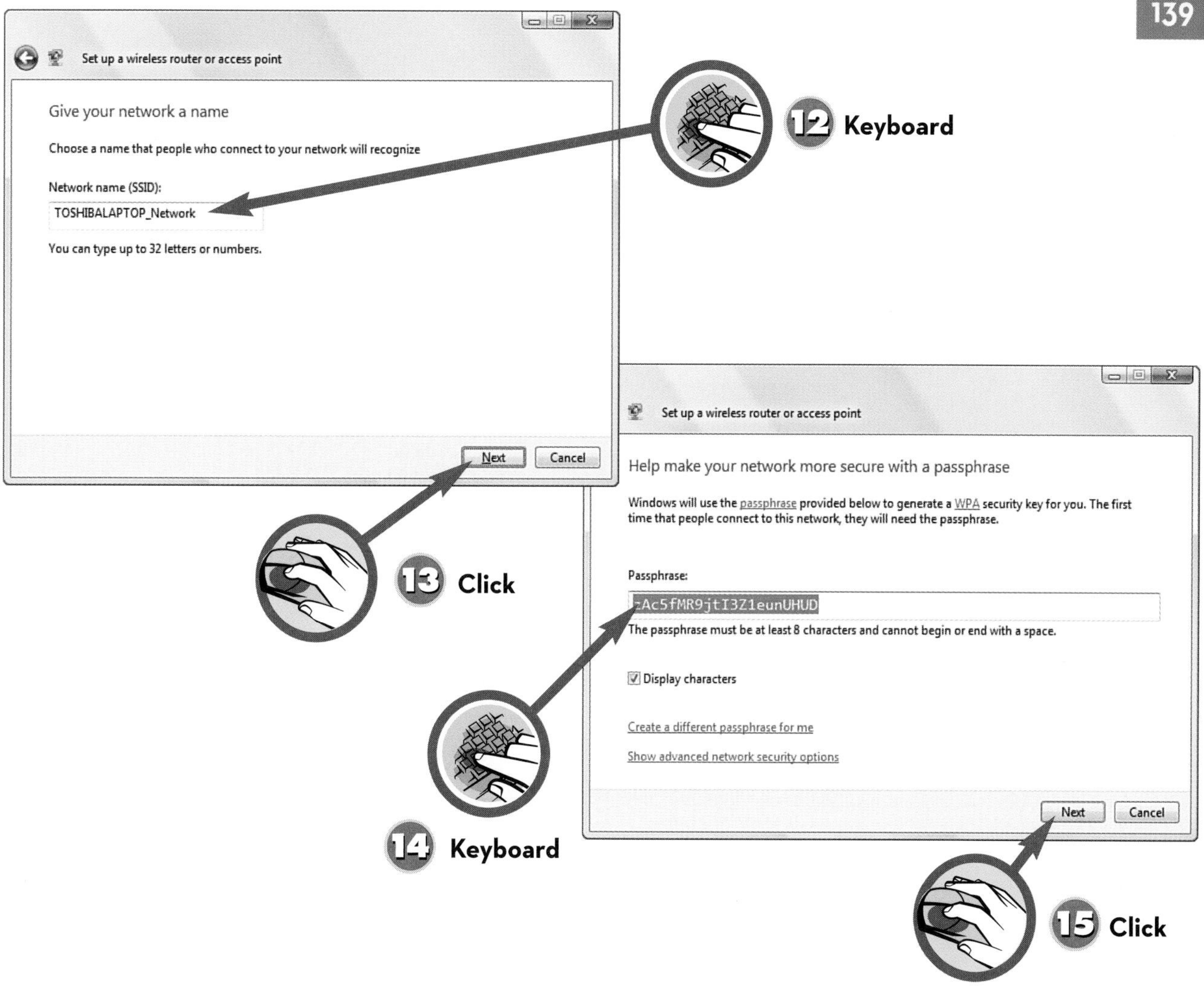

12 Enter a name (SSID) for your network.

13 Click **Next**.

14 Enter a password or passphrase for your network's security. You can accept the passphrase that Windows generates for you, or you can enter something easier for you to remember; the passphrase must be at least 8 characters long.

15 Click **Next**.

Continued

NOTE

SSID

SSID stands for *Service Set Identifier*, which is a set of letters or numbers that identify a particular wireless network.

TIP

Write Down the Key

Write down the passphrase or network key you assign your network. You might need this to connect other computers to the network.

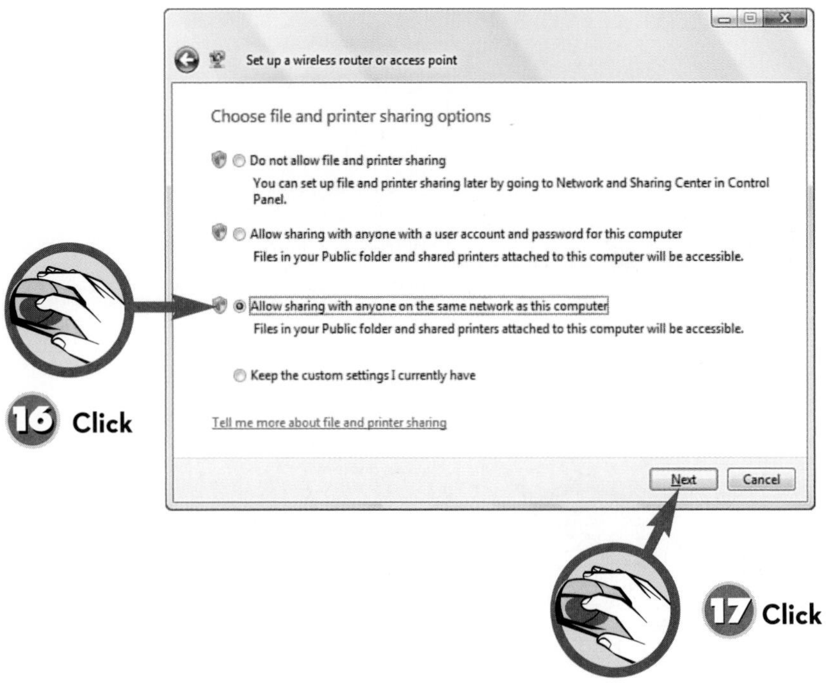

16 You're now prompted to configure the file and printer sharing options for your network. To allow sharing, click **Allow Sharing with Anyone on the Same Network as This Computer**.

17 Click **Next**.

Continued

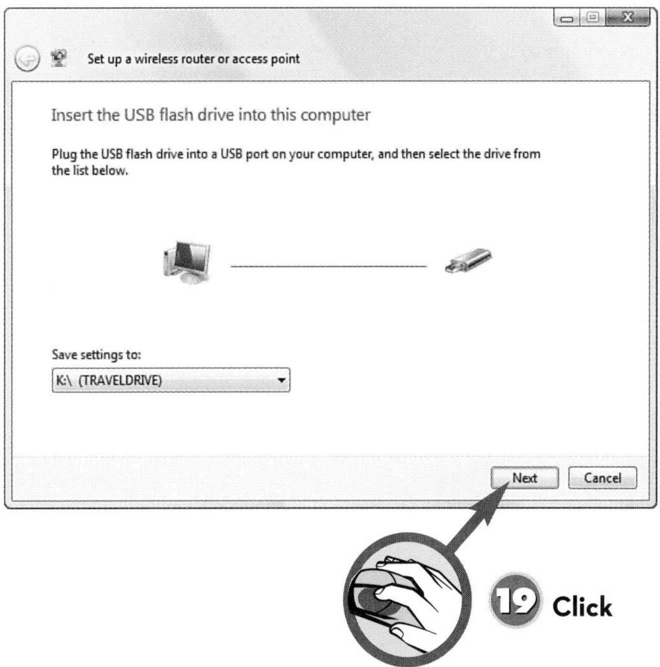

18 Connect

19 Click

18 When prompted, connect a USB flash drive to one of your computer's USB ports. This saves your network setting to the flash drive, which can then be used to transfer those settings to other computers on your network.

19 Click **Next** to finish the procedure.

End

CONNECTING ADDITIONAL PCS TO YOUR WIRELESS NETWORK

Each additional PC on your network requires its own wireless adapter. The easiest way to configure each computer for your new network is to use the USB flash drive you configured when you first set up your network.

Start

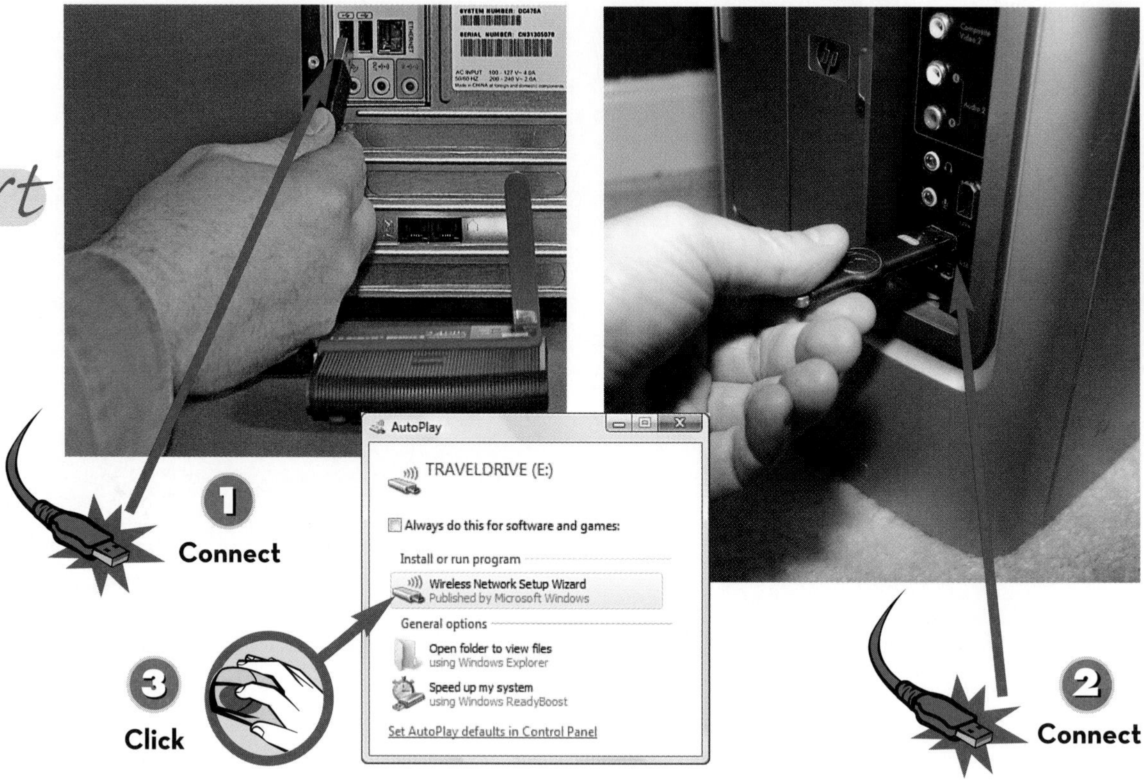

1 Connect

2 Connect

3 Click

AutoPlay

TRAVELDRIVE (E:)

Always do this for software and games:

Install or run program

Wireless Network Setup Wizard
Published by Microsoft Windows

General options

Open folder to view files
using Windows Explorer

Speed up my system
using Windows ReadyBoost

Set AutoPlay defaults in Control Panel

1. If you're connecting a desktop PC, connect a wireless adapter to a USB port on the PC, and then run any necessary installation software. (If you have a notebook PC, it probably has a built-in wireless adapter, no installation necessary.)
2. Insert your configured USB flash drive into the USB port of this computer.
3. When the AutoPlay dialog box appears, click **Wireless Network Setup Wizard**.

Continued

TIP

Wireless Adapters

A wireless adapter can be a small external device that connects to the PC via USB, an expansion card that installs inside your system unit, or a PC card that inserts into a laptop PC's card slot.

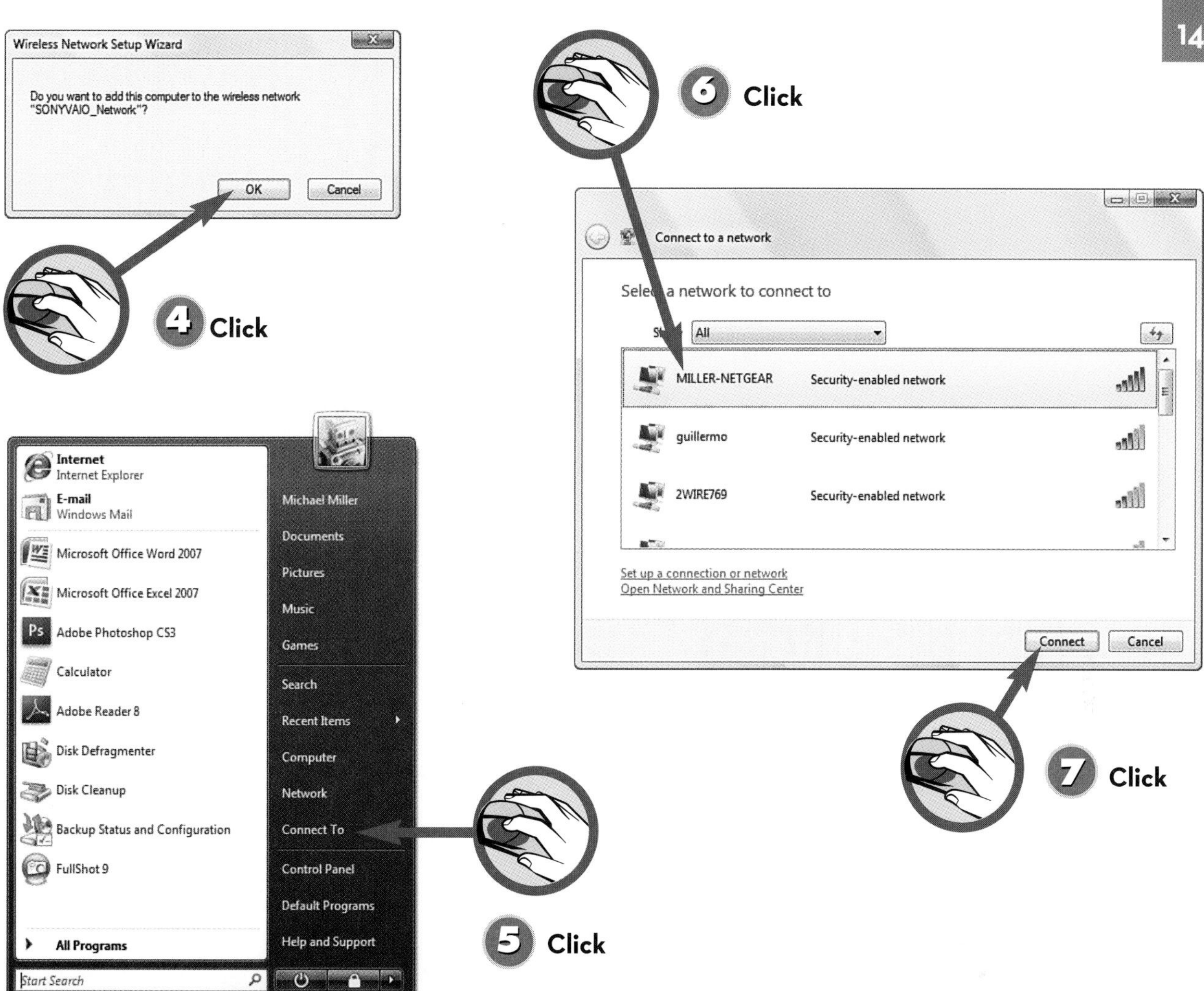

4. When the wizard launches, click **OK** to apply the network settings to this computer.
5. When the wizard is complete, click the **Start** button and then click **Connect To**.
6. Click your network from the list of available wireless networks.
7. Click **Connect**.

End

TIP

Configuring Older PCs

If a computer is running Windows 98, Windows Me, or Windows 2000, you still should be able to configure the computer using the Wireless Network Wizard on your USB flash drive.

MANAGING YOUR NETWORK WITH THE NETWORK AND SHARING CENTER

Just because your network is up and running doesn't mean you're finished with it. In Windows Vista, all network management is accomplished from the new Network and Sharing Center.

Start

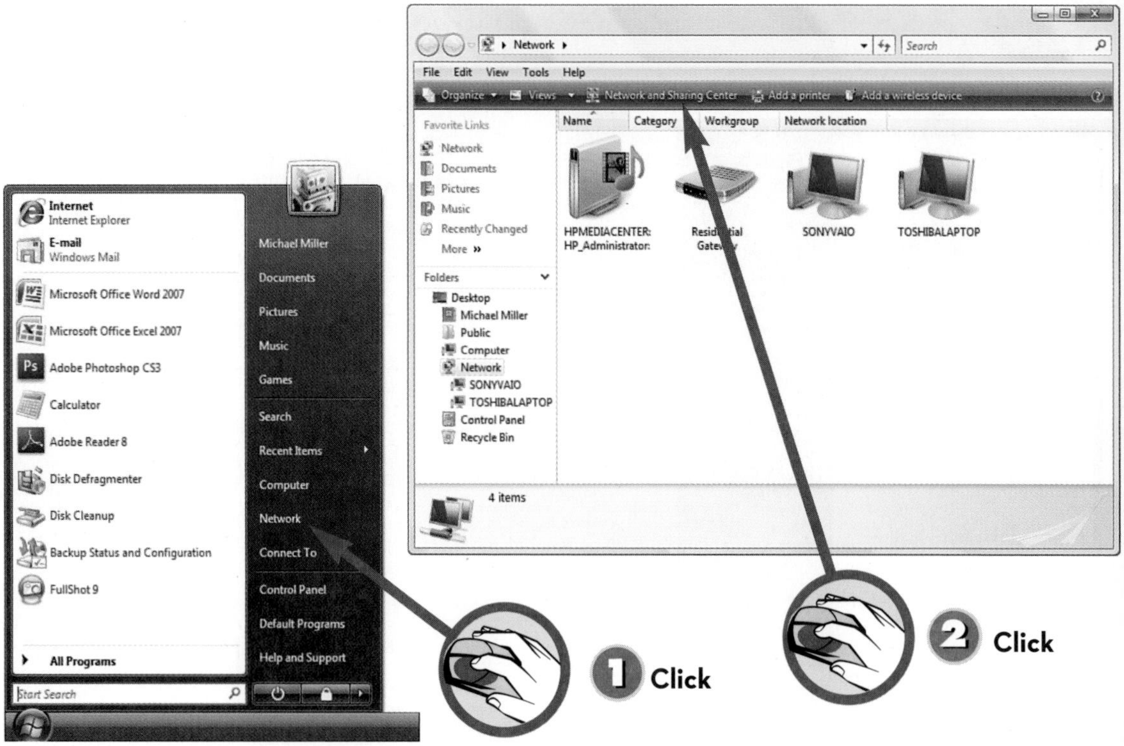

1 Click

2 Click

1 Click the **Start** button and then click **Network**.

2 Click the **Network and Sharing Center** button.

Continued

TIP

Configuration Options

The Network and Sharing Center lets you configure network discovery (to see other PCs on your network), file sharing, public folder sharing, printer sharing, password protected sharing, and media sharing (for music, video, and picture files).

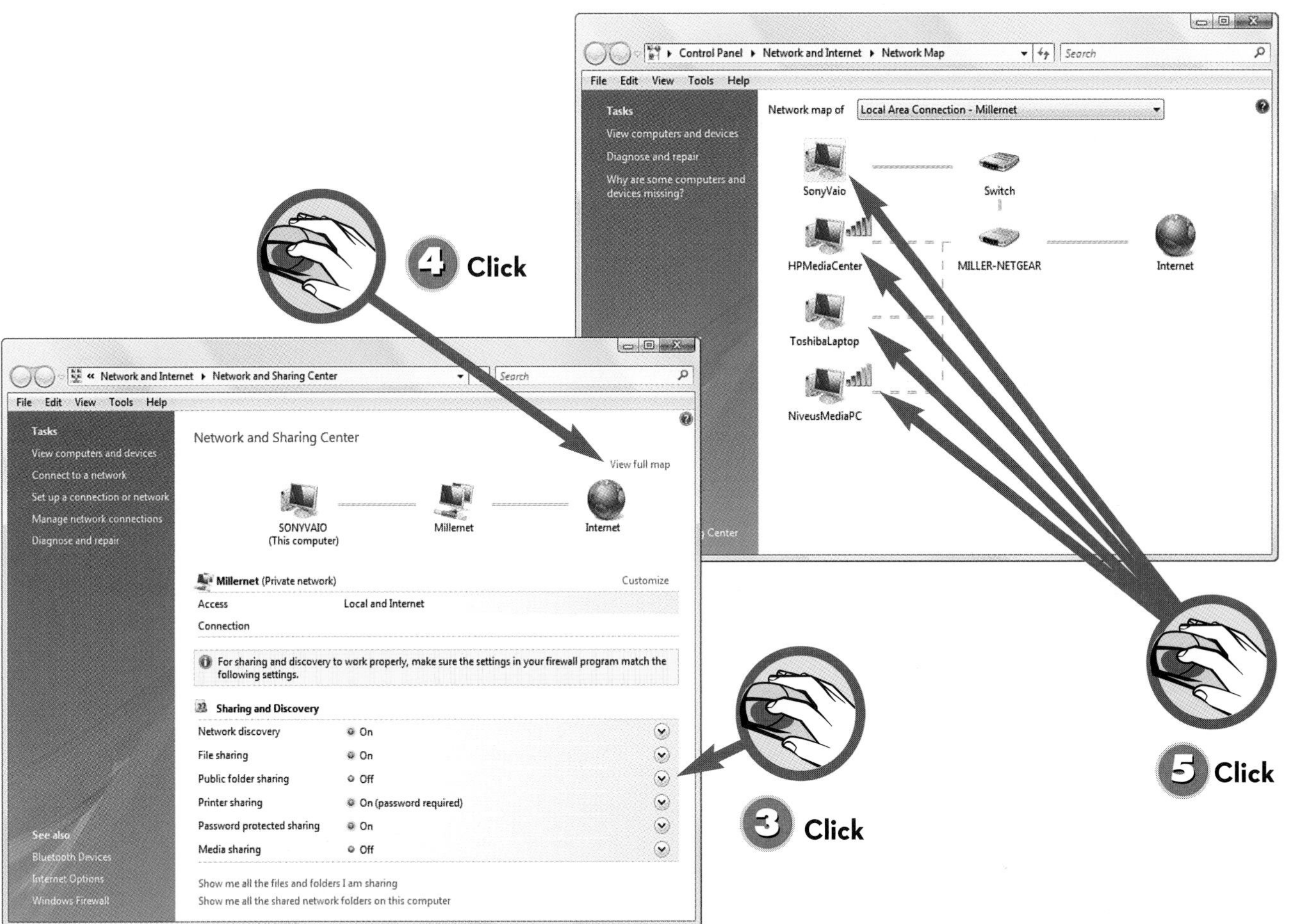

3 The Network and Sharing Center offers easy access to most key network configuration settings; click any section heading to expand the section and see all configuration options.

4 To view a larger and more complete map of your entire network, click the **View Full Map** link in the Network and Sharing Center window.

5 The Network Map opens in a new window; click any network device to see its contents.

End

NOTE

Windows XP Computers

It's likely that only Windows Vista computers and routers will appear in your network map. Computers running Windows XP and older operating systems do not appear by default.

ENABLING PUBLIC FOLDER SHARING

The easiest way to share files between the PCs on your network is to store the files you want to share in Vista's Public folder. To do this, you first have to enable public folder sharing.

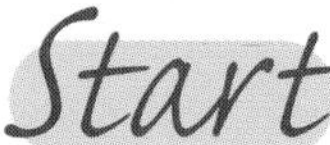

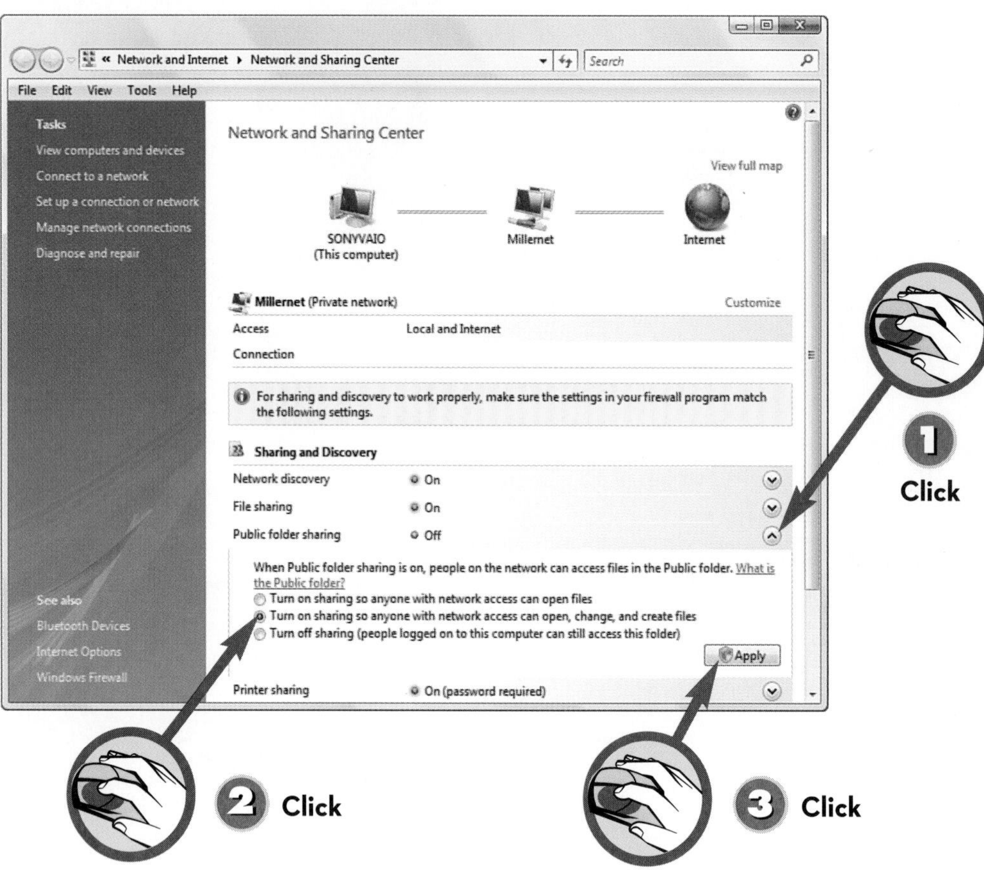

1. From the Network and Sharing Center, click the down arrow next to **Public Folder Sharing**.
2. Click **Turn On Sharing So Anyone with Network Access Can Open, Change, and Create Files**.
3. Click **Apply**.

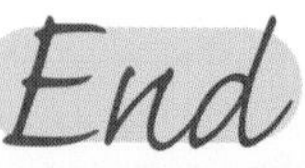

CAUTION

Share Carefully

Be cautious about turning on public folder sharing and file sharing. When you allow a folder to be shared, anyone accessing your network can access the contents of the folder.

TIP

File Sharing

To share files from any folder on your PC, you need to enable file sharing from the Network and Sharing Center. You can then choose to share any individual folder.

ENABLING PRINTER SHARING

To share a single printer between multiple PCs on your network, you have to enable Windows Vista's printer sharing on the PC that is connected to that printer. You can then print to that printer from any other computer on your network.

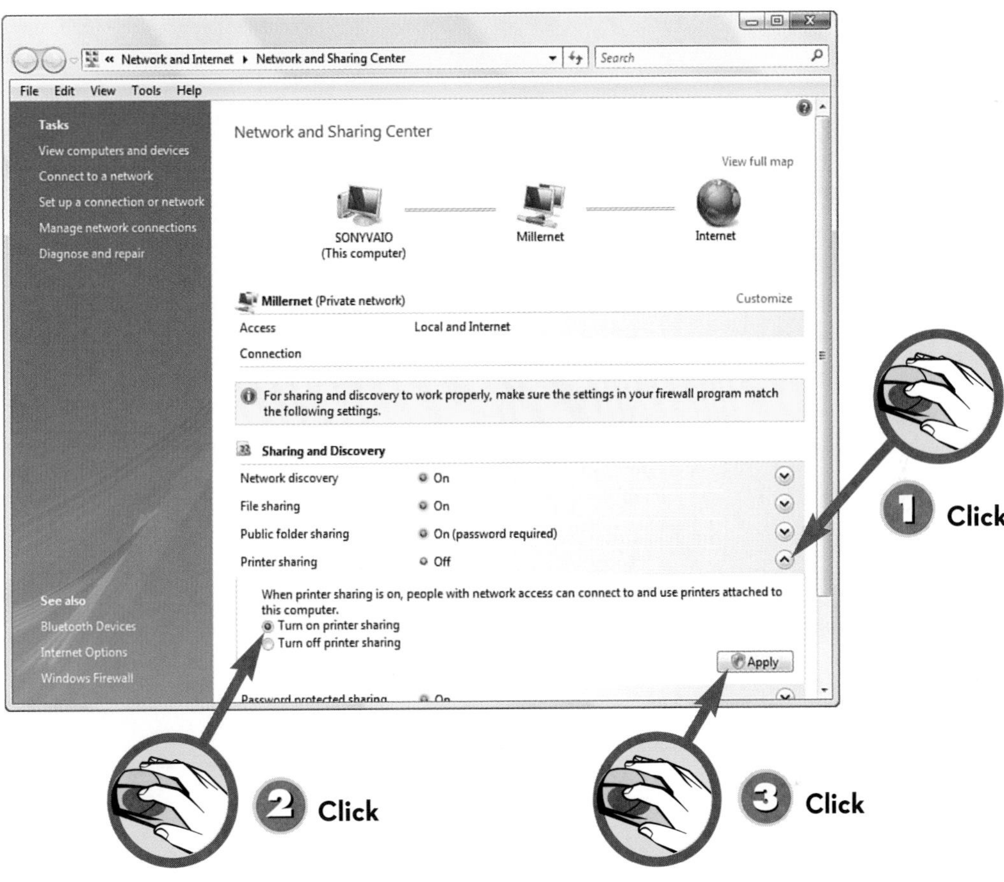

1. From the Network and Sharing Center, click the down arrow next to **Printer Sharing**.
2. Click **Turn On Printer Sharing**.
3. Click **Apply**.

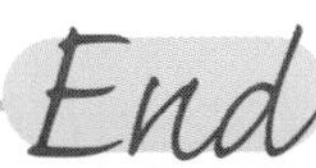

NOTE

Printing to a Network Printer

When you use any program's print function on another network computer, all installed network computers should appear in the program's Print dialog box.

ACCESSING OTHER COMPUTERS ON YOUR NETWORK

After your network is set up and properly configured, it's easy to share files between different computers on the network. In Windows Vista, all your network computers and shared folders are found in the Network window; shared files should be stored in that computer's Public folder.

Start

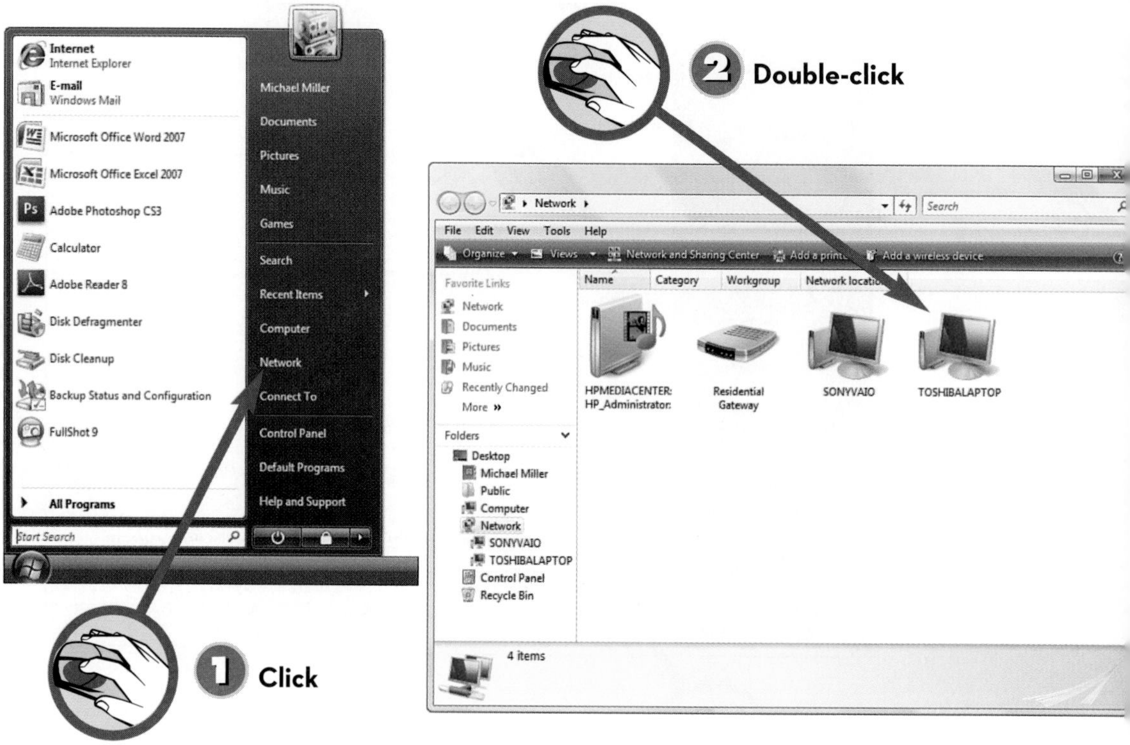

2 Double-click

1 Click

1. Click the **Start** button and then click **Network**.
2. All your network computers are now displayed. Double-click the computer you want to access.

Continued

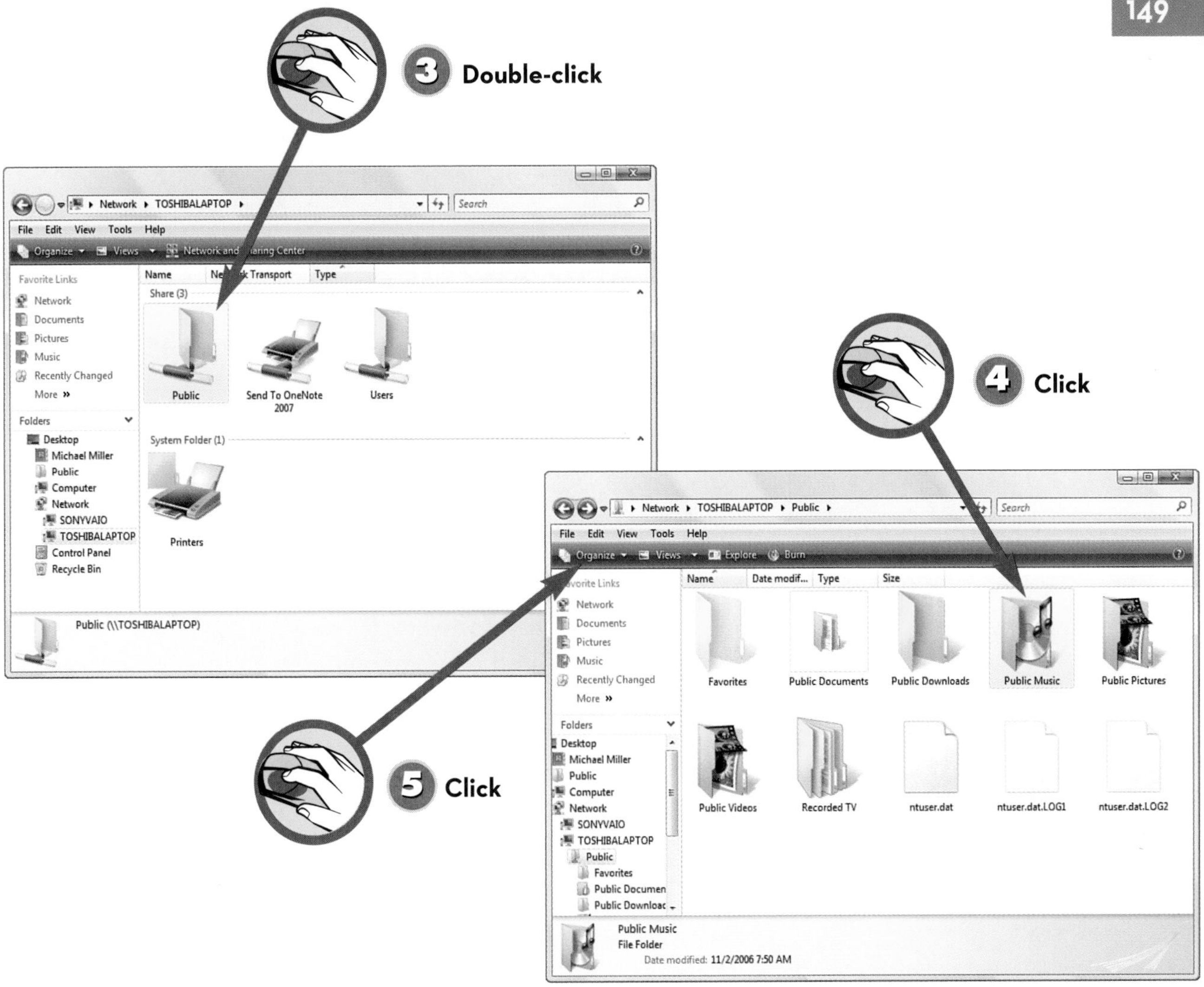

3 Double-click

4 Click

5 Click

3 The shared folders on that computer are now displayed. Double-click a folder to view its contents.

4 Click to select a file or folder.

5 Click the **Organize** menu to cut or copy the selected file or folder to another location or computer.

End

TIP

Look for the Public Folder

On most systems, shared files are stored in the Public folder. Look in this folder first for the files you want.

part 9

PLAYING MUSIC AND MOVIES

Your personal computer can do more than just compute. It can also serve as a fully functional audio/video playback center!

That's right, you can use your PC to listen to your favorite audio CDs and to watch the latest movies on DVD. Vista's Windows Media Player software is a great music player program, and Windows Media Center is a terrific full-screen interface for playing DVD movies. They're both easy to use.

And, if you have an iPod portable music player, you can use your PC to manage all your digital music with the iTunes software. It's easy to download music from the iTunes Store, connect your iPod to your computer, and then transfer your music to your iPod. You can even use the iTunes software to burn your own music CDs!

WINDOWS MEDIA PLAYER

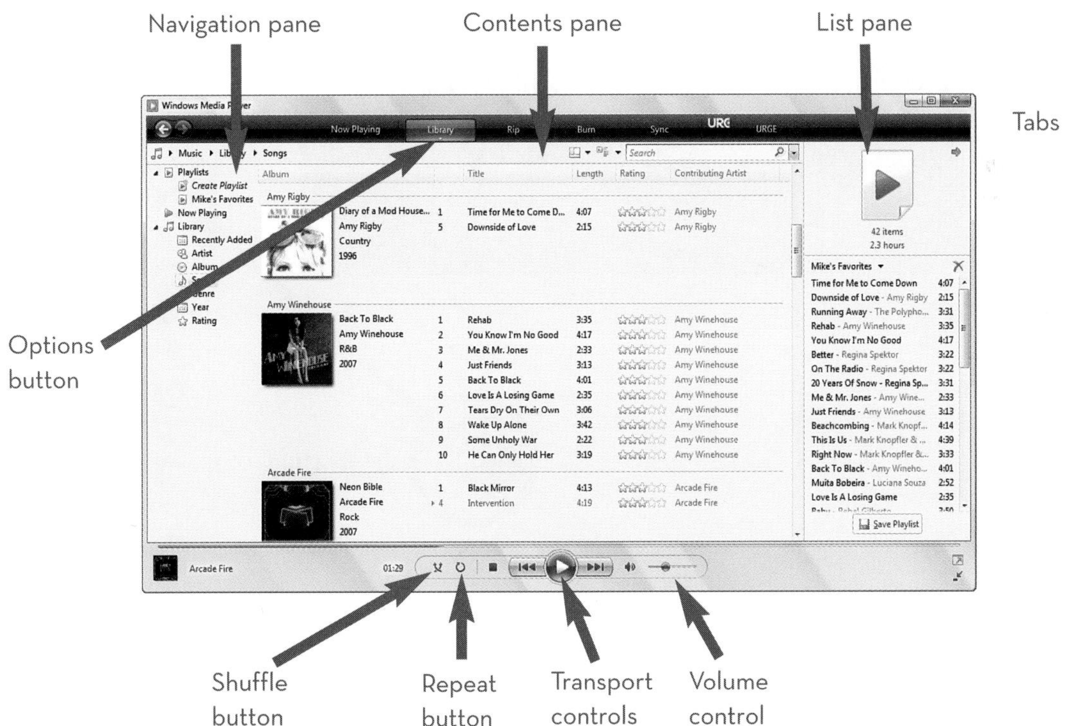

PLAYING A CD WITH WINDOWS MEDIA PLAYER

You play audio CDs using your PC's CD-ROM drive and Windows Media Player (WMP). You can also use WMP to play songs you've downloaded to your PC from the Internet and (if your PC has a DVD drive) to play DVD movies.

Start

1

2 Click

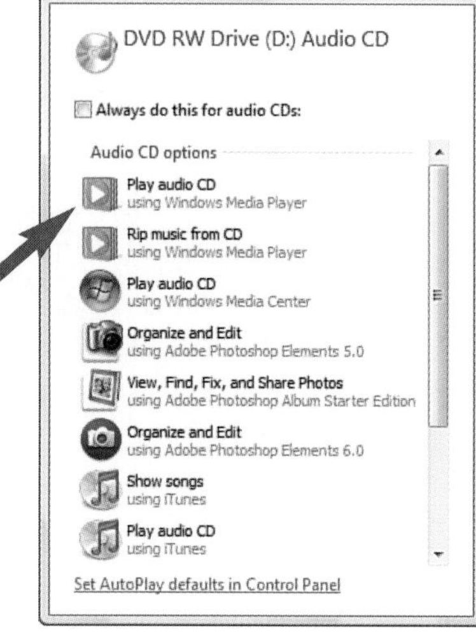

1. Insert a CD into your PC's CD-ROM drive.
2. Windows will ask what you want to do; click **Play Audio CD Using Windows Media Player**.

Continued

—TIP—

Online Music Stores

You can buy downloadable music at many online music stores, including the iTunes Music Store (www.apple.com/itunes/store/), AmazonMP3 (www.amazonmp3.com), Rhapsody (www.rhapsody.com), and Napster (www.napster.com). Most stores charge in the neighborhood of 99¢ per song.

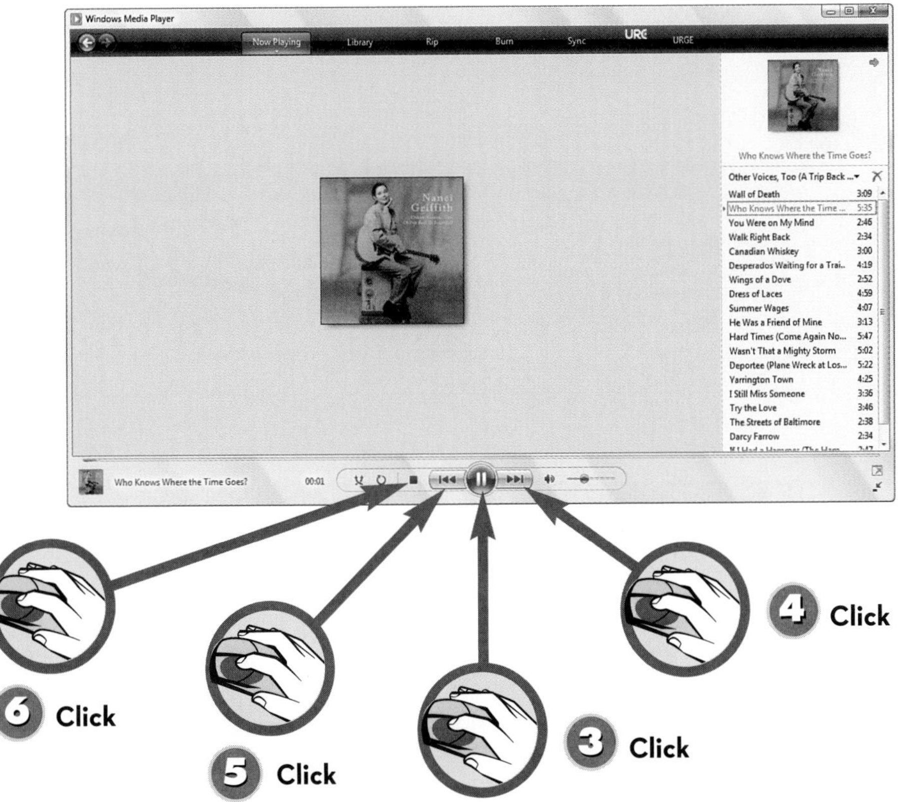

3. The CD should start playing automatically; to pause the CD, click the **Pause** button and then click **Play** to resume playback.
4. To skip to the next track, click the **Next** button.
5. To replay the last track, click the **Previous** button.
6. To stop playback completely, click the **Stop** button.

End

TIP

Download the Latest Version

This book covers Windows Media Player version 11. To download the latest version of Windows Media Player, go to www.microsoft.com/windows/windowsmedia/.

NOTE

Launching Windows Media Player

If WMP doesn't start automatically when you load a CD into your PC's CD-ROM drive, you can launch it manually from the Windows Start menu.

RIPPING A CD TO YOUR HARD DISK

Windows Media Player lets you copy music from your CDs to your PC's hard drive. You can then listen to these digital audio files on your computer, transfer the files to a portable music player, or burn your own custom mix CDs. This process of copying files from a CD to your hard disk is called *ripping*.

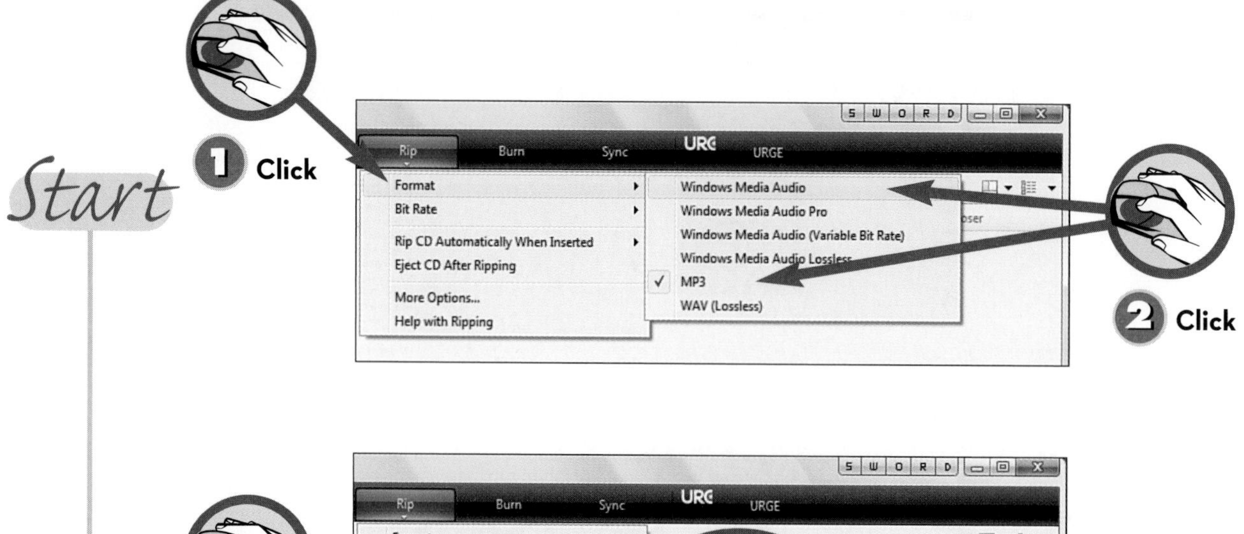

1. Before you rip a CD, you have to set WMP's recording format. Click the **Options** button on the **Rip** tab and select **Format**.
2. Select either **Windows Media Audio** or **MP3** for the recording format.
3. Now you have to set the recording quality. Click the **Options** button on the **Rip** tab and select **Bit Rate**.
4. Select the recording quality you want; 128 Kbps is the default for WMA format files, whereas 192 Kbps is a good setting for MP3 files.

Continued

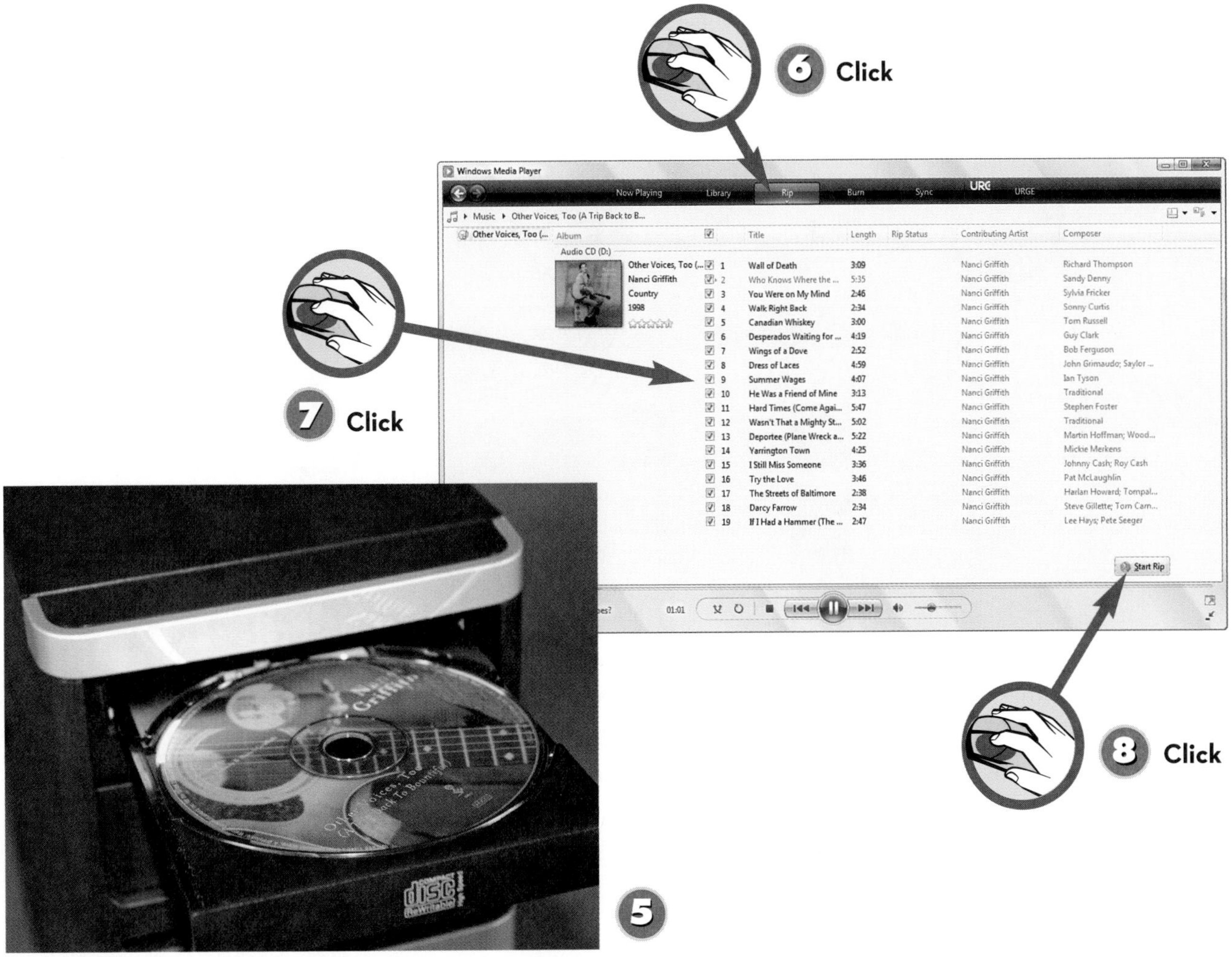

6 Click

7 Click

8 Click

5

5 Insert the CD you want to rip into your PC's CD-ROM drive.

6 In WMP, click the **Rip** tab to show the contents of the CD.

7 Put a check mark by the tracks you want to copy.

8 When you've selected which tracks to rip, click the **Start Rip** button.

End

TIP

Connect to the Internet

Before you rip a CD, you should make sure your PC is connected to the Internet. This lets WMP download track names and CD cover art for the songs you're ripping.

NOTE

Music Files

WMP stores your ripped music files in your Music folder. It creates a subfolder for the artist, and within that another subfolder for each of the artist's CDs.

CREATING A PLAYLIST

Files in your Windows Media Player library can be combined into playlists. You can create playlists from the files you have stored on your hard disk, in any order you want—just like listening to a radio station's playlist.

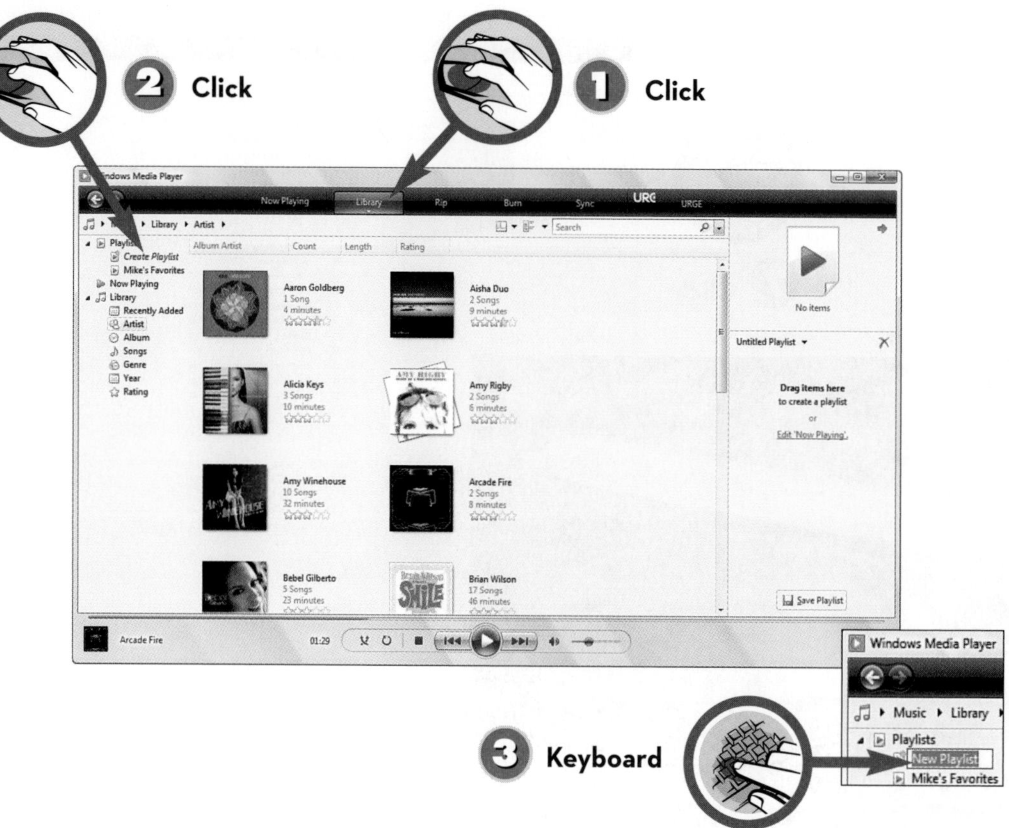

1 Click the **Library** tab.

2 In the Navigation pane, click **Create Playlist**.

3 Enter a title for your new playlist.

Continued

NOTE

Understanding Playlists

When you create a playlist, you don't actually make copies of the individual songs. Instead, the playlist points to the songs where they continue to reside on your hard disk. When you play a playlist, Windows Media Player accesses each song file in turn on the hard drive.

TIP

Auto Playlists

Windows Media Player also includes a feature called *auto playlists*, which are automatically generated based on criteria you specify. To create a new auto playlist, go to the Navigation pane, right-click the playlist item, and select **Create Auto Playlist** from the pop-up menu.

4 Click and drag songs or complete albums from the Contents pane to the List pane.

5 When you're done creating the playlist, click the **Save Playlist** button.

End

—TIP

Editing Playlists

To edit a playlist, click the Playlists item in the Navigation pane; this displays all your playlists in the Content pane. Right-click the playlist you want to edit and select **Edit in List Pane** from the pop-up menu.

PLAYING A PLAYLIST

After you've created a playlist, you can play back any or all songs in that playlist—in any order.

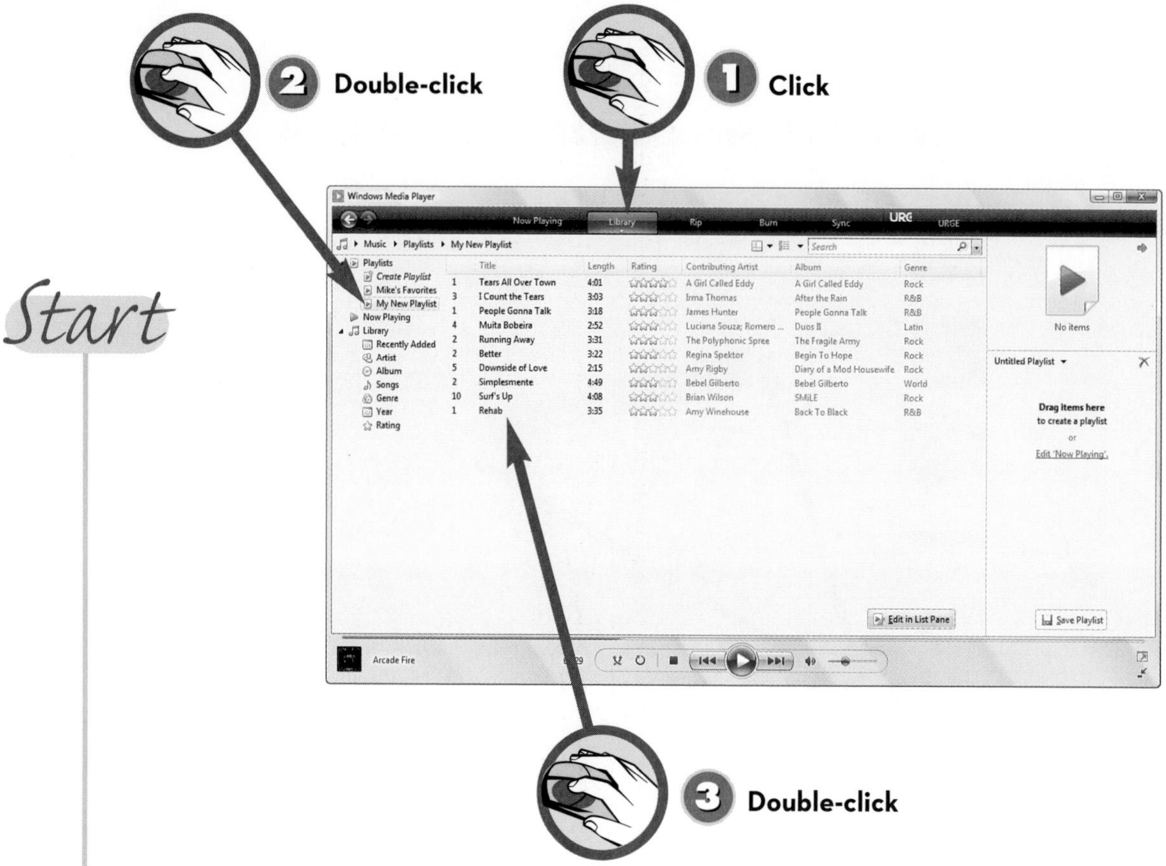

2 Double-click

1 Click

Start

3 Double-click

1. Click the **Library** tab.
2. In the Navigation pane, double-click the playlist name to play the entire playlist.
3. Double-click an individual song to play that song.

End

TIP

Random Play

To play the songs in a playlist in random order, click the **Shuffle** button next to the transport controls.

BURNING A MUSIC CD

If you have a recordable CD drive (called a *CD burner*) in your PC, you can make your own audio mix CDs. You can take any combination of songs on your hard disk; "burn" them onto a blank CD; and then play that CD in your home, car, or portable CD player.

Start

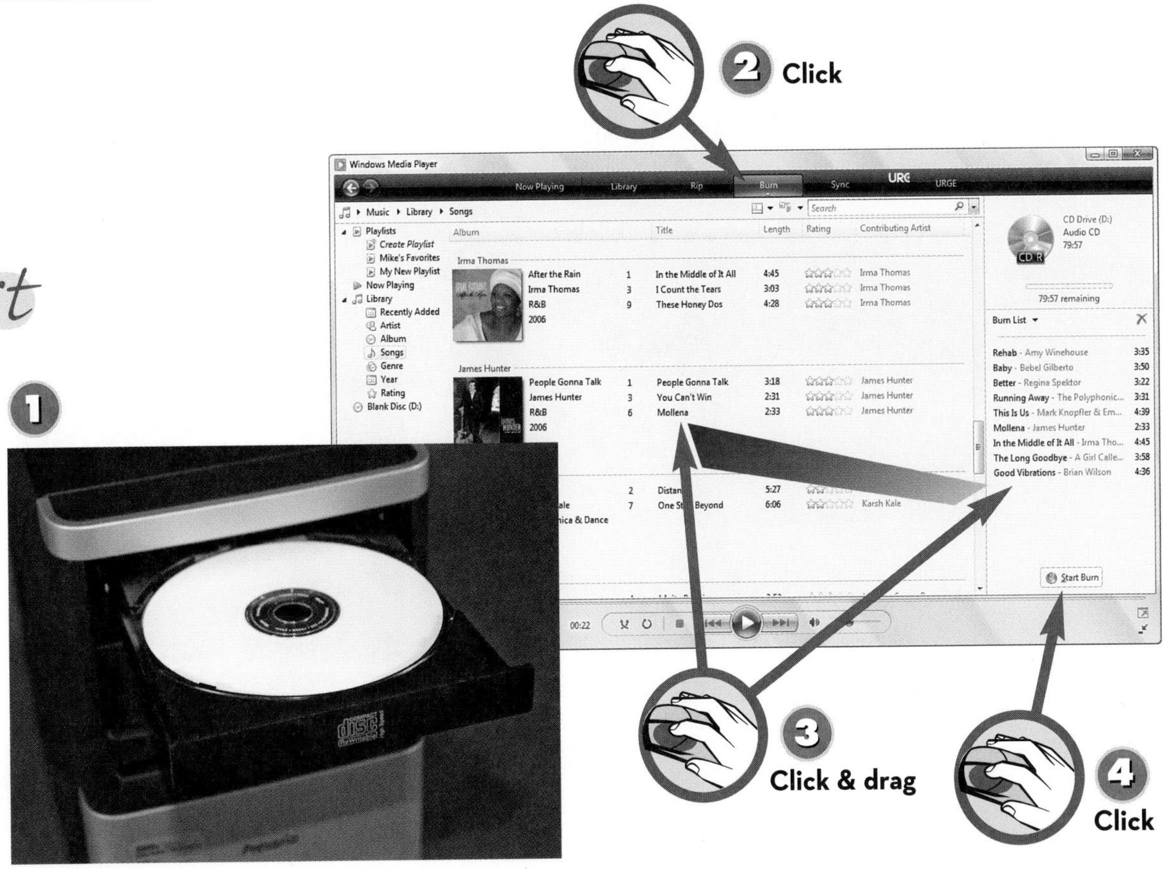

1

2 Click

3 Click & drag

4 Click

1. Insert a blank CD-R disc into your computer's CD-R/RW drive.
2. From within WMP, select the **Burn** tab.
3. Click and drag the songs you want to burn from the Contents pane to the List pane.
4. Click the **Start Burn** button.

End

TIP

Use CD-R Discs

To play your new CD in a regular (non-PC) CD player, record in the CD-R format and use a blank CD-R disc specifically labeled for audio use. (CD-RW discs will not play in most home CD players.)

TIP

Burn a Playlist

A quicker way to select songs to burn is to create a playlist first and then drag that playlist onto the List tab.

CONNECTING AN iPOD TO YOUR PC

To use the iPod with your PC, you first have to install Apple's iTunes software, which comes on the iPod's accompanying CD. When you connect your iPod to your PC, your computer automatically launches the iTunes software and copies any new songs and playlists you've added since the last time you connected.

Start

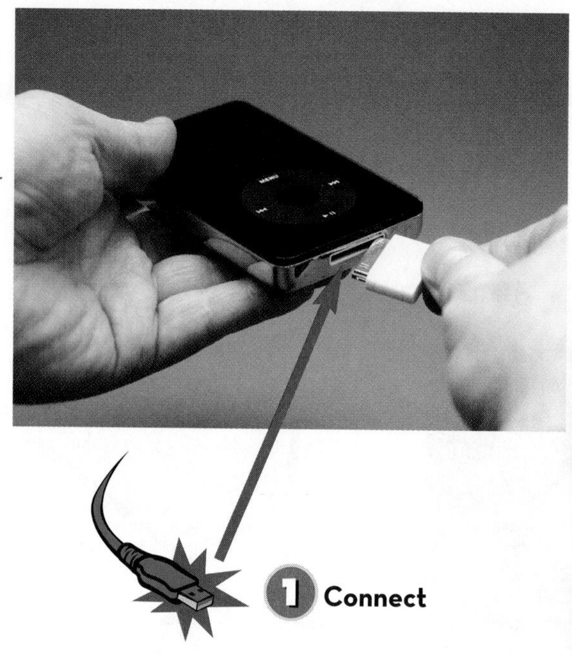

1 Connect

2 Connect

1. Connect one end of the USB cable to your iPod.
2. Connect the other end of the USB cable to a USB port on your PC.

Continued

TIP

Manually Syncing

You can also manually select which tunes are copied to your iPod. Just access the Music tab on the connection screen and opt to sync only selected tracks and playlists—those items checked in your iTunes library.

TIP

Autofill and the iPod shuffle

If you have an iPod shuffle, iTunes offers an Autofill option. This lets the software automatically choose songs to sync to your iPod—which is useful if you have more songs on your hard disk than you have storage capacity on your shuffle.

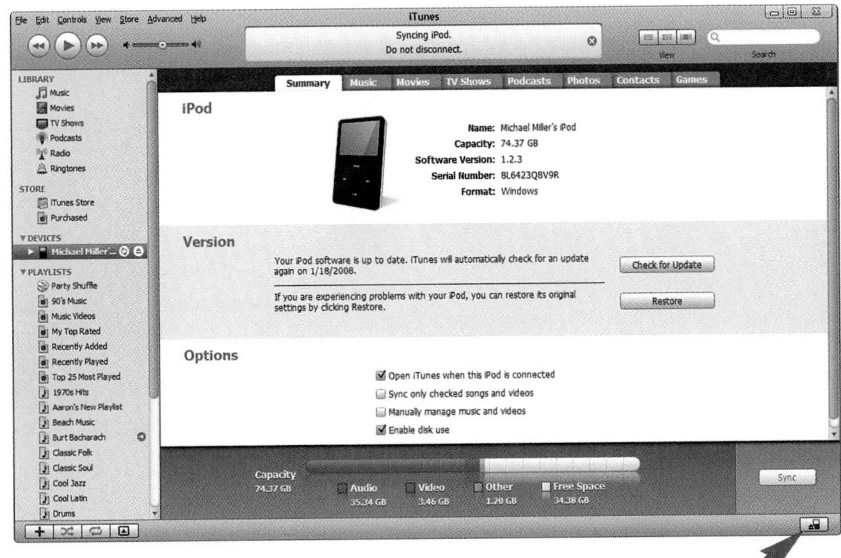

4 click

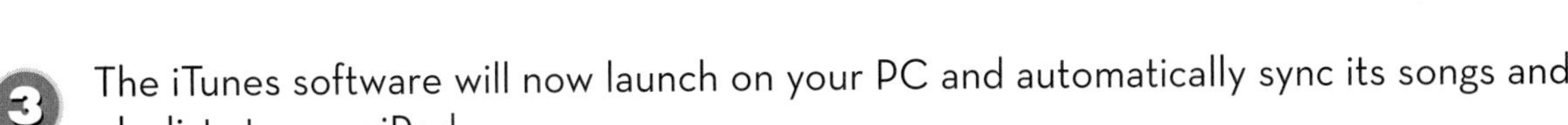

3 The iTunes software will now launch on your PC and automatically sync its songs and playlists to your iPod.

4 When the sync is complete, iTunes will display a message that it's safe to disconnect your iPod. Click the **Eject iPod** button and then disconnect your iPod.

End

TIP

Syncing Videos

If you have an iPod with video capability, you can configure which movies are synced from the Movies tab. From here you can choose to sync all movies, selected movies, or a selected number of unwatched movies. The same option exists for downloaded television shows, which are synced from the TV Shows tab.

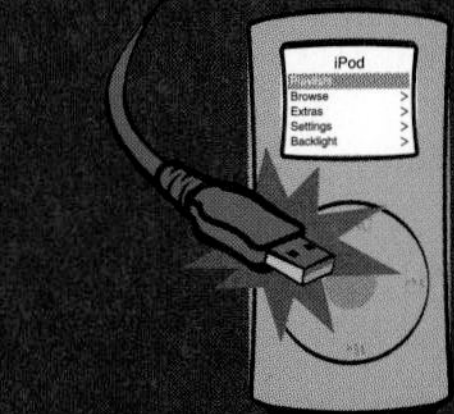

CREATING iPOD PLAYLISTS

You can store thousands of songs on your iPod, which makes it a little difficult to find the music you want. One way to organize your music is to create playlists of your favorite songs.

Start

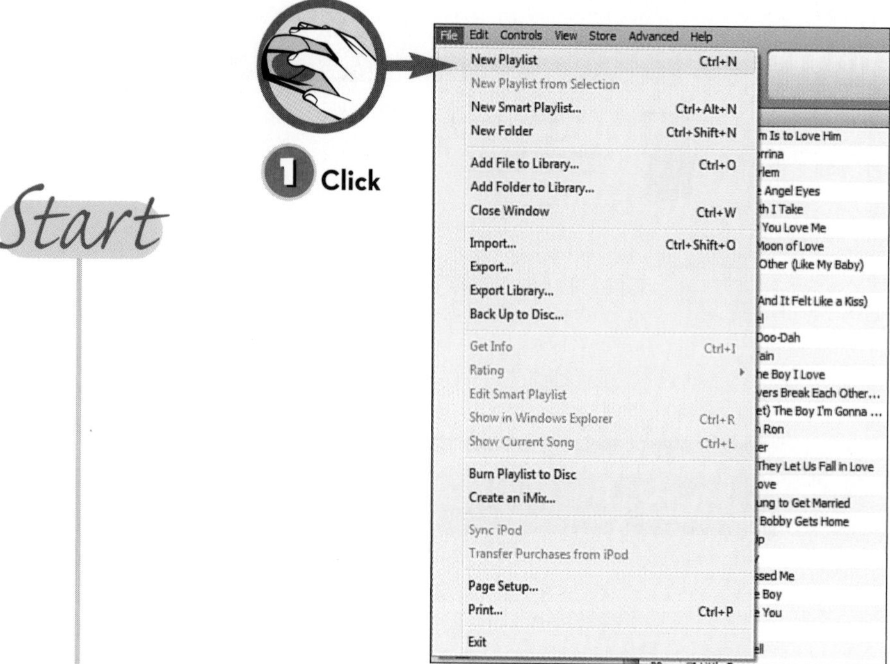

1. From within iTunes, pull down the **File** menu and select **New Playlist**.
2. Enter a name for the new untitled playlist.

Continued

3 Click Music in the Library pane.

4 Click and drag songs from the Contents pane onto the new playlist.

End

TIP
Smart Playlists

You can also create smart playlists (**File**, **New Smart Playlist**) that let you automatically select songs by artist, album, genre, and so on.

TIP
Playing a Playlist

To play an iTunes playlist on your computer, just double-click the playlist name in the Playlists pane.

DOWNLOADING MUSIC FROM THE iTUNES STORE

If you want the latest music for your iPod, it's easy to purchase and download your favorite tunes from Apple's iTunes Store. All you need is an Internet connection and your credit card, and you're ready to shop!

1. In the iTunes software, click **iTunes Store** in the Navigation pane.
2. The iTunes software now connects to the Internet and displays the iTunes Store's main page. To view music for purchase, click **Music** in the iTunes Store box.
3. To search for a specific song or artist, enter your query into the **Search iTunes Store** box and press **Enter**.

Continued

TIP

Browsing by Genre

You can also browse the iTunes store by type of music—Alternative, Country, Classical, and so on. Just scroll down to the Genres section and click the genre you're interested in.

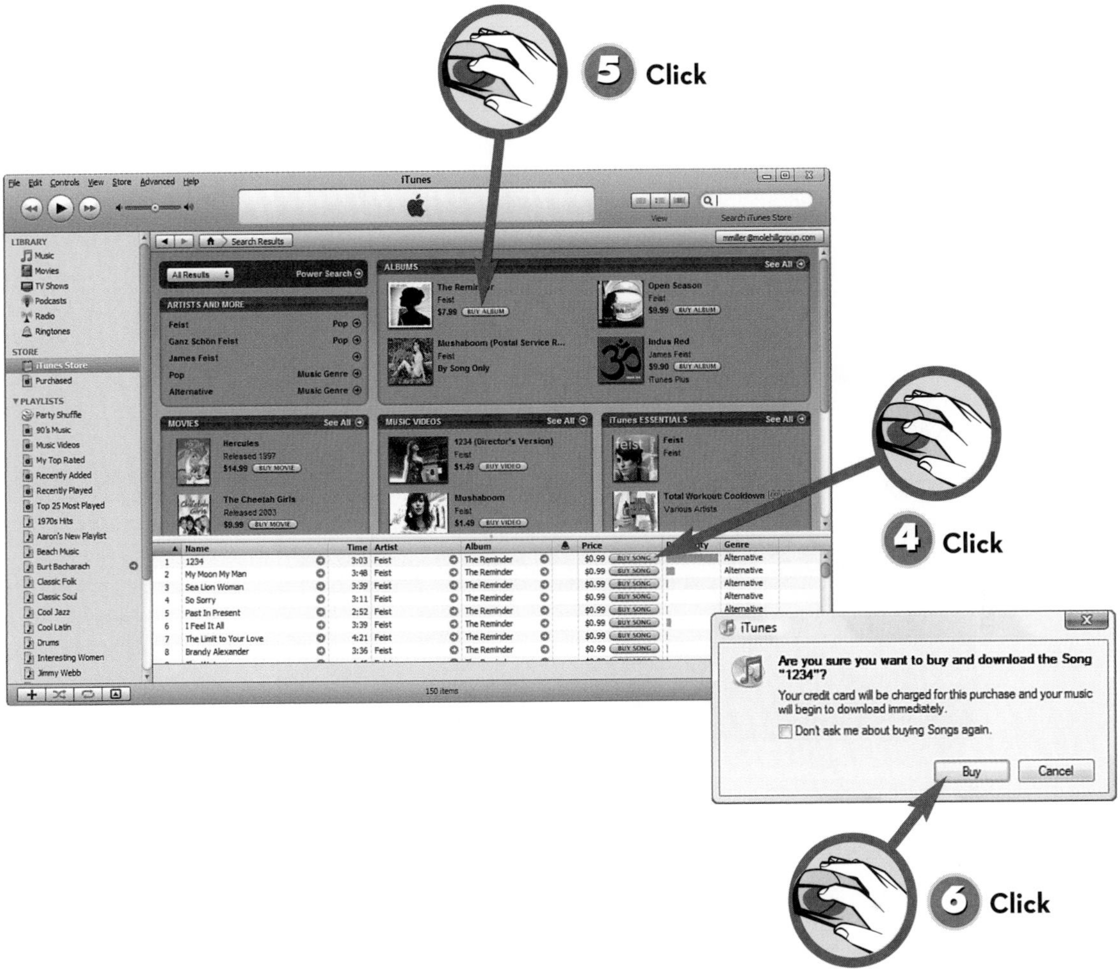

5 Click

4 Click

6 Click

4. The iTunes Store now displays all the music that matches your search. To purchase an individual track, click the **Buy Song** button.
5. To purchase an entire album, click the **Buy Album** button.
6. When prompted if you're sure you want to purchase this item, click the **Buy** button.

End

TIP

Credit Card Required

Before you purchase items from the iTunes Store, you need to enter your credit card information. Pull down the **Store** menu, select **View My Account**, then click the **Edit Payment Information** button and enter the necessary data.

PLAYING A DVD

If your PC has a DVD drive, you can use your PC to watch prerecorded DVD movies. Most versions of Windows Vista include Windows Media Center, a full-screen interface for playing digital media; you use Media Center to watch your DVD movies.

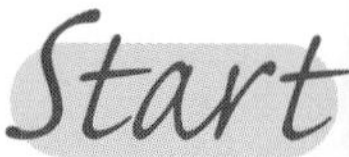

Click

1. Insert the DVD into your PC's DVD drive.
2. When prompted, click **Play DVD Movie Using Windows Media Center**.

Continued

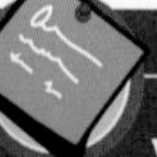

NOTE

Windows Media Center

Windows Media Center is included with the Home Premium and Ultimate versions of Windows Vista, not the Home Basic version.

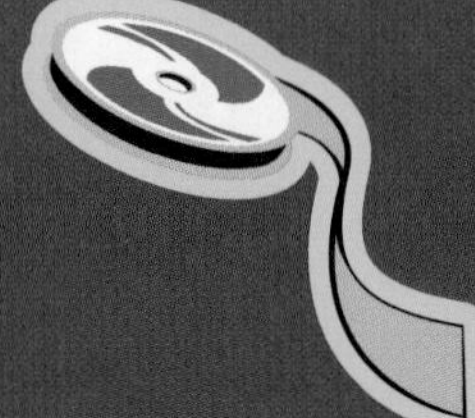

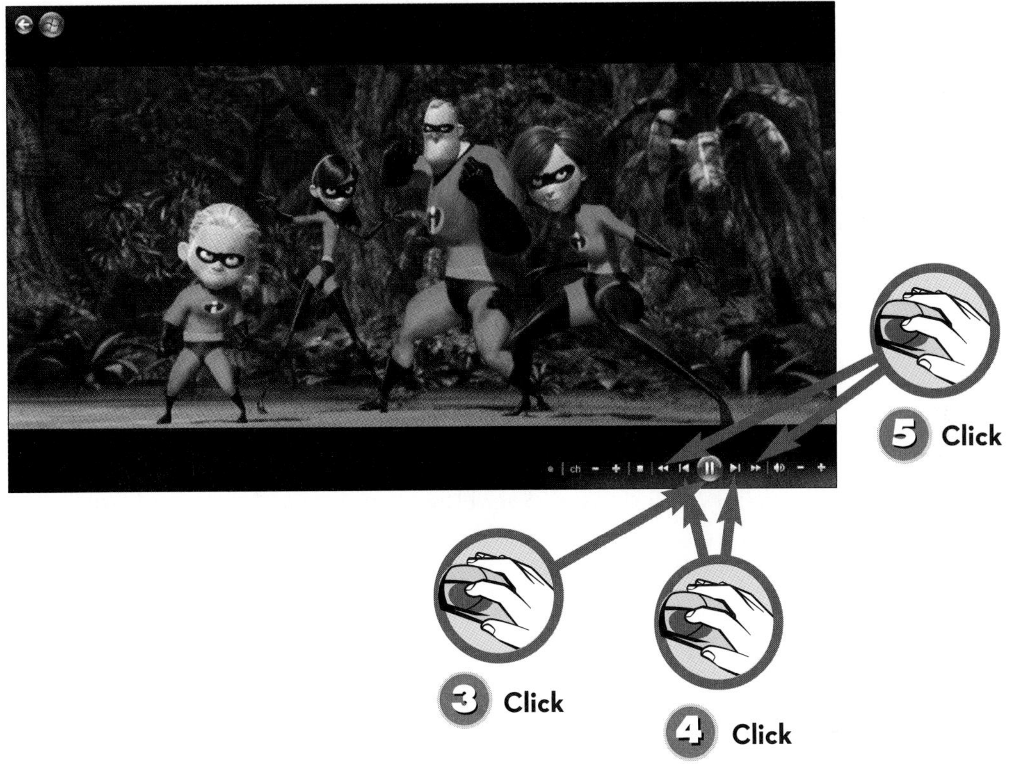

3 The movie should start playing automatically. To pause the movie, click the **Pause** button; then click **Play** to resume playback.

4 Click the **Next** button to go to the next chapter on the DVD, or click the **Previous** button to go to the previous chapter.

5 Click the **Fast Forward** or **Rewind** buttons to speed forward and backward through the movie.

End

TIP

DVDs in Windows Media Player

You can also play DVD movies in Windows Media Player and other media player programs.

part 10

WORKING WITH DIGITAL PHOTOS

More and more people are trading in their old film cameras for new digital cameras—and connecting those cameras to their PCs. You can use your digital camera and PC together to transfer all the photos you take to your hard disk and then edit your pictures to make them look even better.

Windows Vista not only stores your digital photos, but also helps you edit and display those photos. It's all possible due to Vista's new Windows Photo Gallery utility—a combination photo viewer/editor program.

Want to view your photos in a slideshow? Windows Photo Gallery will do it. Want to organize your photos—by date taken, rating, or keyword? Windows Photo Gallery will do that, too. How about printing your photos, or ordering prints online? Also a job for Windows Photo Gallery. Or maybe you need to crop a poorly composed photo, remove a stubborn case of red eye, or adjust brightness or color? These are also things you can do with Windows Photo Gallery; all you need to know is how.

WINDOWS PHOTO GALLERY

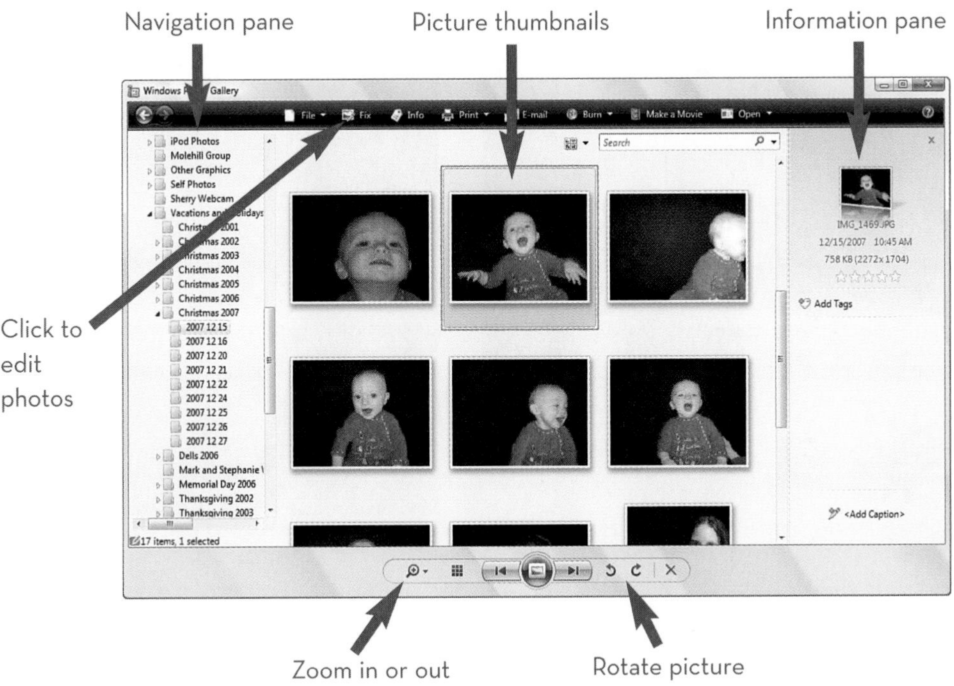

TRANSFERRING PICTURES FROM A DIGITAL CAMERA

Connecting a digital camera to your PC is extremely easy; all you have to do is connect a USB cable between your camera and your computer. With this type of setup, Windows will recognize your camera as soon as you plug it in and will automatically download the camera's contents.

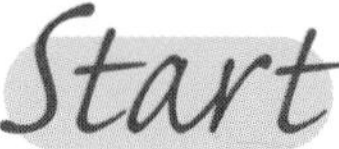

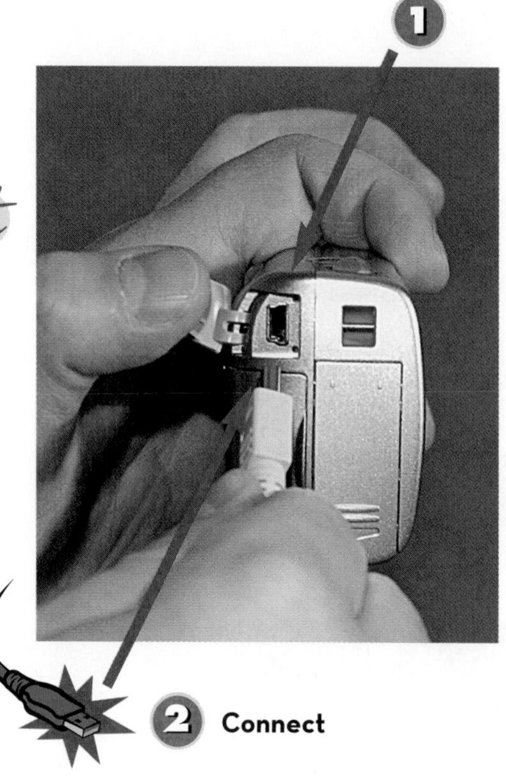

1. On your digital camera, locate and open the cover to the data transfer port.
2. Connect one end of the USB cable to the data transfer port on your digital camera.
3. Connect the other end of the USB cable to a USB port on your PC.

Continued

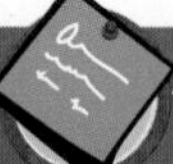

NOTE

Other Photo-Downloading Software

Connecting your camera to your PC may launch other image-transfer programs that may be installed on your computer. This may be a program that came with your digital camera, or perhaps a photo-editing program. You can use any of these programs to transfer pictures from your camera.

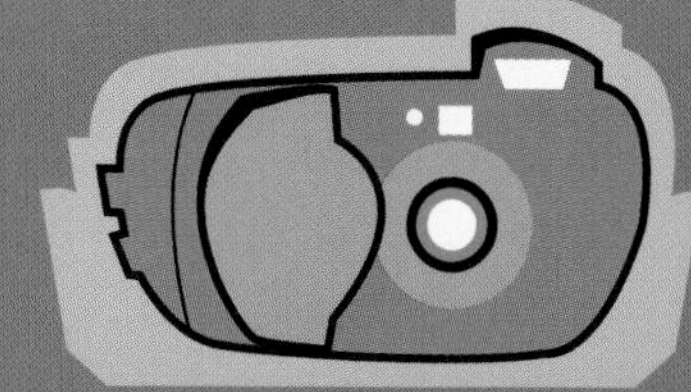

4 Select

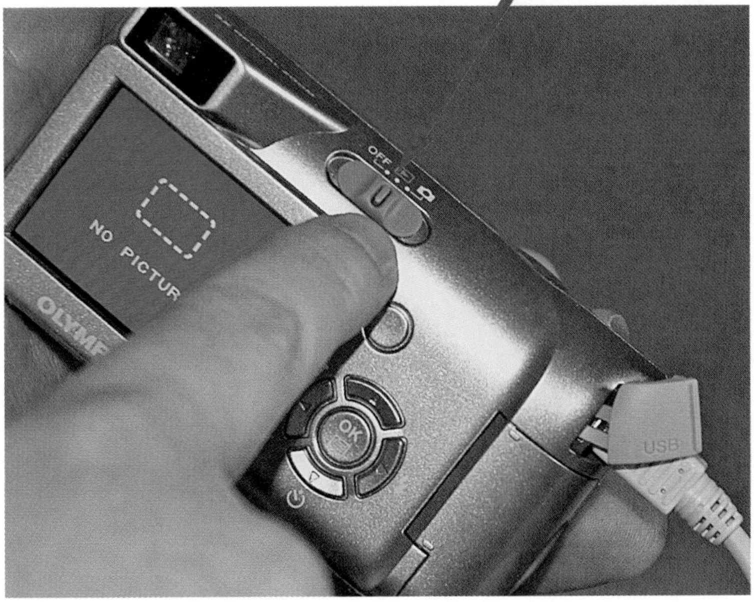

5 Click

4. Turn on your digital camera and (if necessary) move the selection dial or switch to the transfer pictures setting.
5. When the AutoPlay window appears, click **Import Pictures Using Windows**.

End

CAUTION

Turn Off Your Camera

Don't forget to turn off your camera when you're done transferring pictures. If you leave your camera on, you'll drain your batteries!

NOTE

Destination Folder

By default, Windows Vista downloads your digital photos to the Pictures folder, in a subfolder labeled by date.

TRANSFERRING PICTURES FROM A MEMORY CARD

If your PC includes a memory card reader, a faster and easier way to copy your digital photos is via your camera's memory card. When you insert a memory card, your PC recognizes the card as if it were another disk on your system. You can then copy files from the memory card to your computer's hard disk.

Start

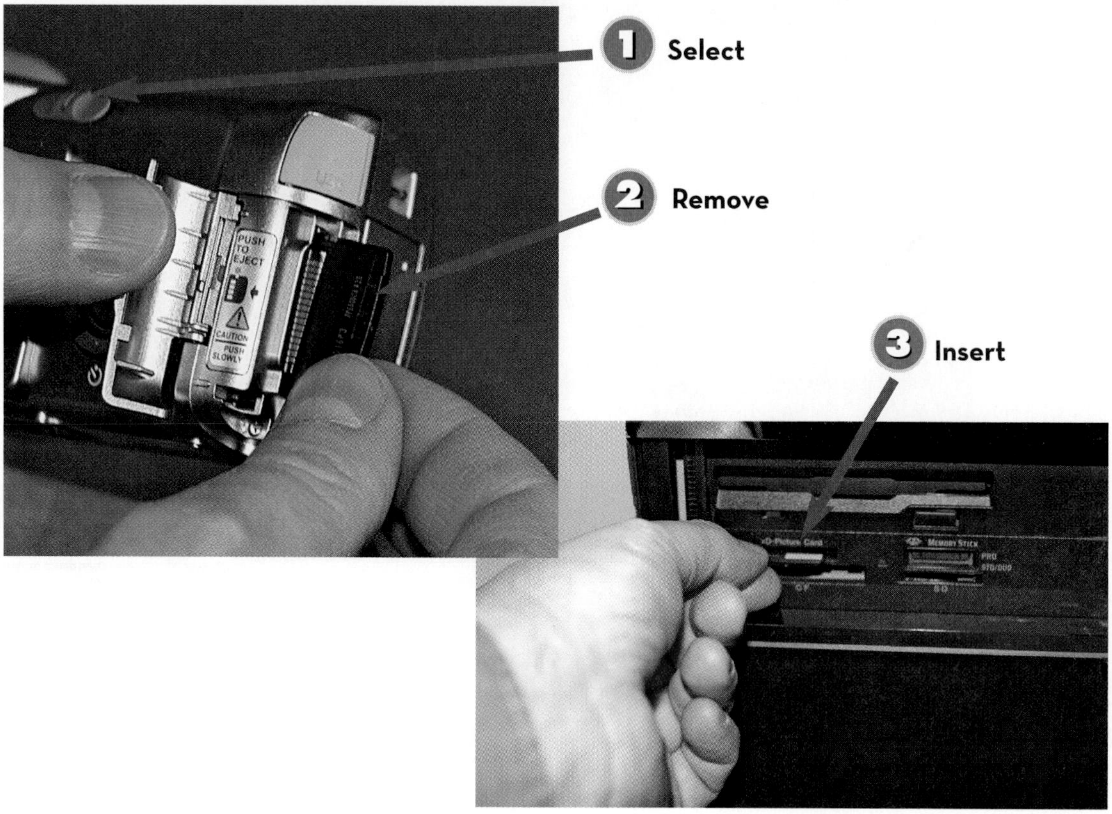

1 Select

2 Remove

3 Insert

1. Turn off your digital camera.
2. Remove the flash memory card.
3. Insert the memory card from your digital camera into the memory card slot on your PC.

Continued

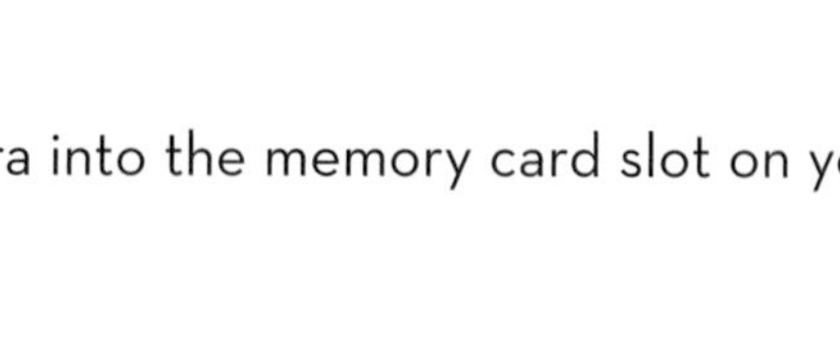

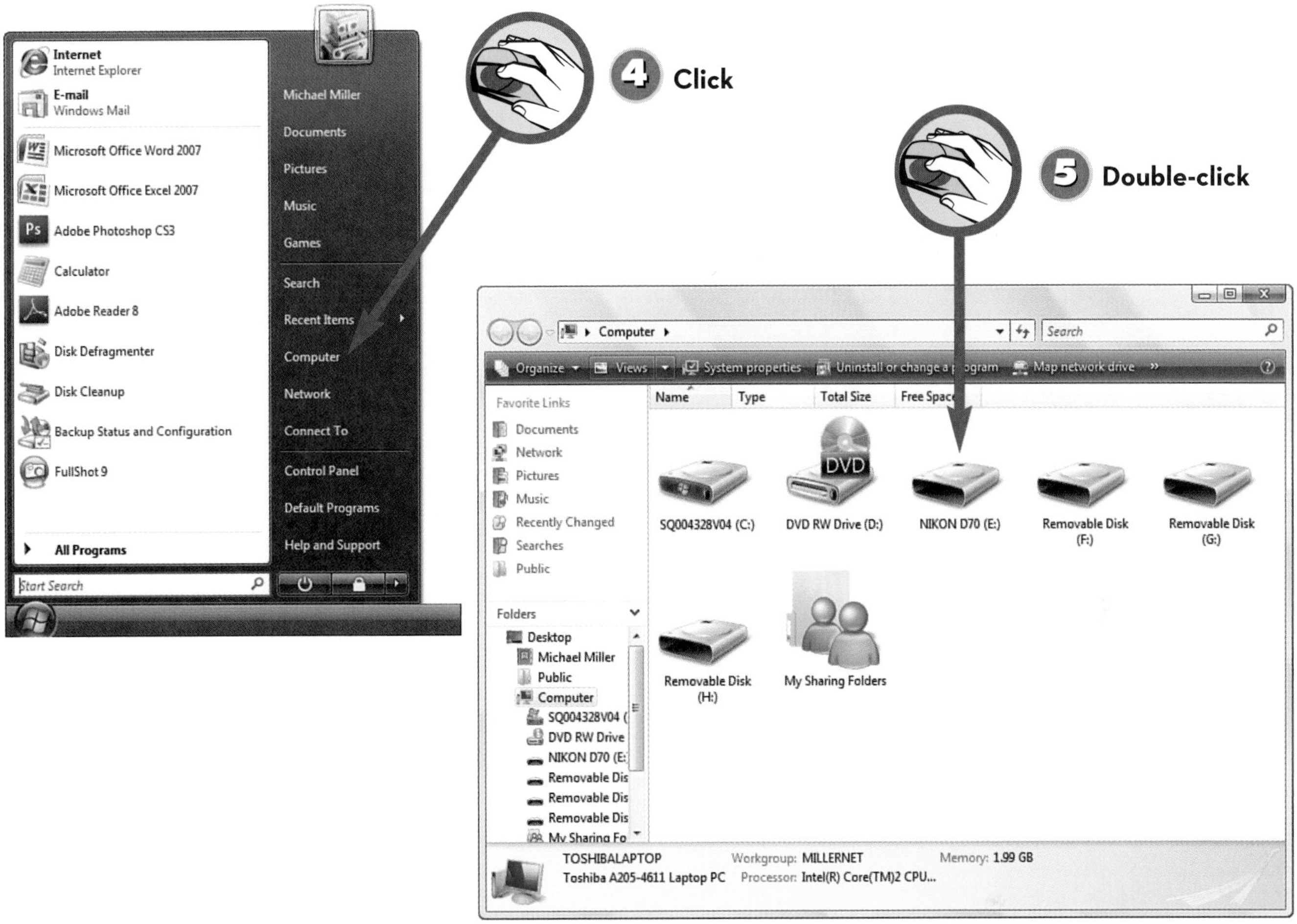

4 Click **Start** and select **Computer**.

5 Double-click the icon for the memory card reader drive.

Continued

NOTE

Copying Automatically

In some instances, Windows may recognize that your memory card contains digital photos and start to download those photos automatically—no manual interaction necessary.

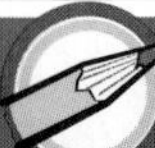

TIP

Printing from a Memory Card

Many color photo printers include memory card slots that let you print directly from your camera's memory card, bypassing your computer entirely.

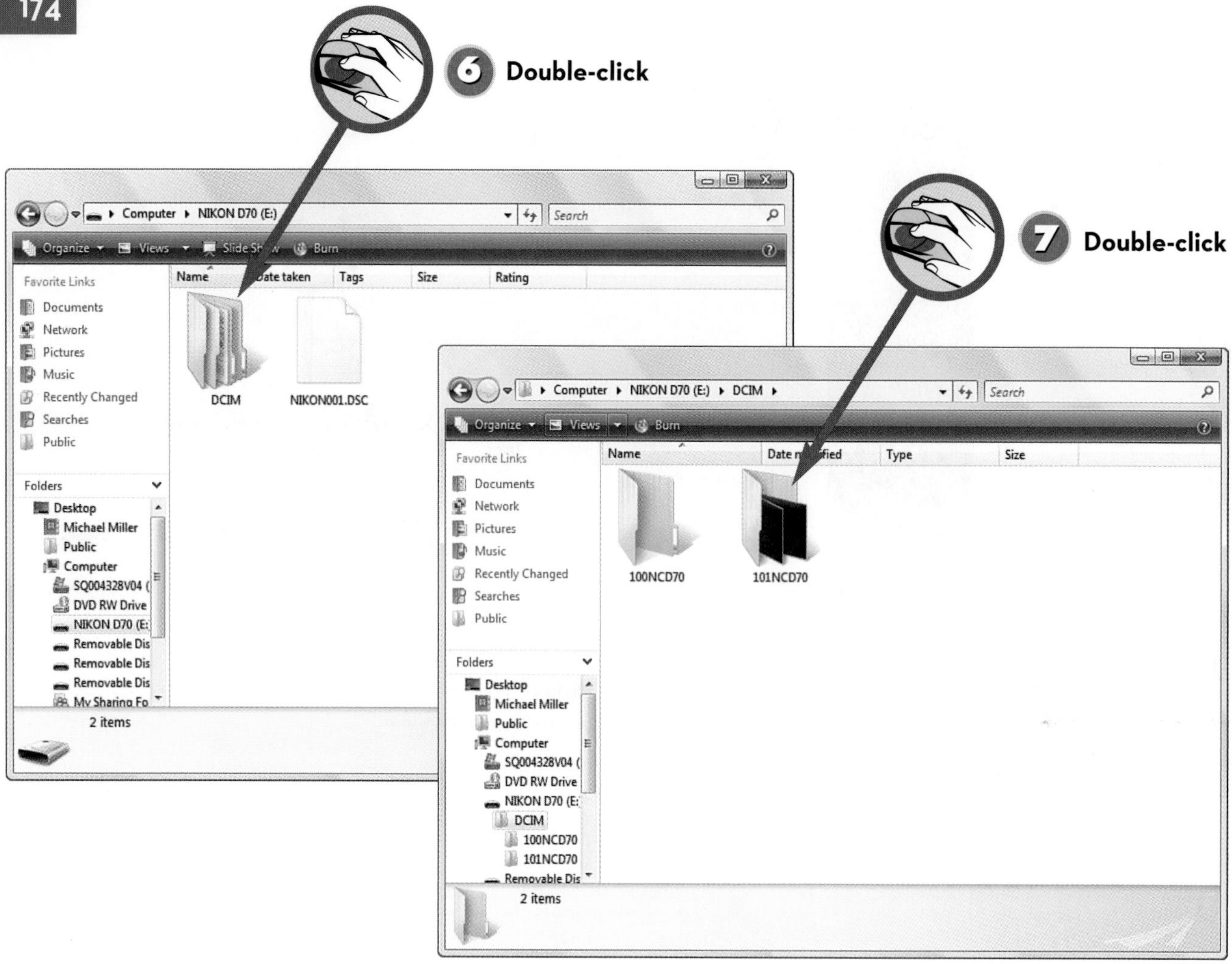

6 Double-click

7 Double-click

6. Double-click the **DCIM** folder. (The folder name may vary depending on your camera manufacturer.)
7. Double-click the appropriate subfolder within the DCIM folder to see your photos.

Continued

TIP

Different Folder Names

Some cameras might use a name other than DCIM for the main folder.

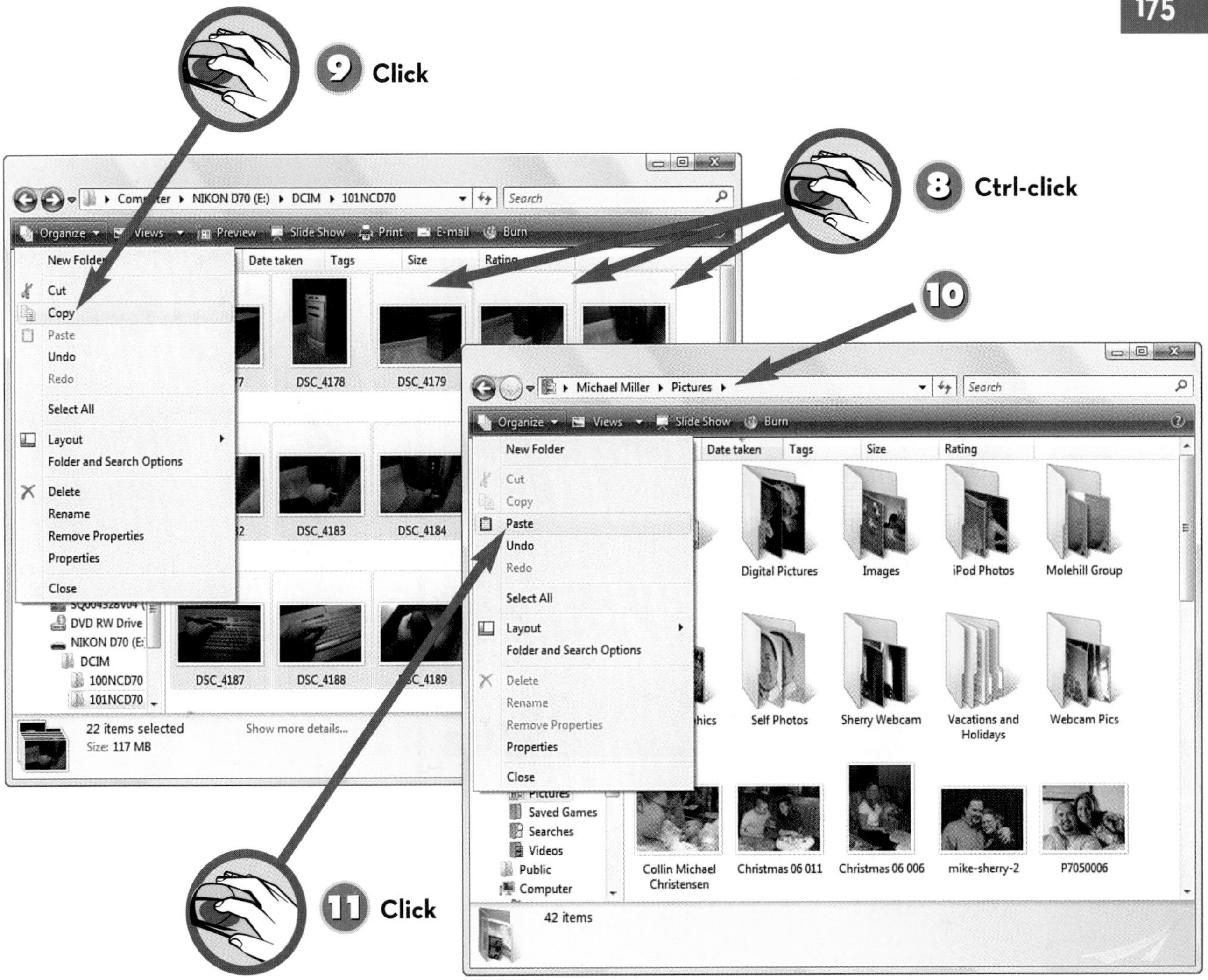

9 Click

8 Ctrl-click

10

11 Click

8 Hold down the **Ctrl** key and click each photo you want to transfer.

9 Click the **Organize** button and click **Copy**.

10 Navigate to your computer's hard disk and open the desired destination folder for the photos.

11 Click the **Organize** button and click **Paste**.

End

TIP

Buy a Bigger Card

To store more pictures (and higher-resolution pictures) on your camera, invest in a higher-capacity flash memory card. The bigger the card, the more photos you can store before transferring to your computer.

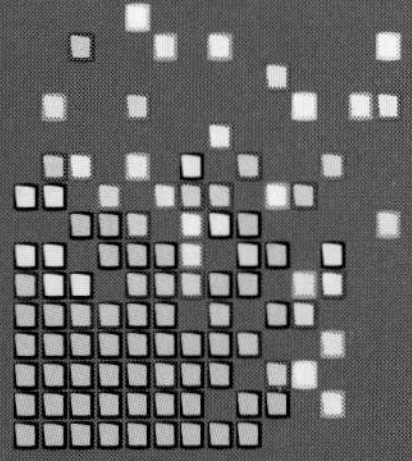

SCANNING A PICTURE

If your photos are of the old-fashioned print variety, you can still turn them into digital files using a flatbed scanner. To import photos from your scanner, you use Vista's Windows Photo Gallery application.

Start

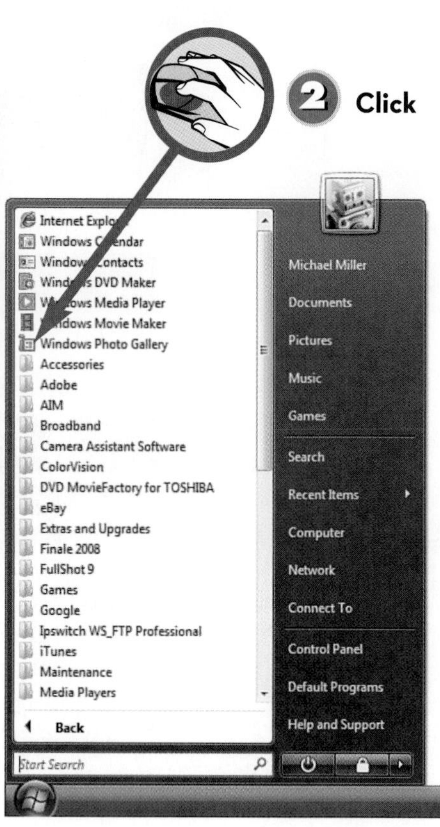

1. Open the scanner lid and place a photo on the scanner glass, face down.
2. Click the **Start** button, then click **All Programs**, **Windows Photo Gallery**.

Continued

TIP

Scan Automatically

Some scanners launch Windows Photo Gallery or some other utility automatically when you press the Scan button on the scanner.

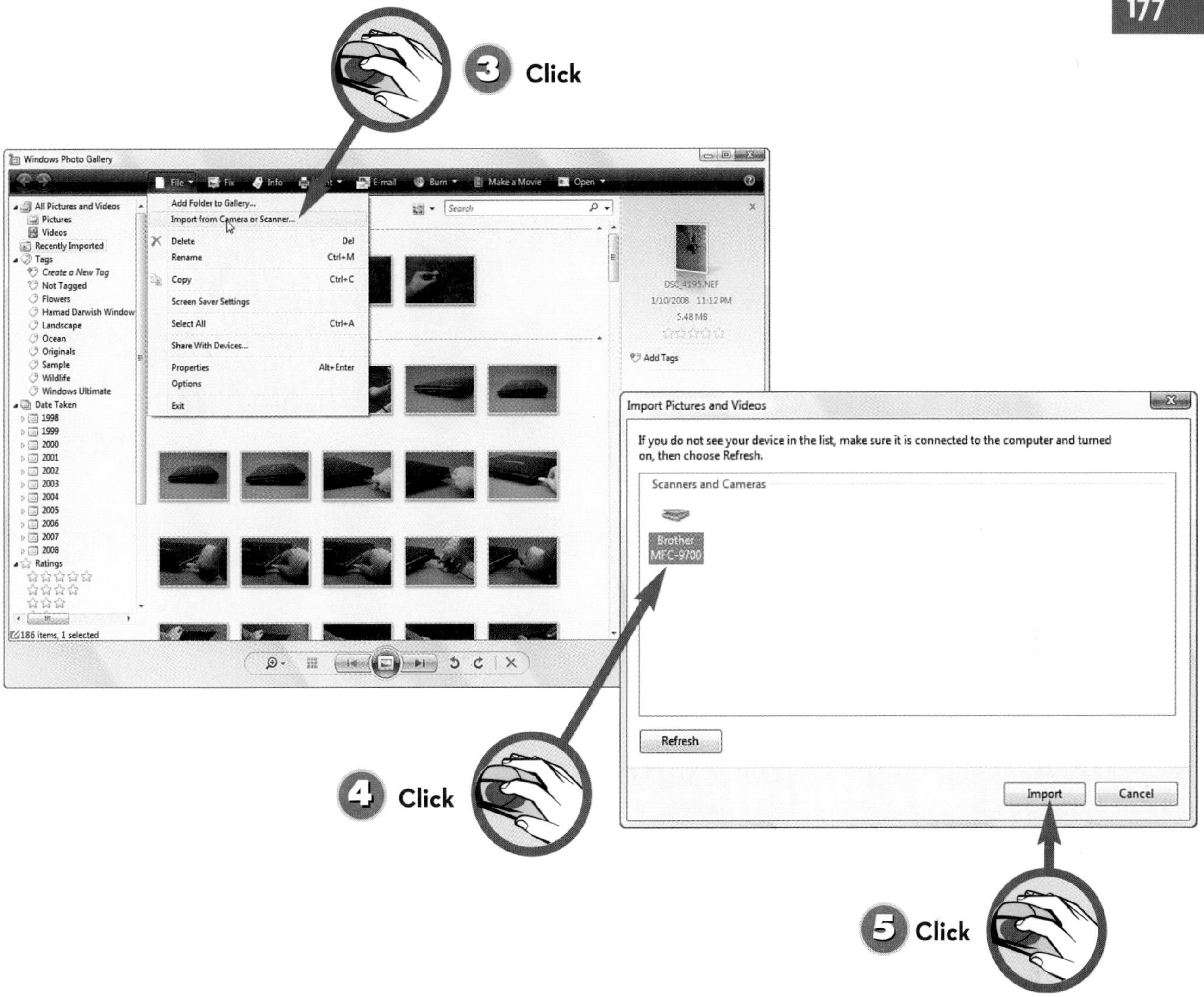

3. Click **File**, then click **Import from Camera or Scanner**.
4. Click the scanner you want to use.
5. Click **Import**.

Continued

NOTE

Other Programs for Scanning

You can also use other programs to import photos from your scanner. For example, Adobe Photoshop CS and Photoshop Elements both include an "acquire from scanner" feature.

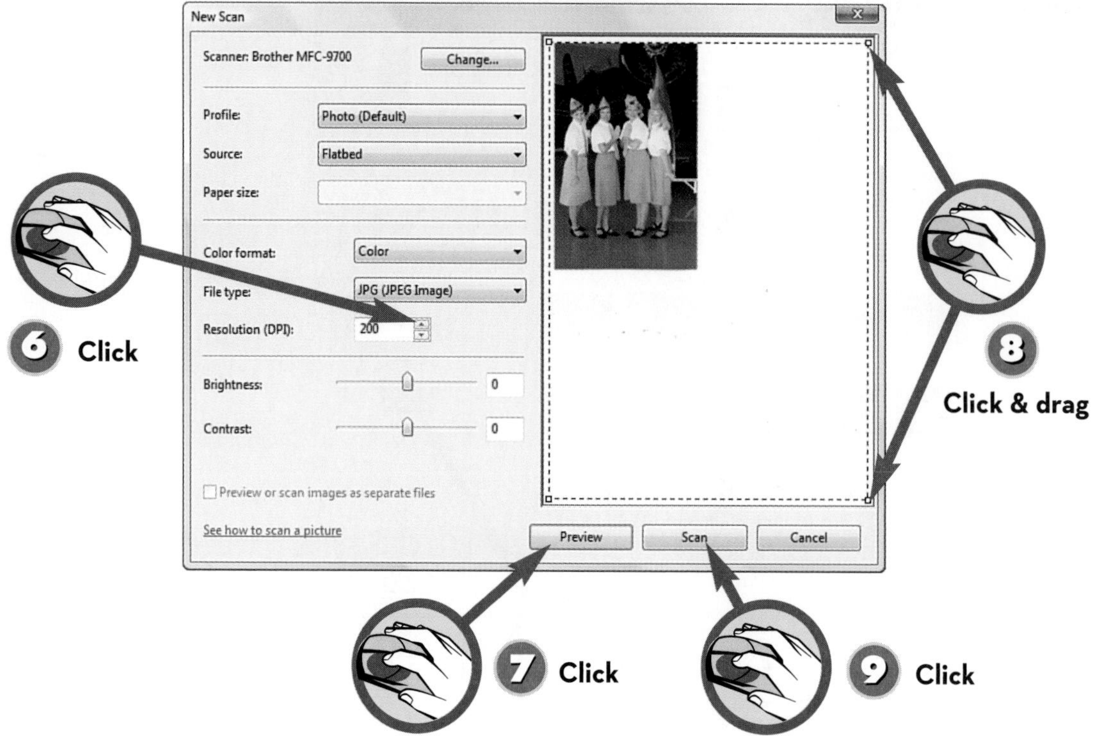

6. Click the **Resolution** list and select the desired scan resolution, in dots per inch (DPI).
7. Click the **Preview** button to preview how your scan will look.
8. Click and drag the border boxes to crop the scan to the size of the picture.
9. When you're satisfied with how your scan will look, click the **Scan** button.

Continued

—TIP—

Higher Resolution

By default, Windows scans your item at 150dpi (dots per inch). If you plan to print the photo, select a higher resolution—such as 300dpi.

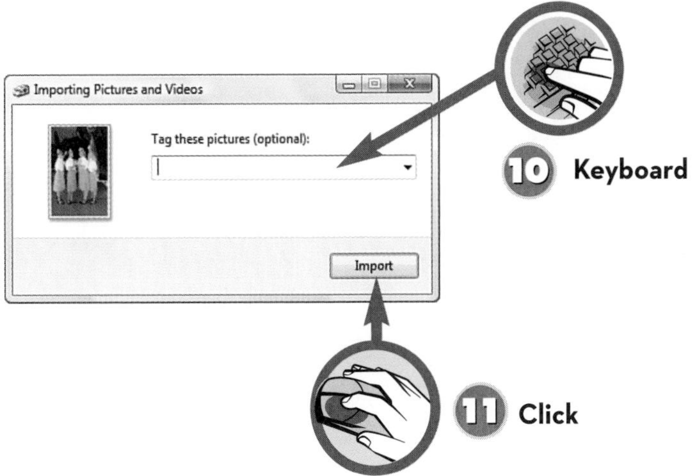

10 Enter any tags (keywords) you want to describe the scanned photo.

11 Click the **Import** button.

End

TIP

Reposition the Item

If you don't like the preview scan, reposition the item on your scanner and click the **Preview** button again to start a new scan.

VIEWING PHOTOS WITH WINDOWS PHOTO GALLERY

You can use Windows Photo Gallery to both view and edit your digital photos. You launch Windows Photo Gallery from the Windows Start menu or by double-clicking any photo in your Pictures folder.

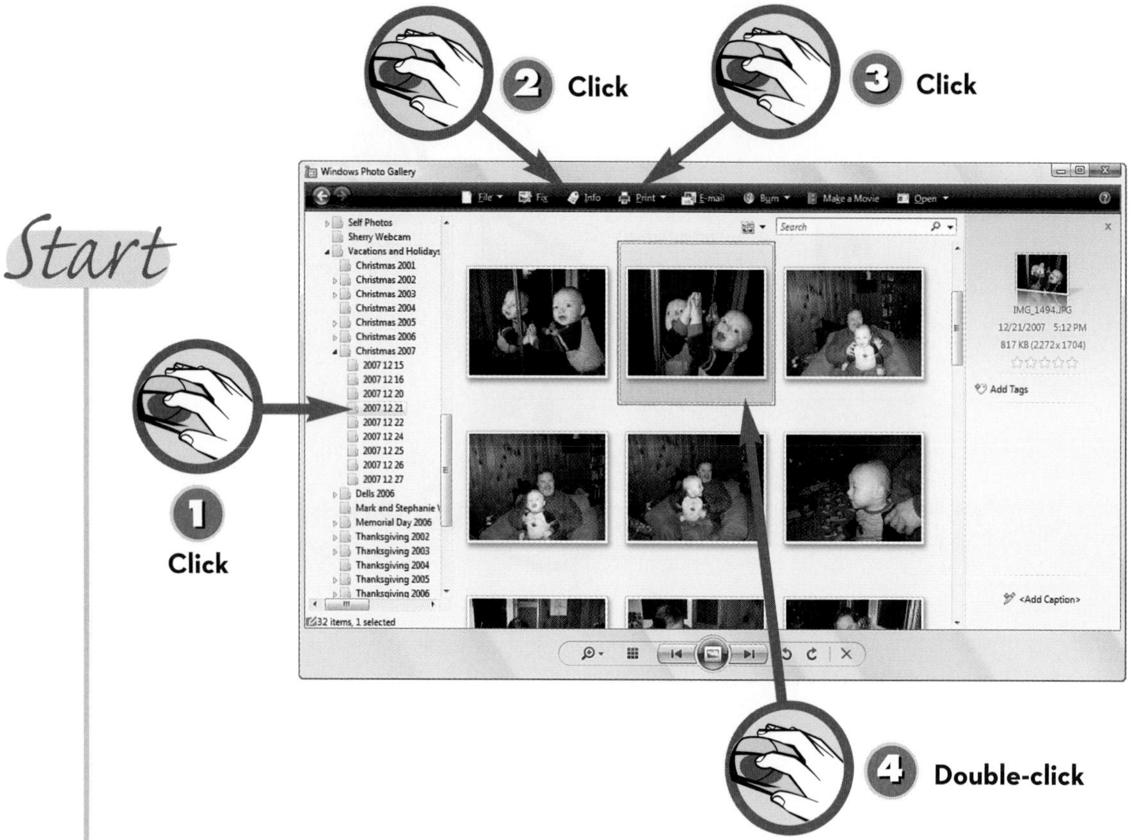

Start

1 Click

2 Click

3 Click

4 Double-click

1. Click any folder or subfolder in the Navigation pane to view the photos stored in that folder.
2. Click the **Info** button to view information about the selected photo in the Information pane.
3. Click the **Print** button to print a copy of the selected photo(s).
4. Double-click any photo to view it larger in the Content pane.

Continued

TIP

Organizing Your Photos

Use the Navigation pane on the left side of the Windows Photo Gallery window to organize photos by date taken, rating, tag (descriptive keyword), or folder location.

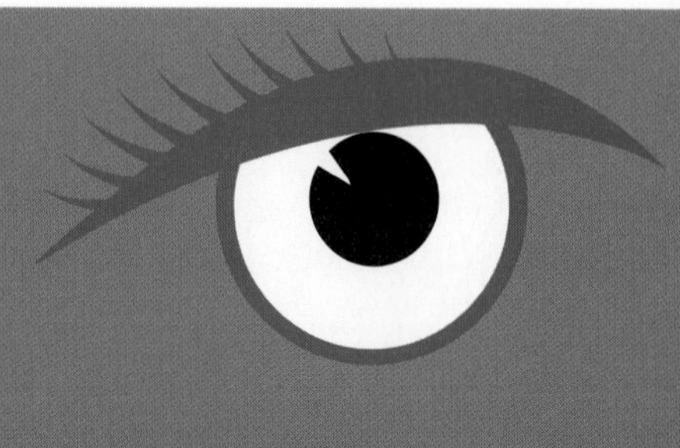

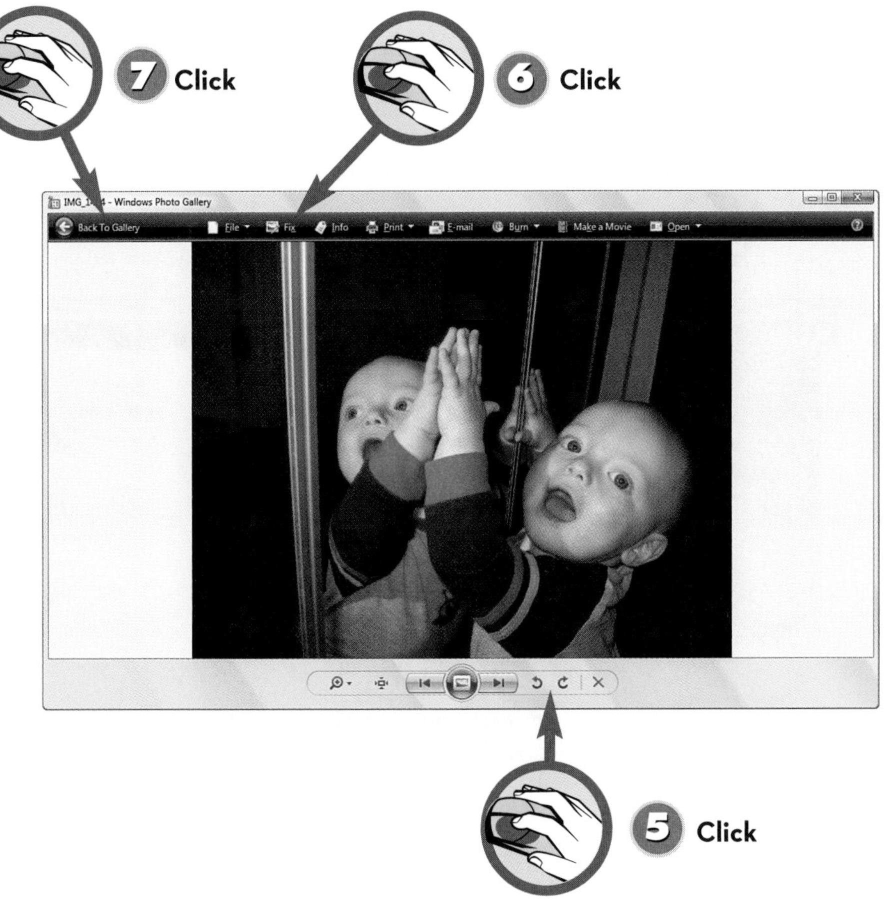

5 Click the left or right **Rotate** buttons to change the photo from landscape to portrait orientation.

6 Click the **Fix** button to edit the selected photo.

7 Click the **Back to Gallery** button to return to the thumbnail view of multiple photos.

End

TIP

Slide Show

You can also use Windows Photo Gallery to view your photos in a slide show. Just click the **Play Slide Show** button in the middle of the transport controls, at the bottom of the window.

CROPPING A PHOTO

One of the most common problems with digital photographs is poor composition, where the subject of the picture is either too far away or off center. You can fix this problem in Windows Photo Gallery by cropping unwanted areas out of the final picture.

Start

1. Click the **Fix** button.
2. Click **Crop Picture**.
3. Click and drag the corners of the onscreen box until the box frames the part of the area you want to keep.
4. Click the **Apply** button.

End

TIP

Crop for Prints

To crop to an exact size, perfect for photo prints, click the **Custom** button and select a print size from the list.

REMOVING RED EYE

Another common problem with pictures of people is red eye, which is sometimes caused by using your camera's built-in flash. Fortunately, Windows Photo Gallery has a tool that lets you quickly and easily fix all red-eye problems.

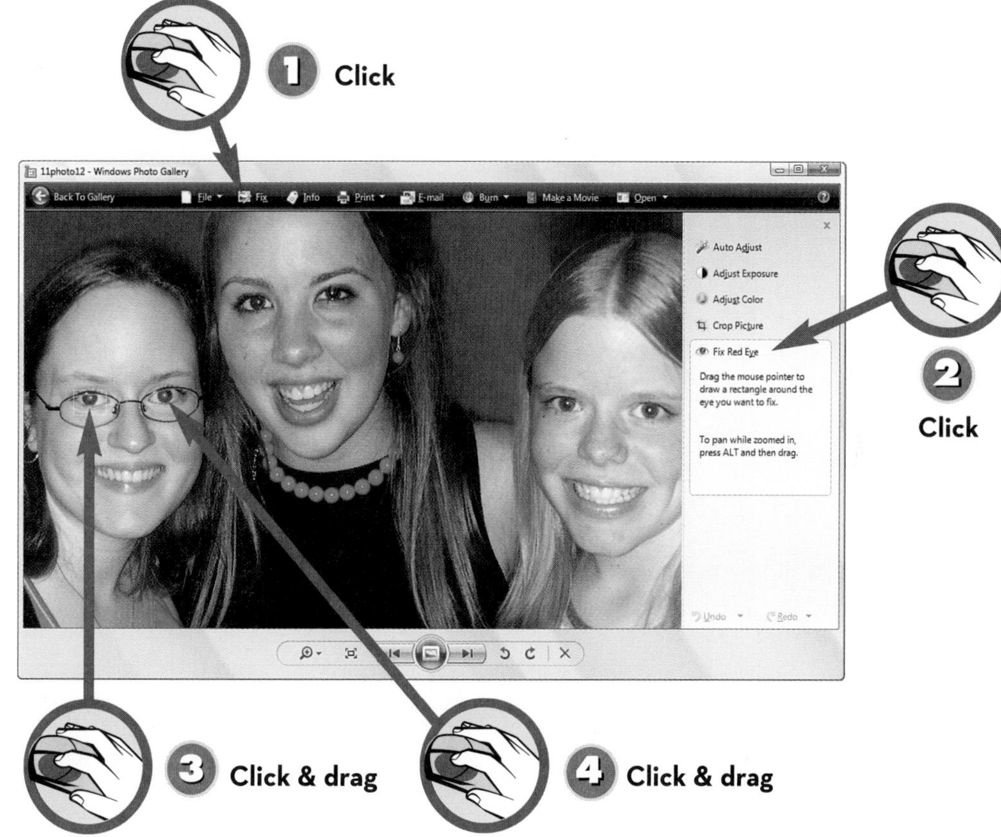

Start

1. Click the **Fix** button.
2. Click **Fix Red Eye**.
3. Click and drag the cursor to draw a rectangle around the first eye you want to fix.
4. Repeat step 3 for the other eye.

End

TIP

Other Photo-Editing Programs

Windows Photo Gallery is good because it's free, but you may need the more powerful editing tools found in other programs, such as Adobe Photoshop Elements (www.adobe.com), Paint Shop Pro Photo (www.corel.com), Picasa (picasa.google.com), and Roxio PhotoSuite (www.roxio.com).

ADJUSTING BRIGHTNESS AND CONTRAST

Many digital photos end up too light or dark, due to poor lighting. Fortunately, you can adjust the lightness of your photos using the Brightness and Contrast controls in Windows Photo Gallery.

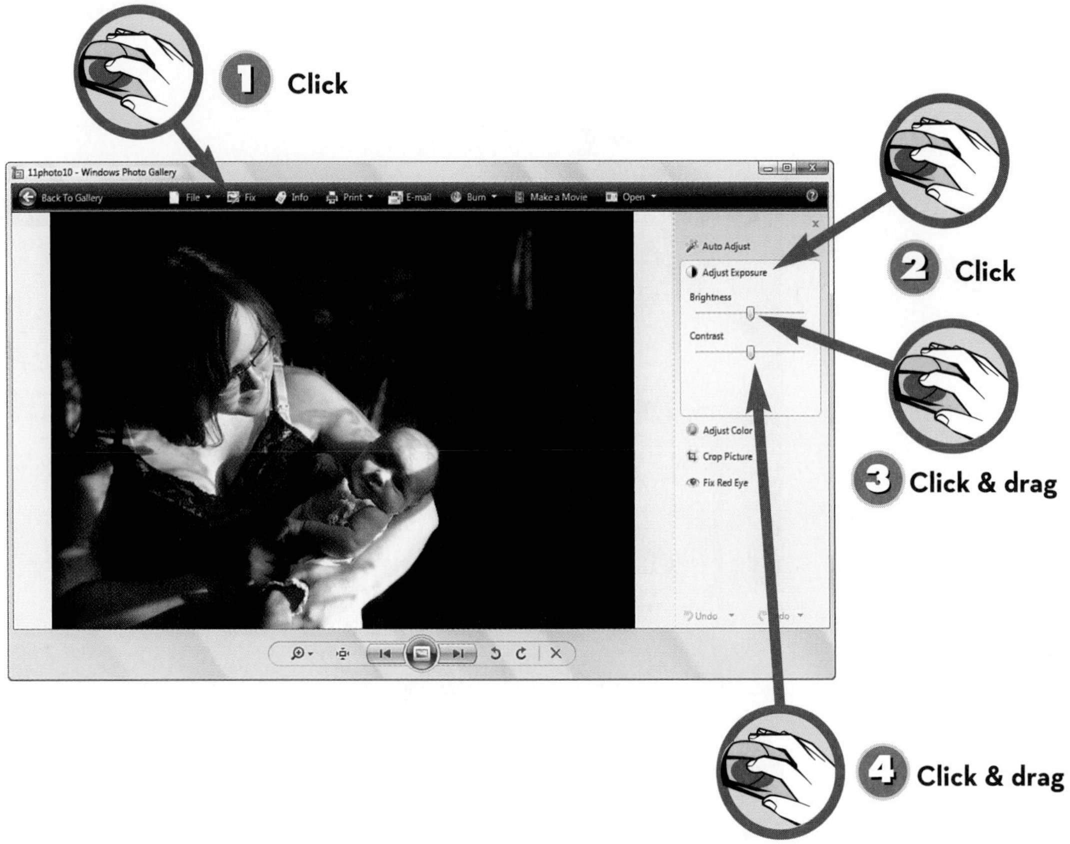

Start

1 Click

2 Click

3 Click & drag

4 Click & drag

1. Click the **Fix** button.
2. Click **Adjust Exposure**.
3. Click and drag the **Brightness** slider to make the picture darker or lighter.
4. Click and drag the **Contrast** slider to increase or decrease the picture's contrast level.

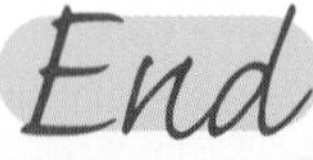

NOTE

Learn More in *Photopedia*

Learn more about taking and editing digital photos in my companion book, *Photopedia: The Ultimate Digital Photography Resource* (Michael Miller, Que, 2007).

ADJUSTING COLOR AND HUE

What do you do when the colors don't turn out right in a photograph? The answer is simple—use Windows Photo Gallery's Color Temperature, Tint, and Saturation controls to fix the problem.

Start

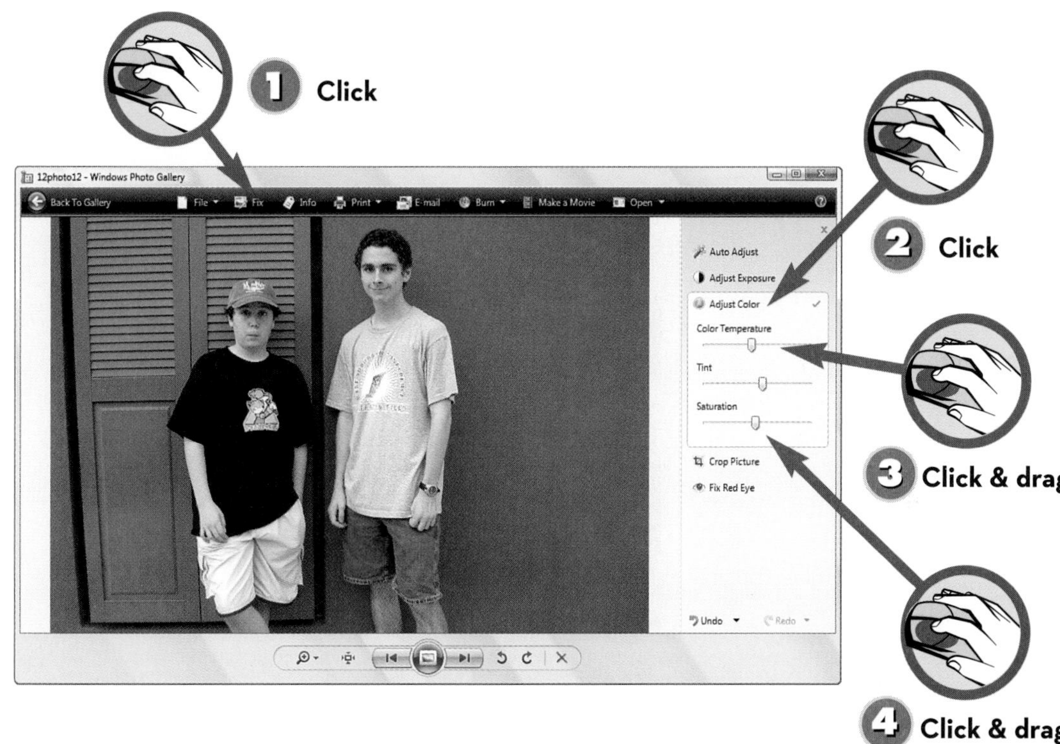

1. Click the **Fix** button.
2. Click **Adjust Color**.
3. Click and drag the **Color Temperature** slider to the left for cooler colors (more blue), or to the right for warmer colors (more orange).
4. Click and drag the **Saturation** slider to the left to decrease the amount of color in the photo, or to the right to increase the amount of color.

End

NOTE

Color and Lighting

Poor color is often caused by the type of lighting you use in your photos. Incandescent lighting often creates an orange cast, while fluorescent lighting creates a bluish-green cast.

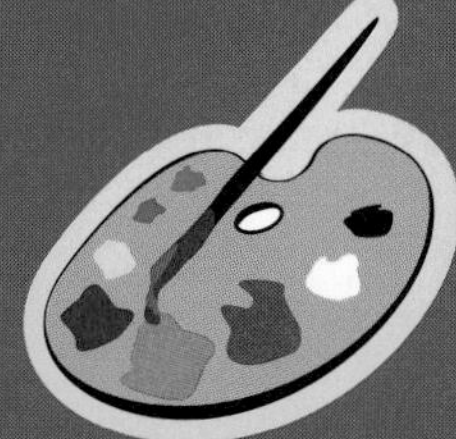

PRINTING A PHOTO

Any photo editing program will let you print your pictures from within the program. You can also print directly from Windows Photo Gallery.

Start

1. Click the pictures you want to print. (To select multiple pictures, hold down the **Ctrl** key while clicking.)
2. Click the **Print** button and click **Print**.

Continued

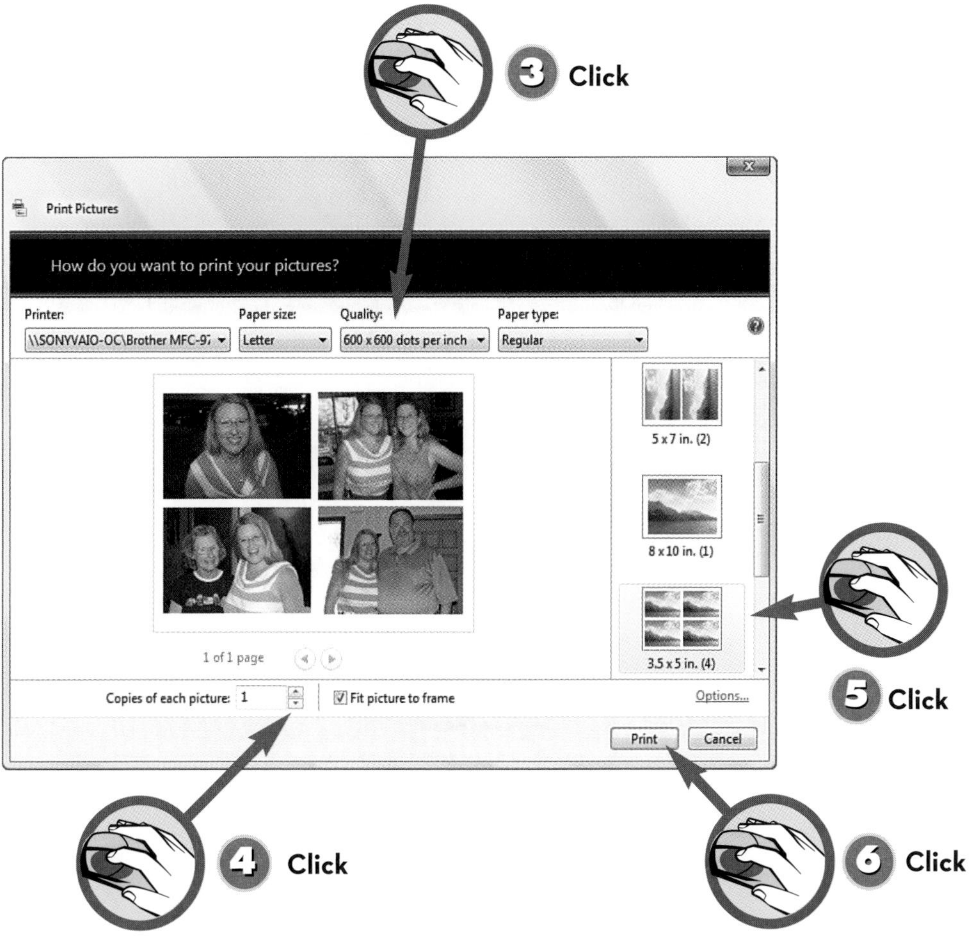

3. Click the **Quality** button and select the quality (DPI) of the print.
4. Select how many **Copies** you want to make of each picture.
5. Scroll down the right-hand list and select what size and type of prints you want—full page photo, two 4" x 6" prints, four 3.5" x 5" prints, and so forth.
6. Click the **Print** button.

End

TIP

Different Sizes

You can choose to print your photos full-page, at a specific print size, or as multiple prints on a single contact sheet.

ORDERING PRINTS ONLINE

If you don't have your own photo-quality printer, you can use a professional photo-processing service to print your photos. You can go directly to one of the Internet's many photo-processing sites, or you can order prints from within Windows Photo Gallery.

Start

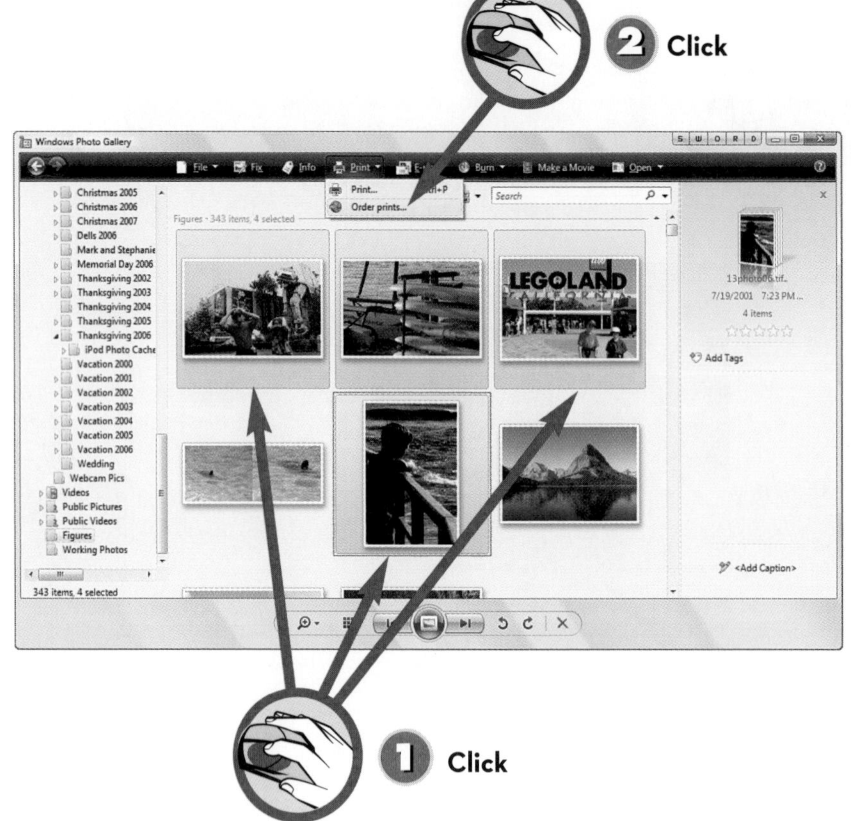

1. Click the pictures you want to print. (To select multiple pictures, hold down the **Ctrl** key while clicking.)
2. Click the **Print** button and click **Order Prints**.

Continued

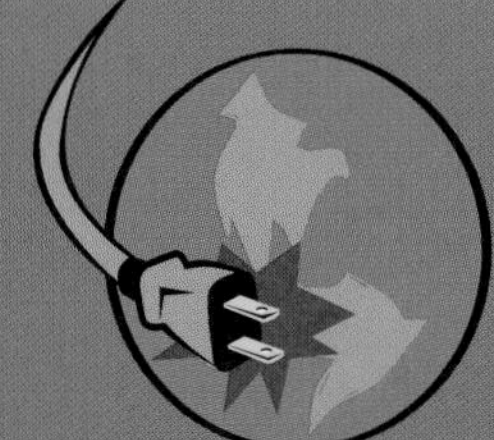

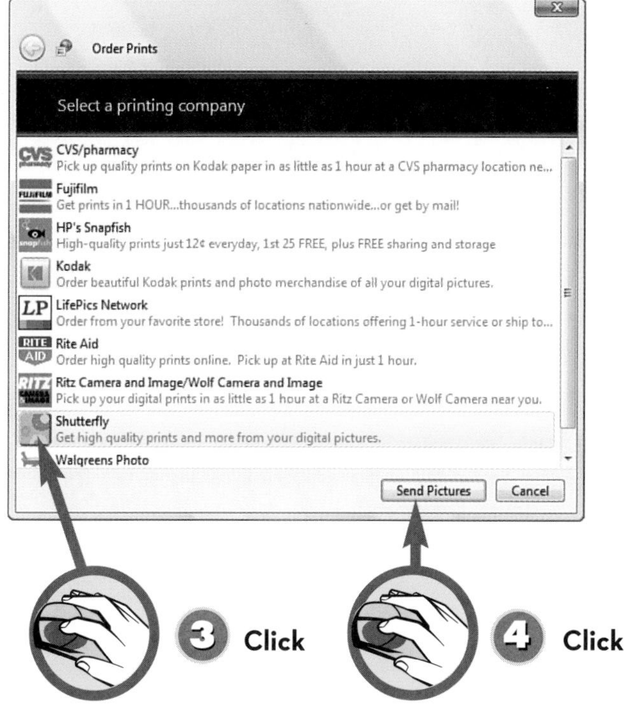

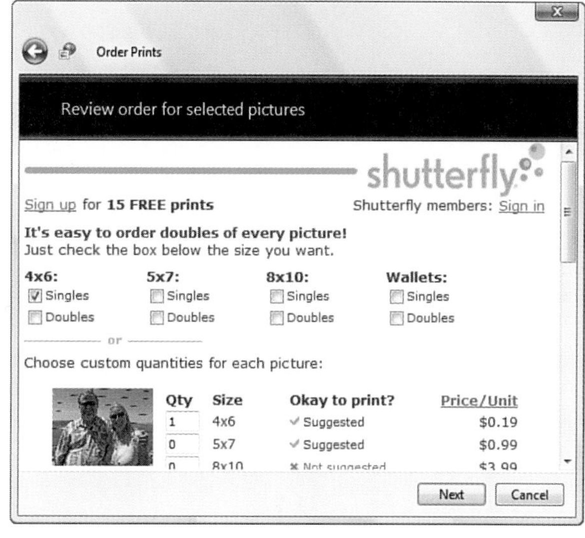

3. Windows now displays a list of online printing companies. Click the company you want to use.
4. Click **Send Pictures**.
5. Complete the rest of the online ordering process from the site you selected. (Each site has its own distinct process!)

End

TIP

Other Online Photo Sites

You can also order prints directly from many online photo sites, including Kodak EasyShare Gallery (www.kodakgallery.com), Shutterfly (www.shutterfly.com), and Snapfish (www.snapfish.com).

part 11

ADDING NEW DEVICES TO YOUR SYSTEM

If you just purchased a brand-new, right-out-of-the-box personal computer, it probably came equipped with all the components you could ever desire—or so you think. At some point in the future, however, you might want to expand your system—by adding a second printer, a scanner, a PC camera, or something equally new and exciting.

Everything that's hooked up to your PC is connected via some type of *port*. Airport is simply an interface between your PC and another device, either internally (inside your PC's system unit) or externally (via a connector on the back of the system unit). Different types of hardware connect via different types of ports.

COMPUTER CONNECTIONS

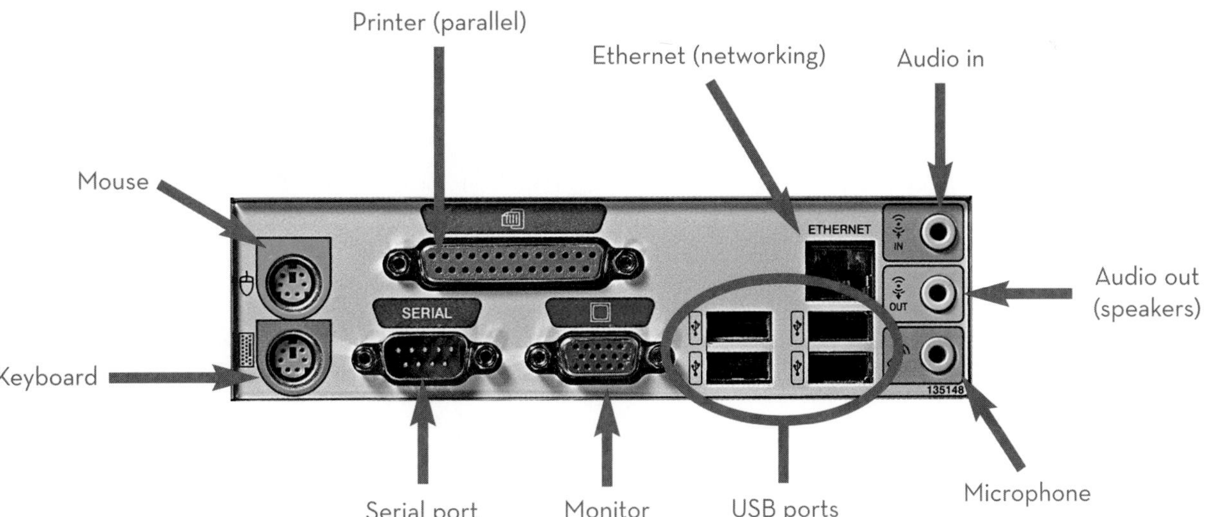

ADDING A NEW EXTERNAL DEVICE VIA USB

The most common external connector today is the USB port; almost every type of peripheral comes in a USB version. USB is popular because it's so easy to use. When you're connecting a USB device, not only do you not have to open your PC's case, but you also don't even have to turn off your system when you add the new device.

Start

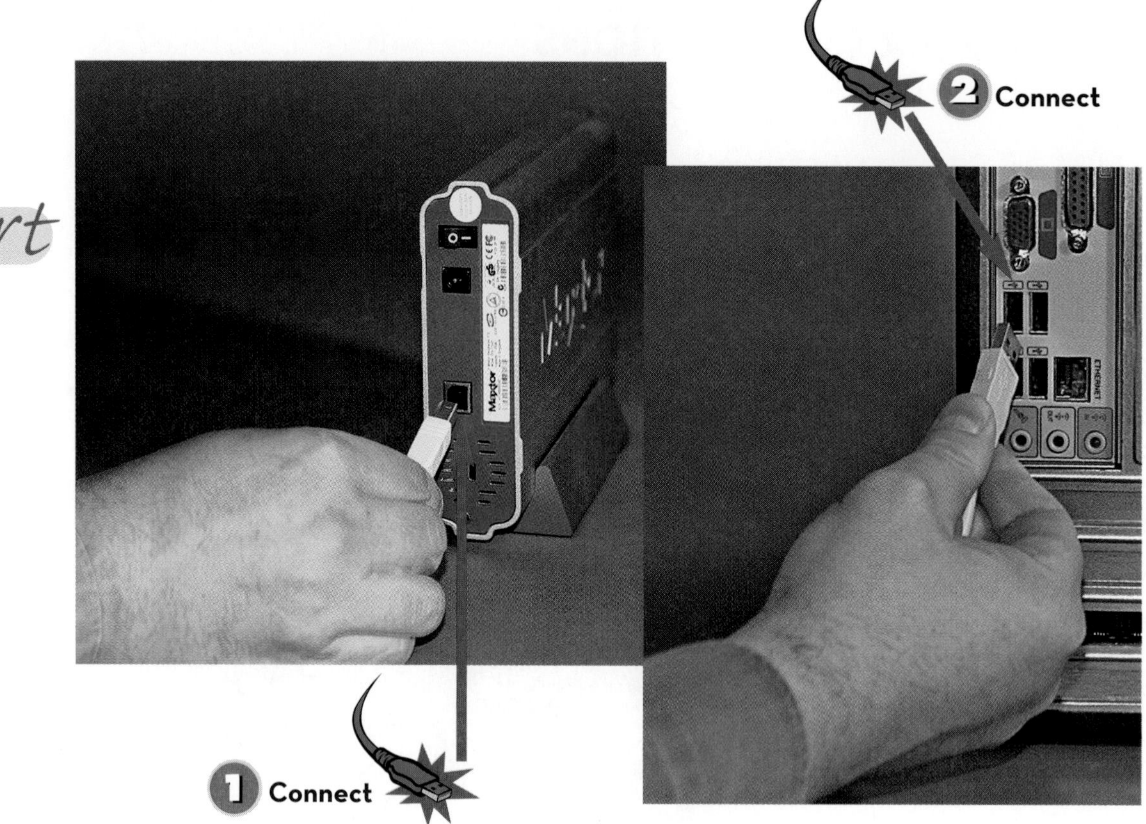

1. Connect one end of the USB cable to your new device.
2. Connect the other end of the cable to a free USB port on your PC.

Continued

TIP

Follow Directions

As easy as most USB devices are to connect, you should still read the device's instructions and follow the manufacturer's directions for installation.

NOTE

FireWire Connections

FireWire is a slightly faster connection than USB, which makes it ideal for connecting devices that move a lot of data, such as hard drives and camcorders. Connecting a device via FireWire is similar to connecting it via USB.

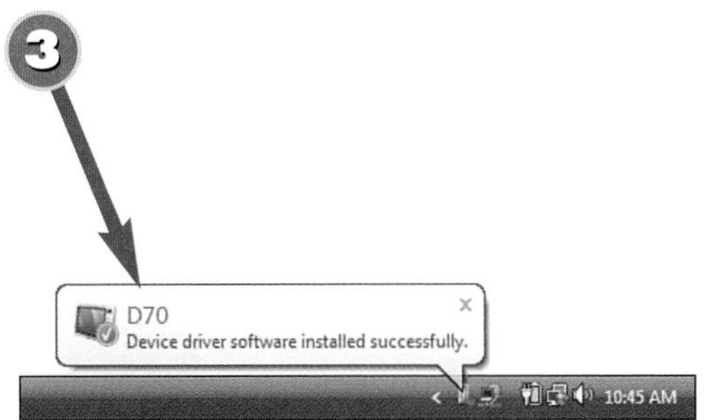

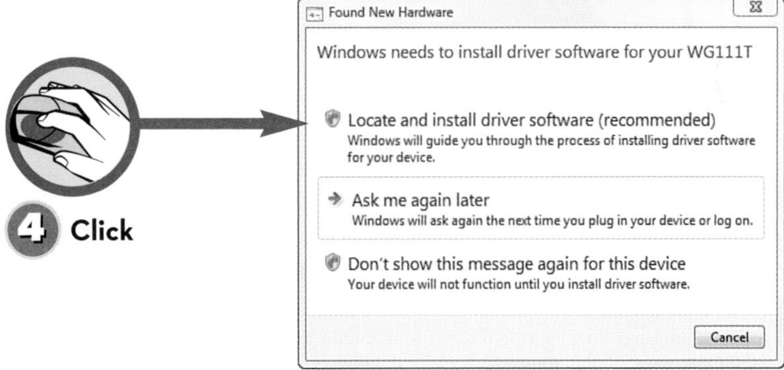

3 Windows should automatically recognize the new peripheral and install the necessary drivers. An onscreen message will notify you when the installation is complete.

4 If Windows can't automatically install the device, you'll see the Found New Hardware window. Click **Locate and Install Driver Software** and follow the onscreen instructions from here.

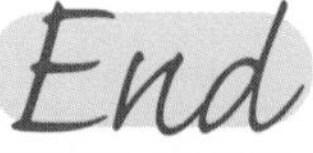

CAUTION

Install Before Connecting?

Windows normally detects a new USB device when you connect it, and then installs the driver automatically. However, some devices require you to install the driver before connecting the device. Again—make sure you read the directions before you install!

TIP

USB Hubs

If you connect too many USB devices, you can run out of USB connectors on your PC. If that happens, buy an add-on USB hub, which lets you plug multiple USB peripherals in to a single USB port.

ADDING NEW INTERNAL HARDWARE

Adding an internal device—usually through a plug-in card—is slightly more difficult than adding an external device, primarily because you have to use a screwdriver and get under the hood of your system unit. Other than the extra screwing and plugging, however, the process is pretty much the same as with external devices.

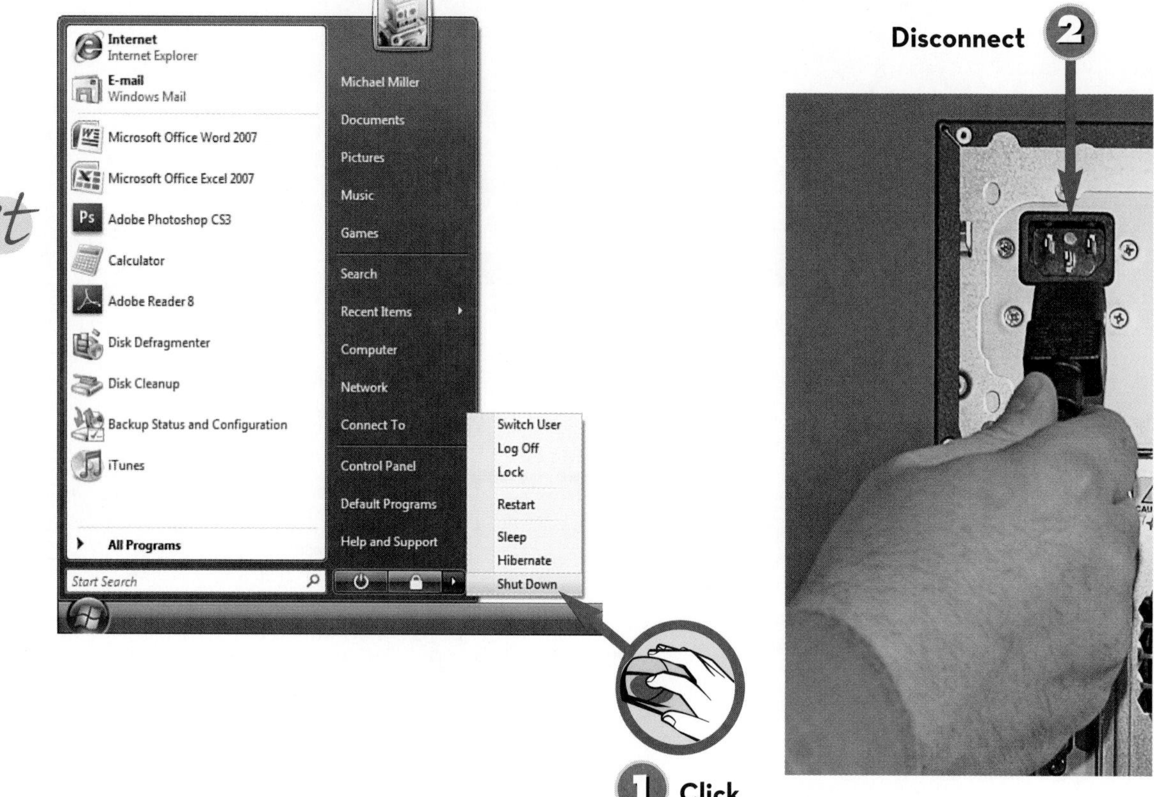

1. Click the **Start** button, click the right-arrow button, and then click **Shut Down**.
2. Unplug the power cable from the back of your system unit.

Continued

3 Unscrew the screws attaching the case of your system unit.

4 Remove the system unit's case.

Continued

CAUTION

Turn Off the Power!

Never touch anything inside your computer while the power is still on and connected. Always turn off your PC and unplug the power cord, just to be safe.

NOTE

Device Drivers

A *device driver* is a small software program that lets your PC control a given device. If Windows doesn't include a particular driver, you typically can find the driver on the installation CD or on the manufacturer's website.

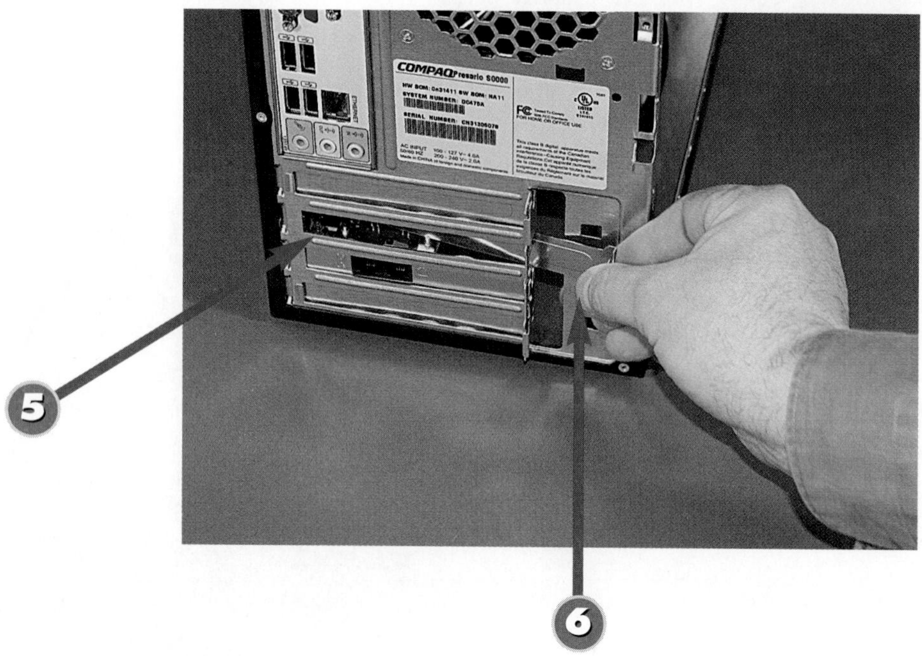

5. Find an open card slot inside the system unit that fits the type of card you'll be installing.
6. Unscrew and remove the cover plate for the open slot. (Save the screw.)

Continued

NOTE

Common Upgrades

The most common types of internal computer upgrades are sound cards, video cards, and networking cards. You can also add cards to provide additional ports for your system—USB, FireWire, serial, or parallel.

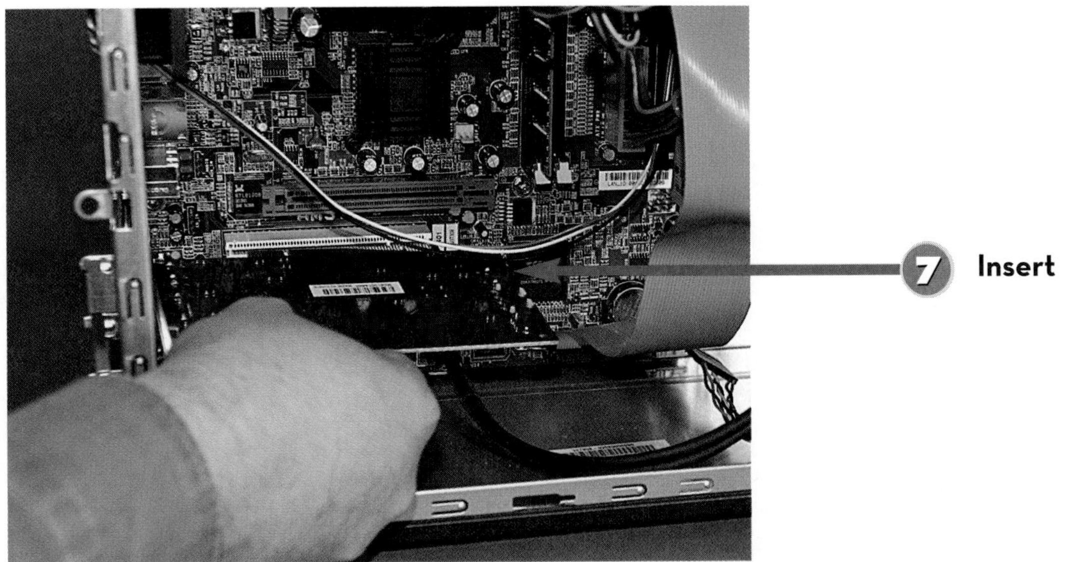

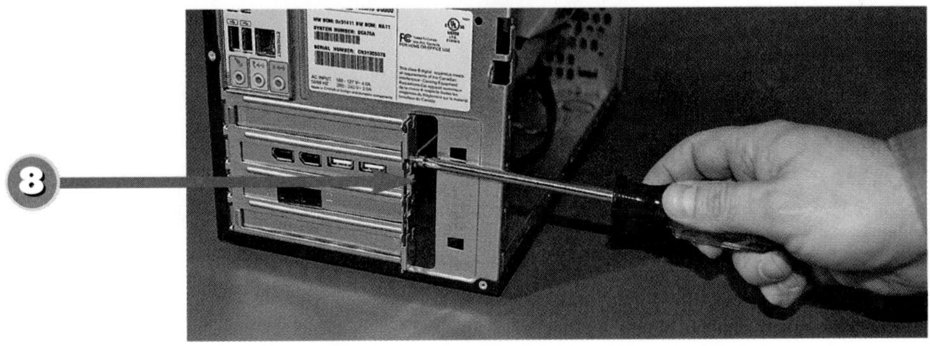

7. Insert the new card into the open slot, making sure it's firmly seated.
8. Screw the card into place.

Continued

CAUTION

Avoid Electrostatic Shock

You should avoid touching any of the sensitive components inside your PC because you might transfer a damaging electrostatic shock. You can minimize this risk by wearing an antistatic wrist band.

9 Put the case back on the system unit.

10 Screw the case back together.

Continued

TIP

Test It Before You Finish It

You probably want to see whether the new component configures and works properly before you close your system unit. For that reason, you might want to leave the case off until you're convinced everything is working okay and you don't need to do any more fiddling around inside your PC.

CAUTION

Downloading New Drivers

If your new device doesn't appear to work, you might have to download updated device drivers from the manufacturer's website.

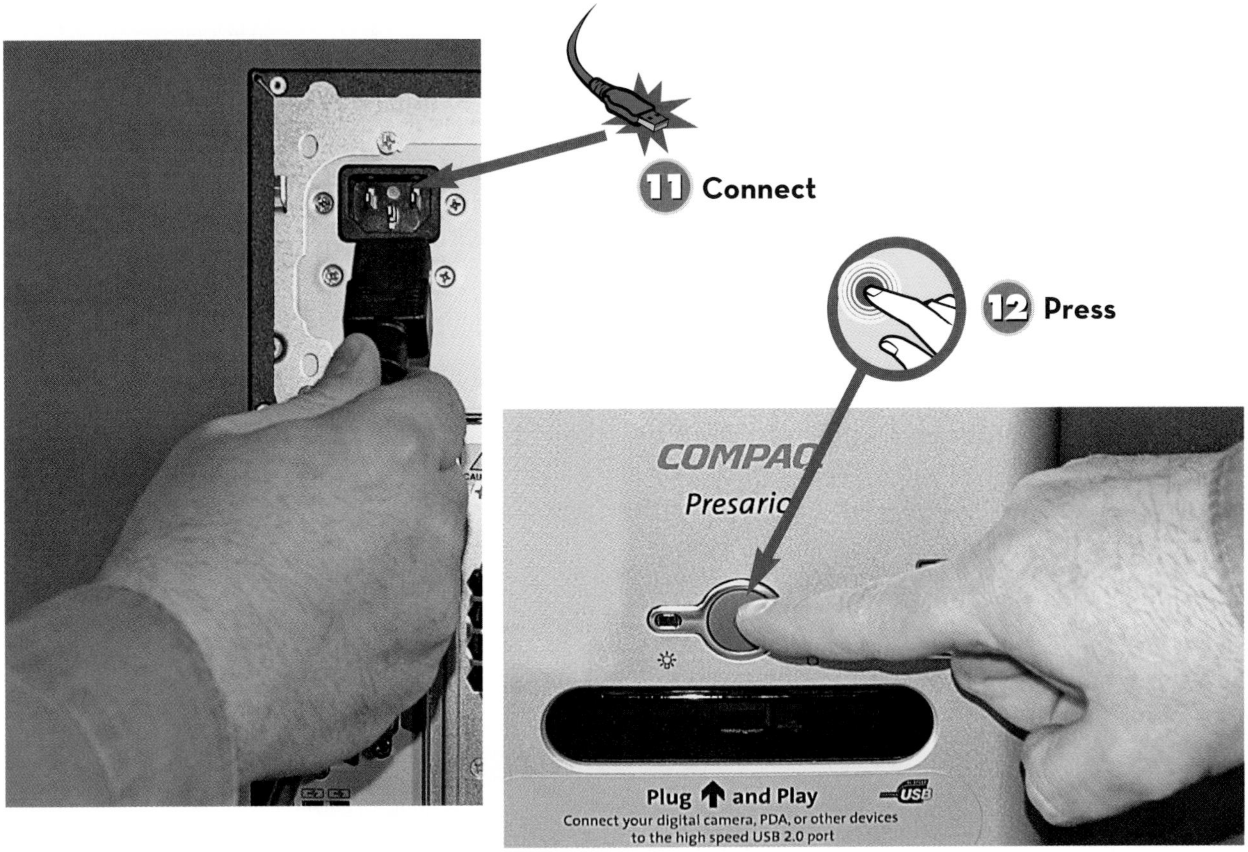

11 Reattach the power cable to the system unit.

12 Turn your computer back on. As Windows starts, it should recognize the new device and either install the proper drivers automatically or ask you to supply the device drivers (via CD-ROM).

End

TIP

Installation Programs

Some peripherals come with their own installation programs either on CD or floppy disk. Always follow the manufacturer's instructions when installing a new device.

part 12

PROTECTING YOUR COMPUTER

When you connect your PC to the Internet, you open up a whole new world of adventure and information for you and your family. Unfortunately, you also open up a new world of potential dangers—viruses, spam, computer attacks, and more.

Fortunately, it's easy to protect your computer and your family from these dangers. All you need are a few software utilities—and a lot of common sense!

To track your PC's security, open the Windows **Control Panel** and select **Security**, then **Security Center**. The Security Center will tell you what steps you need to take to better protect your system.

WINDOWS SECURITY CENTER

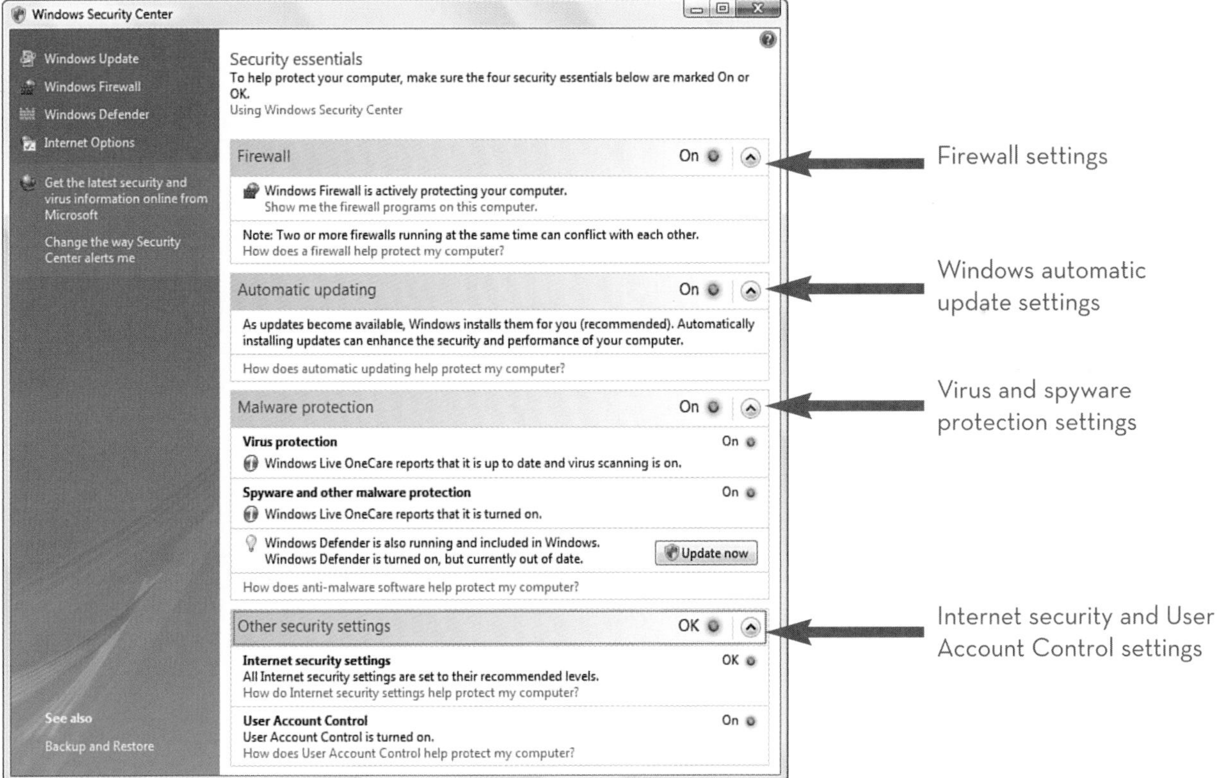

DEFENDING AGAINST COMPUTER ATTACKS WITH WINDOWS FIREWALL

Connecting to the Internet is a two-way street. Not only can your PC access other computers online, but other computers can also access *your* PC—to access your private data or damage your system hardware and software. You protect against attacks with a firewall program, such as the Windows Firewall in Windows Vista.

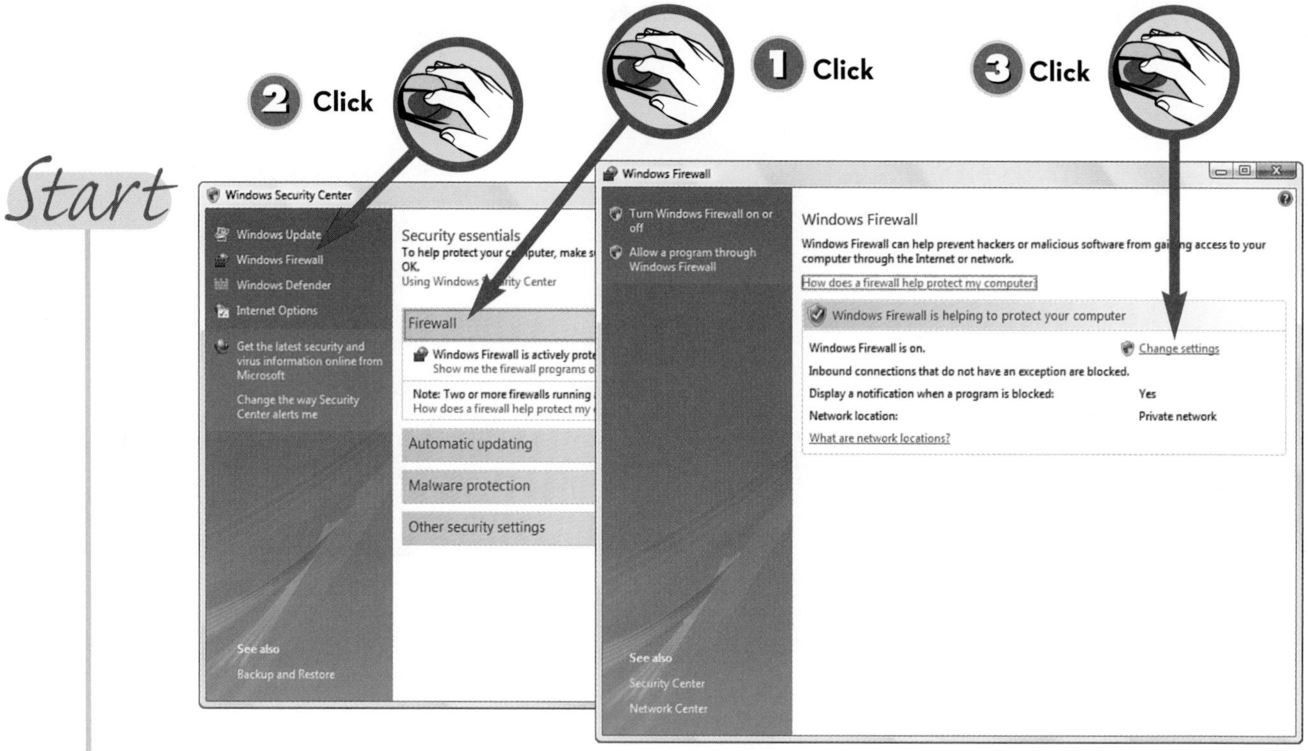

Start

1 From the Security Center, click **Firewall**. This displays the status of currently installed firewall programs.

2 To turn on Windows Firewall, click **Windows Firewall**.

3 Click **Change Settings**.

Continued

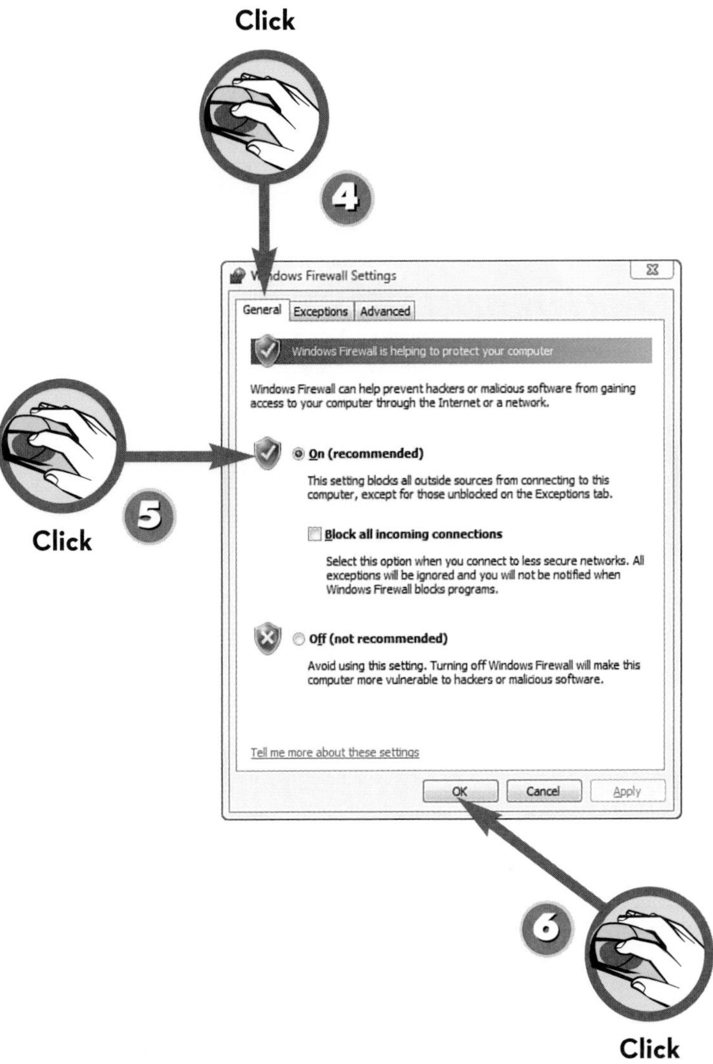

4. Click the **General** tab.
5. Check the **On** option.
6. Click **OK**.

End

TIP

Other Firewall Programs

Many third-party firewalls offer more protection than the Windows Firewall. These programs include McAfee Total Protection (www.mcafee.com), Norton Internet Security (www.symantec.com), Windows Live OneCare (onecare.live.com), and ZoneAlarm Internet Security Suite (www.zonealarm.com).

REMOVING SPYWARE WITH WINDOWS DEFENDER

Spyware programs install themselves on your computer, typically without your knowledge, and then surreptitiously send information about the way you use your PC to some interested third party—to serve advertising or for other, more nefarious purposes. You can protect your system from spyware and remove spyware from your computer by using an anti-spyware program, such as Microsoft's Windows Defender.

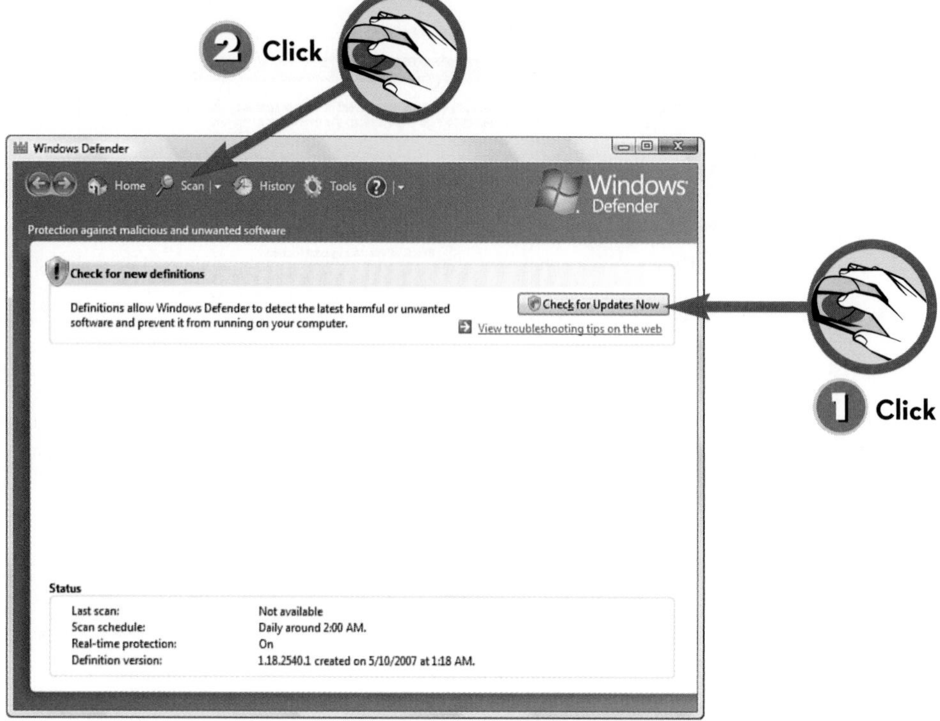

1. To work properly, Windows Defender must be kept updated with the latest list of spyware definitions. To download new definitions, click the **Check for Updates Now** button.
2. To manually scan your system for spyware, click **Scan**.

Continued

TIP

Download Windows Defender

Windows Defender is a free program. You can download it from www.microsoft.com/athome/security/spyware/software/.

TIP

Other Anti-Spyware Utilities

Other popular anti-spyware utilities include Ad-Aware (www.lavasoftusa.com), AVG Anti-Spyware (free.grisoft.com/doc/download-free-anti-spyware/), and Spybot Search & Destroy (www.safer-networking.org).

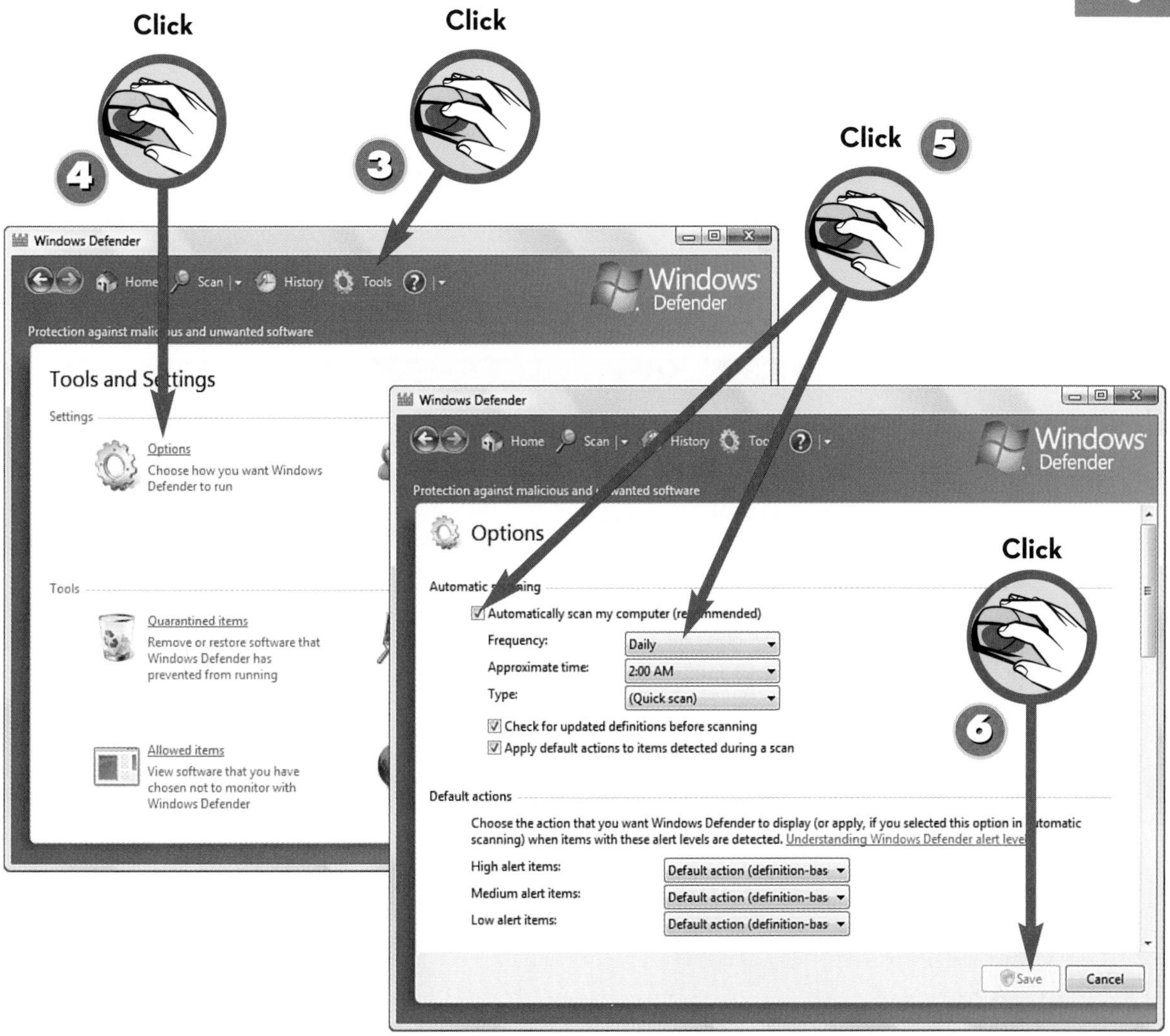

3. To configure Windows Defender for automatic operation, click **Tools**.
4. Click **Options**.
5. Check **Automatically Scan My Computer** and select a frequency and time for the scan.
6. Click **Save**.

End

CAUTION

Avoid File Sharing Networks

Common sources of spyware are files downloaded from peer-to-peer file sharing networks. When you download the software used to download music and movie files, you often download a spyware program, too.

TIP

Other Defender Tools

Windows Defender includes several useful system tools, including System Explorer (monitors all software running), Quarantined Items (view items Defender has stopped from running), and Allowed Items (choose items not to monitor).

PROTECTING AGAINST COMPUTER VIRUSES WITH WINDOWS LIVE ONECARE

A *computer virus* is a malicious software program designed to do damage to your computer system by deleting files or even taking over your PC to launch attacks on other systems. You can protect against computer viruses by using an antivirus program, such as Windows Live OneCare.

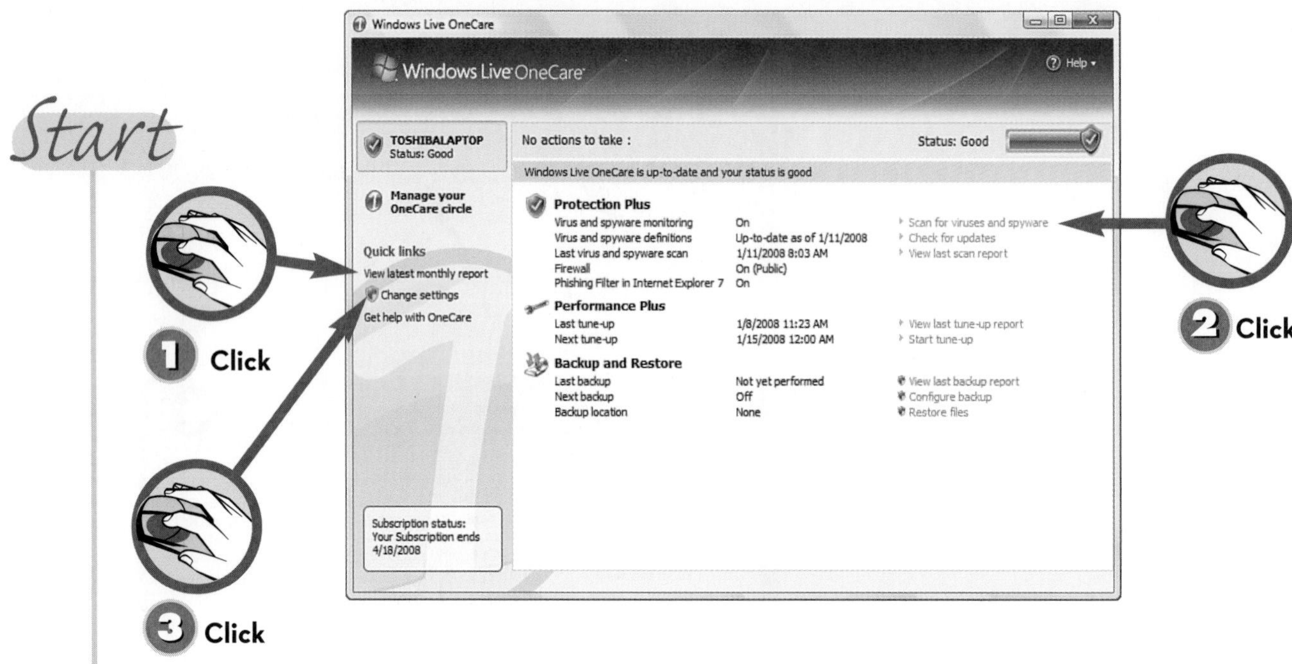

1. The main OneCare screen informs you of your system's security status. To view a report of your system's status, click **View Latest Monthly Report**.
2. To perform a manual virus scan, click **Scan for Viruses and Spyware**.
3. To configure OneCare to perform automatic virus scans, click **Change Settings**.

Continued

TIP

Subscribe to Windows Live OneCare

Windows Live OneCare is available via subscription; a three-PC subscription costs $49.95/year. Learn more and download the software at onecare.live.com.

TIP

More Than Just Antivirus

Windows Live OneCare is more than just an antivirus program. It also functions as an anti-spyware program, performs automatic system tune-ups, and features its own firewall—more robust than the normal Windows Firewall.

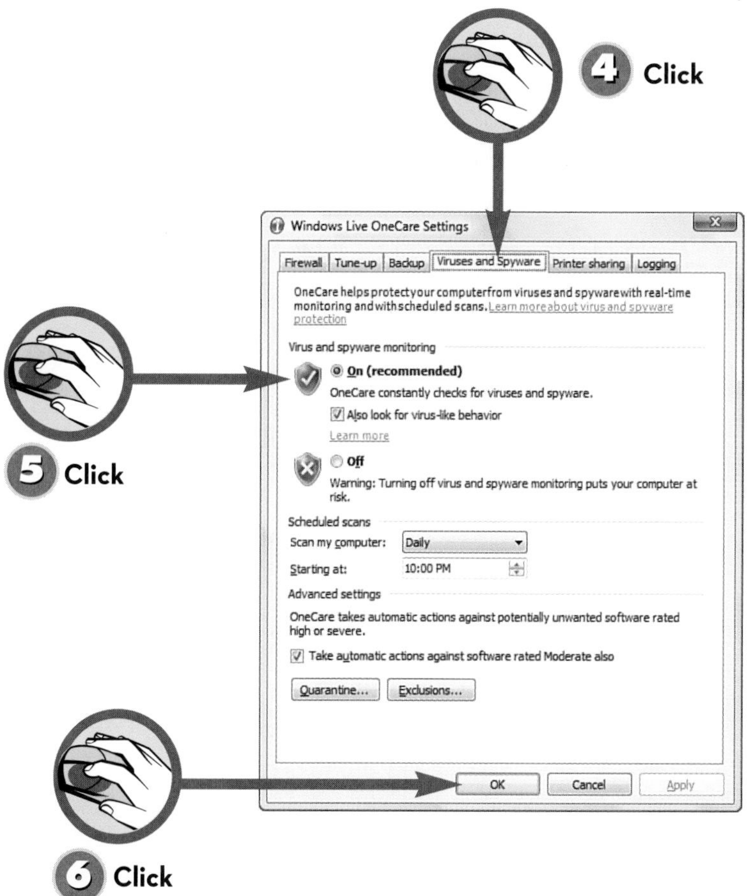

4. Click the **Viruses and Spyware** tab.
5. Check **On** for **Virus and Spyware Monitoring**.
6. Click **OK**.

End

CAUTION

Email Attachments Are Bad!

The single largest source of computer viruses is infected email attachments. If you remember nothing else from this chapter, remember this: *Never open an unexpected file attachment*, even if it's from someone you know. Period!

TIP

Other Antivirus Programs

Other popular antivirus programs include AVG AntiVirus (free.grisoft.com), McAfee VirusScan Plus (www.mcafee.com), Norton AntiVirus (www.symantec.com), and ZoneAlarm Antivirus (www.zonealarm.com).

FIGHTING EMAIL SPAM IN WINDOWS MAIL

If you're like most users, well over half the messages delivered to your email inbox are unsolicited, unauthorized, and unwanted—in other words, *spam*. Fortunately, most email programs—including Windows Mail—include built-in spam filters.

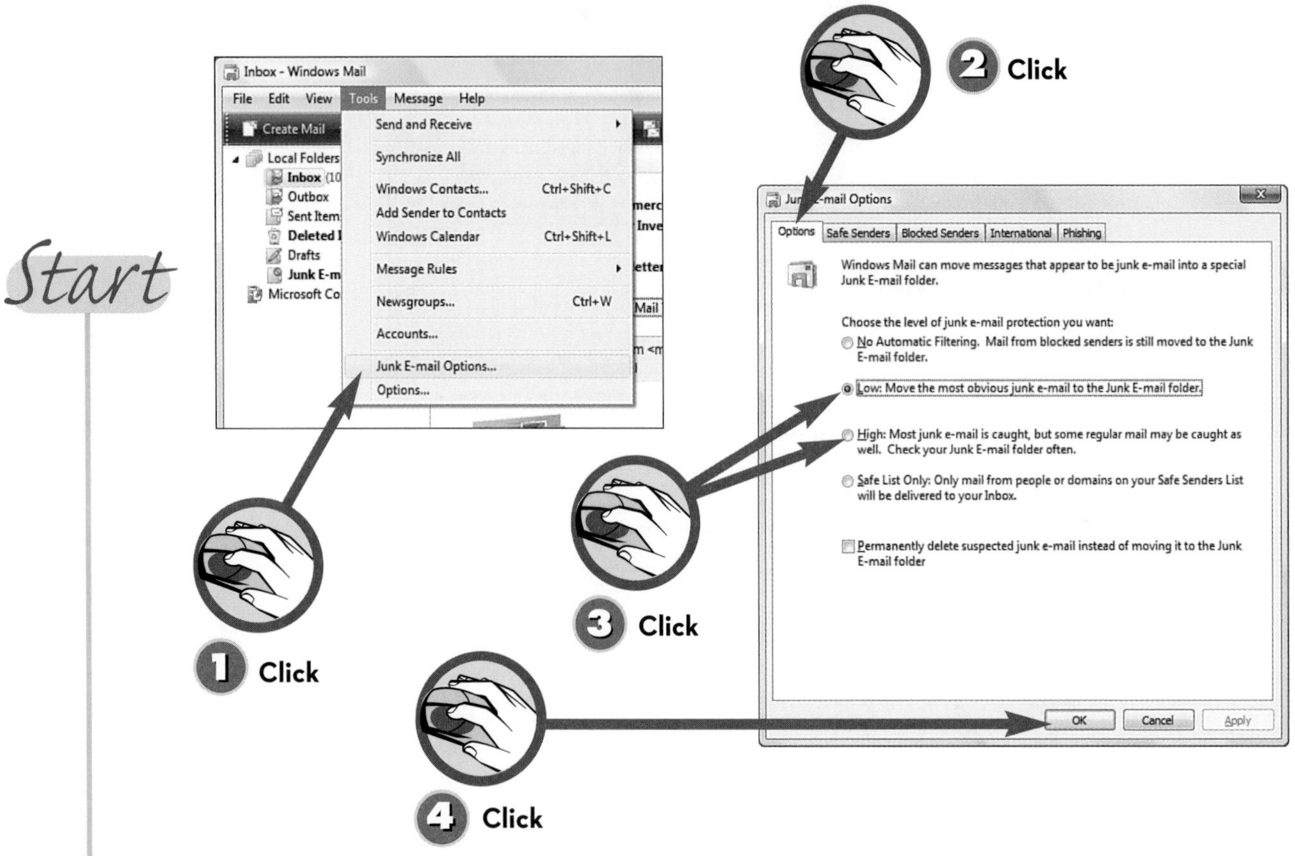

Start

1 Click

2 Click

3 Click

4 Click

1. To configure the spam filter in Windows Mail, pull down the **Tools** menu and select **Junk E-mail Options**.
2. Click the **Options** tab.
3. Click the level of spam protection you want, **Low** or **High**.
4. Click **OK**.

Continued

NOTE

What Level of Protection?

Windows Mail's Low spam protection catches the most obvious junk email messages. The High level catches more spam but may also send some legitimate messages to the Junk E-mail folder.

TIP

Viewing Junk Email

Windows Mail sends all identified spam messages to the Junk E-mail folder. To review these messages, click the **Junk E-mail** folder in the **Folders** list. (It's a good idea to review these messages periodically, to ensure no legitimate messages have been accidentally sent there.)

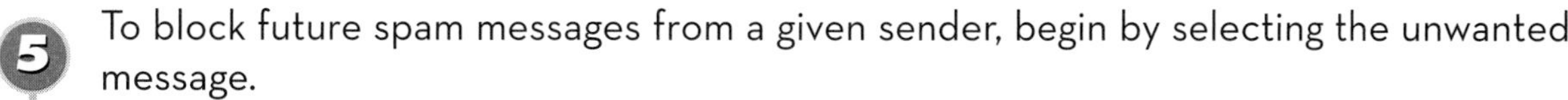

5 To block future spam messages from a given sender, begin by selecting the unwanted message.

6 Pull down the **Message** menu and select **Junk E-mail, Add Sender to Blocked Senders List**.

TIP

Use a Spamblock

To confuse email address-harvesting software, you can insert a spamblock into your email address on any public web page or blog. For example, if your email address is johnjones@myisp.com, you might change the address to read johnSPAMBLOCKjones@myisp.com.

TIP

Avoiding Spammers

You can reduce the chances of spammers finding you by not posting your email address in public forums, message boards, or blogs. You also should avoid posting your email address on your web page, if you have one.

PROTECTING YOUR CHILDREN WITH PARENTAL CONTROLS

As a responsible parent, you want to protect your children from any of the bad stuff that's all too prevalent online. The easiest way to do this is via the Windows Vista Parental Controls feature, which lets you select which websites they can visit, which PC games they can play (based on game ratings), and which specific programs they can or cannot use. You can even set time limits for when they can use the PC!

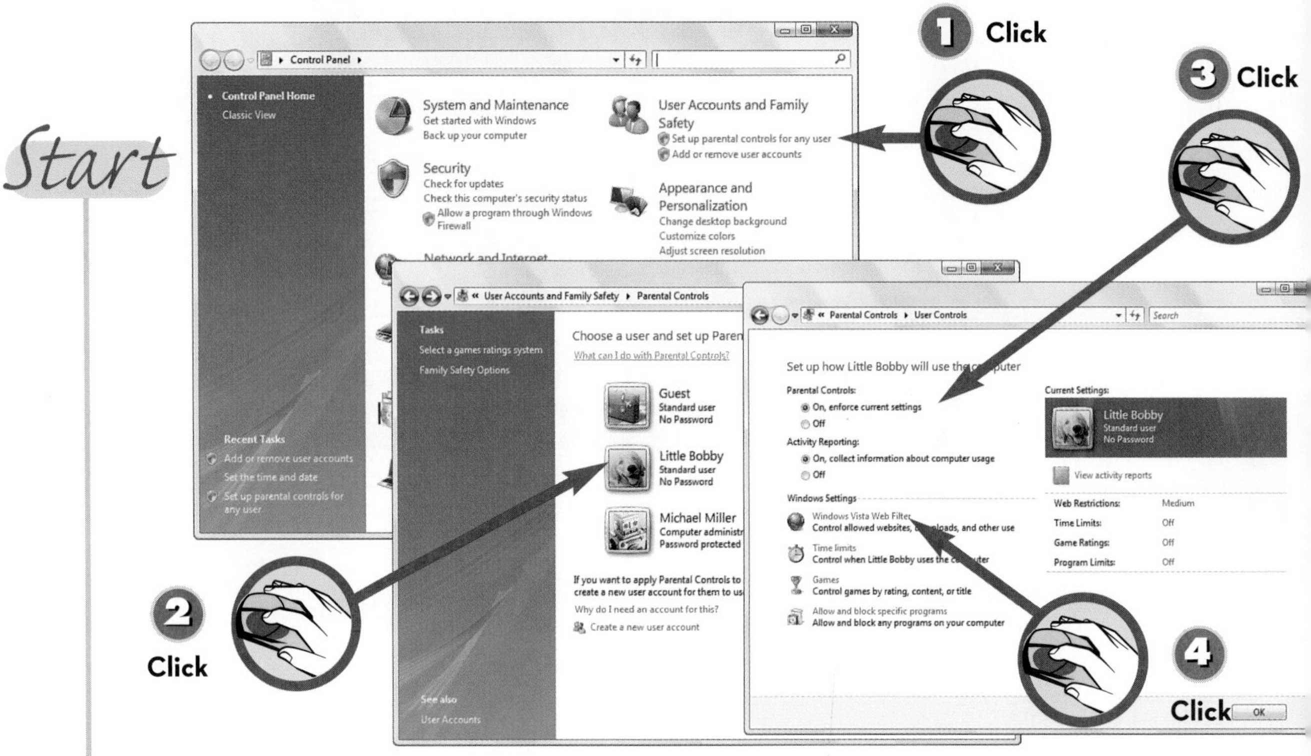

Start

1 Click

3 Click

2 Click

4 Click

1. Open the Windows Control Panel and click **Set Up Parental Controls for Any User**.
2. Click the user for which you want to set up Parental Controls.
3. To turn on Parental Controls, click **On, Enforce Current Settings**.
4. To filter websites, click **Windows Vista Web Filter**.

Continued

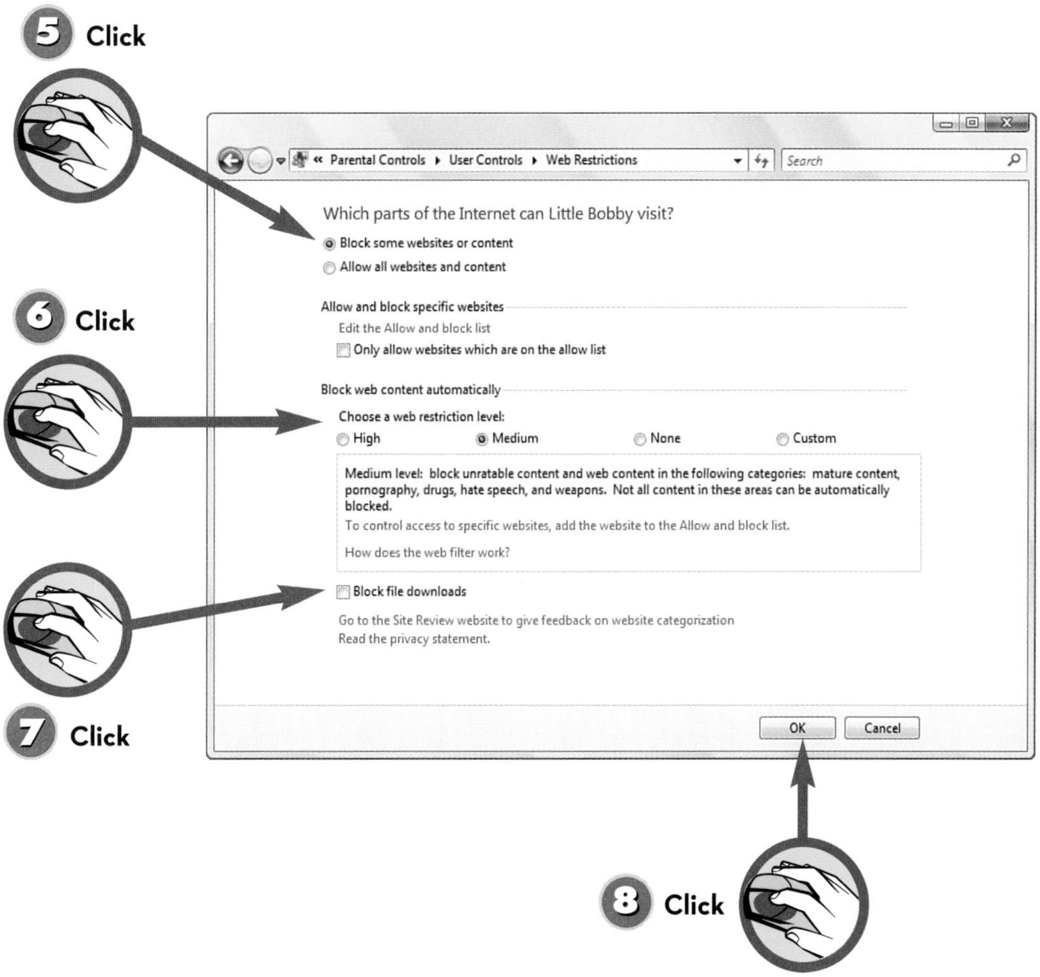

5. Click **Block Some Websites or Content**.
6. In the Block Web Content Automatically section, choose a web restriction level—**High**, **Medium**, or **Custom**.
7. To block potentially harmful file downloads, check **Block File Downloads**.
8. Click **OK**.

End

TIP

Web Restriction Level

How strict should you set Vista's web restrictions? The Medium level blocks mature content, pornography, drugs, hate speech, and weapons. The High level blocks all content except websites specifically approved for children.

DEALING WITH USER ACCOUNT CONTROL

One of the key security features in Vista is User Account Control (UAC). UAC prevents unauthorized people and processes from taking control of your system and installing and running malicious programs. Instead, you're prompted whenever Windows needs to run an administrative-level task, so that these operations aren't executed automatically.

Start

1. When a program or user attempts to perform an administrative-level task, User Account Control presents a dialog box that asks for authorization.
2. Click **Continue** to proceed with the task.

Continued

NOTE

What is Unauthorized?

What types of operations need UAC authorization? Just about anything that could affect the way your system runs, such as installing a new software program, changing system settings, or deleting a system file.

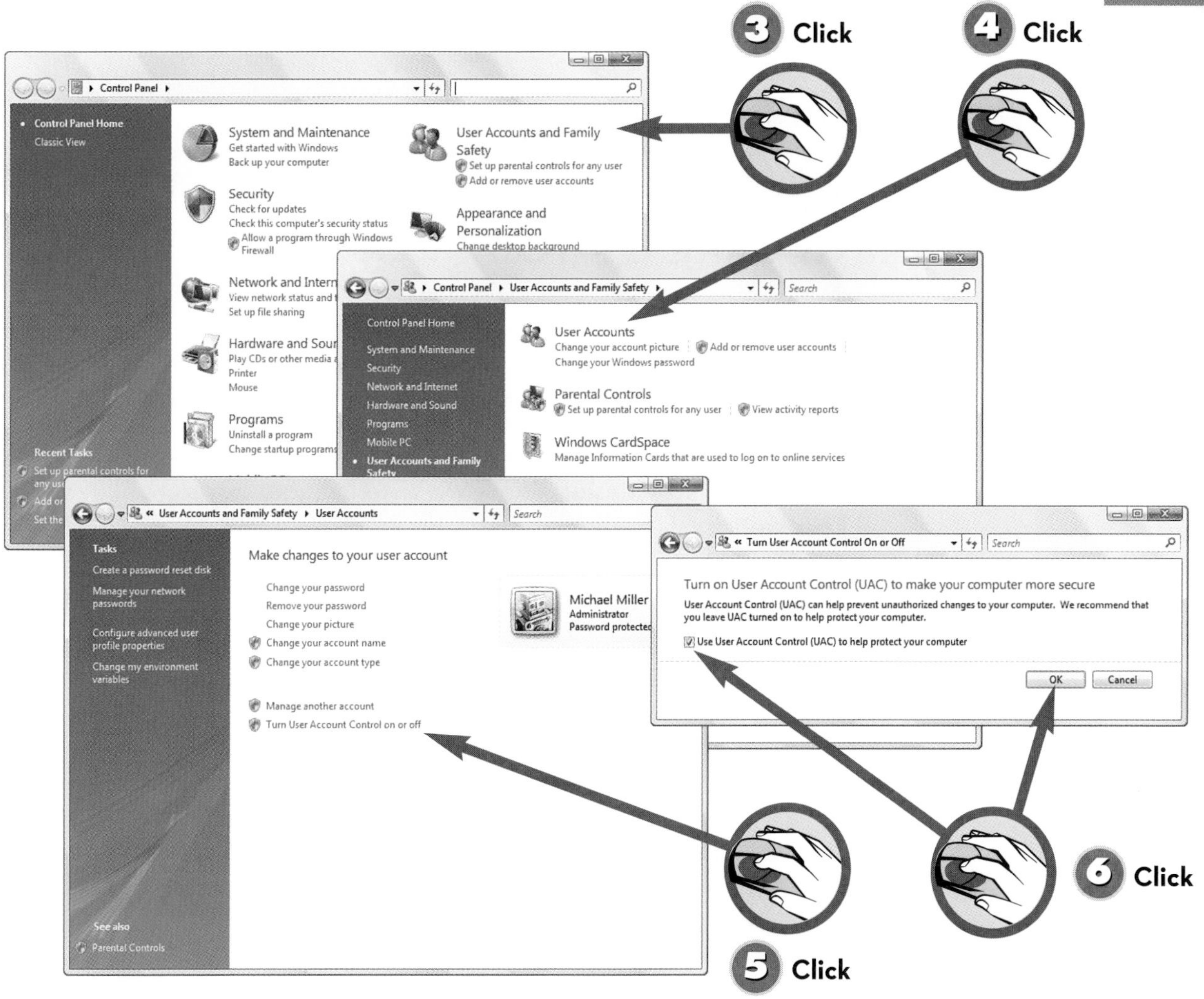

3 Click

4 Click

5 Click

6 Click

3 Some users find UAC unnecessarily annoying. To turn off UAC, open the Control Panel and click **User Accounts and Family Safety**.

4 Click **User Accounts**.

5 Click **Turn User Account Control On or Off**.

6 Uncheck **Use User Account Control (UAC) to Help Protect Your Computer**, and then click **OK**.

part 13

TAKING CARE OF YOUR COMPUTER

"An ounce of prevention is worth a pound of cure" is a bit of a cliché, but it's also true—especially when it comes to your computer system. Spending a few minutes a week on preventive maintenance can save you from costly computer problems in the future.

To make this chore a little easier, Windows Vista includes several utilities to help you keep your system running smoothly. You should use these tools as part of your regular maintenance routine—or if you experience specific problems with your computer system.

WINDOWS VISTA SYSTEM TOOLS

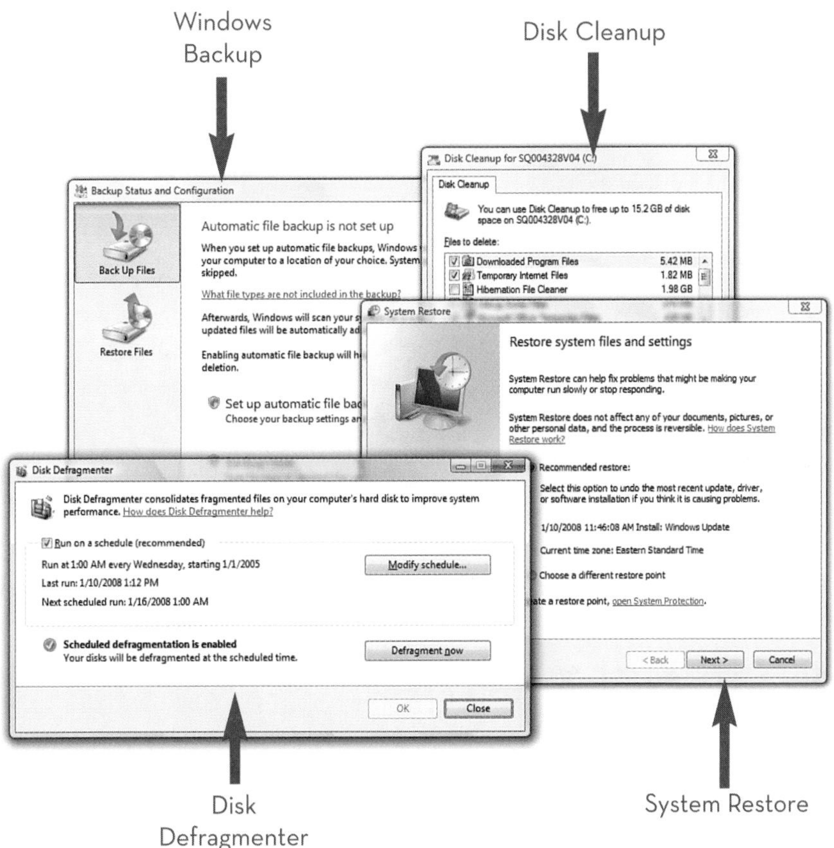

BACKING UP IMPORTANT FILES

The data stored on your computer's hard disk is valuable, and perhaps irreplaceable. That's why you want to keep a backup copy of all these valuable files, preferably on an external hard disk, using Windows Vista's new Backup utility. You can configure the Backup utility to back up your data automatically, on a predefined schedule.

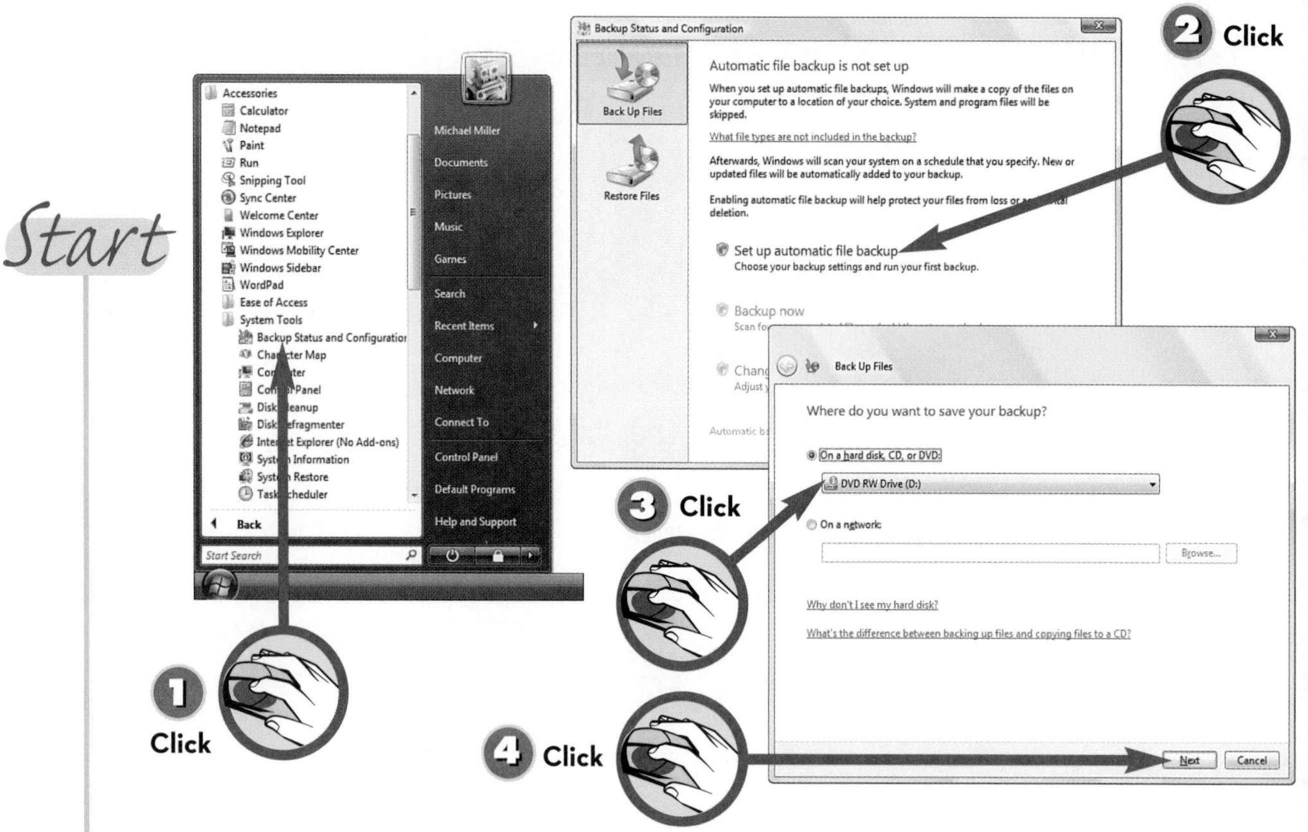

Start

1 Click

2 Click

3 Click

4 Click

1. Click the **Start** button and select **All Programs**, **Accessories**, **System Tools**, **Backup Status and Configuration**.
2. Click **Set Up Automatic File Backup**.
3. Select where you want to back up your data—to an external hard disk, to a CD or DVD disc, or to another computer on your network.
4. Click **Next**.

Continued

TIP

Incremental Backup

Vista's Backup utility performs an incremental backup. That is, it doesn't back up every file every time; it only backs up those files that are new or have changed since the last backup.

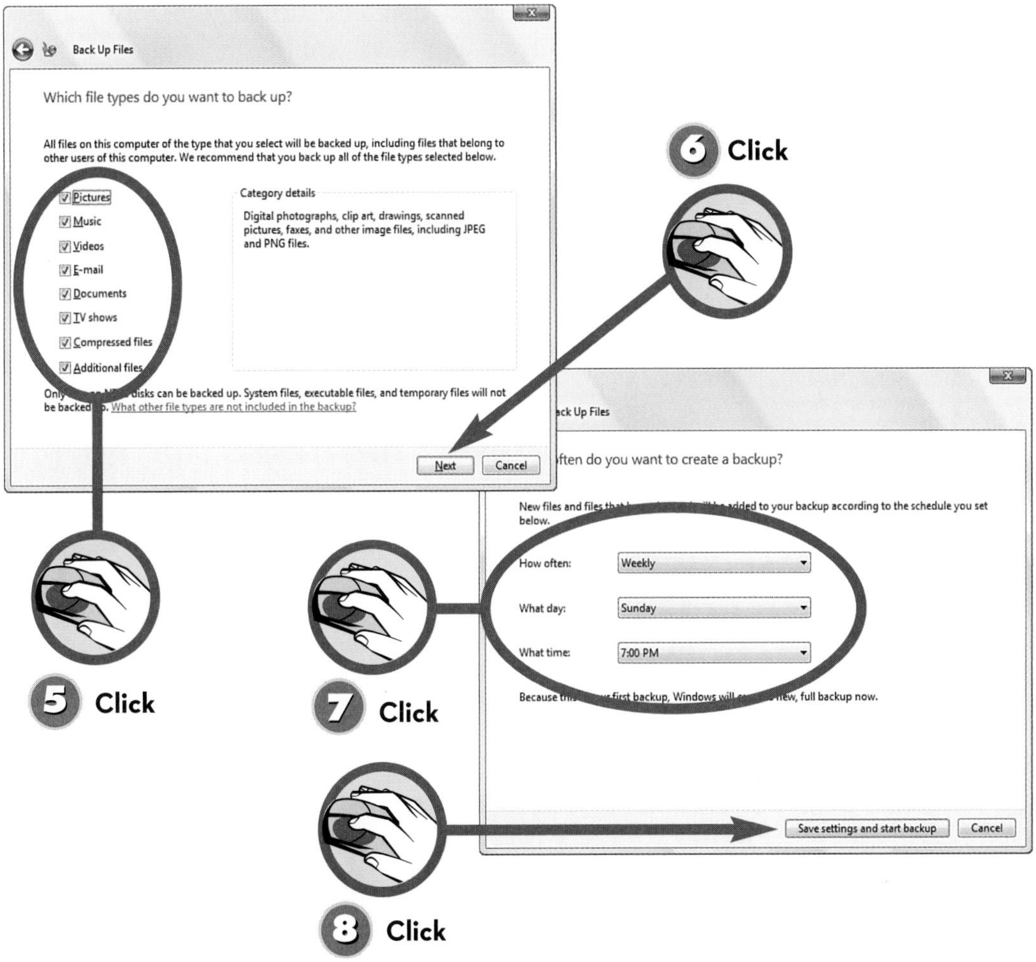

6 Click

5 Click

7 Click

8 Click

1. Select which types of files you want to back up.
2. Click **Next**.
3. Select how often, what day, and what time you want to back up your data.
4. Click **Save Settings and Start Backup** to perform your first backup.

End

—TIP

How Often to Back Up?

Should you back up your data daily, weekly, or monthly? It depends on how often you use your computer and how valuable your data is. There's no harm in performing daily backups—which means that your backup is never more than 24 hours out of date.

RESTORING YOUR COMPUTER AFTER A CRASH

If your computer system ever crashes or freezes, your best course of action is to run the Windows Vista System Restore utility. This utility can automatically restore your system to the state it was in before the crash occurred—and save you the trouble of reinstalling any damaged software programs. It's a great safety net for when things go wrong!

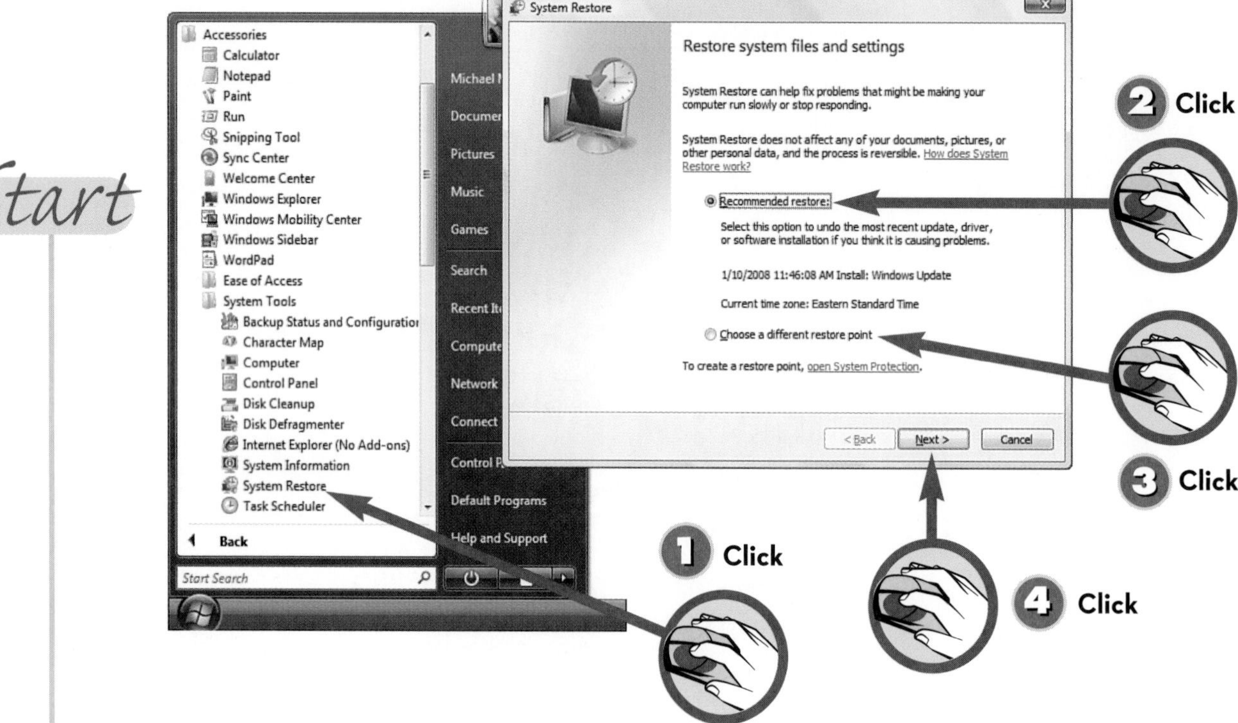

1. Click the **Start** button and select **All Programs**, **Accessories**, **System Tools**, **System Restore**.
2. To accept the default restore point, click **Recommended Restore**.
3. To restore to a different point in time, click **Choose a Different Restore Point**.
4. Click **Next**.

Continued

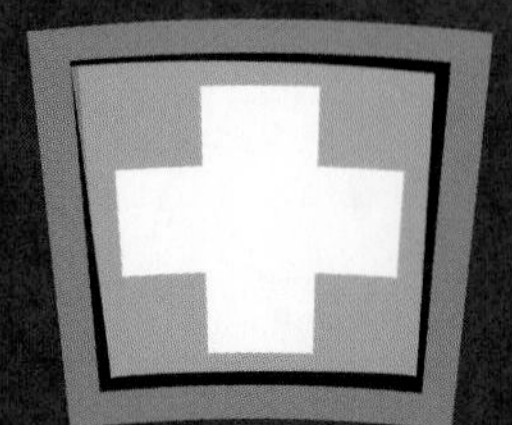

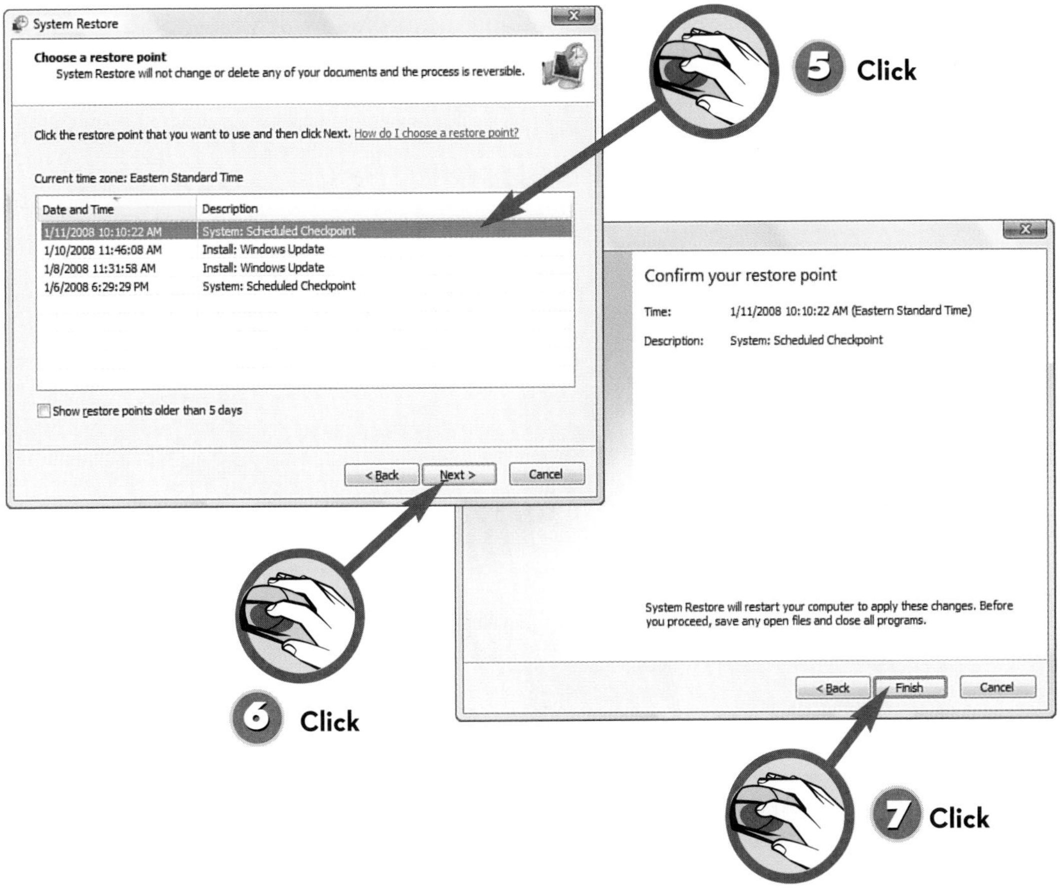

System Restore

Choose a restore point
System Restore will not change or delete any of your documents and the process is reversible.

Click the restore point that you want to use and then click Next. How do I choose a restore point?

Current time zone: Eastern Standard Time

Date and Time	Description
1/11/2008 10:10:22 AM	System: Scheduled Checkpoint
1/10/2008 11:46:08 AM	Install: Windows Update
1/8/2008 11:31:58 AM	Install: Windows Update
1/6/2008 6:29:29 PM	System: Scheduled Checkpoint

Show restore points older than 5 days

< Back | Next > | Cancel

Confirm your restore point

Time: 1/11/2008 10:10:22 AM (Eastern Standard Time)

Description: System: Scheduled Checkpoint

System Restore will restart your computer to apply these changes. Before you proceed, save any open files and close all programs.

< Back | Finish | Cancel

5 Click

6 Click

7 Click

5. If you opted to choose a different restore point, click a date from the list.
6. Click **Next**.
7. When the confirmation screen appears, click **Finish** to begin the restore process.

End

—TIP

Restoring Your System

Be sure to close all programs before you use System Restore because Windows will need to be restarted when it's done. The full process might take a half-hour or more.

—CAUTION

System Files Only—No Documents

System Restore will help you recover any damaged programs and system files, but it won't help you recover any damaged documents or data files.

DELETING UNNECESSARY FILES

Even with today's humongous hard disks, you can still end up with too many useless files taking up too much hard disk space. Fortunately, Windows Vista includes a utility that identifies and deletes unused files. The Disk Cleanup tool is what you should use when you need to free up extra hard disk space for more frequently used files.

Start

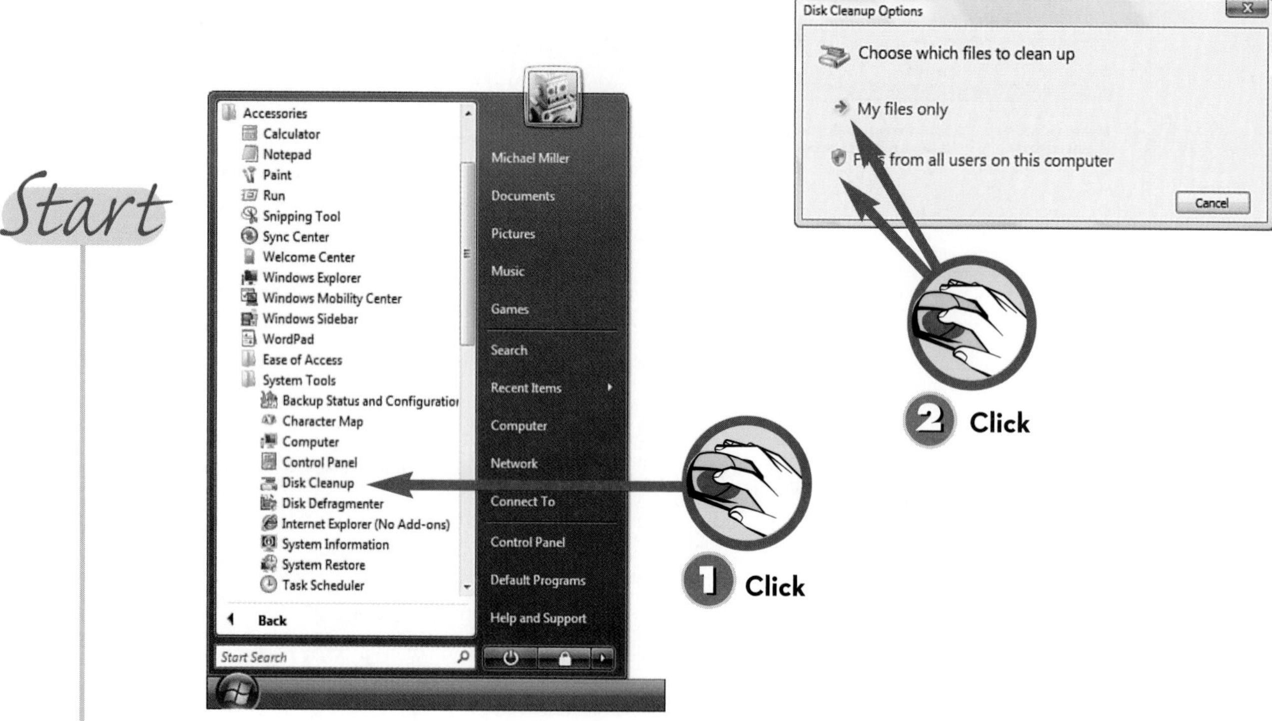

1. Click the **Start** button and select **All Programs**, **Accessories**, **System Tools**, **Disk Cleanup**.
2. Choose whether you want to clean up your files (**My Files Only**) or all files on your PC (**Files from All Users on This Computer**).

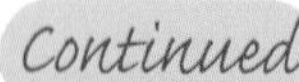
Continued

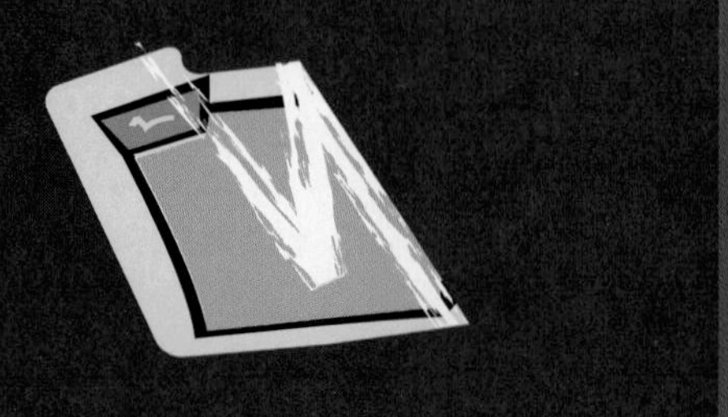

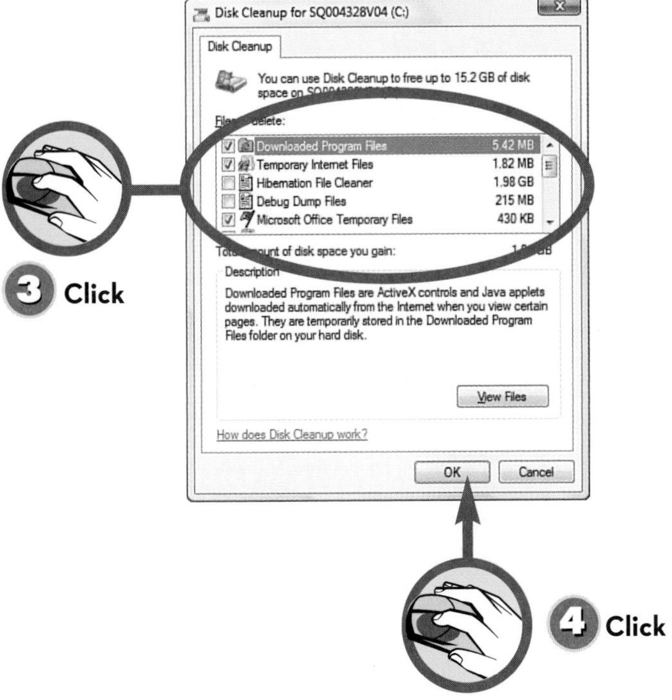

3. Disk Cleanup analyzes the contents of your hard drive and presents its results in the Disk Cleanup dialog box. Check which types of files you want to delete.

4. Click **OK** to delete the files.

End

TIP

Which Files to Delete?

You can safely choose to delete all these files *except* the setup log files, which are often needed by the Windows operating system.

DEFRAGMENTING YOUR HARD DISK

If you notice that your system takes longer and longer to open and close files or run applications, it's probably because little fragments of files are spread all over your hard disk. You fix the problem when you put all the pieces of the puzzle back in the right boxes—which you do by defragmenting your disk.

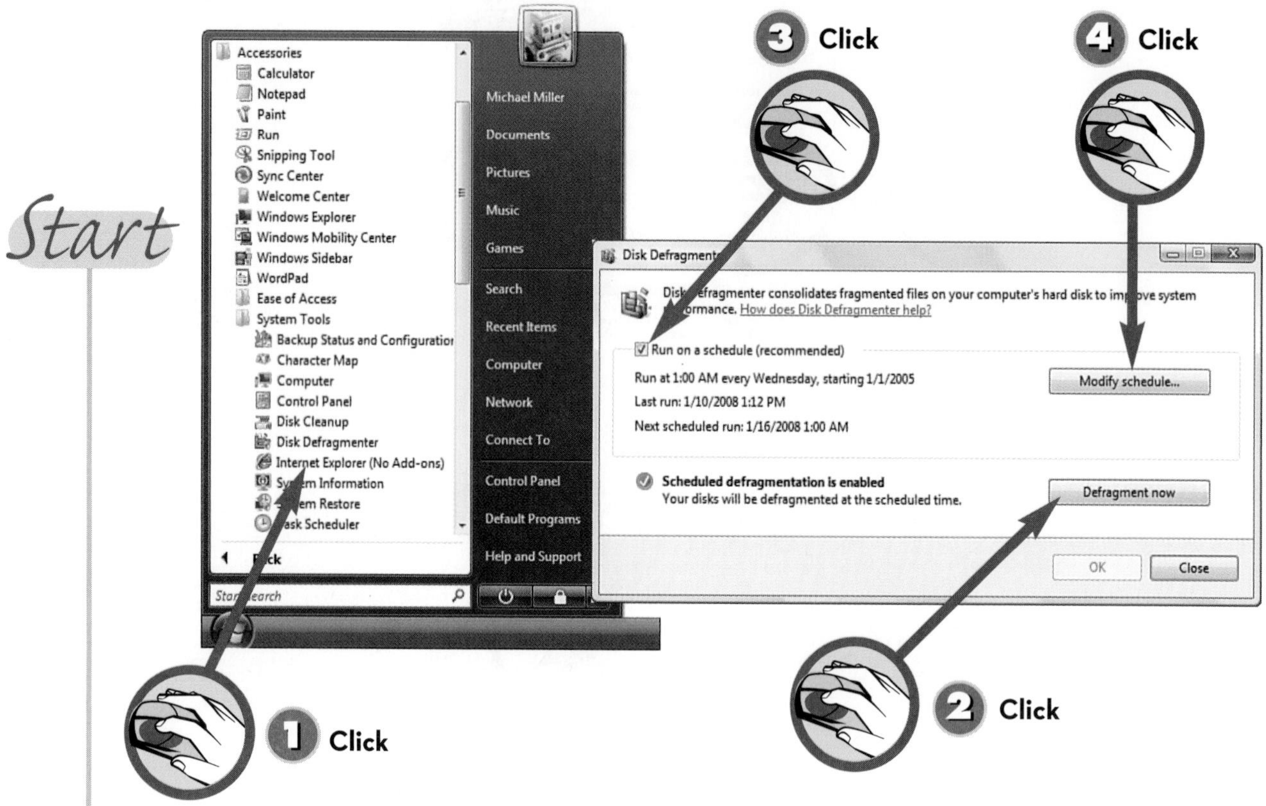

Start

1 Click

2 Click

3 Click

4 Click

1. Click the **Start** button and select **All Programs**, **Accessories**, **System Tools**, **Disk Defragmenter**.
2. To manually defragment your hard drive, click **Defragment Now**.
3. To set up automatic disk defragmenting, click **Run on a Schedule**.
4. Click the **Modify Schedule** button to schedule the defragmenting operation.

Continued

TIP

It Takes Time

Defragmenting your drive can take an hour or more, especially if you have a large hard drive or your drive is really fragmented.

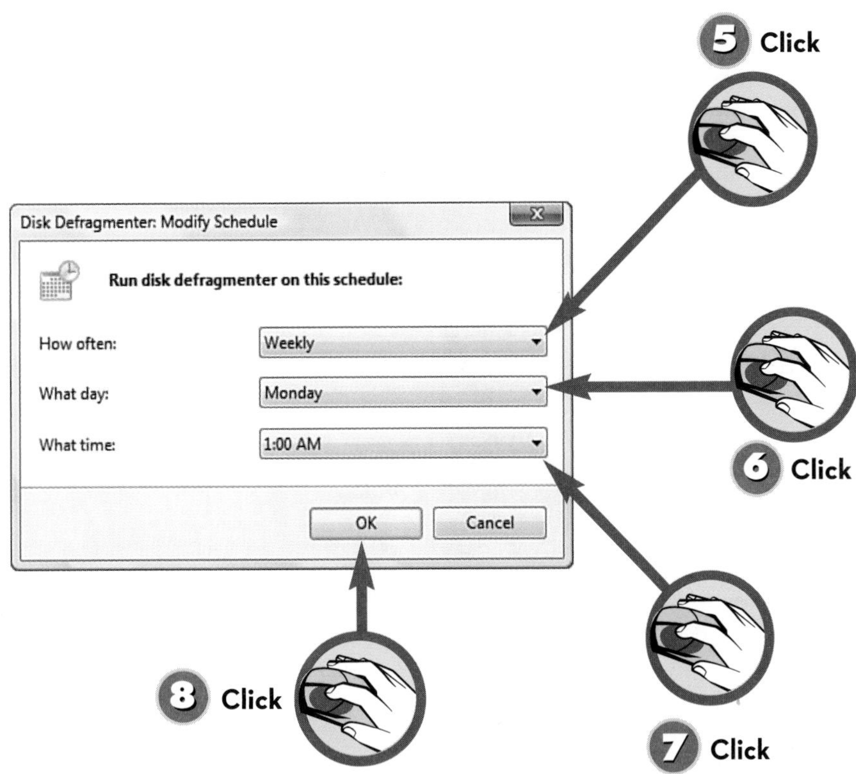

5. Click the **How Often** button and select how often you want to defragment.
6. Click the **What Day** button and select what day of the week you want to defrag your disk.
7. Click the **What Time** button and select at what time of day you want to run the defragmenter utility.
8. Click **OK**.

End

NOTE

Pieces of the Puzzle

File fragmentation is like taking the pieces of a jigsaw puzzle and storing them in different boxes along with pieces from other puzzles. The more dispersed the pieces are, the longer it takes to put the puzzle together.

NOTE

Fragmented Files

Files can get fragmented whenever you install, delete, or run an application, or when you edit, move, copy, or delete a file.

CHECKING YOUR HARD DISK FOR ERRORS

Any time you move or delete a file, or accidentally turn off the power while the system is running, you run the risk of introducing errors to your hard disk. Fortunately, you can find and fix most of these errors directly from within Windows Vista, using the ScanDisk utility.

Start

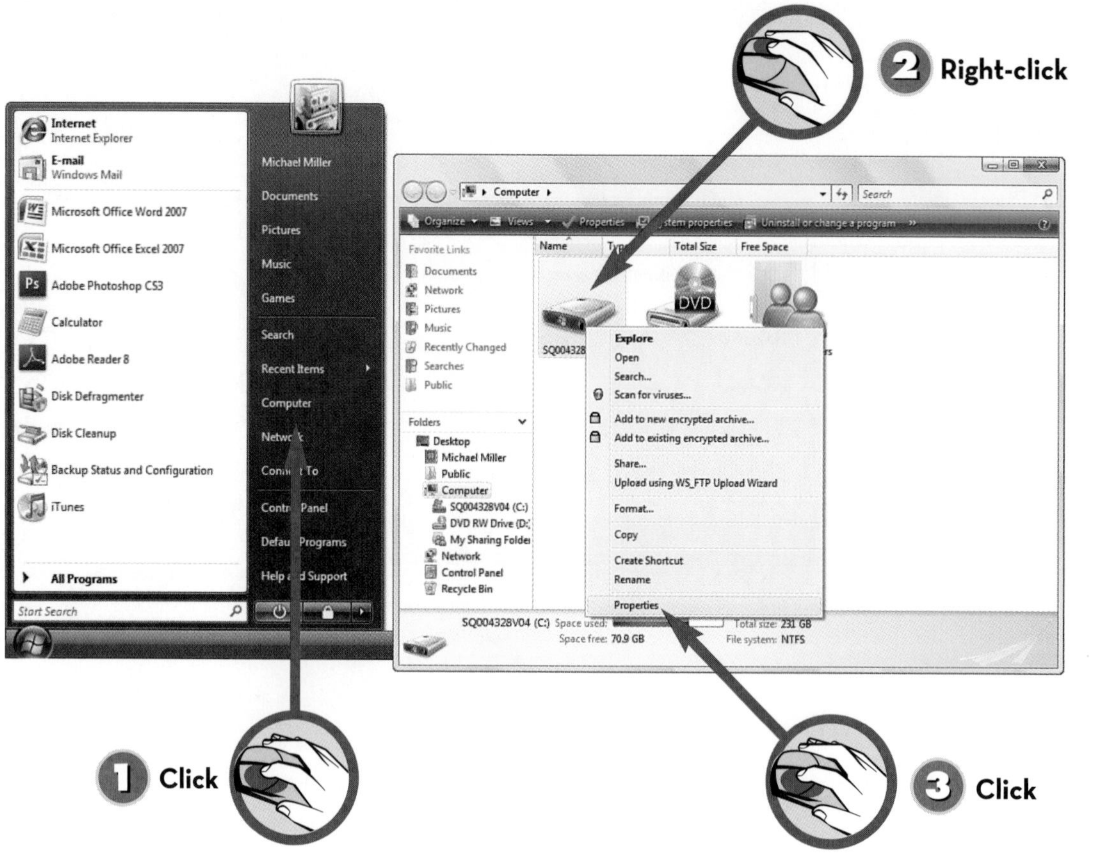

1. Click the **Start** button and select **Computer**.
2. Right-click the icon for the drive you want to scan.
3. Select **Properties** from the pop-up menu.

Continued

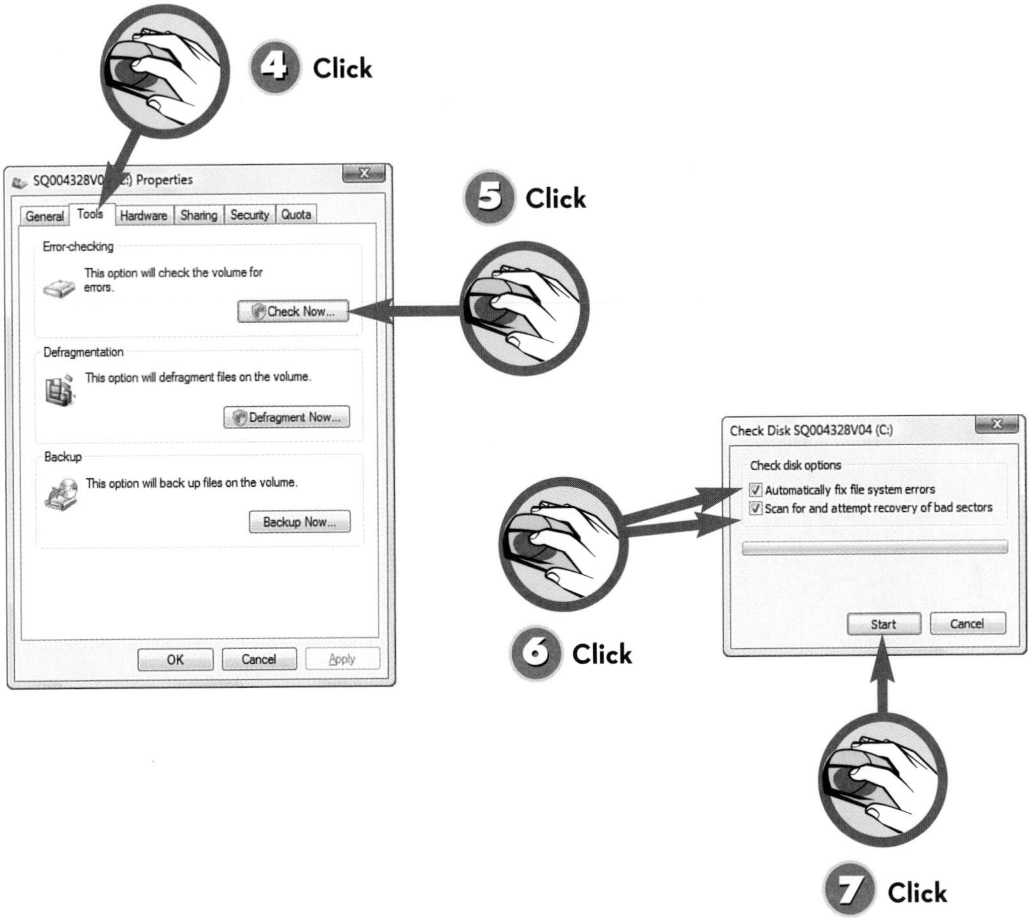

4. When the Properties utility opens, click the **Tools** tab.
5. Click the **Check Now** button in the Error-Checking section.
6. Check **Automatically Fix File System Errors** and **Scan for and Attempt Recovery of Bad Sectors**.
7. Click **Start**.

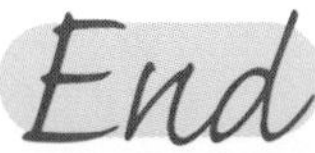

TIP

Scanning and Fixing

ScanDisk not only scans your hard disk for errors but also automatically fixes any errors it finds.

TIP

How Often to Run?

It's a good idea to run all these system utilities at least once a month, just to ensure that your system stays in tip-top condition.

KEEPING YOUR COMPUTER IN TIP-TOP SHAPE

Not all preventive maintenance takes place from within Windows. There are also some physical things you should do to keep your computer operating in tip-top shape.

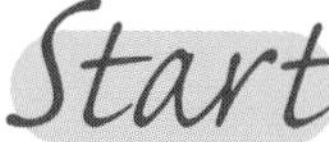

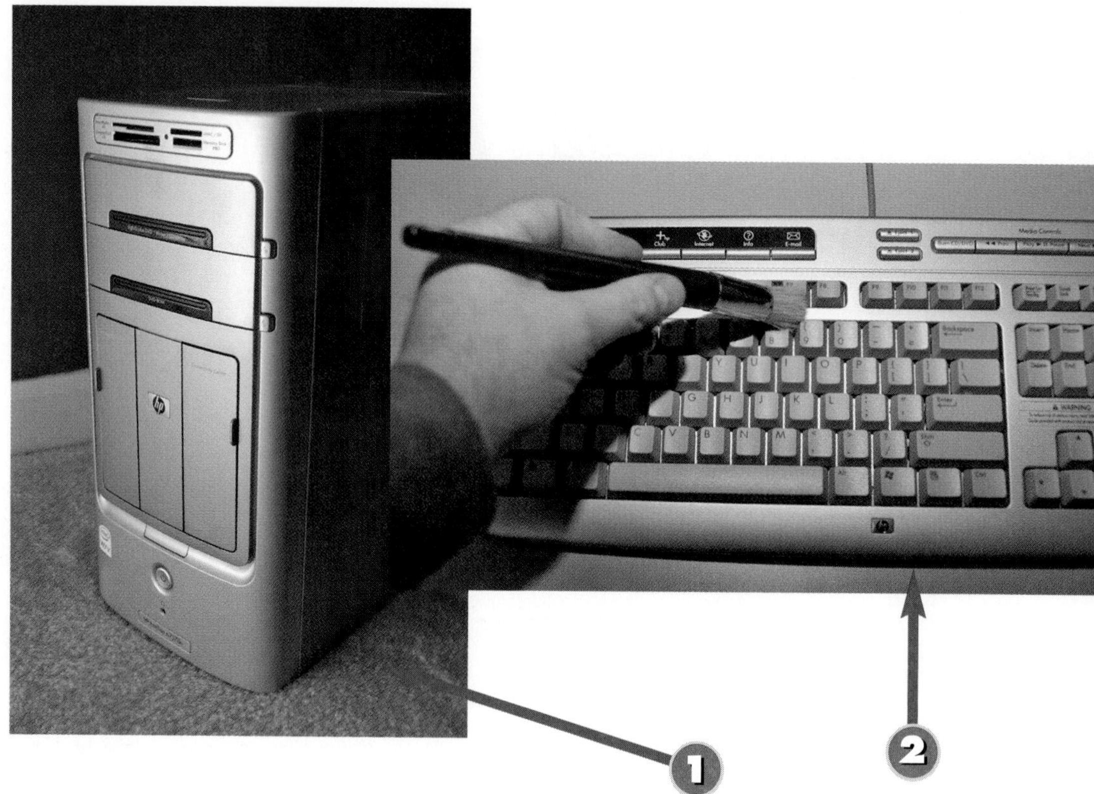

1. Position your system unit in a clean, dust-free environment with plenty of air flow around it, and dust it on a regular basis.
2. Use a small vacuum cleaner to periodically sweep the dirt from your computer keyboard. Use a cotton swab, soft cloth, or small brush to clean between the keys.

Continued

TIP

Compressed Air

Another good way to clean your keyboard is to use a can of compressed air to *blow* the dirt away.

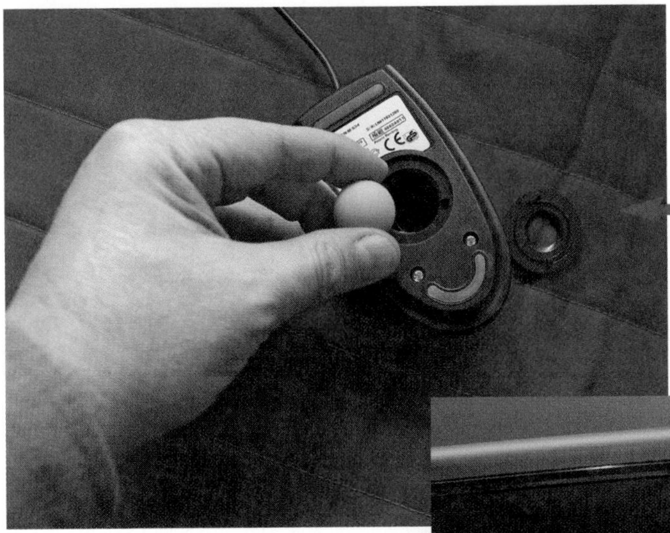

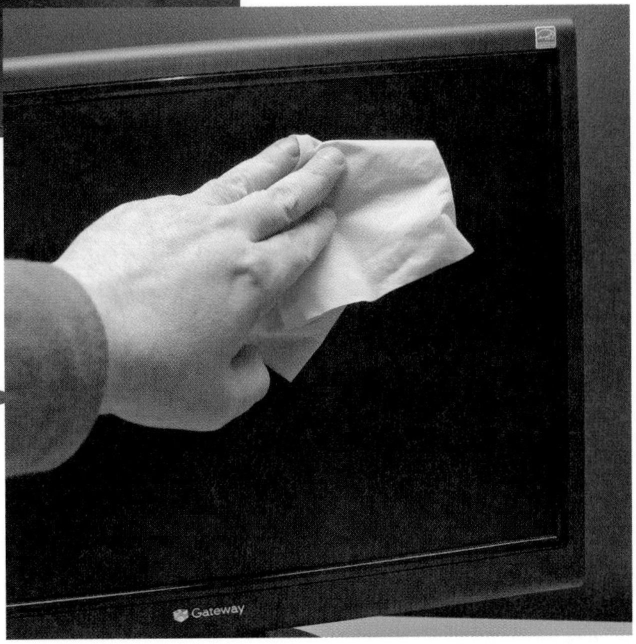

3 If your mouse has a roller ball, remove the ball periodically to clean the roller mechanism. If you have an optical mouse, keep the bottom of the mouse free from dust and dirt.

4 Clean a traditional CRT monitor with standard glass cleaner; clean an LCD flat-panel monitor with water or specially formulated display cleaner on a lint-free cloth. Spray the cleaner on the cloth, not directly on the screen.

End

CAUTION

Turn It Off

Always turn off your monitor before you clean its screen.

CAUTION

Avoid Alcohol and Ammonia

When cleaning your monitor, do not use any cleaner that contains alcohol or ammonia; these chemicals may damage an LCD screen. You can, however, use commercial cleaning wipes specially formulated for LCD screens.

Glossary

A

add-in board A device that plugs in to your computer's system unit and provides auxiliary functions. (Also called a *card*.)

address The location of an Internet host. An email address might take the form johndoe@xyz.com; a web address might look like www.xyztech.com. See also *URL*.

Aero The new translucent desktop interface in Windows Vista.

application A computer program designed for a specific task or use, such as word processing, accounting, or missile guidance.

attachment A file, such as a Word document or graphic image, attached to an email message.

B

backup A copy of important data files.

boot The process of turning on your computer system.

broadband A high-speed Internet connection; it's faster than the older dial-up connection.

browser A program, such as Internet Explorer, that translates the Hypertext Markup Language of the Web into viewable web pages.

bug An error in a software program or the hardware.

burner A device that writes CD-ROMs or DVD-ROMs.

C

cable modem A high-speed, broadband Internet connection via digital cable TV lines.

card Also called an *add-in board*, this is a device that plugs in to your computer's system unit and provides auxiliary functions.

CD-R (compact disc recordable) A type of CD drive that lets you record only once onto a disc, which can then be read by any CD-ROM drive or audio CD player.

CD-ROM (compact disc read-only memory) A CD that can be used to store computer data. A CD-ROM, similar to an audio CD, stores data in a form readable by a laser, resulting in a storage device of great capacity and quick accessibility.

CD-RW (compact disc rewritable) A type of CD that can be recorded, erased, and rewritten to by the user, multiple times.

computer A programmable device that can store, retrieve, and process data.

(CPU) central processing unit The group of circuits that directs the entire computer system by (1) interpreting and executing program instruction and (2) coordinating the interaction of input, output, and storage devices.

CRT Cathode ray tube is a type of video display device that uses a vacuum tube display.

cursor The highlighted area or pointer that tracks with the movement of your mouse or arrow keys onscreen.

D

data Information that is convenient to move or process.

database A program for arranging facts in the computer and retrieving them—the computer equivalent of a filing system.

desktop The entire screen area on which you display all your computer work. A typical computer desktop can contain icons, a taskbar, menus, and individual application windows.

device A computer file that represents some object—physical or nonphysical—installed on your system.

disk A device that stores data in magnetic or optical format.

disk drive A mechanism for retrieving information stored on a magnetic disk. The drive rotates the disk at high speed and reads the data with a magnetic head similar to those used in tape recorders.

diskette A portable or removable disk.

domain The identifying portion of an Internet address. In email addresses, the domain name follows the @ sign; in website addresses, the domain name follows the www.

download A way to transfer files, graphics, or other information from the Internet to your computer.

dpi (dots per inch) A measurement of printer resolution; the more dots per inch, the higher the resolution.

driver A support file that tells a program how to interact with a specific hardware device, such as a hard disk controller or video display card.

(DSL) digital subscriber line A high-speed Internet connection that uses the ultra-high frequency portion of ordinary telephone lines, allowing users to send and receive voice and data on the same line at the same time.

DVD An optical disc, similar to a CD, that can hold a minimum of 4.7GB, enough for a full-length movie.

E

email Electronic mail; a means of corresponding with other computer users over the Internet through digital messages.

encryption A method of encoding files so only the recipient can read the information.

Ethernet The most common computer networking protocol; Ethernet is used to network, or hook together, computers so they can share information.

executable file A program you run on your computer system.

F

favorite A bookmarked site in Internet Explorer.

file Any group of data treated as a single entity by the computer, such as a word processor document, a program, or a database.

firewall Computer hardware or software with special security features to safeguard a computer connected to a network or to the Internet.

FireWire A high-speed bus used to connect digital devices, such as digital cameras and video cameras, to a computer system. Also known as *i.Link* and *IEEE-1394*.

folder A way to group files on a disk; each folder can contain multiple files or other folders (called *subfolders*). Folders are sometimes called *directories*.

freeware Free software available over the Internet. This is in contrast with *shareware*, which is available freely but usually asks the user to send payment for using the software.

G

gigabyte (GB) One billion bytes.

graphics Pictures, photographs, and clip art.

H

hard disk A sealed cartridge containing a magnetic storage disk(s) that holds much more memory than removable disks—up to 400GB or more.

hardware The physical equipment, as opposed to the programs and procedures, used in computing.

home page The first or main page of a website.

hover The act of selecting an item by placing your cursor over an icon without clicking.

hub Hardware used to network computers together, usually over an Ethernet connection.

hyperlink A connection between two tagged elements in a web page, or separate sites, that makes it possible to click from one to the other.

I–J

icon A graphic symbol on the display screen that represents a file, peripheral, or some other object or function.

instant messaging Text-based, real-time one-on-one communication over the Internet.

Internet The global network of networks that connects millions of computers and other devices around the world.

Internet service provider (ISP) A company that provides end-user access to the Internet via its central computers and local access lines.

K–L

keyboard The typewriter-like device used to type instructions to a personal computer.

kilobyte (KB) A unit of measure for data storage or transmission equivalent to 1,024 bytes; often rounded to 1,000.

LAN (local area network) A system that enables users to connect PCs to one another or to minicomputers or mainframes.

laptop A portable computer small enough to operate on one's lap. Also known as a *notebook* computer.

LCD (liquid crystal display) A flat-screen display where images are created by light transmitted through a layer of liquid crystals.

M–N

megabyte (MB) One million bytes.

megahertz (MHz) A measure of microprocessing speed; 1MHz equals 1 million electrical cycles per second.

memory Temporary electronic storage for data and instructions, via electronic impulses on a chip.

microcomputer A computer based on a microprocessor chip. Also known as a *personal computer*.

microprocessor A complete central processing unit assembled on a single silicon chip.

modem (modulator demodulator) A device capable of converting a digital signal into an analog signal, which can be transmitted via a telephone line, reconverted, and then "read" by another computer.

monitor The display device on a computer, similar to a television screen.

motherboard Typically the largest printed circuit board in a computer, housing the CPU chip and controlling circuitry.

mouse A small handheld input device connected to a computer and featuring one or more button-style switches. When moved around on a flat surface, the mouse causes a symbol on the computer screen to make corresponding movements.

network An interconnected group of computers.

O–P

operating system A sequence of programming codes that instructs a computer about its various parts and peripherals and how to operate them. Operating systems, such as Windows, deal only with the workings of the hardware and are separate from software programs.

parallel A type of external port used to connect printers and other similar devices.

Parental Controls Windows Vista's collection of utilities that help parents monitor and control their children's PC, game, and Internet use.

path The collection of folders and subfolders (listed in order of hierarchy) that hold a particular file.

peripheral A device connected to the computer that provides communication or auxiliary functions.

phishing The act of trying to "fish" for personal information via means of a deliberately deceptive email or website.

pixel The individual picture elements that combine to create a video image.

Plug and Play (PnP) Hardware that includes its manufacturer and model information in its ROM, enabling Windows to recognize it immediately upon startup and install the necessary drivers if not already set up.

pop-up A small browser window, typically without menus or other navigational elements, that opens seemingly of its own accord when you visit or leave another website.

port An interface on a computer to which you can connect a device, either internally or externally.

printer The piece of computer hardware that creates hard copy printouts of documents.

Q–R

RAM (random access memory) A temporary storage space in which data can be held on a chip rather than being stored on disk or tape. The contents of RAM can be accessed or altered at any time during a session but will be lost when the computer is turned off.

resolution The degree of clarity an image displays, typically expressed by the number of horizontal and vertical pixels or the number of dots per inch (dpi).

ROM (read-only memory) A type of chip memory, the contents of which have been permanently recorded in a computer by the manufacturer and cannot be altered by the user.

root The main directory or folder on a disk.

router A piece of hardware or software that handles the connection between two or more networks.

S

scanner A device that converts paper documents or photos into a format that can be viewed on a computer and manipulated by the user.

serial A type of external port used to connect communication devices, such as modems, PalmPilots, and so on.

server The central computer in a network, providing a service or data access to client computers on the network.

shareware A software program distributed on the honor system; providers make their programs freely accessible over the Internet, with the understanding that those who use them will send payment to the provider after using them. See also *freeware*.

software The programs and procedures, as opposed to the physical equipment, used in computing.

spam Junk email. As a verb, it means to send thousands of copies of a junk email message.

spreadsheet A program that performs mathematical operations on numbers arranged in large arrays; used mainly for accounting and other record keeping.

spyware Software used to surreptitiously monitor computer use (that is, spy on other users).

system unit The part of your computer system that looks like a big beige or black box. The system unit typically contains the microprocessor, system memory, hard disk drive, floppy disk drives, and various cards.

T-U-V

terabyte (TB) One trillion bytes.

upgrade To add a new or improved peripheral or part to your system hardware. Also to install a newer version of an existing piece of software.

upload The act of copying a file from a personal computer to a website or Internet server. The opposite of *download*.

URL (uniform resource locator) The address that identifies a web page to a browser. Also known as a *web address*.

USB (universal serial bus) An external bus standard that supports data transfer rates up to 480Mbps; an individual computer can connect up to 127 peripheral devices via USB.

User Account Control (UAC) A Windows Vista security feature that requires administrator authorization before major operations are allowed to run.

virus A computer program segment or string of code that can attach itself to another program or file, reproduce itself, and spread from one computer to another. Viruses can destroy or change data and in other ways sabotage computer systems.

W-X-Y-Z

web page An HTML file, containing text, graphics, and/or mini-applications, viewed with a web browser.

website An organized, linked collection of web pages stored on an Internet server and read using a web browser. The opening page of a site is called a *home page*.

Wi-Fi The radio frequency (RF)-based technology used for home and small business wireless networks, and for most public wireless Internet connections. It operates at 11Mbps (802.11b), 54Mbps (802.11g), or 248Mbps (802.11n). Short for "wireless fidelity."

window A portion of the screen display used to view simultaneously a different part of the file in use or a part of a different file than the one in use.

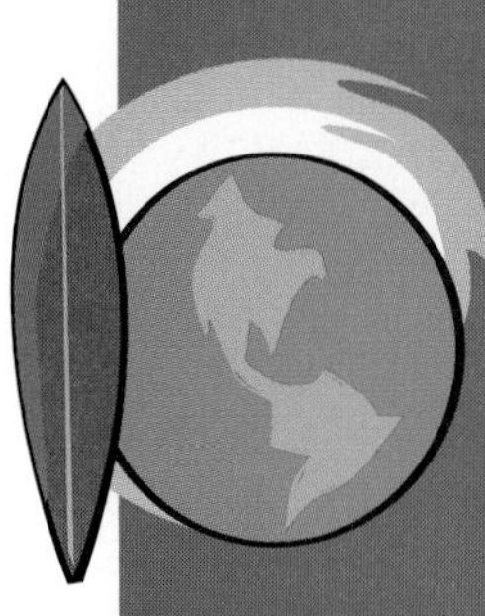

Windows The generic name for all versions of Microsoft's graphical operating system.

World Wide Web (WWW) A vast network of information, particularly business, commercial, and government resources, that uses a hypertext system for quickly transmitting graphics, sound, and video over the Internet.

Zip file A file that has been compressed for easier transmission.

Index

A

B

C

D

Index

G-H

I

J-K-L

Index

M

N

O

P

Q-R

Index

T

U

V

W

X-Y-Z

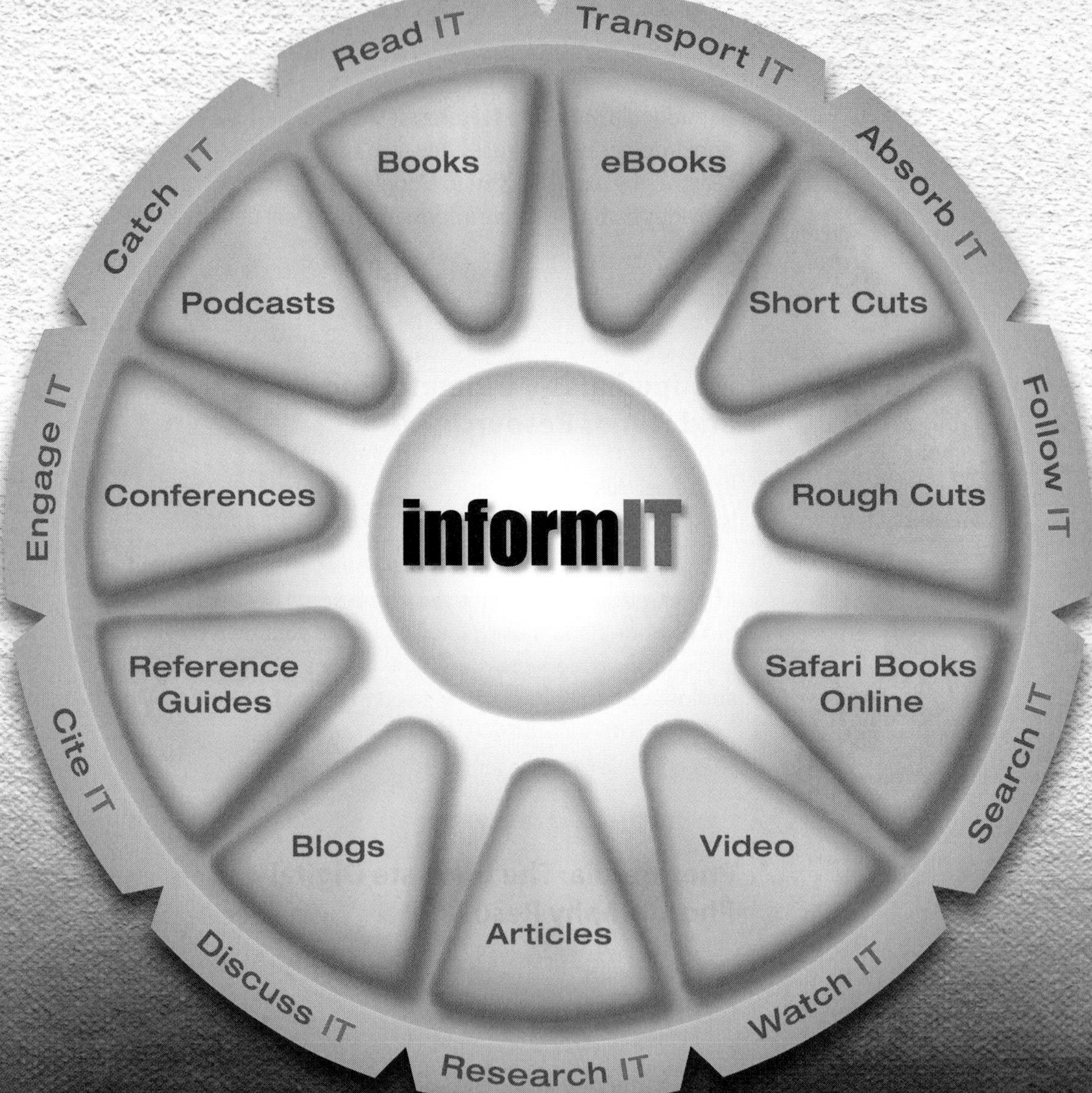

THIS BOOK IS SAFARI ENABLED

INCLUDES FREE 45-DAY ACCESS TO THE ONLINE EDITION

The Safari® Enabled icon on the cover of your favorite technology book means the book is available through Safari Bookshelf. When you buy this book, you get free access to the online edition for 45 days.

Safari Bookshelf is an electronic reference library that lets you easily search thousands of technical books, find code samples, download chapters, and access technical information whenever and wherever you need it.

TO GAIN 45-DAY SAFARI ENABLED ACCESS TO THIS BOOK:

- Go to **informit.com/safarienabled**
- Complete the brief registration form
- Enter the coupon code found in the front of this book on the "Copyright" page

If you have difficulty registering on Safari Bookshelf or accessing the online edition, please e-mail customer-service@safaribooksonline.com.